STRANGE FOOTING

STRANGE FOOTING

Poetic Form and Dance in the Late Middle Ages

SEETA CHAGANTI

THE UNIVERSITY OF CHICAGO PRESS

CHICAGO AND LONDON

The University of Chicago Press, Chicago 60637
The University of Chicago Press, Ltd., London
Published 2018
Printed in the United States of America

27 26 25 24 23 22 21 20 19 18   1 2 3 4 5

ISBN-13: 978-0-226-54799-2 (cloth)
ISBN-13: 978-0-226-54804-3 (paper)
ISBN-13: 978-0-226-54818-0 (e-book)
DOI: https://doi.org/10.7208/chicago/9780226548180.001.0001

The University of Chicago Press gratefully acknowledges the generous support of
the University of California, Davis, toward the publication of this book.

Library of Congress Cataloging-in-Publication Data

Names: Chaganti, Seeta, author.
Title: Strange footing : poetic form and dance in the late Middle Ages /
    Seeta Chaganti.
Description: Chicago ; London : The University of Chicago Press, 2018. |
    Includes index.
Identifiers: LCCN 2017040608 | ISBN 9780226547992 (cloth : alk. paper) |
    ISBN 9780226548043 (pbk. : alk. paper) | ISBN 9780226548180 (e-book)
Subjects: LCSH: Poetry, Medieval—History and criticism. | Literature and dance.
Classification: LCC PN1161.C47 2018 | DDC 809.1/02—dc23
LC record available at https://lccn.loc.gov/2017040608

♾ This paper meets the requirements of ANSI/NISO Z39.48–1992
(Permanence of Paper).

For Joshua Clover

CONTENTS

ILLUSTRATIONS

COLOR PLATES (FOLLOWING PAGE 134)

BLACK-AND-WHITE FIGURES

INTRODUCTION

This newe daunce / is to me so straunge
Wonder dyuerse / and passyngli contrarie
The dredful fotyng / doth so ofte chaunge
And the mesures / so ofte sithes varie. . . .[1]

One might assume that a book proposing to examine dance and poetic form together would subscribe to a rationale of analogy between these two art forms. As modern readers, we have internalized a tendency to think in terms of analogy when considering the relation of poetic form to other arts: the structure of verse is—or is not—like a building, like a painting, like a circle of dancers. In many instances, analogy is a useful strategy in formal reading. From New Criticism to political formalism, comparison—how, for instance, do walled enclosures and literary forms both constrain?—provides a language with which to describe effects and functions, patterns and affordances.[2] When espoused in reading medieval poetry and dance, analogy tends to create a mutually reinforcing expectation of dance and poetic form as two correspondingly regular and harmonious kinds of expression. This occurs in part because dance affirms such symmetry. Witness, for instance, the thirteenth-century *Hali Meiðhad*'s ring of dancing virgins in heaven: "In heore ring . . . þe heouenliche cwen leat i þet eadi trume of shimminde meidnes, ne moten nane buten heo hoppin ne singen" [In their ring . . . the

---

1. John Lydgate, "The Dance of Death," in Florence Warren and Beatrice White, eds., *The Dance of Death, Edited from MSS Ellesmere 26/A.13 and BM Lansdowne 699, Collated with the Other Extant MSS*, EETS o.s. 181 (New York: Kraus Reprint, 1971), 62; subsequent citations in text.

2. Caroline Levine, *Forms: Whole, Rhythm, Hierarchy, Network* (Princeton: Princeton University Press, 2015), 6, 11.

heavenly queen lead(s) in that fortunate company of shining maidens, nor might any except they dance or sing].[3] That heavenly circle makes concrete the parallel Nicholas Oresme draws between danced movement and the intricate order of the heavens.[4] Dance and poetry equally draw out these attributes in each other. Hermannus Alemannus, for example, compares the component of poetic discourse he calls "measure" [pondus] to the isolable "rhythm in dancing" [pondus in saltatione].[5] Medieval poetry and dance fit a neoplatonic template for rhythmic measure and evoke those expectations in each other when compared.

This narrative, however, obfuscates the depth of material collusion between these two arts. Medieval dance and poetry do not exist in the infinite nonintersection of parallelism, nor as the overlaying of one harmonious ideal upon another. Rather, these media occur in situations that more dynamically integrate them.[6] Most obvious is the subtle complexity of reciprocal reaction in situations where sung verse accompanies dance. But this is far from the only mode of interaction between premodern dance and poetry. Even when poetry is not vocally performed with dances, the stanzaic structures of various lyric genres reflect their origins as constituted by certain choreographic patterns. Some medieval lyrics familiar to us as modern read-

3. Bella Millett, ed., *Hali Meiðhad*, EETS o.s. 284 (Oxford: Oxford University Press, 1982), 11; my translation. Alan J. Fletcher associates this dance with the ideal of harmony and order implied in the medieval concept of *musica* and compares it to Dante's *carole* of the saints in the Heaven of the Fixed Stars. "The Dancing Virgins of *Hali Meiðhad*," *Notes and Queries* 40.4 (1993): 439. On *musica, armonia*, and "the pleasure of proportional sound," see John Stevens, *Words and Music in the Middle Ages: Song, Narrative, Dance and Drama, 1050–1350* (Cambridge: Cambridge University Press, 1986), 385.

4. Nicole Oresme, *Le livre du ciel et du monde*, ed. and trans. Albert D. Menut, ed. Alexander J. Denomy (Milwaukee: University of Wisconsin Press, 1968), 342–44. (Book II, ch. 6, fols. 86b–86c.) Christopher Stampone argues that in the *Troilus*, dance operates as a figure for the intricacies of rhetorical practice, so much so that literal and rhetorical dance replace each other rather than coexisting throughout. "Choreographing *Fin'amor*: Dance and the Game of Love in Geoffrey Chaucer's *Troilus and Criseyde*," *Chaucer Review* 50.3/4 (2015): 394, 416.

5. Hermannus translates Averroes's Arabic commentary on the *Poetics*. A. J. Minnis, A. B. Scott, and David Wallace, eds., *Medieval Literary Theory and Criticism c. 1100–c. 1375: The Commentary-Tradition*, rev. ed. (Oxford: Clarendon Press, 2003), 290; Laurentius Minio-Paluello,. ed., *De arte poetica, translatio Guillelmi de Moerbeka, accedunt expositio media Averrois sive 'Poetria' Hermanno Alemanno Interprete et specimina translationis Petri Leonii*, Corpus philosophorum medii aevi academiarum consociatarum auspiciis et consilio editum . . . , vol. xxxiii *editio altera* (Bruxelles-Paris: Desclée de Brouwer, 1968), 42.

6. This period inherits classical integrations of dance and poetry. On the complexity of this relationship in ancient Greece, the spectrum that ranges from poetry performed as dance to poetry that represents dance, and the questions surrounding "choral self-referentiality" in new performances of existing choreography, see F. G. Naerebout, *Attractive Performances: Ancient Greek Dance: Three Preliminary Studies* (Amsterdam: J. C. Gieben, 1997), 196–206.

ers thus sustain elaborate relationships to dance; the dialogue of these two media is sometimes only faintly audible because it is so deeply embedded. And the direct interaction of dance and poetry occurs in another kind of medial context as well: the dance-themed paintings and site-specific installations that include poetic inscriptions in their visual programs.

Strange Footing will show that by interweaving media in these ways, all the situations above construe poetic form not as comparable to dance but rather as constituted within the perceptual habits produced by dance. In the contexts to which I refer, the form of a poem is not a textual attribute. Rather, it is an experience reliant upon a consciousness of medial multiplicity, an experience generated when an audience familiar with the spectatorship of, and participation in, dance encounters poetic text. In diverse medieval arenas, interactions with textual material are shaped and informed by the social structures and forces surrounding those confrontations with text.[7] A highly visible and deeply ingrained aesthetic and social practice, dance operates as such a force, conditioning an audience's perceptual and aesthetic experiences of textual objects whether or not that audience is, at the moment of textual encounter, physically engaged in dance.

Within that structure of relation, *Strange Footing* argues, medieval dance and poetry produce not only harmony but also arrhythmia, disorientation, and strangeness. Through a set of case studies, this book will demonstrate that in bringing dance-based perceptual practices to bear upon the apprehension of poetry, a medieval audience experiences a poem's form as a virtual manifestation, hovering askew of worldly measures of time and space, existing between the real and unreal. When we read dance and poetry as collaborative media, this is the experience that medieval poetic form reveals itself to offer: a strange footing. Certain medieval taxonomies acknowledge medieval verse's capacity to build into itself a sense of formal discord.[8] But what I investigate here is a subtler, less codified sense of strangeness shadowing the emphasis on symmetry and harmony that occurs when dance and poetry are compared. *Strange Footing* proposes a methodology that elucidates the collaboration of dance and text to produce an experience of poetic

7. Rebecca Krug, *Reading Families: Women's Literate Practice in Late-Medieval England* (Ithaca: Cornell University Press, 2002), 5–6.

8. See, for instance, Johannes de Grocheio's reference to the *cantus*'s occasional closure with a verse discordant from the others ("clauditur per versum ab aliis . . . discordantem"). *Ars musice*, ed. and trans. Constant J. Mews et al. (Kalamazoo, MI: TEAMS Varia, 2011), 70. Medieval music theory also understands and refers to temporal qualities like syncopation; see Gilbert Reaney, "The Anonymous Treatise 'De origine et effectu musicae,' an Early Fifteenth-Century Commonplace Book of Music Theory," *Musica Disciplina* 37 (1983): 107.

form. In what follows I shall introduce that method, which begins by for-
mulating new readings of medieval dance and then articulates the role of
those readings in understanding the medieval experience of poetic form.

Why configure this methodology to proceed in one direction, from dance
to poetry? If medieval dance and poetic form exist in the dynamic relation I
claim, that interaction of arts is almost certainly more reciprocal than sin-
gly vectored. Making a case about dance and poetry in an argument-based
structure that requires progression in one direction might thus appear to
consign us to an interpretive linearity that restricts our view of such reciprocity. In response to this potential constraint, my analysis will consider
at specific moments how the strange form of a poem might reinflect an experience of spectacle. But in the enterprise of deriving insights about form,
a procedure that starts with dance and proceeds to poetry offers important
advantages. Analyzing dance by means of poetry—moving, that is, from poetry to dance—can encourage the perception of periodicities and harmonies
in common across the two arts. Reversing that order to begin with the analysis of movement-based spectacle, in contrast, creates a space in which to
perceive and entertain the strangeness that I suggest is crucial to understanding the medieval nexus of dance and poetry.

ON MEDIEVAL DANCE

Before embarking upon this study's approach to medieval dance, we must acknowledge the limitations that we, from our postmodern perspective, bring
to such an endeavor. There is the obvious evidentiary constraint—how do we
employ necessarily static vestiges of the past to understand a kinetic tradition?—but this is not our deepest problem. Rather, we need to recognize that
our ability to perceive dance as a central and familiar cultural practice, one
woven into various aspects of social life, might also be limited. In the present day, when a person lets on that they have studied dance, the question they
most often receive in response is not about what, when, and where they performed, or to which genres of musical accompaniment they responded most
deeply. Instead, almost every nondancer asks whether the dancer began to
train as a very young child. People seek that frame of reference for a dancer's self-identification because they understand access to this art as limited
by stringent and rarified requirements. Since the early modern period's accelerated production of dancing manuals and masters, Western dance has
cleaved to protocols of professionalization that have, over time, become so
absorbing and extreme that in many spheres they reconfigure the very phys-

iology of the dancer.[9] In growing accustomed to thinking of dance this way, we often separate it from the realm of our daily experience. Even popular entertainment involving dance—such as reality television shows that set dancers in competition—emphasizes the training underlying the practice of every style. Whether vernacular or concert-based, many types of Western dance exist at a remove from their audience, a foundation in hard-won knowledge enforcing this distance.

For this reason, it is challenging for us to imagine not only the intimacy that earlier audiences felt with dance but also dance's resultant ability to inform their perceptual habits and practices more broadly. Our modern perspective, that is, compromises our ability fully to see how dance could shape encounters with other expressive media. As Jennifer Nevile asserts, "dance was ever-present in the lives of Western Europeans from the late medieval period to the middle of the eighteenth century."[10] It crosses social and vocational lines to include aristocrats, clerics, students, and participants in civic festivities.[11] Nevile also asserts that in early-period dance, to be an amateur does not necessarily imply occupying one side of a wide "gulf" whose opposite shore is lined with professionals; rather, to be a nonprofessional in a more universally dance-literate culture could as easily involve degrees of expertise and familiarity difficult for us to envision.[12] Early dance is an aspect of habitual social practice.[13] As such, it urges us to ask how informed practices of dance spectatorship and participation might inflect other acts of response, decoding, and interpretation, particularly those aimed at the poetry with which dance coexists. To answer this main question, we must also

9. Sally Ann Ness reads the reconfiguration the ballet dancer's ligaments and bones as an inscription upon the body. "The Inscription of Gesture: Inward Migrations in Dance," in *Migrations of Gesture*, ed. Carrie Noland and Sally Ann Ness (Minneapolis: University of Minnesota Press, 2008), 19. On the sixteenth-century emergence of the figure who reflects "the modern sense of a person engaged solely in the dance profession," see Jennifer Nevile, "Introduction and Overview," in *Dance, Spectacle, and the Body Politick, 1250–1750*, ed. Jennifer Nevile (Bloomington, IN: Indiana University Press, 2008), 6.

10. Nevile, "Introduction," 2. On the inclusion of dance in fifteenth-century Italian wedding celebrations and state visits, see Barbara Sparti, ed., trans., and intr., *On the Practice or Art of Dancing* (Oxford: Clarendon Press, 1993), 51–53, 54–55.

11. On clerical and student dance in the Middle Ages, see Karen Silen, "Dance in Late Thirteenth-Century Paris," in *Dance, Spectacle*, 72–74.

12. Nevile, "Introduction," 4.

13. It is perhaps because of this sense of habituation and familiarity that the anonymous late-medieval theorist of music who mentions musical *caroles* (*carollis*), along with other dance music, dismisses them all as "fantastica et frivola" and not worthy of the consideration of serious music scholarship. Reaney, 117–18.

consider a few subsidiary ones. Besides its allegorization as verbal, divine, or political harmony, what is the experience of watching or participating in dance to its sophisticated medieval audiences?[14] How do these audiences theorize and understand their own engagement with danced spectacle?

Dance scholars and those with specialized training in dance have formulated ways to describe the experience of dance spectatorship in their own modern context. Influential in this discourse is the concept that spectators perceive *virtuality* when presented with danced performance. This idea finds expression in numerous arenas, perhaps most prominently throughout the work of the philosopher Susanne K. Langer. Langer argues that dance inheres not in the muscles and movements of dancers but rather in the "display of interacting forces" that these create in the spectator's perception. Dancers' bodies are doing something when they dance, but what we see is, in Langer's terms, a "virtual entity."[15] Elsewhere she suggests that when we watch two dancers together, we perceive the relation between them not entirely as spatial but rather as a "relation of forces . . . virtual powers."[16] Accounts of dance spectatorship beyond the fields of aesthetic philosophy or performance studies reflect this same idea. The dancer Darcey Bussell explains, "Dancers have to leave shapes in the air," like a "sparkler" does, as they move through space.[17] Her words offer a vernacular idiom for Langer's principle: that a medium apprehensible but intangible, a force (expressed in the light of the sparkler), accompanies the bodily medium of dance. In a review of the Courtauld exhibition *Rodin and Dance*, Anne Wagner comments that Rodin's images of Alda Moreno distill themselves until "what remains of Moreno's muscularity is lightness, an elusive line of movement, that has left her body behind."[18] Wagner employs another image that con-

---

14. Skiles Howard argues that even when early dance intends to allegorize political or social order, it sustains a number of complex and contradictory elements beneath its harmonious ideological surface. *The Politics of Courtly Dancing in Early Modern England* (Amherst, MA: University of Massachusetts Press, 1998), 2–3.

15. Susanne K. Langer, "The Dynamic Image: Some Philosophical Reflections on Dance," in *Aesthetics and the Arts*, ed. Lee A. Jacobus (New York: McGraw-Hill, 1968), 78. Dance theorists and practitioners have taken up Langer's evocation of virtuality. See, for instance, Kim Vics and John McCormick, "Touching Space: Using Motion Capture and Stereo Projection to Create a 'Virtual Haptics' of Dance," *Leonardo* 43.4 (2010): 359–66. Vics and McCormick argue that what "Langer was describing . . . might . . . be re-visioned as a form of virtual haptics—a metaphorical 'touching' of the space around a dancer" (359).

16. Susanne K. Langer, *Feeling and Form: A Theory of Art* (New York: Scribner's, 1953), 175–76.

17. Royal Ballet livecast, World Ballet Day 2016, https://www.youtube.com/watch?v=J31ci5lJ2Bw, 42:46–43:04.

18. Anne Wagner, "At the Courtauld," *London Review of Books*, 17 November 2016, 36.

veys what Langer calls the virtuality in dance: a trajectory of energy born of body and muscle but also traced outside its material realm.

Such virtual force is relevant to both modern and medieval worlds. One might be inclined to attribute modern evocations of virtuality to their authors' familiarity with electronic technology in games, art, and other environments. But theorists of dance seem to understand virtuality as force, both tied to materiality and cast beyond it. As force, this sense of virtuality equally obtains in medieval cultural locales. The medieval terms *virtus* and *vertu* (descended from Latin *vir*) represent forces originating within but also supplementary to that which is embodied and material.[19] Most familiar to us might be the *vertu* that drives forward the agitated spring of Chaucer's General Prologue, the force that is both of the physical rain and, at the same time, exerting impact beyond it to the flowers' engendering.[20] Furthermore, in the fourteenth century, theological disputation employs the term *virtus sermonis* to stand for what had been called the *vis*, the "force," of a word.[21] *Virtus sermonis*, or *de virtute sermonis*, is widely used to convey the notion of what is *intended* by a word or by the speaker of that word.[22] As intention, it is a force always stretching forth, the energy of potential that both hums within and acts as anticipatory supplement to the word. When I use the term *supplement* to refer to such virtual elements, I have in mind a version of the Derridean model: an element that operates as secondary and integral at once and that thus negotiates between presence and absence.[23]

Strange Footing proposes an approach to medieval dance whereby the modern account of dance's virtuality illuminates the medieval awareness of virtual supplements around, ahead of, and behind the body in choreographed motion. Reconstructing premodern dances based solely on their archival evidence cannot expose this aspect of their viewing experience.

19. *Middle English Dictionary*, https://quod.lib.umich.edu/m/med/ (hereafter *MED*), s.v. *vertu*; Rev. F. E. J. Valpy, *Etymological Dictionary of the Latin Language* (London: Longman, 1828), 513, s.v. *virtus*; James J. O'Hara, *True Names: Vergil and the Alexandrian Tradition of Etymological Wordplay* (Ann Arbor: University of Michigan Press, 2017), 107.

20. Larry D. Benson, ed., *The Riverside Chaucer* (Boston: Houghton Mifflin, 1987), 23, *Canterbury Tales* I.1–4. Hereafter all Chaucer texts cited from this edition.

21. William J. Courtenay, "Force of Words and Figures of Speech: The Crisis over *Virtus Sermonis* in the Fourteenth Century," *Franciscan Studies* 44 (1984): 113–14.

22. Maarten J. F. M. Hoenen, "*Virtus Sermonis* and the Trinity: Marsilius of Inghen and the Semantics of Late Fourteenth-Century Theology," *Medieval Philosophy and Theology* 20 (2001): 158–59. That intention can originate with a standard meaning dictated by logic or with the individual speaker's perspective, which might not be the same.

23. Jacques Derrida, *Of Grammatology*, trans. Gayatri Chakravorty Spivak (Baltimore: Johns Hopkins University Press, 2016), 156–58, 324, and *passim*.

I therefore offer a technique, which I term *narrative reenactment*, to generate a space between what is accessible to us in our understanding of dance spectatorship and what the medieval example offers. I have chosen works of contemporary dance by Lucinda Childs and Mark Morris to stage this narrative reenactment because they make distinctive use of multimedia settings, processional aesthetics, and round dance, all of which play an important role in the medieval dance traditions on which I focus. It should be emphasized that Childs and Morris do not reconstruct medieval dance or espouse "neomedievalism"; rather, they position bodies in round and processional configurations that are common in medieval dance traditions.[24] The accessibility of Childs's and Morris's work makes it possible to speak about certain perceptual and participatory experiences these configurations produce.[25] In discussing these experiences, I draw upon both my own position as a spectator and interviews with company members who have danced both pieces. These two sources of evidence might appear to separate participation and spectatorship in a manner incompatible with the medieval setting, foregrounding the distinction between premodern social dance, on the one hand, and modern proscenium-based concert dance, on the other. Mindful of this issue, I asked the dancers throughout the interviews to reflect upon spectatorship even as they discussed their performance experiences. In addition, my perspective as a spectator is informed by several years of dance training. With these responses to contemporary dance as a template, I consider how visual and verbal representations of medieval dance subtly indicate corresponding perceptual experiences for the audiences of and participants in those premodern spectacles. The goal here is not to contend that choreography or our encounters with it possess some transhistorical quality—we watch and participate in dance in ways unfathomably distinct from a medieval agent. Rather, it is to demarcate sites for interpretation between what is at best a hazily discernible scene of medieval experience, on the one hand, and what we as postmodern subjects might understand

24. *Neomedievalism* might be described as a self-conscious and agenda-driven adaptation. See, for instance, Umberto Eco, "Dreaming of the Middle Ages," in *Travels in Hyperreality: Essays*, trans. William Weaver (New York: Harcourt Brace & Company, 1986), 61–72; and Züleyha Çetiner-Öktem, "Dreaming the Middle Ages: American Neomedievalism in *A Knight's Tale* and *Timeline*," *Interactions* 18.1 (2009): 43–45.

25. Even as contemporary works, these dances raise their own questions about reconstruction and reenactment; see chapter 3. On related questions concerning the categories of archive and repertoire, see Diana Taylor, *The Archive and the Repertoire: Performing Cultural Memory in the Americas* (Durham: Duke University Press, 2007), 19–52.

to obtain in our experiences of watching dance, on the other. That space's parameters are set by our awareness of both the past's inaccessibility and our confinement within present modes of seeing. But within these bounds, my juxtaposition of different temporal moments will reveal the possibility of virtualities in the medieval experience of spectatorship that would otherwise be undetectable to us.

To gain access to any aspect—virtual or otherwise—of an *experience* is a vexed endeavor but not one entirely lacking interpretive possibilities. As Dominick LaCapra suggests, experience can operate as "black box."[26] This term refers to a site whose very naturalization of function obscures its means of functioning to those outside it.[27] Such inaccessibility does not result exclusively from an experience's historical distance: the experience of someone immediately adjacent to us can be equally obscure. In addition, the implications of this problem involve not only the invisibility of an experience's perceptual and analytical process itself, but also the obfuscation of the ideologies that produce that experience.[28] But as Philipp von Hilgers argues, the impenetrable façades of the black box do not necessarily require capitulation to those barriers to knowing. Rather, the black box emphasizes our responsibility to be thoughtful about the "mode of perceiving and working" at play even when its mechanics cannot be visible.[29] The viewing experience of an other is equally inaccessible whether across the temporal distance to the Middle Ages or across the spatial distance to the spectator in the next seat. That situation, however, does not preclude considering the perceptual modes that dictate experience by juxtaposing what is and is not available to one's knowledge and producing insight in the interstice.

Within this context, the medieval experience of dance emerges as the perception of virtual forces supplementing bodily movement. To reenact this experience, and briefly illustrate my method, I shall juxtapose a modern instance with a medieval one. Bill T. Jones, Paul Kaiser, and Shelley Eshkar's

26. Dominick LaCapra, *History in Transit: Experience, Identity, Critical Theory* (Ithaca: Cornell University Press, 2004), 38.

27. Bruno Latour, *Pandora's Hope: Essays on the Reality of Science Studies* (Cambridge, MA: Harvard University Press, 1999), 304.

28. Joan W. Scott, "The Evidence of Experience," *Critical Inquiry* 17.4 (1991): 778. Scott draws upon Michel de Certeau's observation that what seems a dominant historical reality to us "serves precisely to camouflage the practice which in fact determines it." Michel de Certeau, "History: Science and Fiction," in *Heterologies: Discourse on the Other*, trans. Brian Massumi (Minneapolis: University of Minnesota Press, 1986), 203.

29. Philipp von Hilgers, "The History of the Black Box: The Clash of a Thing and Its Concept," trans. William Rauscher, *Cultural Politics* 7.1 (2011): 45–46.

Ghostcatching (1999) experiments with motion capture technology to comment on virtuality in dance.[30] Throughout, the dancer's body appears as outlined in light. In some sections, this piece additionally uses its technologies to generate supplementary lines of light and energy that spectators can see as the outlined dancing body traces them (figure 1).[31] By making these luminous vectors and curves visible to the audience as they are cast from the dancer's gestures, *Ghostcatching* manifests the forces that supplement the body's movement. Criticism discussing the piece understands those visible forces as "virtual"; *Ghostcatching* emblematizes the concept that dance spectatorship consists in the awareness of such forces supplementing the body.[32]

Ghostcatching productively complicates our sense of what medieval texts convey when describing dance. In a fourteenth-century sermon, John Bromyard offers an *exemplum* that portrays a circular *carole* performed by demon dancers. He calls these dancers *viri*: "Coram quo apparuerunt quatuor viri fetidi nigri et horribiles, quasi conducentes coream. . . ." [before whom there appeared four men, stinking, black, and monstrous, as though leading a dance. . . .].[33] Echoing etymologically the qualities of force and potency in *virtus*, each *vir* is indeed potent in his ability to terrify. But these figures also speak to virtuality more broadly construed: the *viri* are forces whose relationship to the material world is indeterminate; they situate themselves within it but do not occupy quite the same plane as the embodied world. Their dancing is *quasi*; the nature of their spectacle's apprehensibility is ambiguous. This sermon, then, sees dance as force and entertains the possibility that dance-based spectacle does not fully entail or even require physical bodies. But another version of the *exemplum* expands the story further, replacing a group of human dancers with the demons and thus momentarily setting the two danced manifestations into one scene:

30. See, for instance, https://www.youtube.com/watch?v=aL5w_b-F8ig. A related piece of similar vintage is Merce Cunningham's *Hand-Drawn Spaces* (1998). See also the later revision of Jones et al., *After Ghostcatching* (2010).

31. Tiffany E. Barber describes these as "the arced lines the figure marks in space." "*Ghostcatching* and *After Ghostcatching*, Dances in the Dark," *Dance Research Journal* 47.1 (2015): 50.

32. Danielle Goldman argues that while this experiment with the "virtual . . . *beyond* the body" represents a "formal turn," its use of technology is also part of a "powerful . . . line in which the dancing body intersects with race, labor, and technology." "*Ghostcatching*: An Intersection of Technology, Labor, and Race," *Dance Research Journal* 35.2/36.1 (2003–2004): 69. See also Barber, 45: "his bodies in virtual and physical form remain inextricably linked."

33. Siegfried Wenzel, "The 'Gay' Carol and Exemplum," *Neuphilologische Mitteilungen* 77.1 (1976): 86; my translation.

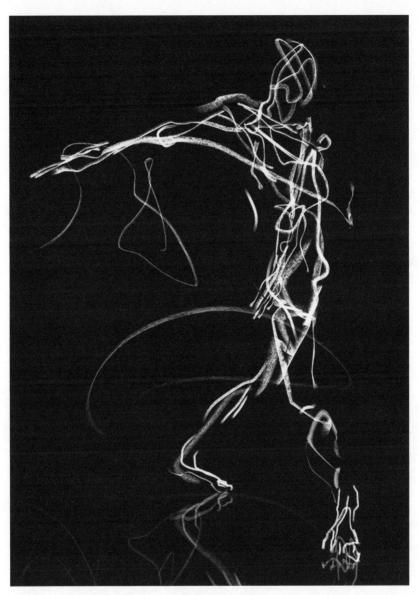

Fig. 1. Bill T. Jones, Shelley Eshkar, and Paul Kaiser, *Ghostcatching* (1999).
Photograph: Courtesy Paul Kaiser / OpenEndedGroup.

"[Gaius] iussit familie sue coriam circa ignem ducere et cantare. . . . Quo peracto, ecce supervenit corea demonum" [Gaius commanded his household to lead a dance around the fire and to sing. . . . Which thing having been completed, behold there came up a dance of demons].[34] In its transition between one circle and another, this revised narrative conveys the intangible forces of danced movement as supplements to embodied dance. As Ingrid Nelson argues, what an *exemplum* does is more complex than it might appear, and lyric (which this *exemplum* includes in the form of its carol text) lives in the "gap" that the *exemplum*'s ambiguity creates.[35] Didactically, the dancing's demonic aspect might emphasize what is already understood as immorality and dissolution. But in light of *Ghostcatching*, the supernatural elements in these medieval dances fulfill another function. The demon *caroles* imply entities in medieval dance that hover at the periphery of the material and that assert themselves as forces that are apprehensible but of ambiguous reality. In this capacity, the demon dances are not alone: we might think also of the Wife of Bath's fairy carolers and the Franklin's illusory dancing lovers. In all these cases, to narrate the experience of medieval dance is to acknowledge an implicit habituation to a virtual supplement that modernity—less universally habituated to dance—must name explicitly or illuminate technologically.

Juxtaposing *Ghostcatching* and the *exemplum* tradition foregrounds another important point about medieval dance's virtual forces, which is that they exist off the axes of order and expectation: they are uncanny (what Todorov calls *l'étrange*).[36] Jones's titular reference to ghosts functions in part to name the specifically preternatural quality of that effect. In identifying dance as an activity that captures ghosts and ghostliness, Jones emphasizes to us that Bromyard's *viri*, and the other version's demons, identify the forces within dance as apparitional, outside the bounds of normalcy.[37] Bromyard seems interested in associating dance with the supernatural; another *exemplum* of his imagines a demon gesturing to human dances as evidence

34. Ibid., 89; my translation. For a more detailed discussion of these *exempla*, see my "Dance in a Haunted Space: Genre, Form, and the Middle English Carol," *Exemplaria* 27.1–2 (2015): 133–35.

35. Ingrid Nelson, *Lyric Tactics: Poetry, Genre, and Practice in Later Medieval England* (Philadelphia: University of Pennsylvania Press, 2017), 118–19.

36. I evoke Tzvetan Todorov's structuralist term; its duality maps onto my discussion of the virtual not simply as immateriality but rather as born from an interaction of the bodily with immaterial force. *The Fantastic: A Structural Approach to a Literary Genre*, trans. Richard Howard (Ithaca: Cornell University Press, 1975), 41–57.

37. On the medieval conflation of ghosts and demons, see my "Haunted," 134.

of subjection to unholy powers.[38] Jones again articulates a nexus implicitly at work in medieval representations of dance, one that will assert itself in different ways throughout this study: in perceiving dance's virtuality, the spectator often understands this manifestation to be *étrange*, something that disrupts ordinary structures of time and space.

Medieval representations of dance—whether they include demons, fairies, magical illusions, or virginal visions—communicate this virtuality, the forces that tip away from conventional materiality but that, like the uncanny, are at the same time familiar to audiences as well as tethered to the material body. Sensitizing oneself to forces and energies that anticipate or lag behind the dancer's body, that hover around it or off its center, becomes part of the experience of dance for medieval audiences. Not only is virtuality integral to medieval experiences of dance, but premodern audiences also expect those experiences to produce disorientation, forces not centered within the body but manifesting themselves as adjacent paranormalcies in time and space.

ON MEDIEVAL POETIC FORM

In each of my case studies, experiences of danced virtuality are the mode by which audiences experience poetic form as strange footing. The medieval audience's attunement to the strange forces of dance, I will show, functions as a perceptual practice that leads them through an experience of poetic form. Strange footing thus emerges for us not by comparing dance to poetry as separate entities but instead by construing poetic form as constituted in dance's perceptual habits. Strangeness as a medieval category wields multifarious power and meaning. Its sense of distance in space or time evokes a concomitant unintelligibility that in the end can be more compellingly salient than the distance itself, as Ardis Butterfield argues.[39] The *House of Fame's* use of *straunge* to describe German dance tunes seems to reflect the foreign nature of these idioms; however, the environment's plethora of bizarre stimuli might equally permit *straunge* to convey such performances as curious or bewildering.[40] Susan Crane argues that the Middle English

38. Silen, "Dance," 70, 76n12.

39. Ardis Butterfield, *The Familiar Enemy: Chaucer, Language and Nation in the Hundred Years War* (New York: Oxford University Press, 2009), 198. See her comments that *straunge* could stand in for *alien* as a legal term but could also refer to origin elsewhere in England (203–4); as well as for "disengagement" from ownership (294).

40. ". . . Pipers of the Duche tonge / To lerne love-daunces, sprynges, / Reyes, and these straunge thynges" (*HF* ll. 1234–36). The performer preceding these dance accompanists is a skinless satyr (ll. 1229–30).

descriptor *straunge* moves beyond "foreignness" or "distance" to signal indeterminacy across many ontological categories.[41] When Cynthia Hahn refers to reliquaries as "strange" in medieval and modern eyes, she conveys qualities of wonder-inducement and unexpectedness.[42] Finally, as Joyce Coleman suggests through the example of Robert Mannyng, strangeness in poetic language might even evoke "unauthorized fascination" on an author's part.[43] Attending to medieval poetry's relationship with dance identifies this multifaceted quality of strangeness not just within the plot, theme, or structural attributes of a poem but also within an audience's experience of verse form.

My investigation of danced virtuality extracts a theory of medieval poetic form from a culture that does not always make such theories explicit. Bruce Holsinger has argued that traditional readings of medieval music, which often privilege music's relationship to harmony, and the perfections of numerical or cosmological order, risk obscuring important aspects of embodied music practice.[44] I similarly rethink dance practice but additionally point out that to do so reconfigures our understanding of medieval poetic form. In assembling my claim thus, I respond to Nicolette Zeeman's challenge that we must carefully seek the Middle Ages' " 'imaginative' articulations of literary theory," because these are often not explicitly named as such.[45] A perceptual habituation—as conditioned by dance—to uncanniness and disorientation in poetic form offers itself as a theory of medieval verse structure that may not name itself that way.

In this sense, *Strange Footing* intervenes broadly into theories of poetic form. It speaks back to the specific critical phenomenon of New Formalism, but its stakes also lie in a more capacious set of issues. These concern our habits as modern formalist readers of the past, the history of formalist practice that has produced these, and the ways these habits intersect with strangeness. It is important to recognize that the contemporary formalist analysis of a premodern poem brings ingrained modern reading habits to

41. Susan Crane, *Animal Encounters: Contacts and Concepts in Medieval Britain* (Philadelphia: University of Pennsylvania Press, 2013), 127–30.

42. Cynthia Hahn, *Strange Beauty: Issues in the Making and Meaning of Reliquaries, 400–circa 1204* (University Park, PA: Penn State University Press, 2014), 8. See also Butterfield, *Familiar*, 336–37, on predominantly nonlinguistic strangeness as intricacy or obscurity.

43. Joyce Coleman, "Strange Rhyme: Prosody and Nationhood in Robert Mannyng's 'Story of England,'" *Speculum* 78.2 (2003): 1218.

44. Bruce W. Holsinger, *Music, Body, and Desire in Medieval Culture: Hildegard of Bingen to Chaucer* (Stanford: Stanford University Press, 2001), 5–6.

45. Nicolette Zeeman, "Imaginative Theory," in *Oxford Twenty-First Century Approaches to Literature: Middle English*, ed. Paul Strohm (Oxford: Oxford University Press, 2007), 222.

the encounter with the medieval.[46] One such habit involves the modernist and postmodern desire to trouble or "break" poetic form's apparent regularities; this stance finds poetry's deepest revelations in those places where it is most recalcitrant or discordant.[47] Sometimes as contemporary readers we perceive this modern sense of poetic form to exist in opposition to the aesthetics of medieval verse. At other times we work to locate moments of disorientation within medieval poetry. We make such effort because it is productive to bring certain developments in formalist study—like the attention to destabilizing irregularity—to bear on objects that predate them. Christopher Cannon demonstrates that the most confusing formal elements of some medieval texts are the ones that contribute integrally to their comprehensive logics.[48] *Strange Footing* builds upon this approach to ask how the postmodern reading habits developed from a critical legacy of formalist practice can decode those medieval sensibilities and where the limitations of those modern reading habits lie. While to some degree this book reproduces the protocols of modern formalist reading, its two-stage methodology—dance to poetry—creates a context for reading that requires acknowledgment of and response to the particularities of a medieval cultural situation. Reading by this method reveals that in its intersection with dance, a medieval poem can trouble, destabilize, or break its structure in ways that reach beyond modernity's understanding of what formal rupture might mean. *Strange Footing* thus positions itself to speak back to postmodernity's formalist work. In excavating some foundations underlying our contemporary formalist priorities, *Strange Footing* asserts that a deeper understanding of premodern poetic form is essential to literary studies' present endeavors to see formalism anew.

46. Valerie Allen points out the importance of distinguishing medieval and modern poetics within the context of ekphrastic discourse, noting that their difference "rests on different understandings of form and of the category of the aesthetic, and on the relationship between materiality and textuality." "Ekphrasis and the Object," in *The Art of Vision: Ekphrasis in Medieval Literature and Culture*, ed. Andrew James Johnston, Ethan Knapp, and Margitta Rouse (Columbus, OH: The Ohio State University Press, 2015), 17.

47. Harold Bloom, "The Breaking of Form" (1979), in *The Lyric Theory Reader: A Critical Anthology*, ed. Virginia Jackson and Yopie Prins (Baltimore: The Johns Hopkins University Press, 2014), 275–86; Yopie Prins, "'What Is Historical Poetics?'" *Modern Language Quarterly* 77.1 (2016): 28, 30 (and see chapters 4 and 6).

48. Christopher Cannon, "Form," in *Middle English: Oxford Twenty-First Century Approaches to Literature*, ed. Paul Strohm (New York: Oxford University Press, 2007), 189–90; and Cannon, *The Grounds of English Literature* (New York: Oxford University Press, 2004), 3–10. See also Cannon's discussion of the Bayeux Tapestry as illuminating history's tendency, in collusion with our "desiring mind," to manufacture "coherence" (*Grounds*, 22–24).

Geoffrey Chaucer's *ballade* "To Rosemounde" will demonstrate, in closing, how danced virtuality produces an experience of poetic form. Readers of this poem have tended to explain its famously peculiar images—the tub of tears and sauced fish—as existing along a spectrum that runs from the disproportion of exaggeration to elusively discernible parody to the disorientation of generic instability.[49] Jill Mann advocates for the need to find explanations for this poem's "oddly discordant" imagery that do not rely on the complexities of genre; her solution is to posit Rosemounde as a child addressee, making the poem a "courtly amusement."[50] I suggest a different explanation for these ill-fitting images. Spoken by someone who watches a dance, "To Rosemounde," I argue, reveals a process of poetic encounter configured in the practices of dance spectatorship. In a context of a sensitivity to danced virtuality, what seems the strangeness of "To Rosemounde"'s imagery reveals instead a more deeply embedded experience of strange form.

Madame, ye ben of al beaute shryne
As fer as cercled is the mapamounde,
For as the cristal glorious ye shyne,
And lyke ruby ben your chekes rounde.
Therwith ye ben so mery and so jocounde   5
That at a revel whan that I see you daunce,
It is an oynement unto my wounde,
Thogh ye to me ne do no daliaunce.

For thogh I wepe of teres ful a tyne,
Yet may that wo myn herte nat confounde;   10
Your semy voys that ye so smal out twyne
Maketh my thoght in joy and blis habounde.
So curtaysly I go with love bounde
That to myself I sey in my penaunce,
"Suffyseth me to love you, Rosemounde,   15
Thogh ye to me ne do no daliaunce."

49. See, respectively, Edmund Reiss, "Dusting off the Cobwebs: A Look at Chaucer's Lyrics," *Chaucer Review* 1.1 (1966): 64; T. L. Burton, "'The Fair Maid of Ribbesdale' and the Problem of Parody," *Essays in Criticism* 31 (1981): 282; and Alfred Hiatt, "Genre without System," in *Middle English*, 277–78.
50. Jill Mann, "The Inescapability of Form," in *Readings in Medieval Textuality: Essays in Honour of A. C. Spearing*, ed. Cristina Maria Cervone and D. Vance Smith (Cambridge: D. S. Brewer, 2016), 130.

Nas neuer pyk walwed in galauntyne
As I in love am walwed and ywounde,
For which ful ofte I of myself devyne
That I am trewe Tristam the secounde.   20
My love may not refreyde nor affounde,
I brenne ay in an amorous plesaunce.
Do what you lyst, I wyl your thral be founde,
Thogh ye to me ne do no daliaunce.
tregentil . . . . // . . . . chaucer[51]

This poem describes a scene of dance, draws for its form upon the tradition of lyric accompaniment to dance, and is produced in a dance-attuned literary setting. While "To Rosemounde" most likely did not accompany an actual dance, Chaucer's influences and interlocutors, like Machaut and Deschamps, wrote lyrics that were mindful of the aesthetics of dance and dance accompaniment.[52] Within this context, the lyric not only narrates a brief dance-based episode but also employs a form—the *ballade*—tied to dance practice. The origins of the *ballade* form situate themselves in the refrain-structured poetry that accompanied both folk and aristocratic dances earlier in the Middle Ages.[53] We might begin, then, by considering what happens if we use certain attributes of "To Rosemounde"—such as its verse structure—to *reconstruct* its dance. In this enterprise, the poem's resolving stanzaic structure provides a template for a vision of orderly dance. It might furthermore be tempting to map the symmetrical roundness of Rosemounde's cheeks and the *mapamounde* onto this imagined choreography, reinforcing a sense of harmonious concentricity between the dance and the poetic stanzas. If, then, we wanted to use the poem to imagine the dance to which it gestures, we would generate a tableau of circularity regarded from outside. From the concatenated poem with its repeating refrain,

51. Benson, 649.
52. See chapter 2.
53. Helen Louise Cohen, *The Ballade* (New York: Columbia University Press, 1915), 45. Julia Boffey and Paula Simpson bring to light another Middle English *ballade*, addressed to "Susan." This poem intensifies the epistolary intimation that Martin Camargo identifies in "To Rosemounde"; both additionally share the coy use of "daliaunce." Both also directly refer to dance, with Susan "in daunsyng, sport, and curtesie / Wele demeand." "A Middle English Poem on a Binding Fragment: Early Valentine?" *Review of English Studies* 67.282 (2016): 851; Martin Camargo, *The Middle English Verse Love Epistle* (Tübingen: Max Niemayer Verlag, 1991), 44.

we would create—like the *mapamounde*—a dance that is also a whole, bracelet-like object.

But to travel interpretively from "To Rosemounde"'s most evident formal attributes to a choreographic idea (from poetry to dance) occludes the more intensely experiential component of dance to which the poem refers. For ". . . at a revel, whan that I see you daunce," the speaker says, "It is an oynement unto my wounde" (ll. 7–8).[54] In its speaker's positioning, "To Rosemounde" invites us to *reenact* an experience of participatory spectatorship particular to medieval social dance. In this scenario, the spectator of dance is habituated to its conventions and requirements, fluctuating between the roles of participant and spectator. As Frances Eustace and Pamela M. King argue, both participation and observation are "an essential part of the experience of dance in the medieval period."[55] Invested in her unattainability, "To Rosemounde"'s speaker appears to emphasize spectatorship without active partnership. At the same time, however, a speaker who describes himself watching a dance at a party is potentially educated and conditioned in the ways of social dance, habituated to what it presents perceptually. In another example, Christine de Pisan's early fifteenth-century *Livre du duc des vrais amans* precedes the speaker's leading of the lady into the dance ("Si la prins et la menay / A la dance" [Therefore I took her and led her to the dance]) with the statement that at the commencement of the *danse*, "tout homme s'esgaye / La belle feste esgardant" [every man gladdened watching the beautiful revel].[56] Narrating a social dance involves blurring the boundaries between spectatorship and participation; the pleasure of "tout homme" is the speaker's pleasure as well.[57] While the evidence cannot be definitive, it implies that even if the Chaucerian speaker is not

54. Chaucer's Black Knight, surely educated in dance practice himself, also watches his lady dance in the *Book of the Duchess*: "I sawgh hyr daunce so comlily, / Carole and synge so swetely" (*BD* ll. 848–49).

55. Frances Eustace with Pamela M. King, "Dances of the Living and the Dead: A Study of *Danse Macabre* Imagery within the Context of Late-Medieval Dance Culture" in *Mixed Metaphors: The Danse Macabre in Medieval and Early Modern Europe*, ed. Sophie Oosterwijk and Stefanie Knöll (Newcastle Upon Tyne: Cambridge Scholars, 2011), 47.

56. Maurice Roy, ed., *Le Livre du duc des vrais amans*, in *Oeuvres poétiques de Christine de Pisan*, vol. 3 (Paris: Firmin Didiot, 1846), page 82, ll. 780–81, 774–75. She later favors him with "doulz regart," l. 797.

57. As Laura Weigert argues, the participatory experience of medieval performance is perceptible even in certain forms of medieval evidence, and such evidence does not necessarily reify performance. *French Visual Culture and the Making of Medieval Theatre* (New York: Cambridge University Press, 2015), 10.

partnered with Rosemounde in the dance, we might still understand his experience as that of as an engaged, informed, and even immersed spectator.[58]

What, then, appears to the medieval viewer in this state of habituation to, and familiarity with, the bodily imagery of dance? A brief return to modernity offers a means to reenact an answer to this question. *Ghostcatching*, as we saw, brings to light the possibility of medieval dance spectatorship as attuned to the forces that exist between and around embodied dancers; in addition, it conveys the strangeness of those virtualities. Because "To Rosemounde" focuses our attention upon a particular spectator, it prompts us to investigate the nature of that strangeness perceived. Here, as throughout this study, danced virtuality consists of forces cast from the body and suspended between material gestures, registering impulsion not centered within the body. Langer the theorist, along with Bussell the dancer, imply in their descriptions of perceived force a destabilizing of spatial regularity. The trace of the metaphoric sparkler can be detected only by hovering in a space adjacent to the body that produces it. The forces between and around two dancers necessarily affect their operations of reciprocity or symmetry with each other. Indeed, watching *Ghostcatching*'s dancer produce his arcs of force is a spatially disorienting experience: those lines cross, complicate, and interfere with the body's symmetry and center. "To Rosemounde" presents a medieval viewer who watches the dance from an involved and attuned position. In response, we might combine the insights gleaned from the accessible experiences of dancer, spectator, and theorist to reenact—in the space between medieval and modern occurrence—such a medieval viewer's apprehension of virtuality's strange forces.

In the reenactment exercise, introducing virtuality to Chaucer's *ballade* might seem entirely speculative; however, the poem's use of the word *oynement* reveals itself to indicate the presence of such virtuality. For Middle English poets endow healing substances like *oynement* with the force of *vertu*.[59] Ardis Butterfield compares Chaucer's line about ointment to Gower's healing stone in No. 45 of his *Cinkante Balades*, a *ballade* that bears

---

58. Gazing and spectatorship (sometimes thematized as narcissistic self-regard) have been identified elsewhere as important concepts in this poem. Nicolette Zeeman, "The Gender of Song in Chaucer," *Studies in the Age of Chaucer* 29 (2007): 142; John Stephens, "The Uses of Personae and the Art of Obliqueness in Some Chaucer Lyrics: Part III," *Chaucer Review* 22.1 (1987): 43–44.

59. Rossell Hope Robbins groups *oynement* with *walwed* and *galantyne* as terms conventionalized by their appearance in the *Romance of the Rose*. But that grouping suggests that *oynement* registers as off-putting and peculiar in the same ways that those other words are

other similarities to "To Rosemounde": "Car celle piere qui la poet toucher /
De sa vertu reçoit sa medicine" [for whoever can touch that stone receives
its cure through its *vertu*, its power].[60] Associated with the healing object,
then, is the force of *vertu*. In the fifteenth century, the word *oynement* itself
appears paired with *vertu*: Lydgate observes in an allegorical capacity that
"Oynemente ys a soote thyng, And ryht vertuous in werkyng To woundys
cloos & ope also," while Capgrave likens St. Gilbert's "vertu" to an "oynement" that must be stirred and rolled with tribulation in order to enhance
its pungency.[61] The metaphor in "To Rosemounde"—when I see you dance,
it is an ointment to my wound—is not quite straightforward. Not the dance
itself but the *activity* of watching of Rosemounde dance is comparable to
salve as an *object* that will heal the wound of his love. *Oynement*'s virtuality, however, allows it to function as an object whose qualities can map
onto an activity. In one sense, *oynement* is simply a virtuous object. But its
usages suggest equally that such objects of healing, the stone or the salve,
operate through force, something sensible but not tangible, something supplementary to the object. In "To Rosemounde," the *vertu* of *oynement* thus
permits the metaphor to signal the apprehension of not only the body but
also the forces of virtuality that appear in the activity of watching it in motion. The force and activity of the body—the *vertu* necessary to the functioning of *oynement*—enable the sight of Rosemounde dancing to be the
ointment dressing the wound.

Having discerned the presence of virtuality in the poem's dance spectatorship, we become aware that virtuality underlies "To Rosemounde"'s pervasive sense of conflict. If dance as *oynement* speaks to the *vertu* hovering in
the interstices between material bodies, limbs, or folds of flesh, those forces
operate dually and even oppositionally. In Lydgate's later terms, the *vertu* of
oynement knits things together, but it also opens them up, stretches them
apart. To call the sight of dance an *oynement* conveys not only its sense
of force but also the multiple and even conflicting functions of that force.
The *ballade*'s refrain makes explicit this sense of tension between drawing
together and pushing apart: "though ye to me ne do no daliaunce." The pang

---

often perceived to be. "Chaucer's 'To Rosemounde,'" *Studies in the Literary Imagination* 4
(1971): 75.

60. Butterfield, *Familiar*, 255.

61. John Lydgate, trans., *The Pilgrimage of the Life of Man*, ed. F. J. Furnivall and K. B. Locock,
EETS e.s. 77, 83, 92 (Millwood, NY: Kraus, repr. 1973), l. 1513; J. J. Munro, ed., *John Capgrave's
Lives of St. Augustine and St. Gilbert of Sempringham*, EETS o.s. 140 (London: Oxford University
Press, 1910), 93.

of the *though* with which the refrain repeatedly begins is our familiar cue that the lady seems both near and far to the speaker, in his world but out of his reach. In this sense, its forces of *vertu* render the dance relevant to the speaker's manifest conundrum. Virtuality's disorientations, the forces pulling in different directions from their interstitial spaces, estrange.

But I would also suggest that the perception of danced virtuality does deeper and subtler work: medieval dance and its virtualities constitute a perceptual practice that leads the reader through the poem. In this process, poetic form becomes an experience rather than an entity. I began this reading by considering what I called the formal attributes of "To Rosemounde": the structure of the stanza, the insertion of the refrain, even the sense of concentricity derived in the play of round imagery and concatenating verse. Here and throughout this study, however, I maintain that there exists an experience of poetic form that is not entirely accounted for, and does not entirely line up with, what its attributes might appear to do. When "To Rosemounde" 's first stanza refers to dance, it articulates a perceptual practice for the rest of the poem. Signaling the virtualities of dance, this stanza awakens an attunement to forces that hover between things visible and material. In a process of leading that I will later explore through the medieval language of *ductus*, this dance-inflected attunement conducts the reader through the poem to produce an experience of form.

In this process of leading, "To Rosemounde" reveals that the strangeness of the poem does not instantiate itself in the second and third stanzas' actual images of tear-filled tubs and sauced fish; rather, it lies in the interstitial forces between stanzas. For it is important to note that those motifs with which readers have struggled are each positioned at a stanza's opening (ll. 9 and 17). In each instance, the image follows the refrain, whose diction, rhythm, and repetition emphasize periodicity, proportion, and expectation fulfilled. The stanzas' initiating images—the tub, the rolled fish—seem to respond with roundness of their own, but they evoke, as many have opined, roundness that is pronouncedly off-kilter. Proceeding through the poem, the reader recognizes something impelling the text away from the resolving mechanism of refrain and ultimately expressing itself in the misalignment with which the next stanza begins. That something is the force of *vertu*, the virtual traces that twist and disrupt. The strangeness that we have always detected in "To Rosemounde" 's images expresses materially an even stranger, intangible force hovering between one stanza and the next. In this way, "To Rosemounde" illustrates poetic form as an experience constituted in the medieval engagement with danced virtuality.

PLAN OF THE BOOK

Strange Footing begins with a section that defines the argument's structuring terms and elaborates on the book's theory of poetic form. Chapter 1 considers in detail the meanings of *reenactment, experience,* and *virtuality* as they operate in my argument. Chapter 2 deploys these three terms to explain the book's theory of medieval poetic form. This chapter investigates medieval poetic form as an experience of strange time and space shaped by readers' habituation to the untimely and materially ambiguous elements— the virtualities—of dance. The chapter's foundation is the concept of *ductus* as a process that leads an agent through a formal network of dance and other visual media in producing an experience of poetic form. The book's first section is followed by two case studies, one on *danse macabre* art and poetry and one on the danced *carole* and the poetic carol. Each case study will begin by reenacting the experience of its dance tradition, thus identifying the experience of that tradition and the virtualities that supplement it. Each case study will then proceed to consider how the perceptual practices of that dance tradition produce the audience's experience of the associated poetry's form.

Danse macabre is not conventionally understood as an embodied performance tradition, often involving instead site-specific installations that integrate painting, architecture, and ambulatory spectators. Chapter 3 argues, however, that while its lack of choreographed dancers might prevent us from seeing *danse macabre* as dance, *danse macabre* appears as such to its premodern audiences because it creates the virtual supplements that characterize medieval dance. To reenact *danse macabre,* I juxtapose it with Lucinda Childs's iconic avant-garde piece *Dance* (1979). The resulting reenactment reveals that what is terrifying and compelling about *danse macabre* is not simply its reminder of death's inevitability; it is, more comprehensively, the suggestion that confronting death involves an agglomeration of multiple rates and structures of temporal passage at once. Chapter 4 turns to John Lydgate's fifteenth-century *danse macabre* poem, whose inscription often accompanies the painted installation. This chapter brings to bear the perceptual experience to which *danse macabre* imagery habituates its viewers—one of temporal and spatial ambiguity in the dynamic force of virtuality—upon *danse macabre* poetry's form. Its resulting claim is that what superficially appear as relentlessly serial and predictable *huitain* verses are experienced as untimely and disorienting.

The next case study comprises a diptych of chapters concerning the round dance often referred to as *carole* and the Middle English poetic carol.

In Chapter 5, I reenact the medieval *carole* by setting it next to Mark Morris's round dances in *L'Allegro, il Penseroso ed il Moderato* (1988). In the space between medieval and postmodern dance, I demonstrate that the embodied circle of the *carole* casts out from itself virtual circles, arcs, and trajectories of force that decenter the dance's apparently perfect circularity and syncopate its time. Chapter 6 argues that the skewed, hovering virtual supplements of the *carole* inform readers' experiences of the Middle English poetic carol's structure in two fourteenth-century examples. In different ways, perceptual attunements to virtual circles destabilize the resolution and closure of each poetic carol's ostensible structure.

By beginning with *danse macabre* and proceeding to the Middle English carols I have chosen, I reverse the chronological order of these texts; I have structured this reversal for specific expositional purposes. Beginning with *danse macabre* offers readers what can be (though is not always) a concrete intersection of visual spectacle, text, and audience. Once we learn to outline the contours of the resultant interactions in a setting of multiple material media, we then move to a case study—*carole* and carol—in which the status of dance as an embodied medium relative to the poem is more vexed, sliding along a scale between accompaniment and ideational trace.[62] But even in this latter case, dance lends its habits of perception with equal force to the experience of poetic form. In addition, while *danse macabre* requires its interpretations to address a particular preoccupation with death, the carol is a lyric genre whose examples treat a variety of topics. Proceeding from a narrower to a wider interpretive field showcases my reading method's capacity to accommodate a range of interpretive ends. Finally, moving from the fifteenth century to the fourteenth reminds us that dance and poetry's relationship does not plot—as modernity's perspective can lead us to believe—a clear course from intimacy to distance, but is rather a moving target throughout the Middle Ages. The relation of dance to other media equally complicates the notion of progression along a single trajectory. While *danse macabre* itself postdates the *carole*, its model of a multimedia environment that refers to and includes kinetic practices would certainly have existed earlier in the Middle Ages, whether in drama, liturgical or paraliturgical performance against the backdrop of church art and

62. This perspective on media engages a different set of concerns from the play of transparency and opacity that informs many discussions of postmodern media. See, for instance, Jay David Bolter and Richard Grusin, *Remediation: Understanding New Media*, rev. ed. (Cambridge, MA: MIT Press, 2000), 21.

architecture, or other idioms of installation art.[63] The section order reinforces the point that dance and poetry's relation is not a linear trajectory;
it also reminds us to recognize the plurality of specific relations that the
general category of multimediacy might include.

My conclusion addresses the questions the readings raise concerning the
role of hermeneutic value in the reading of form. In some instances, conceiving of poetic form as an experience constituted in the perceptual practices of dance answers questions about particular poems—as both texts and
manuscript objects—that have hitherto puzzled us. Those interpretations
yield the kind of hermeneutic payoff we traditionally seek in literary and
historical analysis. But I am equally interested in the exercise of naming the
contributions of formal readings independently of the interventions often
valued in literary and historical fields. In deploying dance to expand and
even alter our sense of what poetic form means in a premodern context, I
aim finally for the strange footing of medieval poetic form to pace some new
avenues of approach to poetic form in other realms as well.

---

63. On dance in churches, churchyards, and other sacred and devotional architecture, see, for
instance, L. Gougaud, "La danse dans les églises," *Revue d'histoire ecclésiastique* 15.1 (1914): 5–
22 and 15.2 (1914): 229–45; Peter Dronke, *The Medieval Lyric* (London: Hutchinson & Co., 1968),
186–88; Jeannine Horowitz, "Les danses cléricales dans les églises au Moyen âge," *Le Moyen Âge* 2
(1989): 279–92; and Karen Silen, "Elisabeth of Spalbeek: Dancing the Passion," in *Women's Work:
Making Dance in Europe before 1800*, ed. Lynn Matluck Brooks (Madison: University of Wisconsin Press, 2007), which describes thirteenth-century dance performance "held in a specially built
round chapel" (207, 215).

PART I

CHAPTER ONE

"Vanysshed Was This Daunce": Reenactment, Experience, Virtuality

This chapter explains *Strange Footing*'s approach to medieval dance by defining that approach's major terms: reenactment, experience, virtuality. My method for analyzing medieval dance invokes several subdisciplines across performance studies, history, and philosophy, and my nomenclature will signify differently to readers of different disciplinary backgrounds. For these reasons term definition becomes especially important. I begin by elaborating upon *reenactment* as an experimental methodology by which to deepen our understanding of premodern scenes of dance as these were both performed and watched. I proceed to consider the implications of identifying, through reenactment, the *experience* of participatory spectatorship in medieval dance. What emerges in these experiences is the presence of *virtual* environments perceptible to medieval dance audiences and participants. I end by reading a lyric from Boccaccio's *Decameron* to illustrate the experience of virtuality that we can discern in the reenactment of dance. This text does not number among the poems I read closely for the experience of form; rather, it illustrates the need for experimental reenactment and portrays the virtuality that supplements experiences of dance. But by ending with a brief look at a lyric, I draw attention to an inextricable relation of dance and verse and set the stage for the ensuing readings that reenact poetic form as an experience produced in interactions among media.

NARRATIVE REENACTMENT

This section will describe the activity I term *narrative reenactment*. My approach is conceptually indebted to performance theory's approaches to reenactment, which confront the issues of temporality and historicity that arise in the process of representing a performance of the past. In particular

I respond to Mark Franko's formulation of dance reenactment as not only theorizing but also problematizing the archive, time, the alignment of historical subjects, and the history of reenactment itself.[1] Reenactments *as* performances contribute to his investigation, such as a piece that compels attention to the space between past and present by featuring visible costume changes during its reperformance of historical choreography; and a piece that incorporates archival encounter into the performance.[2] Freddie Rokem further examines the performance-based work of reenactment in terms of the "hyper-historian," the performer who negotiates past and present, sometimes through metatheatrical means. This performer does not "'scientific[ally]'" replicate past performance but rather reenacts, through consciousness of his own location in the present, the "conditions" characteristic of historical performance or event.[3] While my method draws on concepts resonant with Franko's and Rokem's, it differs in producing *narrative reenactments* rather than considering performance objects. These narratives elucidate—through an awareness of the postmodern perspective—the conditions of spectatorship and participation characteristic of vanished medieval performance.

Performance reconstruction contends with the difficulty of accounting fully for the body's historical contingency. Dance and music historians like Margit Sahlin, Ann Harding, Ingrid Brainard, Mabel Dolmetsch, and, more recently, Joan Rimmer and Robert Mullally have meticulously researched various movement components of early dance; their work provides an indispensable foundation for my readings throughout this study.[4] Dance scholarship has sometimes pursued its goals through reconstruction projects and

1. Mark Franko, "Epilogue to an Epilogue: Historicizing the Re- in Danced Reenactment," in *The Oxford Handbook of Dance and Reenactment*, ed. Mark Franko (New York: Oxford University Press, 2017), 487–503. Franko reconsiders his earlier proposal of "construction" as an alternative to traditional reconstruction in 1993's *Dance as Text: Ideologies of the Baroque Body*, rev. ed. (New York: Oxford University Press, 2015), 131–51.

2. The two pieces, Susanne Linke's *Hommage à Dore Hoyer* (1987) and Martin Nachbar's *Urheben Aufheben* (2008), explore Dore Hoyer's *Affectos Humanos* (1962). Franko, "Epilogue," 494–95.

3. Freddie Rokem, *Performing History: Theatrical Representations of the Past in Contemporary Theatre* (Iowa City: University of Iowa Press, 2000), 13.

4. Brainard and Dolmetsch were both married to musicologists, the latter to Arnold Dolmetsch, a proponent of historical instrument use in the reconstruction of early music. Arnold might have influenced the historian R. G. Collingwood in developing his theory of historical reenactment: Collingwood's father hosted members of the Early Music Revival, "pioneered" by Arnold, in England. Kate Bowan, "R. G. Collingwood, Historical Reenactment and the Early Music Revival," in *Historical Reenactment: From Realism to the Affective Turn*, ed. Iain McCalman and Paul A. Pickering (New York: Palgrave Macmillan, 2010), 134–37.

performances, as did Brainard with her Cambridge Court Dancers ensemble (founded in 1969). But ultimately, no matter the level of detail at which we might understand an early dance, the fact of historical contingency renders it partial to us.[5] As Skiles Howard argues, "there is no 'body' that is not shaped by historical forces."[6] Furthermore, archival evidence can be unreliable even when it purports to represent dance. Sharon Fermor points out, for instance, that fifteenth-century Italian painters who depicted dance often did not do so with the goal of recording dance techniques and practices accurately; rather, they drew upon conventions influenced by classical models or else exaggerated movements for emphasis or idealization, presenting a highly mediated representation of dance.[7] Finally, it is important to bear in mind that a "master conceit" of traditional reconstruction methodology has been "to evoke what no longer is."[8] As such, it must create the sensation of having entered a past world, a sensation perforce undermined by any element drawing attention to its incompleteness or contingency. And indeed, the staging of medieval performance has moved increasingly away from the purely reconstructive goal.[9]

5. Many dance reconstructions are rigorous and thoughtful in their use of the available information. But it can be difficult to ignore the performers' postmedieval dance training living in their bodies, as well as differences in factors, like costume, that dictate movement practices. For example, modern shoes diverge in both construction and purpose from the footwear of the late Middle Ages. In the *Roman de la rose*'s depiction of a danced *carole*, the narrator specifies the type of shoe that the dancer Mirth wears. Chaucer renders this as "And shod he was with gret maistrie, / With shoon decoped, and with lass" (*RR* ll. 842–43) ["Chauciez refu par grant metrisse / D'un solers decopez a laz"]; see Guillaume de Lorris et Jean de Meun, *Le Roman de la rose*, ed. Armand Strubel (Paris: Livre de poche, 1992), ll. 825–26. This account recalls the attention paid the shoes of the Miller's Absalon (*CT* 1.3318), also a dancer (*CT* 1.3328–30). These medieval descriptions suggest a different set of functions—and effects—for dancing shoes than those associated with, for instance, ballet flats or modern character shoes.

6. Howard, *Politics*, 4. See also Asa Simon Mittman's articulation of the more general problem that "In no cases can we have unmediated views of 'medieval' or 'early modern objects,' since the periods have passed (and it is dubious to argue that even medieval viewers could have some sort of 'pure' experience of an object, since all experience is mediated by numerous non-technological factors and frameworks)." "Of Wood and Bone: Crafting Living Things," *Preternature: Critical and Historical Studies on the Preternatural* 4.1 (2015): 114.

7. Sharon Fermor, "On the Question of Pictorial 'Evidence' for Fifteenth-Century Dance Technique," *Dance Research Journal* 5.2 (1987): 18–19, 23, 27, 29. Fermor refers mainly to fifteenth-century court dance, whose understated, naturalized (28) dignity would have been difficult to convey as dance in a representation. But her point reminds us of the mediating factors in any representation of early dance.

8. Franko, *Dance*, 133. See also Franko, "Authenticity in Dance," in *Encyclopedia of Aesthetics*, vol. 2, ed. Michael Kelly (New York: Oxford University Press), 268–71.

9. Lofton Durham, for instance, explains that he is less interested in using performance to "replicate" a medieval circumstance than to bring contemporary approaches to the medieval

The present study converses with other scholarship in medieval studies that considers these issues in the study of the Middle Ages more broadly. A number of medieval subfields foreground a self-conscious perspective on modernity and postmodernity as the filter through which to analyze the Middle Ages. Scholars of medieval theatrical performance such as John R. Elliott and Margaret Rogerson have, for instance, focused on the twentieth-century restaging of medieval mystery plays, following David Lowenthal's encouragement to question the dismissal of "heritage industries" and instead acknowledge the political and economic ideologies underlying reenactment.[10] Claire Sponsler, meanwhile, examines the self-conscious use of reconstructed and nostalgic performances of the medieval in the early assertion of American identity.[11] Jody Enders looks to contemporary constructs like "snuff" to consider questions about "where theatre ends and life begins" (or vice versa) in the Middle Ages.[12] Elsewhere, she investigates this question further in terms of accident, intentionality, crime, and consequence by juxtaposing pre- and early-modern performance events with contemporary media spectacles.[13] Alexander Nagel revises our understanding of medieval and modern art's relation by questioning the reifying assumptions that separate them. He reexamines artistic modernity through the lens of certain premodern conventions. By his account, multimedia installation art reflects a more fully representative artistic condition than modern easel art because of the installation's place in a longer history of "multimedia environments."[14] Finally, Carolyn Dinshaw challenges the temporal structures medievalists have traditionally legitimized in studying our period, offering as an alternative a modern amateur desire for the Middle Ages that

---

archive. "Q&A: Meeting the Mostly Medieval Theater Festival," 8 May 2017. http://finearts .wmich.edu/blog/qa-meeting-the-mostly-medieval-theatre-festival.

10. David Lowenthal, *Possessed by the Past: The Heritage Crusade and the Spoils of History* (New York: The Free Press, 1996), x-xiii; John R. Elliott, Jr., *Playing God: Medieval Mysteries and the Modern Stage* (Toronto: University of Toronto Press, 1989); Margaret Rogerson, *Playing a Part in History: The York Mysteries* (Toronto: University of Toronto Press, 2009).

11. Claire Sponsler, *Ritual Imports: Performing Medieval Drama in America* (Ithaca: Cornell University Press, 2004).

12. Jody Enders, *Death by Drama and Other Medieval Urban Legends* (Chicago: University of Chicago Press, 2005), 2.

13. Jody Enders, *Murder by Accident: Medieval Theater, Modern Media, Critical Intentions* (Chicago: University of Chicago Press, 2009); see especially her chapter on accidental death in a dance (89–107).

14. Alexander Nagel, *Medieval Modern: Art out of Time* (London: Thames and Hudson, 2012), 18.

accommodates queer forms of cross-temporality.[15] My approach intersects with these other strategies in a few ways. Like Dinshaw, I privilege the category of the nonprofessional, though I do so within the context of premodern dance. There, as my introduction notes, the condition of amateurism allows certain medieval practices to exist as quotidian and habitual in ways not easily visible to us. Like Nagel, I capitalize upon multimedia environments as sites to consider the premodern and the postmodern in each other's terms. For me, these themes underlie a reenactment process distinct from the recreation of a past event.

To lay a foundation for my reenactment process, I will examine some established uses of the term *reenactment*. One use refers to the performance of historical scenes, especially battles. Rebecca Schneider, for instance, reads Civil War reenactment as a performance mode that seeks both to evoke the past and to meditate upon the implications of this activity; it is "an intense, embodied inquiry into temporal repetition, temporal reoccurrence."[16] Even as a battle reenactor depicts a vivid past through detailed accuracy, he might at the same time annotate the battle with a refrain of continued ideological weight: "the Civil War isn't over."[17] In this case, a specific agenda requires the reenactment to acknowledge a metadiscursive frame, a dialogue between past and present. More generally, such frames rely upon the body's temporal ambiguity within the reenactment project. The very inaccessibility of experiential evidence both foregrounds the conundrum of the irretrievable past and enables the reenactment process to explore the situating of the body—historical and present—across time.

To articulate these complexities, reenactment practices sometimes incorporate a theory of historical study also known as *reenactment*.[18] R. G. Collingwood apparently first began to consider the historian's reenacting

---

15. Carolyn Dinshaw, *How Soon Is Now? Medieval Texts, Amateur Readers, and the Queerness of Time* (Durham: Duke University Press, 2012), xiv, 23–24.

16. Rebecca Schneider, *Performing Remains: Art and War in Times of Theatrical Reenactment* (New York: Routledge, 2011), 2. See also Schneider's discussion of the problematic nature of this term in the context of contemporary high-culture and gallery art (29). Another reenactment model appears in the work of Mary-Kay Gamel, who experiments with contemporary settings and scripts for ancient Greek drama. "From *Thesmophoriazousai* to *The Julie Thesmo Show*: Adaptation, Performance, Reception," *American Journal of Philology* 123.3 (2002): 466–67.

17. Schneider, 32–33.

18. Bowan, 134–58. Collingwood himself may have used the terms *reenactment* and *reconstruction* interchangeably, while I assign different meanings to each. See David Boucher, "The Significance of R. G. Collingwood's *Principles of History*," *Journal of the History of Ideas* 58.2 (1997): 326.

work while wondering how to listen to a piece of music played in the present but composed in the past. His theory, however, developed to address not performance in particular but rather the philosophy of historical inquiry more broadly.[19] For Collingwood, *reenactment* characterizes the historian's consciousness in the act of scholarly investigation into the past. The historian, he contends, is looking for "processes of thought. All history is the history of thought."[20] Collingwood acknowledges the inevitable contribution of the historian's own consciousness to this dynamic, terming this process "re-enactment": "the historian brings to bear on the problem all the powers of his own mind. . . . It is not a passive surrender to the spell of another's mind. . . . The historian not only re-enacts past thought, he re-enacts it in the context of his own knowledge."[21] Historical understanding perceives the difference between the historian's perspective and that of the historical agent, even while considering the implications of inhabiting that distant perspective. Karsten R. Stueber argues that fundamental to Collingwood's theory is the idea of an "indexical" perspective on history.[22] Reenactment, that is to say, acknowledges that while the historian can describe the processes and activities of the past, these descriptions are profoundly shaped by his own "habits of thought."[23]

Reenactment in the theory of historical study reminds us that performance-based reenactment can be vulnerable to some of the same problems as traditional reconstruction, and such performance must therefore ensure that it investigate its own processes and involve the frame of the present in its reenactment of the past. When performance reenactment limits itself to privileging what Vanessa Agnew calls "body-based testimony," it produces an excessively narrow focus on the "minutiae" of experience without questioning the inevitable mediation of this experience. Agnew suggests that Collingwood and other historians introduce a useful awareness of the "essential otherness of historical agents" through their own engagement with reenactment.[24] As a historical theory, reenactment exhorts

---

19. On the idea's origin in a question about musical performance, and its shift into realms "more central to the interests of historians," see William H. Dray, *History as Re-enactment: R. G. Collingwood's Idea of History* (Oxford: Clarendon, 1995), 33.

20. R. G. Collingwood, *The Idea of History*, rev. ed. (Oxford: Clarendon Press, 1993), 215.

21. Ibid.

22. Karsten R. Stueber, "The Psychological Basis of Historical Explanation: Reenactment, Simulation, and the Fusion of Horizons," *History and Theory* 41.1 (2002): 26.

23. Ibid., 41.

24. Vanessa Agnew, "Introduction: What Is Reenactment?" *Criticism* 46.3 (2004): 329.

the reenacted spectacle to accommodate critical self-awareness concerning the spectacle's mediations across time and subjective perspective.[25]

Dance-based reenactment can reflect upon these temporal and perspectival mediations with particular efficacy. To make this point, I turn to the choreographer Doris Humphrey's *The Shakers* (1931). This piece reenacts historic Shaker devotional dance in the sense that it embeds a historic movement practice within choreography that reflects other conceptual and aesthetic agendas that are specific to Humphrey in her own time. Richard Schechner uses this dance to illuminate the pathways by which performance-based behaviors travel and recur, developing his model of performance as "twice-behaved behavior."[26] Specifically, he compares Shaker dances as historic originals to Humphrey's *The Shakers* as well as to Robin Evanchuk's reconstruction of the "authentic" original dances. Humphrey's piece, Schechner notes, does not present itself as an "ethnographic reconstruction."[27] Indeed, the dance is distinctively Humphrey's, featuring her signature *cambré* and her unmistakable *port de bras* that presents as at once curved and angular, as well as her modernist ensemble ethos.[28] And yet, this performance prompts an anthropologist specializing in the Shakers to opine: "Humphrey's choreography embodies a wide range of Shaker culture." In Schechner's terms it is "able to actualize something of Shaker culture"; it "comes close to expressing the heart of the sect." The piece's 1955 revival deeply moved one of the last two surviving Shaker brothers.[29] Evanchuk's stated goal of authenticity in her reconstruction, in contrast, elicits from Schechner some questions that elucidate the problematic nature of reconstruction: if "'authentic' . . . which dances, performed on which occasions, before what audiences, with what dancers?"[30]

---

25. Ibid., 330.

26. Richard Schechner, "Restoration of Behavior," *Between Theater and Anthropology* (Philadelphia: University of Pennsylvania Press, 2010), 36.

27. Ibid., 49.

28. Similar movement motifs appear, for instance, in Humphrey's *Air on the G String* (1934). Humphrey comments that in *The Shakers*, "the strongest and most important movement was given to the group, and it was their collective strength which gave power to the dance." In her statement, Humphrey represents the choreography of *The Shakers* as characteristic not only of her own style but also of modern dance's recognition of a "change in social attitude"; in this way as well the dance asserts its own time in its construction of Shaker heritage. *The Art of Making Dances* (New York: Grove Press, 1959), 92.

29. Schechner, 47–49. On dance's complex engagements with the idioms that it quotes, see Peter W. Travis's argument (drawing on Mary Orr) that parody can exist in choreographic relation to its target text. *Disseminal Chaucer: Rereading the "Nun's Priest's Tale"* (Notre Dame, IN: University of Notre Dame Press, 2010), 14–15.

30. Schechner, 50.

As a frame for a historical past, Humphrey's modernist perspective thus enhances, rather than obscures, the audience's encounter with and understanding of that past. Schechner's discernment of the "heart of the sect" in Humphrey's piece tells us something important. Humphrey demonstrates here what Franko has described in his theory of dance reenactment: she "sacrifices the reproduction of a work to the replication of its most powerful intended effects."[31] Humphrey, that is, employs gestural vocabularies to enter two temporalities—her present and the past object—into conversation. That conversation promotes our understanding not of the minutiae of historical gesture but rather of the gesture's meaning through its very mediation. Humphrey's model foregrounds commingled temporalities, meditating on a historical devotional idiom through a modernist ideal of community expressed in movement practice. This quality grants spectators access to effects that a performance preoccupied with the details of its own authenticity might occlude.

Unlike Humphrey, a book cannot make a dance; *Strange Footing* instead proposes a method of narrative reenactment that draws upon *The Shakers'* danced response to the problems and possibilities of reenactment. My method juxtaposes the performance occasions of the past and the present in order to narrate the effects of medieval spectacle in the space between the two occasions. Acknowledging that archives are only one aspect of a performance's complicated reality, Jeff Friedman argues that the "gaps" between archive and other, more experiential, sites of information are interpretively productive.[32] I shift this model from the realm of performance practice to that of narrative to explore what lies in the interstice between a medieval representation of dance and an accessible viewing experience of a contemporary dance that shares certain structural features with the earlier example. To give a brief example, I ask in chapter 5 what spectatorial effects medieval round dance created for its participants and audiences. In answer, I align medieval round dance's visual and textual representations with a contemporary performance that makes abundant use of choreography in the round, Mark Morris's *L'Allegro, il Penseroso ed il Moderato* (1988). In the space between the two performances, I narrate the presence and effects of virtuality by considering the medieval representations of dancers in terms

31. Franko, *Dance*, 133.

32. Jeff Friedman, "Minding the Gap: The Choreographer as Hyper-Historian in Oral History-Based Performance," in *History, Memory, Performance*, ed. David Dean, Yana Meerzon, and Kathryn Prince (New York: Palgrave Macmillan, 2015), 54, 67.

of the movement dynamics and gazing trajectories that Morris's circling dancers and their audiences create. This account encapsulates my process of *narrative reenactment*: a description of participatory spectatorship in the interstice between medieval and modern examples.

My method has a few implications that will be important to keep in mind. First, unlike studies that read the Middle Ages through modernity by tracing a trajectory of cultural or intellectual influence between them, I do not focus upon causal progressions that might link medieval and contemporary dance.[33] As stated above, I choose contemporary choreography for its structural similarities to medieval scenes, not for similarities of theme or preoccupations of subject matter. As chapter 5 will discuss, the thematic and narrative preoccupations of *L'Allegro* differ from what is at stake in a medieval round dance. I have an interest, however, in the capacity of modern choreographic configurations (circles, processions, partnerings) to evoke, as does Humphrey in *The Shakers*, the interpretive, aesthetic, or affective experience of medieval danced scenes with similar structures. Second, it is dangerous to assume that medieval audiences saw in the ways that we see, and I do not make this contention.[34] I instead place my claims about medieval performance within a negotiating interstice—like the one Humphrey's reenactment creates—that exists between modernity and premodernity and maintains our awareness of the temporal distance between them. Even as I acknowledge the impossibility of lining up sightlines or micromuscular ocular habits between a Mark Morris audience and the participatory watcher of a *carole*, I maintain that the unearthly forces traced in the spaces between Morris's round dancers can cast into relief some elusive aspects of the medieval experience of round dance. Third, I propose here a method of reading whose heuristic device can adapt to suit other interpretive situations. The conditions of my encounter with *L'Allegro* clearly play a role in my interpretation of the medieval dance juxtaposed with it. The reenactment method itself, however, accommodates the possibility that other readers might use other performances that strike them as relevant in choreographic structure to premodern spectacles.

---

33. See, for instance, Bruce Holsinger, *The Premodern Condition: Medievalism and the Making of Theory* (Chicago: University of Chicago Press, 2005), which "traces the shaping force of the medieval" as the "foundation" for an influential body of modern critical theory (x, 4).

34. Kate Giles has noted that "current approaches tend to impose our own, modern ways of seeing and thinking, as a means of understanding perceptions and experiences in the past," occluding the historicity of seeing and space themselves. "Seeing and Believing: Visuality and Space in Pre-Modern England," *World Archaeology* 39.1 (2007): 106.

Ultimately, historical dance encourages acute consciousness of the enterprise of regarding the past. *The Shakers* provides a model for reenacting
the experience of a movement practice through its basketweave of the contemporary and the historical. Medieval dance's very recalcitrance where archives are concerned, meanwhile, can work in its analytical favor. Claire
Sponsler has acknowledged that "whenever dance enters into systems
of signification, it does so in haphazard, partial, and inevitably distorted
ways." She goes on, however, to argue that the distorting "entanglement"
of medieval Morris dance with later traditions provides useful opportunities to challenge entrenched assumptions about historical periodization by
rethinking our ways of understanding and defining performance.[35] Medieval dance's lacunae provide opportunities to thread contemporaneity and
theory through it as part of the narrative reenactment process.

EXPERIENCE

What I reenact through my juxtapositional method is not simply dance as
a reified occurrence or self-contained moving diorama. Rather, in reenacting dance I reenact the experience of participating in and watching it. My
deployment of the term *experience* to discuss dance correlates with some of
its medieval senses. Medieval experience emphasizes habitual practice and
the acquisition of skill. Middle English *experience* conveys not only sensory
intake but also participatory engagement involving practice, skill, and investigation. Experience implies the habituation that accompanies repeated
behavior, conveyed in the doctor who should have "vse and experience"
(*MED* 3), as well as the interactivity of experiment (*MED* 2a) and discovery
(*MED* 2b).[36] As the introduction suggested, these senses of *experience* hold
particular relevance to a culture whose familiarity with dance allows it not
only to observe but also to participate. These definitions, that is, reflect the
habituation, responsiveness and interactivity that characterize medieval
dance-based experience.

35. Claire Sponsler, "Writing the Unwritten: Morris Dance and Theatre History," in
Representing the Past: Essays in Performance Historiography, ed. Charlotte Canning and Thomas
Postlewait (Iowa City: University of Iowa Press, 2010), 86–7.

36. See also Curtis R. H. Jirsa, "*Piers Plowman*'s Lyric Poetics," *Yearbook of Langland
Studies* 26 (2012): 80 on the "experiential compositional process" outlined in *Piers Plowman*
that relies on "experiential modes of inquiry" (94); here as well, the experience of sensory intake
involves not only the awareness of such information but also the act of "extract[ing] significance"
from it (94).

At the same time, however, *experience* is a vexed term in both medieval and modern arenas.[37] As does LaCapra with the *OED*, Derek Pearsall critically examines the senses of *experience* in the *MED* (and the *OED*), suggesting that such taxonomies necessarily fail to convey the ambiguities of a word's signifying potential in the Middle Ages.[38] Inflected by a long history of critical perceptions of *experience*'s meaning, the *Wife of Bath's Prologue*'s fame draws itself largely from the shifting relation her words posit between experience and authority in the Middle English context. Karma Lochrie argues that the ostensible dichotomy of written authority and lived experience is considerably complicated by the Wife's strategies to authorize herself even as her lived and affective experience provide avenues for disrupting authoritative codes.[39] Modernity also frames the ambiguities of experience in terms of authority. When, for instance, Agnew considers the role of experience in reenactment, she suggests that the multiplicity of experiential responses within a scene of reenactment risks constituting a "crisis of authority." Participants experience an event in different ways without a "means of adjudicating" among the spectrum of responses, whether in terms of the legitimacy of one reeanctor's experiential response relative to another, or in terms of the correlation of a reenactor's experience with that of a historical subject.[40] In a sense, both periods ask what kind of authority experience can wield.

In the modern history of theorizing experience, this question has tended to fold itself into another concerning how the historian handles the inevitable mediation of experience. Different perspectives upon this latter question proliferated during the 1990s; the analysis of individual experience and its mediation responds to a broader debate in this period concerning identity politics and ideology.[41] Within this arena of historical analysis, Joan W.

37. LaCapra enumerates the ambiguities lying within the senses of *experience* as the *OED* defines them (38–46).

38. Derek Pearsall, "The Wife of Bath's 'Experience': Some Lexicographical Reflections," in *Readings in Medieval Textuality*, 8–11.

39. Karma Lochrie, *Covert Operations: The Medieval Uses of Secrecy* (Philadelphia: University of Pennsylvania Press, 1999), 57–58. See also Helen Cushman's argument that certain cycle plays "expose clerical learning's dependence on and proximity to lay experiential knowledge," rendering experience as constitutive of theological knowledge. "Handling Knowledge: Holy Bodies in the Middle English Mystery Plays," *Journal of Medieval and Early Modern Studies* 47.2 (2017): 281.

40. Agnew, 331.

41. On the conservative anxiety about scholarly techniques for gaining access to marginalized perspectives and how these might reflect the ideology of the historian more than the "truth" of history, see Reuel E. Schiller, "The Strawhorsemen of the Apocalypse: Relativism and the Historian as Expert Witness," *Hastings Law Journal* 49 (1998): 1173–74.

Scott cautions against a critical tendency to allow experience to "essential-ize identity and reify the subject." Privileging experience as evidence not only values certain categories of experience over others but also occludes the ideologies that have constituted particular experiences. Scott therefore recalibrates the relation between evidence and experience, designating ex-perience not as evidence itself but rather as "that which we seek to ex-plain, that about which knowledge is produced."[42] By the time Martin Jay intervenes into this debate, it has become, in his eyes, a "sterile" conflict between "naïve experiential immediacy and the no less naïve discursive mediation of that experience."[43] But the issue of historical experience con-tinues to pose challenges, as William Guynn, for instance, has more re-cently discussed.[44] This is partly because, as we saw Collingwood's work suggest, the experience to which one might gain access in either a mental or physical exercise of reenactment involves the mediated perspective not only of the historical agent but also of the observing and analyzing histo-rian; Scott combines these factors in her investigation of "the evidence by which 'experience' can be grasped and by which the historian's relationship to the past he or she writes about can be articulated."[45] Thus, from a variety of angles, experience as an authoritative source of evidence demands a set of self-aware questions and is never entirely stable.

Narratively reenacting dance at once draws attention to and addresses the problem of historical experience. In one sense, to focus on dance is simply to foreground a conundrum at issue in all historical study. As the previous section suggested, many aspects of premodern dance are irrecoverable by the usual evidentiary channels. One of those aspects is the experience of kinetic spectatorship and participation, which might remain obscure even within a detailed depiction of choreographic feature or pattern. But while dance's evanescence might make this problem seem especially severe, it in fact merely emblematizes the limit of any present inquiry into any past experi-ence, whether one of reading, composing, ruling, praying, and so on. By ask-ing my reader constantly to shift between modern and medieval experiences in the reenactment process, I keep the dilemma of experiential mediation in a place where—as one tries to do with a wasp in the room—we can see it. On the one hand, bringing my experiential account of contemporary dance

42. Scott, 797, 780.

43. Martin Jay, "The Limits of Limit-Experience: Bataille and Foucault," *Constellations* 2.2 (1995): 157, 169.

44. William Guynn, *Unspeakable Histories: Film and the Experience of Catastrophe* (New York: Columbia University Press, 2016), 1–6.

45. Scott, 796.

into dialogue with a medieval scene simply underscores the limits of my own perspective; Elizabeth J. Bellamy and Artemis Leontis note that "as a report about itself," such an experiential account "will always be self-validating—without goal or method."[46] On the other hand, my juxtaposition of medieval and modern experience brings to light possibilities in the medieval occurrence that would otherwise remain invisible. As I proceed to explain my use of *experience*, I do so within the framework I have presented here that acknowledges the more intractable aspects of this term and my method's response to them.

Evoking a perceiver's experience implies a concern with sensation, and phenomenology provides perhaps the most obvious means to address that topic; however, while this discourse has some use, I ultimately distinguish my approach from it. Both performance studies and other arenas of literary and cultural studies have employed the language of phenomenology to articulate insights about what I here refer to as experience. For this reason my discussion of experience will turn at this point to phenomenology. Because my study overall is concerned with the relationship between dance and poetry, I will briefly sketch major phenomenological approaches to both performance and literature. But in the end I set certain aspects of phenomenology aside in favor of a concept of experience based in both medieval and modern terminologies.

Performance and dance studies have for some time described experience in terms of phenomenality and phenomenology, adopting this philosophical discourse to centralize acts of perception and sensation in the process of spectatorship and the construction of the spectacle. Phenomenological concepts, such as Husserl's primacy of the subject's consciousness and perception and Maurice Merleau-Ponty's integral network of bodily senses constituting experience, influence performance theory's accounts of the spectator's experience. Bert O. States illustrates the phenomenological reading of performance, which looks past theories of mimesis and semiosis to discern performance as a "theater phenomenon." Theater, States argues, "*mak[es] itself* out of . . . speech, sound, movement, scenery, text, etc." and depends on the individual's "own perceptual encounters" with it.[47] Dance theory has also assimilated phenomenology as a means to describe experience. Anna Pakes, for instance, shows how in contemporary dance performance,

46. Elizabeth J. Bellamy, Artemis Leontis, "A Genealogy of Experience: From Epistemology to Politics," *Yale Journal of Criticism* 6.1 (1993): 168.
47. Bert O. States, *Great Reckonings in Little Rooms: On the Phenomenology of Theater* (Berkeley: University of California Press, 1985), 1, emphasis in original.

according to Husserl's brand of phenomenology, "the experienced elements, the performance, even the dance work itself, are constituted in the process of being seen, noted, reflected upon, and described. . . . The dance appears as it does by virtue of how it is apprehended and described."[48] Here as well, the experience (this word appears throughout her essay) of performance is understood in terms of the sensory apprehension of phenomena and the phenomenon of that apprehension.

Phenomenology's manifestation in literary studies, meanwhile, stresses the constitutive role of the experiencing subject but distances itself from the arsenal of senses that watching a performance requires. The work of Georges Poulet illustrates this point. His treatise on the phenomenology of reading influenced literary studies broadly, tracing conceptual lines of descent, for example, to reader-response criticism.[49] Because he asks, "What happens when I read a book?" rather than what happens when he watches a dance, Poulet's understanding of phenomenological perception differs from that of a performance theorist. Poulet's formulation of the reader's experience encountering a text instead turns on the conflation of interior and exterior locales. What happens when he reads a book is "as though reading were the act by which a thought managed to bestow itself within me with a subject not myself."[50] Whereas the book itself might have been an exterior object, it relocates itself in an "interior world" where its words and images swim around like "fish in an aquarium," "dependent on [the reader's] consciousness" to house them.[51] Poulet ultimately describes art as a transcendent subject that reveals itself to itself and to the reader in its requirement of "subjectivity without objectivity." A book's universe forsakes objects and objective forms.[52] The important location becomes the interiority of the mind itself and its own transcendent potential. Poulet's literary phenom-

48. Anna Pakes, "Phenomenology and Dance: Husserlian Moves," *Dance Research Journal* 43.2 (2011): 34.

49. Poulet's "Phenomenology of Reading" is excerpted as "Criticism and the Experience of Interiority" in Jane Tompkins's volume on reader-response criticism for its emphasis on "the intimate personal quality of the relation between author and reader and not on the text and its formal features." Jane P. Tompkins, ed., *Reader-Response Criticism: From Formalism to Post-Structuralism* (Baltimore: Johns Hopkins University Press, 1980), xiv. I focus on Poulet here rather than on more recent scholars of phenomenology, like Sara Ahmed, because I want to identify the conceptual structures underlying our contemporary approaches. Poulet's work influences a variety of literary critics. See, for instance, J. Hillis Miller, "The Literary Criticism of Georges Poulet," *MLN* 78.5 (1963): 488. An important medievalist study referring to Poulet is V. A. Kolve's *The Play Called Corpus Christi* (Stanford: Stanford University Press, 1966), 102.

50. Georges Poulet, "Phenomenology of Reading," *New Literary History* 1.1 (1969): 56.

51. Ibid., 54–55.

52. Ibid., 68.

enology, where the perceiving subject organizes the experience of the world, de-emphasizes sensory array in favor of a dynamic interiority.

Bruce Smith's "historical phenomenology" resolves these different ways of understanding experiences of art by drawing on an archive of Shakespeare plays, which must be read as both text and performance. Smith coins the term "historical phenomenology" in an essay that takes up literary representations of sensory experience.[53] Historical phenomenology, according to Smith, counteracts the "distrust of sense experience" evident in both new historicist and poststructuralist methodologies. It is relational (drawing upon Michel Serres), a way of reading "among" rather than against, which uses the sense of immersion within the body and sensory stimuli to "reconstruct" temporally inaccessible experience.[54] Elsewhere, Smith proposes to begin with an "approved" historicist method that examines ancillary archival evidence but then to deviate deliberately into "a performative space . . . inhabited by phenomenology as a critical method." In this space, the experience of sexual sensation "will take place just outside the frame of the fiction" as the play's final couplet points in its rhyme to "another time and another place."[55] Thus the play's features as both spectacle and poetic text contribute to a sense-based performance experience. Historical phenomenology provides access to historically vanished sensory experience not simply by reconstructing performance objects but rather by identifying interstitial spaces—offstage, between and around texts—that accommodate the constitutive nature of the perceiver's experience, the "sentient body . . . positioned among the cultural variables set in place by new historicism and cultural materialism."[56]

Philosophical, literary, and historical phenomenologies all provide insights that inform my argument. They remind us of spectatorship's capacity as an aesthetic object itself, expanding the focus from the artistic object to a sensory dynamic of participation and even absorption. Medieval readers and thinkers did not suffer from any lack of self-awareness about their acts of sensory perception.[57] Phenomenonology helps us recognize their

53. Bruce R. Smith, "Premodern Sexualities," *PMLA* 115.3 (2000): 319–20.

54. Ibid., 325–26. See also Michel Serres, *The Troubadour of Knowledge*, trans. Sheila Faria Glaser with William Paulson (Ann Arbor, MI: University of Michigan Press, 1997), 146, on the preposition as an expression of relational work.

55. Bruce R. Smith, "L[o]cating the Sexual Subject," in *Alternative Shakespeares*, vol. 2, ed. Terence Hawkes (New York: Routledge, 1996), 112–14.

56. Smith, "Premodern," 326.

57. Mary Carruthers, *The Experience of Beauty in the Middle Ages* (Oxford: Oxford University Press, 2013), 47–48.

attunement to sensory process and its role in constituting aesthetic experience. In addition, historical phenomenology's attention to interstitial space is particularly important to my reenactment methodology. In the previous section, I proposed examining what appears in the spaces between the archival evidence of performance and an accessible performance. To the extent to which historical phenomenology also presents itself in terms of interstitial configurations, this approach affects my method's constitution. Both my approach and that of historical phenomenology pose questions about what lies in the material or conceptual territories between one event or archival object and another.

But as useful as certain of phenomenology's insights might be, the term *experience* is ultimately a more effective instrument in constructing my argument. One reason is the critique of phenomenology's potential unpreparedness to recognize what Michel Foucault calls the "dissociation" of the perceiving subject from itself.[58] *Experience* as a critical term has developed to confront questions concerning the subject's mediated position. There is also a difference in the methodological approaches that historical phenomenology and experiential reenactment, respectively, entail. Smith describes historical phenomenology as a method that "depends on the materialities of new historicist investigations."[59] For Smith, this means drawing upon textual archives—conduct and character books, legal treatises—that circulate contemporaneously around the poetic and performance object. My interpretive technique, as I have described it, distinguishes itself more completely from new historicist protocols by using contemporary performance—like Mark Morris's work—rather than materials extant at the moment of the medieval performance. In a sense, I wish to extend further Smith's quest for alternatives to new historicist practice by turning away from the performance object's surrounding archives and toward other performance experiences that would explicate it differently. While I do set contemporaneous traditions of dance and poetry in conversation with each other, I derive meaning from them not through traditional historicist interpretive practice but rather through a turn outward to the present's perspective on performance.

In defining *experience*, I thus draw out its capacity to set past and present in dialogue and to foreground its elusiveness in our attempts to name

58. Michel Foucault, "How an Experience-Book is Born," in *Remarks on Marx: Conversations with Duccio Trombadori*, trans. R. James Goldstein and James Cascaito (New York: Semiotext[e], 1991), 31. Cited in Jay, 158.

59. Smith, "Premodern," 327.

it; within these contexts, however, it is also important to specify how a premodern audience describes its own processes of encountering dance, poetry, and other art. In fact, the medieval lexicon offers a term for an experience of participatory engagement with artistic objects: *ductus*. As it suggests, this word casts the viewer's experience of a work of art as a process through which one is led. In Mary Carruthers's formulation, it addresses "the way in which a work guides those experiencing it through itself."[60] *Ductus* acknowledges that the experience of the work engages the viewer's participation, skill, habituation, and perception. As such a participatory mechanism, *ductus* gives us a language to describe relationships among medieval experiences of apprehending visual, kinetic, and textual modes of expression. In chapter 2, I will discuss this idea in detail, proposing that the condition of being led through an artistic object or spectacle allows the perceiver to deploy different perceptual faculties associated with multiple media simultaneously, so that the perceptual practices associated with one art can inflect the apprehension of another. Here, however, I focus on *ductus*'s relevance to experiences of spectacle that are not primarily verbal in order to continue exploring the experience of medieval dance.

While it often describes processes of textual creation and reception, *ductus* asserts its relevance as well to other kinds of aesthetic expression in general and dance in particular. Certain discourses theorize the effects of *ductus* in a broadly performance- or spectacle-based capacity. An example appears in Augustine's meditation on Psalm 41 (discussed by Carruthers), which describes the psalmist walking around God's earthly *tabernaculum* and being led (*perductus est*) to his heavenly one. This process of leading is enabled by the psalmist's discernment of musical sounds, which draw him inward and toward the heavenly house.[61] While this music might not be real, and the sensory experience it entails is internal, *ductus* refers for Augustine to an experience of being led by a nontextual stimulus that engages a spectrum of sense and that involves participation and even transformation on the part of the agent being led by the features of the aesthetic environment. Within this general context appear diverse specifications of dance as a ductile experience. For example, the reference to *Hali Meiðhad* with which the introduction began specifies that "þe heouenliche cwen *leat*" her

---

60. Mary Carruthers, "Editor's Introduction," in *Rhetoric beyond Words: Delight and Persuasion in the Arts of the Middle Ages*, ed. Mary Carruthers (Cambridge: Cambridge University Press, 2010), 10–11.
61. Mary Carruthers, "The Concept of *Ductus*, or Journeying through a Work of Art," in *Rhetoric beyond Words*, 194–95.

company. Round dances often rely upon a dance leader singing the stanzas
and the rest of the company singing the burden according to their cue.[62]
In the thirteenth century, Johannes de Grocheio labels certain vocal and
instrumental dance accompaniments *ductia*; Robert Mullally suggests that
Grocheio derives this word from the phrase "choreas ducere."[63] And as we
shall see elsewhere in this study, lyrics describing or otherwise associated
with dance sometimes name leading as a central motif.[64]

Ductus emphasizes participation rather than passive reception, an aspect that has implications for reenacting the experience of dance. Underlying accounts of scriptural reading as well as theories of composition, *ductus*
characterizes both response and intervention.[65] Carruthers suggests that
both works of art and their perceivers bring to their shared situation a sense
of agency, "directed desires" that the Middle Ages term *intentio*. For the
perceiver, this means interacting with the work's own agency rather than
merely receiving the work. "Aesthetic experiences," as Carruthers puts it,
are "at least two-way"; our attention to what our senses perceive represents
the *intentio* of interaction as the work leads us through itself.[66] As a ductile
experience, medieval dance therefore produces a sense of engagement, response, and even creativity in a multidimensional network of leading, moving, and watching. The instances I reenact do not cast being led as passive,
but rather evoke responses that crucially contribute to the constitution of
the danced work itself.

Another aspect of *ductus*—as a term to refine our account of medieval
dance-based experience—is the opportunity it provides for habituation. Eliz-

62. Karl Reichl, "The Middle English Carol," in *A Companion to the Middle English Lyric*,
ed. Thomas G. Duncan (Cambridge: D. S. Brewer, 2005), 158.

63. Robert Mullally, "de Grocheo's 'Musica Vulgaris,'" *Music & Letters* 79.1 (1998): 21. See
also Grocheio, 68–69: "Ductia vero est cantilena levis et velox et ascensu et descensu que in
choreis a iuvenibus et pouellis decantatur" [But *ductia* is a *cantilena* light and swift in both
ascent and descent, which is sung in *caroles* by young men and girls]. Elsewhere Grocheio
discusses the way that this type of song turns back on itself and ends where it began (68–69); its
verse structure (70–71); and its instrumental version for leading dances (72–73). See also Mullally,
"Dance Terminology in the Works of Machaut and Froissart," *Medium Ævum* 59.2 (1990): 252,
on the similarity of the *ductia* to the English vocal carol. Mullally additionally notes that the
ductia's structure resembles the *virelai*, suggesting that "by Grocheo's time, songs in some kind
of *virelai* form had come to rival or replace the *rondeau* as a musical accompaniment of the
carole." He also reads from Grocheio's tract evidence that instrumental *ductia* differs from the
vocal form. "'Musica Vulgaris,'" 10–11, 16–17.

64. See chapter 2.

65. Carruthers, "Concept," 196–97, 204.

66. Carruthers, *Experience*, 53, 51–52.

abeth Fowler's work on aesthetic experience draws upon *ductus* to empha-size the sense of habit that accompanies it. In its "ductile space," "art does more than provide this experience once: it is destined to be used again and again, even to become a habit."[67] For Fowler, the formation of these habits has consequences for reading the world and the self: "understanding pat-terns and following the patterns and codes embodied in art comprise the process that habituates us to cultural meaning."[68] As an aspect of dance-based experience, habituation is important because in structuring an audi-ence's perceptual work within dance, it also creates the potential for an audience to deploy those ingrained perceptual practices and expectations in other encounters.

So, to sum up this sequence, *experience* means the following. It can be described in terms of phenomenology to the extent that understanding experience requires acknowledging the ways that sensory perception can organize the world. And historical phenomenology's technique of locating experiences in the interstitial spaces between and around the archives that represent those experiences will prove crucial to my argument. But while the lexical category of the phenomenal plays a role in defining experience as I invoke it, I preserve a distinction between these terms in order to focus on the resonances that *experience* holds for the medieval world through that world's own concept of *ductus*. Within this context, the medieval experi-ence of dance involves an interactive dynamic that unites the perceiver's impulse toward knowledge, skill, practice, and habituation with the work's own corresponding impulse to lead its perceiver. At the same time, *experi-ence* is to some extent always a "black box." Throughout this study, my juxtapositions of medieval and modern experiences of dance spectatorship rest upon the conceptual foundations I provide here regarding experience. That interpretive structure will underlie the investigation of medieval ex-perience while at the same time maintaining awareness of the complexities inherent to our attempts to gain access to it.

VIRTUALITY

What kind of spectacle did the ductile experience of dance produce? The answer to this question involves *virtuality*, a term that resonates, as the introduction suggested, as much in premodern as in postmodern arenas. The last section proposed that the ductile experience of dance habituates

67. Elizabeth Fowler, "Art and Orientation," *New Literary History* 44.4 (2013): 596–97.
68. Ibid., 596.

viewers to a process in which they respond to and participate in the constitution of the danced spectacle. The current section will propose that in its reenactment, that *ductus* of dance reveals itself to create environments of ambiguous materiality and kinetic force: virtuality. Virtuality here describes a complex interaction of material and immaterial components. It is not synonymous with immateriality but is rather, as Brian Massumi characterizes it, "a *dimension* of reality, not its illusionary opponent or artificial overcoming."[69] I will argue throughout that this definition of the virtual, a manifestation integrated with the real world but occupying another plane, produces strangeness for medieval audiences.

Medievalists frequently invoke virtuality in describing premodern culture. It might be especially important, in fact, to retain the word *virtuality* as part of an arsenal of terms to describe the medieval world. As Michelle Karnes argues, that world readily accommodates the possibility that the inventions of the imagination, apprehensible but not located in the material world, are just as powerful, just as generative of effects, as their material counterparts.[70] Medievalists have also employed virtuality to describe a variety of literary and artistic phenomena. For example, Elizabeth Fowler proposes the summoning of a "virtual subject" to accommodate emotional experience in the reading process.[71] Laura Hughes construes virtuality as a force that disrupts the material present of Machaut's *Voir Dit* in order to project its futurity in an immaterial mode.[72] Hughes's virtual *Voir Dit*—one that resists the manuscript's hierarchical ordering—influences my sense of virtuality's ability to accommodate deviation from order and pattern. While for Hughes, however, virtuality characterizes the life of the compilation beyond its time, I explain virtuality as spatiotemporal force recognizable to medieval audiences.[73] In another medievalist evocation of virtuality, Martin K. Foys has shown that the discourses of new media, digital humanities, and virtuality provide more accurate and productive platforms from which to understand Old English literary and textual practices than do the

69. Brian Massumi, "Envisioning the Virtual," in *The Oxford Handbook of Virtuality*, ed. Mark Grimshaw (New York: Oxford University Press, 2014), 55–56.

70. Michelle Karnes, "Marvels in the Medieval Imagination," *Speculum* 90.2 (2015): 330.

71. Elizabeth Fowler, "The Proximity of the Virtual: A. C. Spearing's Experientiality (or, Roaming with Palamon and Arcite)," in *Readings in Medieval Textuality*, 30.

72. Laura Hughes, "Machaut's Virtual *Voir Dit* and the Moment of Heidegger's Poetry," *Exemplaria* 25.3 (2013): 192–210.

73. Ibid., 199–202, 207.

interpretive tools that print culture has imposed on them.[74] Martha Dana Rust's theory of the "manuscript matrix" suggests that the reader's encounter with a manuscript generates a "virtual space" in which the envisioned realm takes on dimensionality "'within' the physical space of the book at hand."[75] Emma Dillon has described the encounter with past performance as revisiting a place "in the virtual realm."[76] Christopher Cannon compares the genre of medieval romance to a holograph to make the case that it projects a "virtual" image of itself.[77] This brief survey indicates the broad spectrum of uses that medieval studies have assigned this term.

My narrower category of dance sets parameters around what I, meanwhile, mean by *virtuality*. The introduction briefly mentions two familiar Chaucerian examples of danced virtuality: the scene in which the Franklin's *tregetour* offers an illusion of dance that Aurelius watches himself join and the circle of dancing ladies in the *Wife of Bath's Tale* whose detection by the knight causes them to vanish.[78] In calling these examples virtual manifestations, I mean that both tales depict performers who are apprehensible but not locatable on the same material plane as their viewers, and that both tales feature not only the immaterial performance itself but also a constitutive interaction between it and the actual world. I would further apply to this term to static objects that appear to become animated in the context of danced performance. The statue of the Virgin Mary that begins to move in response to the Tumbler of Notre Dame's virtuoso performance offers one instance.[79] In this example, movement itself registers as both real and unreal. The indeterminate forces of Mary's movement supplement the Tumbler's embodied dance, her statue not only animating itself in response to his dance but also fanning the overexerted acrobat to cool him.[80] The Tumbler's story is, of course, miraculous, while the others are not. Despite

74. Martin K. Foys, *Virtually Anglo-Saxon: Old Media, New Media, and Early Medieval Studies in the Late Age of Print* (Gainesville: University Press of Florida, 2007), 3 and *passim*.

75. Martha Dana Rust, *Imaginary Worlds in Medieval Books: Exploring the Manuscript Matrix* (New York: Palgrave Macmillan, 2007), 4. Rust goes on to propose the idea of a "virtual cell" as operative in medieval imaginative practice (5).

76. Emma Dillon, *The Sense of Sound: Musical Meaning in France, 1260–1330* (New York: Oxford University Press, 2012), 5.

77. Cannon, *Grounds*, 198–200.

78. *CT* V.1199–201; *CT* III.989–96.

79. Paul Bretel, ed. and trans., *Le Jongleur de Notre-Dame* (Paris: Honoré Champion, 2003), 66–67 (ll. 408–26). For Jan M. Ziolkowski, this dance represents a "silent oration that accomplishes effectively the aim of persuasion." "Do Actions Speak Louder than Words? The Scope and Role of *Pronuntiatio* in the Latin Rhetorical Tradition, with Special Reference to the Cistercians," in *Rhetoric beyond Words*, 141.

80. Bretel, 67 (ll. 425–33).

this difference, however, I would maintain that in all three cases, the experience of choreographed performance depends upon a component supplementary to physical bodies, one that seems to occupy a space between the material and immaterial and that weaves itself into the spectating dynamic.

To explain why I see this supplement to the embodied aspects of medieval dance as particularly *virtual*, as opposed to some other quality, will require an outline of certain critical contexts in both medieval studies and dance theory. This outline begins by clarifying what virtuality does *not* mean in my argument. Just as, in my parlance, reenactment is not reconstruction, so the purpose of virtuality is not, for me, reconstructive. I do not employ the tools of virtual reality and the digital humanities to reconstruct the past or discuss simulating medieval dance practices with the implements of virtuality. The one virtual reality model to which my study refers, in chapter 3, pointedly reenacts the past, theorizing its own activity, rather than reconstructing the past in reified form.

Virtuality is useful to me not for any aspiration it has to resuscitate the past but rather for its obtrusive anachronism and defamiliarization. Invoking the modern conception of virtuality in narrating medieval spectatorial effects draws attention, like both reenactment and experience, to the historical divide being negotiated. Our familiarity with virtuality in the contemporary sphere prevents us from imposing ourselves unreflectingly on the medieval reenactment process; incorporating virtuality prevents us from lulling ourselves into thinking that we encounter the medieval on its own terms. Contemporary dance in particular has employed virtual elements not to recapture lost movement but rather to defamiliarize the very mechanics of movement perception. Johannes Birringer, for instance, points out that while video games use virtuality to strive for realistic effects, the "virtual bodies" projected into experimental choreography (like *Ghostcatching*) often fulfill the opposite function, making the body strange, "denaturalis[ed]," and abstract.[81] Incorporating this critical discourse into a study of the Middle Ages therefore puts pressure on us to acknowledge, and to be precise in describing, the strangeness or otherness of medieval perceptual experiences in performance. Virtuality is a useful methodological tool because the weirdness of danced virtuality effectively communicates the nature of medieval experiences of dance while maintaining our awareness of these spectacles' alterity.

81. Johannes Birringer, "*Saira Virous*: Game Choreography in Multiplayer Online Performance Spaces," in *Performance and Technology: Practices of Virtual Embodiment and Interactivity*, ed. Susan Broadhurst and Josephine Machon (New York: Palgrave Macmillan, 2006), 46.

When I use virtuality to name an experiential effect in dance and to emphasize the spatiotemporal strangeness of the medieval danced scene, I draw upon a set of principles originating in virtuality studies. For some, the most familiar critical accounts of virtuality refer to its use in a game or "reality" environment, which presents elements that are apprehensible but not materially tangible in a conventional way, an environment that constructs itself through its interaction with the viewer. That sense of immersion is important to virtuality as a technological and recreational manifestation. Ken Hillis, for instance, describes the experience as a perceptual collusion between the spectating participant and the virtual environment: "when I turn my head to look around the virtual space, the space reconfigures before my eyes."[82] This description, reminiscent of the familiar idiom of gaming, might provide us with a place to start, acknowledging immersion and ontological ambiguity as recognizable aspects of virtuality.

Theories of virtuality also elaborate upon the conceptual substance beneath these electronic trappings, explaining virtuality as a temporal and spatial construct. For Massumi, the force of intent or potential is explicitly a temporal occurrence, "the press of the next, coming to pass." It "concerns the potency in what is, by virtue of which it really comes to be." In order to participate in reality, virtuality, in other words, must articulate itself in terms of time. The force of its existence is always "untimely" because of its perpetual potentiality.[83] As a force of potential, virtuality has a spatial element as well in Marcos Novak's characterization. An aspect of our reality that nevertheless does not inhabit quite the same plane as that reality, the virtual environment can contain what Novak calls the "sensed-form," "a precise sense-shape . . . exact, but invisible, a region of activated, hypersensitive space."[84] Virtual manifestations draw our attention to the nature of the space that surrounds us and to our reciprocal relationship with it. Novak's formulation, following upon Massumi's, suggests that virtuality is not simply synonymous with immateriality or artificiality; rather, it participates

---

82. Ken Hillis, *Digital Sensations: Space, Identity, and Embodiment in Virtual Reality* (Minneapolis: University of Minnesota Press, 1999), 71. This discourse has applications in the realm of dance: as Birringer notes: "If [the dancer] performs in conjunction with video or 3D projections, she animates these virtual image-spaces that are constantly emerging and also unpredictable. Her movement, if it affects and responds to the image movement, crosses real and virtual spaces" ("*Saira Virous*," 51).

83. Massumi, "Envisioning," 55–56.

84. Marcos Novak, "Eversion: Brushing against Avatars, Aliens, and Angels," in *From Energy to Information: Representation in Science and Technology*, ed. Bruce Clarke and Linda Dalrymple Henderson (Stanford: Stanford University Press, 2002), 316.

in material and embodied realms even as it positions itself in a different ontological space and a different temporal structure.

Encompassing these concepts, virtuality plays a crucial role in dance theory's descriptions of not only what an audience sees when watching a dance but also the dancer's experience. To Langer, dance is an "apparition," inhering not in the muscles and movements of dancers but rather in the "display of interacting forces" that these create in the spectator's perception.[85] Alain Badiou adopts the language of virtuality to describe dance as well. Badiou's analogy between dance and thought foregrounds the ambiguous ontology and the potential force of dance. Dance, like the Nietzschean conception of thought, is "the movement of its own intensity." Badiou suggests that while dance, like thought, possesses the intensity of internalized generation (a circle, he says, that draws itself), it is additionally shaped by the consciousness of restraint: "In dance thus conceived, movement finds its essence *in what has not taken place*, in what has remained either ineffective or restrained within movement itself."[86] For Badiou, this ambiguous oscillation between movement's generation and restraint is the space of virtuality; "the essence of dance is virtual, rather than actual movement."[87] Langer and Badiou understand the virtual supplement as an integral part of dance and an aspect of spectatorship that collaborates with but also distinguishes itself from the decisive materiality of moving bodies. Writing as both a spectator and a performer, Erin Manning argues that the indeterminacy of the dancing body itself admits it to the realm of the virtual: "c'est un corps indéfini qui danse, qui pense, qui articule le virtuel" [it is an undefined body that dances, that thinks, that articulates the virtual].[88] Elsewhere, Manning addresses the virtual as manifested in the time of dance, the way that the forces between motions exist in anticipation and potential. She identifies, in the process of dance performance, what she terms "intervals," in which the body anticipates and shapes movement before it happens. In these intervals, the body experiences a state of "preacceleration," when movement is virtual rather than actual.[89] Virtuality's untimely and ontologically indeterminate force of potential, construed as implicit

85. Langer, "Dynamic," 78.

86. Alain Badiou, "Dance as a Metaphor for Thought," in *Handbook of Inaesthetics*, trans. Alberto Toscano (Stanford: Stanford University Press, 2005), 57–60.

87. Ibid., 61.

88. Erin Manning, "Danser le virtuel," *Jeu: revue de théâtre* 119.2 (2006): 68.

89. Erin Manning, *Relationscapes: Movement, Art, Philosophy* (Cambridge: MIT Press, 2009), 13–19.

to the experience of watching danced movement, also asserts itself in the performance of dance.

Contemporary dance theory furthermore identifies the presence of virtuality within experimental performance reenactments: virtuality names the vestigial force of the past dance that the present performance evokes. Virtuality characterizes not only an effect located in an experience of spectacle, but also the dynamic, in dance theory's conception of reenactment, of a present spectator encountering the idea of a past dance. Virtuality describes the spectral traces that make themselves apparent when a past dance is incorporated into a present piece of choreography. As André Lepecki argues, when contemporary experimental dance self-consciously embeds earlier twentieth-century choreography within itself, it does so not nostalgically but rather with the desire to "identify in past work still non-exhaustive creative fields of 'impalpable possibilities' (to use an expression from Brian Massumi)."[90] This "will to archive" casts into relief virtual elements that "are always present in any past work and are that which re-enactments activate."[91] A past performance is not only what its archival record represents; it also includes "ghostly matters, those impalpable virtuals willing actualization."[92] For Lepecki, the reenactment of a historically absent dance activates the virtualities—as forces of potential—in the present audience's experience of a reenacted past. In the terms I have laid out here, the Shaker movement traditions embedded within Humphrey's modernist piece *The Shakers* exist as virtualities, forces that travel through and supplement her dancers' actions.

With these foundations in the concept of virtuality and its general relation to dance in place, we might now investigate virtuality's role specifically in medieval movement practice. Most importantly, the construct of *ductus*, evoked earlier to specify a medieval experience of dance, relies upon the possibility of virtuality. What Carruthers calls the *intentio* at work in *ductus* carries the sense of force that virtuality conveys; Carruthers elsewhere associates intention and the medieval sense of *virtue* as related to "movement, desire pressing itself from within outward into the world, as it intends . . . toward an object."[93] Fowler's account of participatory aesthetic experience also

90. André Lepecki, "The Body as Archive: Will to Re-Enact and the Afterlives of Dances," *Dance Research Journal* 42.2 (2010): 31. Lepecki refers to Brian Massumi, *Parables of the Virtual: Movement, Affect, Sensation* (Durham, NC: Duke University Press, 2002), 91.

91. Lepecki, 31.

92. Ibid., 43.

93. Mary Carruthers, "Virtue, Intention, and the Mind's Eye in Chaucer's *Troilus and Criseyde*," in *Traditions and Innovations in the Study of Middle English Literature*, ed. Charlotte

associates *ductus* with virtuality. She suggests that the experiential process of being led through a work of art necessarily "conjures" a desired virtual space.[94] *Ductus*, she specifies, "leans . . . away" from a virtual environment where we might simply observe the ductile space without participating in it; the virtual supplement is, again, constituted in participatory acts that integrate material bodies and other forces.[95] *Strange Footing*'s case studies will explore how virtuality's strange time and space inform *ductus* in the medieval context. In the *ductus* of medieval dance, as we shall see, the sensation of force always places the agent—who is himself often both observer and participant—a little out of time, anticipating and syncopated. Furthermore, as an experience of leading, *ductus* constantly presents its audience with transitions and spaces between the tangible and the intangible, as well as between movement and stasis. Such spaces house the virtual supplements that Langer and others describe in the encounter with dance.

In their occupation of both space and time, the forces of virtuality discussed in this book produce largely visual experiences for their audiences; for this reason it will be useful to outline briefly how medieval seeing practices might accommodate the possibility of such virtuality before moving onward. Both medievalists and scholars of the contemporary have equally attested that it is crucial to integrate studies of performance with those of visual culture.[96] But premodern seeing appears to possess a tactile, dynamic, and affective quality that modern discourses of seeing do not always assume.[97] Medieval seeing is, Rachel Dressler argues, "an active and reciprocal process" whose medieval theorization is based on antique and Near Eastern as well as Western philosophy. In this reciprocal process, the wound in a Man of Sorrows image, for instance, might implicitly invite the viewer to penetrate Christ's body.[98] Theories of intromission address the medieval understanding of visual process as material, allowing for an active and kinetic

---

Brewer and Barry Windeatt (Cambridge: D.S. Brewer, 2013), 87. Also in a medieval context, Jeffrey Jerome Cohen discusses a related possibility of force as "geologic." Holding the possibility of motion within its "lapidary" stillness, force's dialectic involves kinesis and stasis. *Stone: An Ecology of the Inhuman* (Minneapolis: University of Minnesota Press, 2015), 158.

94. Fowler, "Art," 595, 596.

95. Ibid., 603.

96. See, for instance, Elina Gertsman and Jill Stevenson, "Limning the Field," in *Thresholds of Medieval Visual Culture: Liminal Spaces*, ed. Elina Gertsman and Jill Stevenson (Woodbridge: Boydell, 2010), 6; and Catherine Soussloff and Mark Franko, "Visual and Performance Studies: A New History of Interdisciplinarity," *Social Text* 20.4 (2002): 29–46.

97. Giles, "Seeing," 107.

98. Rachel Dressler, "Sculptural Representation and Spatial Appropriation in a Medieval Chantry Chapel," in *Thresholds*, 234–35.

conception of the object being perceived. As Suzanne Conklin Akbari shows, Dante, for instance, speaks of the visible form's *discorso* [progress or movement] as it travels toward the water in the eye.[99] Seeing a still image is thus a lively process. We might think as well of Michael Baxandall's characterization of the fifteenth-century "public mind" as an "active institution of interior visualization" that incorporates the "beholder's previous visualizing activity."[100] His account indicates a premodern understanding of seeing as active and images as vivified by their interaction with viewers. This context might help us to comprehend the visual apprehension of animate forces and traces, those that supplement and weave themselves into spectacles, as a practice available and perhaps even unremarkable to medieval audiences.

Dance theorists identify virtuality in the dances they watch in their present; I shall narratively reenact virtual supplements in experiences of dance at great historical distance from us. In both cases, virtuality names the traces of movement in the interstices between embodied gestures as well as between other material and immaterial media. Let us then sum up this term's meaning. The virtual supplement appears in the spectator's integration of material and immaterial medial components. Virtuality is spatially and temporally ambiguous, always out of its own time in its anticipatory forces and occupying spatial planes both apprehensible and inaccessible. In these capacities, virtuality asserts its strangeness. The ductile experience of medieval dance incorporates forces of virtuality that operate in temporal and spatial registers off the kilter of conventional materiality and not quite aligned with the ostensible harmony, periodicity, and symmetry of the embodied dance. These aspects of *virtuality* provide a definition upon which to base this study's analyses.

LAURETTA LEADS US ONWARD

A familiar late-medieval account of dance puts our three terms—reenactment, experience, virtuality—into action. As their first day of storytelling ends, the characters in the *Decameron* turn to an entertainment that they habitually repeat throughout the text: the performance of a dance to poetic accompaniment. Lauretta concludes Day One by leading a dance to a lyric sung by Emilia, with a refrain that the dancers repeat after each stanza:

99. Suzanne Conklin Akbari, *Seeing through the Veil: Optical Theory and Medieval Allegory* (Toronto: University of Toronto Press, 2012), 130–31.

100. Michael Baxandall, *Painting and Experience in Fifteenth-Century Italy: A Primer in the Social History of Pictorial Style*, 2nd ed. (New York: Oxford University Press, 1988), 45.

Io son sì vaga della mia bellezza,
che d'altro amor già mai
non curerò né credo aver vaghezza.

Io veggio in quella, ognora ch'io mi specchio,
quel ben che fa contento lo 'ntelletto:
né accidente nuovo o pensier vecchio
mi può privar di sì caro diletto.
Quale altro dunque piacevole obgetto
potrei veder già mai
che mi mettesse in cuor nuova vaghezza?

Non fugge questo ben qualor disio
di rimirarlo in mia consolazione:
anzi si fa incontro al piacer mio
tanto soave a sentir, che sermone
dir nol poria, né prendere intenzione
d'alcun mortal già mai,
che non ardesse di cotal vaghezza.

E io, che ciascuna ora più m'accendo
quanto più fisi tengo gli occhi in esso,
tutta mi dono a lui, tutta mi rendo,
gustando già di ciò ch'el m'ha promesso:
e maggior gioia spero più dappresso
sì fatta, che già mai
simil non si sentì qui da vaghezza.[101]

[*I am so dazed by my own beauty*
That I will never care for other loves,
Nor will I feel any besottedness with them.

Every time I look at my reflection, I see in it
That good that makes the mind content,
Nor can any new happenstance or old thought
Deprive me of such dear delight.

---

101. Giovanni Boccaccio, *Decameron*, ed. Amedeo Quondam, Maurizio Fiorilla, and Giancarlo Alfano (Milan: BUR Classici, 2013), 278–79. I.*Concl.*18–21. On the musical structure of Boccaccio's *ballate*, see Margot Fassler, *Music in the Medieval West* (New York: Norton, 2014), 231.

What other pleasing object, then,
Could I ever see
That would place new besottedness in my heart?

This good will not flee whenever I should desire
To see it again as my consolation.
On the contrary, it comes to encounter my pleasure,
So sweet to feel that no speech could express
Nor could any mortal comprehend
If he did not burn with the same besottedness.

And I, who every hour, as I burn more,
So much more do I keep my eyes fixed on it,
I give all of myself to it (this good), I surrender all,
Already tasting that which it has promised me.
And I hope for an even greater joy, even closer,
Made such that no one
Has ever before felt such besottedness.][102]

Michaela Paasche Grudin and Robert Grudin read this poem, and in particular Emilia's repeated reference to "vaghezza," as signaling the *Decameron*'s ties to Cicero and Dante. They suggest that the poem's valuation of passion conveys Emilia's "dazzling realization of her own intellectual excellence," a kind of paean to "self-knowledge and creativity."[103] This exploration of creativity is mediated through classical *ingenium*. As a dance accompaniment, the lyric draws movement practice into this exploration of aesthetic and creative prowess, and it says more about dance as an aesthetic experience than might be initially apparent.

    In revealing some limits of traditional dance reconstruction, criticism concerning Boccaccio's dance scenes makes evident the need for reenactment as an alternative. Boccaccio has long attracted dance historical attention because the *Decameron*'s periodic references to social dancing confirm the significance of this practice in certain milieux. But as Jennifer Nevile notes, "we do not know anything about the dances [Boccaccio's characters] did, let alone what sort of movements were considered aesthetically pleasing

102. I thank Sara M. Petrosillo for assistance with this translation.
103. Michaela Paasche Grudin and Robert Grudin, *Boccaccio's "Decameron" and the Ciceronian Renaissance* (New York: Palgrave Macmillan, 2012), 26.

to them."[104] It is difficult to determine, for example, whether this dance was performed in a circle or with partners in a procession. Historians of dance have ventured to address these and other questions with what resources the medieval archive provides. W. Thomas Marrocco, for instance, emphasizes the distinctions among the names of dances throughout the *Decameron*: *danza, carola, ballo*. According to Marrocco's model, what Boccaccio calls any particular dance determines its choreographic character: round, processional, stately, lively. But as other critics have noted, basing choreographic reconstruction on medieval nomenclature might constitute an unreliable strategy. The evidence could suggest that such terms were used interchangeably as easily as it suggests distinct usages.[105] The very familiarity and informal integration of these danced practices into their audiences' lives might obviate the Middle Ages' need for the kind of precise taxonomy that would help us to identify these distant choreographies. Emma Lewis Thomas, meanwhile, proposes recreating choreographic patterns for Boccaccio's dances through the dance manuals that began to appear in the fifteenth century. [106] But while aspects of the general culture of social dance might obtain across the fourteenth and fifteenth centuries, specific reconstructions of earlier dances based on later models necessarily leave some questions open. Furthermore, both Marrocco and Thomas's analyses lack comment on the poetry itself. If Boccaccio's account makes anything clear, it is the interdependence of these two arts in performance, but this relationship does not seem substantively to inform these instances of traditional dance reconstruction.

Redressing this last omission by attending to the text seems, at first glance, to emphasize poetry and dance's similar affirmation of a harmonious ideal. In the parallel progression of dance and song, the return to the

104. Jennifer Nevile, "The Platonic Theory of Ethos in Fifteenth-Century Italian Court Dance," *Literature and Aesthetics* 3 (1993): 42. See also Nevile's comment that "The natural alliance between dancing and a patrician lifestyle is found throughout the literature of the fourteenth century." *The Eloquent Body: Dance and Humanist Culture in Fifteenth-Century Italy* (Bloomington: Indiana University Press, 2004), 17.

105. W. Thomas Marrocco, "Music and Dance in Boccaccio's Time, Part I: Fact and Speculation," *Dance Research Journal* 10.2 (1978): 20. Hanns Gutman, "Der Decamerone des Boccaccio als musikgeschichtliche Quelle," *Zeitschrift für Musikwissenschaft* 11 (1928): 399. Robert Mullally's study of the *carole*, as another instance, outlines this term's highly complex and ambiguous relationship to another dance label: the *tresche*. *The Carole: A Study of a Medieval Dance* (Burlington, VT: Ashgate, 2011), 60–61.

106. Emma Lewis Thomas, "Music and Dance in Boccaccio's Time, Part II: Reconstruction of 'Danze and Balli' (Including Three Dances with Music and Labanotation)," *Dance Research Journal* 10.2 (1978): 23–42. For an analysis of poetic text integrated into dance reconstruction, see Robert Nosow, "Dancing the Righoletto," *Journal of Musicology* 24.3 (2007): 420–35.

refrain gracefully echoes, over an extended temporal and spatial arc, the small, immediate circuitry of return represented in Emilia's reflexive self-regard. Other such coherences of structure exist in the poem's formal attributes as a dance-song. For example, as one kind of tripling periodicity exists within the three-line refrain itself, another appears in the repeated attachment of the refrain to the end of the previous stanza, which creates the rhyme *vaghezza/bellezza/vaghezza*. The motion of performance generates an intricate symmetry in the interlocking of these two kinds of triad. In this way, the dance and song create pleasingly elaborate patterns that speak to more powerful forces ordering the universe according to similar design. To place this effect in the context of Boccaccio's whole text, Eleanora M. Beck notes that this scene emblematizes a motif connecting mirrors to music throughout the *Decameron*, reinforcing ideals of "balance, judgment, and transcendence."[107] In itself and the dance, the poetic text can thus affirm order, proportion, and harmony.

Reading for this concordant relationship between dance and poem can even specify the choreography further, though in doing so it might present us with more than one possibility. Perhaps this is a round dance that allegorizes each turn toward the mirror as the movement of return. During the round dance known as *carole*, dancers generally step to the left as they mark the leader's singing of the stanzas, following which everyone stops to sing the burden, a refrain external to the strophic text.[108] Sealing the song's circle in its final intonation, the performance of the refrain in a round dance would enact the closed circuit of the gaze in the mirror. Thus, while Boccaccio does not label this dance as a round *carola* (a term he applies to other dances), reconstructing it as such would allow it to respond to its mirror motif. Both the round dance and the confrontation with one's reflection employ the mechanism of circuitry.[109] Alternatively, a processional line of partners could equally respond to the poem's mirror motif. In this case, the doubling structure of partners enacts a pervasive dynamic of alternation: between stanza and refrain, between *bellezza* and *vaghezza*, between the lyric's speaker and her twinned image. Thus, the poem does not necessarily

107. Eleanora M. Beck, "Mirrors and Music in the *Decameron*," *Heliotropia* 7.1–2 (2010): 81.

108. Richard Leighton Greene, ed., *The Early English Carols*, 2nd ed. (Oxford: Clarendon: 1977), xlv–xlvi; hereafter *EEC*. Reichl, 157–58.

109. In some traditions, the leader of the *carole* and the singer of the song seem construed as the same person (see, for instance, *EEC*, xlv), whereas here they are two different women. The other dances that Boccaccio names *carola*, however, exhibit the same pattern of one singer and one dance leader.

give us one choreography only, although its structure bodies forth concepts
that specify these different alternatives.

And yet, as was the case with "To Rosemounde," these strategies for
reconstructing the dance by means of the poem's imagery and formal features do not fully convey what the scene's participants undergo. To make
this case, I turn away from an analytic model that would reconstruct by
moving from poetry to dance. Instead, I *reenact* Boccaccio's dance between
its own unknowable space and the theories of perceptual practice that we
as modern readers might usefully bring to its interpretation. Because my
purpose here is to illustrate the definitions of my terms, I will not engage in
a comprehensive narrative reenactment of the type exemplified in my case
studies (which draw contemporary dance into the investigation). Rather, I
note the necessity of an alternative to more traditional forms of reconstruction, and in what follows I will discuss what becomes apparent in medieval
dance when we entertain such an alternative.

Boccaccio's dance is not simply a choreographic shape wrought by the poem's features: it is constructed of the *experiences* of its participants and spectators. In general, Boccaccio's dance scenes assert one important experiential
aspect of premodern danced tradition, which is the permeability (alluded to
in the introduction) of the categories that we would consider to be performer
and audience. In executing the dance for their own pleasure, the dance's participants function as both performers and spectators. In a fifteenth-century
Italian context, Barbara Sparti notes that our modern distinction between theatrical and social dancing does not exist; a dance that "impress[es] onlookers"
in one instance can function equally to "delight the performers themselves"
in another.[110] The earlier configurations described above—whether a physical
circle that analogizes other imagistic and thematic ones, or the symmetrical
abîmes of partnered gazes—exist in a dynamic where performers watch themselves participate; they contribute by apprehending as well as creating.

This situation makes visible other components of experience related
to both medieval practice itself and our modern perspective on it. For instance, this dance specifies its experience in terms of *ductus*. The dance
shapes itself through the presence of a leader—Lauretta—who conducts the
dance ("quell mendando la Lauretta; prestamente prese una danza e quella
menò") and allows its participants to respond to her structuring activity.[111]
Furthermore, within the larger framework of the *Decameron*, each individ-

---

110. Sparti, *Practice*, 61.
111. Boccaccio, 278. I.*Concl*.17.

ual dance recalls the medieval understanding of experience as habituation, skill, or familiarity through practice or frequent encounter. The ten-day framework miniaturizes or emblematizes this element. If any of the aristocrats feel tentative about their terpsichorean technique on Day One, that is, they might feel less so by Day Ten. The narrative structure establishes a praxis in which one gains experience by repeatedly returning to similar scenes of social dance and song. Thus, we see our sense of *experience* as skill and habituation reflected here. But the dance also raises more specific questions: In the activities of leading and being led, in the shifting possibilities of round and processional dance, what is the experience of looking at the danced spectacle while participating in it? Where and how do those perceptual vectors lie and move? Such questions foreground the issues surrounding our modern vantage point: the experiences within this dance—like all perceptual experiences—occupy a "black box" not only among the dance's participants but also for us. At the same time, focusing on ductile experience makes space for some new thought about perceptual experiences within the dance even when the details of its choreography are unknowable.

In that space for new thought emerges *virtuality*. In the reenactment process, virtuality names a crucial component of the perceptual experience—in all its strangeness—that Boccaccio's dance entails. Emilia's image of the mirror, I will finally suggest, signals virtuality in the experience of the dance. While Beck explains the mirror as participating in a discourse of balance, it can also be understood to introduce more oddity than it does harmony or resolution.[112] In its allusion to a reflected image, Emilia's refrain adds a participant of ambiguous materiality to the performance network of lyric and dance. Every time the company sings the refrain, every time Emilia sings of this insubstantial partner, the performance introduces this other dancer into its midst. The mirror image participates in the intersubjectivity of giving oneself to it (*tutta mi dono a lui, tutta mi rendo*), while tasting (*gustando*) what it has promised one. Lyrically intoned during the dance, the image of the reflection becomes a functioning entity to which the dancing responds. Led in kinetic accompaniment to each stanza's sung performance, the dancers orient and reorient themselves relative to the reflection Emilia's words conjure. A supplement to the scene of dance, the mirror image

---

112. For additional elaboration on the spectrum of symbolic, social, and "metaphysical" (530) meanings that mirrors as material objects carried in the late Middle Ages, see Alexa Sand, "The Fairest of Them All: Reflections on Some Fourteenth-Century Mirrors," in *Push Me, Pull You: Imaginative and Emotional Interaction in Late Medieval and Renaissance Art*, vol. 1, ed. Sarah Blick et al. (Leiden: Brill, 2011), 529–59.

is a force weaving itself into the dance while simultaneously existing on an ontological plane that differs from the one that the *brigata* occupies.

In his account of the mirror image's virtuality, Michel Foucault gives language to the operation of virtuality in Boccaccio's dance. Foucault's narrative of the mirror image focuses on its management of and movement in space. For Foucault, the mirror figures the spatial modes of utopia and heterotopia. On the one hand:

> Dans le miroir, je me vois là où je ne suis pas, dans un espace irréel qui s'ouvre virtuellement derrière la surface, je suis là-bas, là où je ne suis pas, une sorte d'ombre qui me donne à moi-même ma propre visibilité, qui me permet de me regarder là où je suis absent—utopie du miroir.

> [In the mirror, I see myself there where I am not, in an unreal space that opens itself virtually behind the surface, I am over there, there where I am not, a sort of shadow that gives my own visibility to myself, that allows me to see myself there where I am absent—the utopia of the mirror.]

On the other hand:

> . . . c'est églement [*sic*] une hétérotopie, dans la mesure où le miroir existe réellement, et où il a, sur la place que j'occupe, une sorte d'effet en retour; c'est à partir du miroir que je me découvre absent à la place où je suis puisque je me vois là-bas. À partir de ce regard qui en quelque sorte se porte sur moi, du fond de cet espace virtuel qui est de l'autre côté de la glace, je reviens vers moi et je recommence à porter mes yeux vers moi-même et à me reconstituer là où je suis. . . .

> [it is equally a heterotopia, in the capacity where the mirror really exists, and where it has, on the place that I occupy, a sort of returning effect; it is from the mirror that I discover myself absent from the place where I am since I see myself over there. From this gaze which in some sense heads toward me, from the ground of that virtual space which is on the other side of the mirror, I return to me and I begin again to direct my eyes toward myself and to reconstitute myself there where I am. . . .]

In sum, the mirror:

> . . . rend cette place que j'occupe au moment où je me regarde dans la glace, à la fois absolument réelle, en liaison avec tout l'espace qui

l'entoure, et absolument irréelle, puisqu'elle est obligée, pour être per-
çue, de passer par ce point virtuel qui est là-bas.[113]

[makes this place that I occupy, at the moment when I look at myself
in the mirror, at once absolutely real, in contact with all the space that
surrounds it, and absolutely unreal, since to be perceived it is required to
pass through that virtual point that is over there.]

Foucault's account of the mirror in space explicates the work of Emilia's
mirror in the dance. First, if Boccaccio's lyric accompaniment introduces
a mirror into the performance of the dance, Foucault elaborates upon the
nature of the mirror image's motion: it fluctuates between the real and the
unreal. Second, Foucault's mirror image designates the presence of virtual
spaces. The second stanza evokes Emilia's mirror image approaching her
body. This moment constitutes—in light of Foucault—a scenario of return
(*effet du retour*) from the virtual space that the mirror generates and contains.
By existing in an ambiguous space of virtuality, the mirror image at once
asks to be interwoven into the real space around it and always remains on
the other side of a point that distinguishes its reality from ours. Thus, while
on the surface the poem might appear simply to introduce into the dance a
kind of shadow or echo, considering the mirror image in terms of Foucault's
virtuality provides us with a more specific account of the interaction between
lyric and movement. In this account, the image of the mirror introduces a
virtual element by casting itself as both real and unreal in its danced participation: an object at once immaterial and at the same time requiring the rest
of the dance to accommodate it.

Foucault's words further suggest that Emilia's mirror image is not simply an isolated virtual element; rather, it emblematizes the virtual forces
shot through the dance in its entirety. Foucault describes the heterotopia
of mirrors through the effects of returning, passing through, directing his
gaze, and, perhaps most importantly, having to negotiate an awareness of

113. Michel Foucault, "Des espaces autres," in *Dits et écrits*, ed. Daniel Defert et al. (Paris:
Gallimard, 1994), 4.756; my translations. While Foucault wrote this text in 1967, he did not
authorize its publication until close to his death in 1984 (Foucault, 752). Its comments about
the heterotopic spaces point conceptually toward his work on spaces of surveillance and control,
but the essay on its own has a contingent and exploratory quality. Thus, while it may appear
opportunistic to isolate this passage on the image of the mirror, its informality renders it more
purely about the mechanics of moving through space than about the political concerns that frame
this essay when viewed through the prism of Foucault's other work.

simultaneous absence and presence in space. We might not know what the steps of Lauretta's dance look like, or the pace and scale at which the participants execute them, or their choreographic shape, or how exactly they correspond to either the musical accompaniment itself or Emilia's bodily activity in performing it. But we can, aided by Foucault's mirrored virtualities, reenact the perspectival and experiential position of a dancer always occupying and leaving a space at once, gazing at others as he occupies the space from which he himself just gazed, gazing at the space across from him that holds the afterimage of himself as he prepares to return to it. In these activities, he registers all the ambiguously apprehensible force—the *virtus*—at work in the dancers' collaborative participation. The poem's mirror image thus at once asserts the possibility of a virtual presence for its performers and at the same time alerts us to reenact a broadly distributed virtuality to which participants in medieval dance could equally be attuned.

Finally, the dancers' reactions to Emilia's verses indicate how the virtual supplement registers as at once habitual and strange. The rest of the company, Boccaccio tells us, is somewhat puzzled by the meaning of this poem ("alcuni molto alle parole di quella pensar facesse") but cheerfully joins in to repeat the refrain as they dance ("tutti lietamente avean risposto"). While their mild bemusement indicates a sense of the strangeness in what Emilia says, the fact that their reaction does not inhibit their participation intimates that they are registering an aspect of dance that is familiar in its very strangeness. The danced virtuality in Lauretta and Emilia's performance reflects a recognizable characteristic of medieval dance, a virtual supplement acknowledged as strange in aspect but familiar in occurrence.

When the Wife of Bath proclaims, early in her tale, that "vanysshed was this daunce" (*CT* III.996), her comment is both prescient of the future and revealing of its own moment. In one sense, it speaks to the inaccessibility of past experience to us as a modern audience. She frames this section of her story with an acknowledgment that ancient dances in the grass are irretrievable, their preternatural participants no longer visible:

> The elf-queene, with hir joly compaignye
> Daunced ful ofte in many a grene mede. . . .
> But now kan no man se none elves mo. . . .

> (*CT* III.860–64)

In another sense, though, "vanysshed was this daunce" intimates that the spectacle of vanishing—the uncanny pivot between the material and immaterial, between the body and the forces of virtuality that originate from and surround it—represents a component of the encounter with medieval dance. Dance can be mundane or incidentally figural, of course, as when Chaucer's eagle tells Geffrey that he "mayst go in the daunce" of those not favored by Love (*HF* 2.639). But when medieval authors and artists examine dance closely, they seem responsive to its virtual forces. These emerge in a process of reenactment that experimentally construes, in contemporary discourses, what a spectator of, or participant in, medieval dance perceives. In Boccaccio's illustration of reenactment, experience, and virtuality, we realize that medieval dance is always "vanysshed" not only in our access to its historical analysis but also in its own aesthetic identity: in its medieval enactment, dance incorporates vanishings, illusions, and mirrored apparitions, uncanny in their very familiarity, into itself. In reenacting this experience of danced virtuality, I reveal a medieval apprehensional practice that dictates, as the next chapter will suggest, medieval experiences of poetic form.

CHAPTER TWO

Bonaventure and a Strumpet:
A Theory of Medieval Poetic Form

By making strange bedfellows of the thirteenth-century theologian St. Bonaventure and a dance leader in a fifteenth-century English carol, this chapter will outline a theory of poetic form. The theory construes medieval poetic form not as a textual attribute but as an experience constituted in an audience's sensitivity to danced virtuality. As a primer in a formalist reading technique specifically for scripture, St. Bonaventure's prologue to the *Breviloquium* relies, I shall argue, on virtual supplements. With this foundation in place, I shall employ an English carol about a young dance leader to make a further claim: that the experience of poetic form consists in the apprehension of virtuality at the intersection of dance and verse. This carol narrates a process by which medieval readers experience poetic form as the presence of virtuality, a presence to which dance habituates them. This is not to assert that every poem across the entire Middle Ages bears some relation to dance. But it is to suggest that more do than has been evident to us, and that to read medieval poetry through the strange footing of its intersection with dance can recalibrate our sense of medieval poetry for its premodern audience.

This theory of medieval poetic form joins a growing body of work that responds to an observation of Eleanor Johnson's: while formalism has, since around the turn of this century, had "something of a renaissance," it has been slower to "hav[e] a Middle Ages."[1] At the same time, I am mindful of two important caveats. The first is the caution that "the term 'theory' cannot be used in relation to Middle English literature . . . without considerable

---

1. Eleanor Johnson, *Practicing Literary Theory in the Middle Ages: Ethics and the Mixed Form in Chaucer, Gower, Usk, and Hoccleve* (Chicago: University of Chicago Press, 2013), 13.

historical and critical negotiation."[2] The second is the risk that, in an interdisciplinary theory of poetic form, what we categorize as "form" will float imprecisely between visual/performance-based and poetic contexts. The modern response to medieval poetic form has historically treated the relation between verbal and visual form as one of analogy. This analytical structure has ingrained itself in the modern study of medieval poetic form since at least the New Critical era. It not only occludes other possibilities of relation between arts but also obscures the mechanisms by which we move between verbal and visual form. I therefore aim to resist the impulse, shaped by a formalist heritage, to offer an argument of analogy. Rather than describing medieval poetic form by comparing poetry to other arts, I focus on the experiential structure of *ductus* as a means to stage collaboration between poety and other arts. *Ductus* offers an alternative to the account in which form flits between parallel manifestations without a sense of the mechanism by which this migration occurs. This proposed solution requires acknowledging how we have developed modern discourses of medieval poetic form. Thus, while my approach cannot avoid the inevitable "historical and critical negotiation" involved in calling something a "theory" of medieval poetic form, it does deal explicitly with this negotiation between the medieval and the modern.

FORMA

To inquire into poetic form, we ought first to specify some ways that *form* operates conceptually in the Middle Ages. Middle English *forme* encompasses senses that ranged from the aesthetic to the philosophical and hovered in the practical and instrumental realm of behavior, procedure (*MED* s.v. *forme* 8a), and law (*MED* s.v. *forme* 13). Middle English recognizes the Platonic and abstract resonance of *forme* as an idea that gives rise to something (*MED* 14a), a "formative principle," or essence (*MED* 14b). But many more of its meanings in this period pertain to concrete manifestations. *Forme* relates to Aquinas's Aristotelian account of *forma* as one of the three *principia naturae*, along with *materia* and *privatio*. As a principle "per se," *forma* retains a being beyond its process of becoming; that is to say, it can

---

2. Ruth Evans, Andrew Taylor, Nicholas Watson, and Jocelyn Wogan-Brown, "The Notion of Vernacular Theory," in *The Idea of the Vernacular: An Anthology of Middle English Literary Theory, 1280–1520*, ed. Jocelyn Wogan-Brown et al. (University Park, PA: Pennsylvania State University Press, 1999), 315.

be a shape or structure articulated as a result of a process.[3] Thus, one way to understand form is as the created shape itself, and this idea is sometimes distinguished from the process necessary to create this shape. Aquinas, for instance, further emphasizes the sense of form as an already established and perceived shape in his distinction of *forma* from *privatio*, another principle, in *De principiis naturae* 2.9. He notes that *privatio*, unlike form and matter, is a principle only "in fieri et non in esse," in becoming and not in being. "Ad hoc enim quod fiat idolum," he explains, "oportet quod sit aes, et quod ultimo sit figura idoli; et iterum quando iam idolum est, oportet haec duo esse" [in order that a statue come to be, it is necessary that there be bronze, and that in the end there be the shape/form (*figura*) of the statue; and again when the statue already is, it is necessary that these two be].[4] *Figura* is paired with the *materia* of the brass but distinguished from the third principle of nature *privatio*. In such a context, *figura* elucidates form as an attribute of the created material object.

When form as a philosophical concept migrates to the analysis of literary texts, however, it foregrounds the process of articulation that is in fact implicit to it. As Christopher Cannon explains, "at the border between" form as a generative idea and form as a distinguishing attribute "is a way of conceiving of the process of creation or making as movement from one of these states to the other."[5] Among the principles of natural generation, Aquinas specifies that *forma* "est id ad quod est generatio" [is that toward which generation is].[6] The Aristotelian construct, then, reveals itself as what Alastair Minnis calls "the pattern aimed at in a process of generation," reflecting the sense of movement and directionality to which Cannon alludes.[7] In medieval literary theoretical discourse, the rubrics *forma tractandi* and *forma tractatus* communicate this sense of process. A "mode of proceeding," *forma tractandi* emphasizes the process inherent in scriptural authors' theological thought. Minnis notes that exegetical accounts of *formae tractandi* sound increasingly like discussions of the literary

---

3. Joseph Bobik, ed. and trans., *Aquinas on Matter and Form and the Elements: A Translation and Interpretation of the "De Principiis Naturae" and the "De Mixtione Elementorum" of St. Thomas Aquinas* (Notre Dame: University of Notre Dame Press, 1998), 21–22. Here and below I have supplied my own translations in place of Bobik's; mine err on the side of literality rather than grace to avoid occluding certain resonances.

4. Ibid.

5. Cannon, "Form," 177.

6. Bobik, 15 (*De principiis naturae* 2.7).

7. Alastair Minnis, *Medieval Theory of Authorship: Scholastic Literary Attitudes in the Later Middle Ages*, 2nd ed. (Philadelphia: University of Pennsylvania Press, 1988), 118.

(focusing on rhetorical figure) as the Middle Ages progress.[8] The act of tracing a rhetorical figure's occurrence in time emerges as a mode of literary
analysis.[9] And while *forma tractatus*, referring to arrangement and division
within the text, might appear to evoke a more static sense of form, it is so
deeply connected to the doctrinal process that it also preserves this sense of
form plotted over a temporal arc. Hugh of St. Cher notes that the Book of
Isaiah's pattern cannot be discerned in its sequence of historical events at
any given moment, but rather in the activity of reading the whole, "the succession of the book," which will allow its true revelatory order to manifest
itself.[10] In the application of *forma* to literary texts, the pattern by itself
does not represent the fullness of form as an entity; rather, the activity of
being led along a vector of apprehension completes it.

Philosophically and rhetorically, form encompasses the notion of an
ideal even as it speaks to processes—formations—by which formal expression occurs. As Cannon puts it, medieval formalism implies an attunement
to the way "every attribute of text is either the elaboration or entailment
of some originating 'thought.'" "Thoughts become things" for a reader, and
an idea of form is realized across the attributes of a text.[11] Derived from
philosophical discourse, form is a process that plots itself along this trajectory. But while this model articulates a medieval understanding of form, it
leaves some room to consider the mechanics by which poetic form is apprehended. If the conception of form as process is a powerful one in premodernity, does that attunement to process exclusively involve the continuum
between ideal and real? What other kinds of process are apparent to a medieval audience in their perception of formal attributes? Alternatively, how
exactly does a medieval audience perceive poetic form—even in its material
manifestation—*as* process rather than attribute? And what happens when a

8. Ibid., 133.

9. See also ibid., 139–43, on the diminishing gap between analyses of sacred and secular
poetry during the course of the Middle Ages. Minnis ultimately "calls for a qualification of
E. R. Curtius's view that 'Scholasticism is not interested in evaluating poetry. It produced no
poetics and no theory of art.' In fact, thirteenth-century theologians produced a vocabulary which
enabled the literary features of Scriptural texts to be analysed thoroughly and systematically, and
which encouraged the emergence, in the late thirteenth and early fourteenth centuries, of a more
liberal attitude to classical poetry" (144).

10. Hugh of St. Cher, *Cardinalis opera omnia in universum Vetus et Novum Testamentum*,
iv, f. 2r; cited in Minnis, *Theory of Authorship*, 150.

11. "Form," 178, 182, 187. In the cases of both *Handlyng Synne* and *Pearl*, awkwardness,
disproportion, and ill fit in the texts' form become "important moments in which the governing
logic of the whole form only appears to fail because of a boldness that allows that logic to
appear—in those moments—as if in isolation"; in fact they elucidate the logic of the whole
(Cannon, "Form,"185, 187). See also *Grounds*, 3–10.

medieval environment exhorts an audience to apprehend, and even participate in, poetic formal processes across several media at once?

DUCTUS

In response to these questions, the medieval concept of *ductus* (introduced
in chapter 1) represents an important means to understand the experience of
poetic form. What is sometimes elusive to us as modern readers, however,
is *ductus's* further potential as an alternative to the interpretive strategy
that compares the formal features of distinct artistic media. This section
will consider some reasons for that interpretive tendency and then explore
the alternative to it that *ductus* offers. *Ductus* reveals a process in which
the perceptual habits conditioned in encounters with visual spectacle deploy themselves in the encounter with poetic text. These perceptual habits
can obtain whether or not the reader is physically immersed in the site of
spectacle during the poetic encounter.

   Medieval treatises often employ analogies to describe the work of poetic
composition. In the early thirteenth century, Geoffrey of Vinsauf's Ciceronian treatise compares the writing of a poem to the building of a house to
emphasize their mutual dependence upon measure and the need to abolish
impetuosity.[12] He draws upon other analogies as well to describe the nature
of poetic creation and ornamentation, such as the molding of wax, the painting of a picture, and the donning of a garment.[13] This strategy is not universal. In the late-fourteenth-century *Art de dictier*, Eustache Deschamps
outlines composition practices for vernacular poetry mostly by providing
examples of poetic forms and discussing the sound quality of vowels and
consonants.[14] But comparative methods exist in other influential treatises
on vernacular compostion. Dante's *De vulgari eloquentia*, for instance, employs the figure of the *canzone* as a bundle of sticks and cords, another
approach to writerly process as explicated through the language of physical
construction.[15] Dante's debt to Horace furthermore draws our attention to

   12. Geoffrey of Vinsauf, *Poetria Nova*, trans. Margaret F. Nims, rev. ed. (Toronto: Pontifical
Institute of Mediaeval Studies, 2010), 20.
   13. Ibid., 25, 41, 47. As Cannon observes, in this discussion the concept of form is "embedded"
rather than stated explicitly. "Form," 179.
   14. Eustache Deschamps, *L'Art de dictier*, ed. and trans. Deborah N. Sinnreich-Levi (East
Lansing, MI: Colleagues Press, 1994), 67–105.
   15. Steven Botterill, ed. and trans., *Dante: De Vulgari Eloquentia* (Cambridge: Cambridge
University Press, 1996), 68–69 (*fascis*).

that classical precedent, which itself relies significantly upon comparisons among arts to make its claims; recall, for instance, the *Ars poetica*'s famous opening allusion to the painter, who depicts a monstrous hybrid creature, to explain the importance of poetic unity and decorum.[16]

We might reasonably judge such discourses to affect our thinking about poetry only subtly, if at all, especially since these theories are largely compositional. More immediately relevant to our approaches as postmodern formalist readers, however, is a modern history of criticism that also explains poetry through analogies with other arts. Dance numbers among the arts to which poetry is often compared. Stéphane Mallarmé, for instance, crystallizes this approach when he proposes that the dancing woman is in fact neither dancing nor a woman, but rather an "écriture corporelle," a "poëme dégagé de tout appareil du scribe" (a poem freed from any apparatus of the scribe).[17] Barbara Johnson rightly critiques this statement, but the tendency to render the body as a writing has many lives in aesthetic philosophy.[18] Regarding poetic *form* in particular, New Criticism privileges comparison as an expedient method to reveal formal unity. This strategy appears, for example, in Cleanth Brooks's comparison of poetry to architecture and painting in "The Heresy of Paraphrase": "The essential structure of a poem (as distinguished from the rational or logical structure of the 'statement' which we abstract from it) resembles that of architecture or painting; it is a pattern of resolved stresses."[19] We can thus identify a practice in modern criticism—albeit harnessed in quite different ways—of tracing comparisons between poetry and other arts, and in some cases specifying the efficacy of this comparative strategy in the analysis of poetic form. As contemporary formalist readers, we presumably do not subscribe to many of the underlying principles of these older models of formalism—particularly the New Critical commitment to unity—but they represent building blocks in the training and background of many critical readers of poetry.

New Criticism asserts itself in midcentury medieval studies, where it operates—again, perhaps subtly—as an embedded component of the discipline.

16. Horace, *Ars Poetica or Epistle to the Pisos*, in *Satires, Epistles, Art of Poetry*, ed. and trans. H. Rushton Fairclough (Cambridge, MA: Harvard University Press, 1939), 450.

17. Stéphane Mallarmé, *Œuvres complètes*, ed. Henri Mondor and G. Jean-Aubrey (Paris: Gallimard, 1945), 304.

18. Barbara Johnson, "Les Fleurs du mal armé: Some Reflections on Intertextuality," repr. in *Lyric Poetry: Beyond New Criticism*, ed. Chaviva Hošek and Patricia Parker (Ithaca: Cornell University Press, 1985), 274–75. See also Badiou, 57–71.

19. Cleanth Brooks, *The Well Wrought Urn* (New York: Cornwall, 1947), 186.

Here, comparisons among arts identify unity and synthesis in literary texts.[20] Charles Muscatine's *Chaucer and the French Tradition* (1957) illustrates this technique. In his analysis of the *Canterbury Tales*, Muscatine implicitly analogizes processional spectacle to text:

> The procession of the stages in the English mystery cycle, representing the biographical and historical journey of Man from the Creation to the Resurrection, has a . . . public and self-evident meaning. The dual procession of Chaucer's travelers and their tales is given such specific moral significance by the conception of a religious pilgrimage. If Chaucer knew the road through Greenwich, he also knew the one through the *Divine Comedy.* . . . The metaphor permeated medieval consciousness.[21]

The first example is a performance-based journey involving spatial components in a material arena. Watching the Corpus Christi cycle reveals typological echoes, as well as the expansion and contraction of scale in space and time, in following the sequence and being aware of its different components' juxtaposition in performance.[22] This experience thus gives the viewer visual and material access to attributes that one might consider formal: sequence, pattern, and proportion. To discuss his second example, the structure of the *The Canterbury Tales*, Muscatine makes an implicit comparison to cycle drama by referring not only to the traveling company but also to the tales themselves as a "procession" on his way to evoking pilgrimage. By allowing this word to jump from material world to text (a jump reversed in the transition from the road through Greenwich to the "road" through Dante), Muscatine establishes physically immersive, real-time perambulation as a metaphor for textual form (tellers and tales). Within this "coördinatedness and linearity," Chaucer can synthesize the opposing states—heavenly and earthly, for example—that Gothic culture holds in suspension.[23]

---

20. Art historical studies interested in the relation of material and verbal arts continue to rely on analogy and metaphor. See, for instance, Stephen Murray, *Plotting Gothic* (Chicago: University of Chicago Press, 2014), 9, 108–9.

21. Charles Muscatine, *Chaucer and the French Tradition: A Study in Style and Meaning* (Berkeley: University of California Press, 1957), 168.

22. On the formal play of temporal scale in cycle drama, see, for instance, Kolve, esp. chs. 4 and 5.

23. Muscatine, 168–70. In this reading, Muscatine refers to Arthur W. Hoffman, "Chaucer's Prologue to Pilgrimage: The Two Voices," *ELH* 21.1 (1954): 1–16, an essay still cited in studies of *The Canterbury Tales*. Hoffman's essay also exemplifies an old formalist turn away from social and contextual considerations and toward the achievement of "unity"—in both the medieval text and the reading of it—through intricate interpretations of the General Prologue's various

Deepening our backward glance into Muscatine's book reveals that the foundation for his formalist comparison lies within a medieval model of participatory ductile experience. The springboard for Muscatine's reading is Arnold Hauser's *Social History of Art* (1951), which describes the "basic form of Gothic art" as follows:

> The beholder is, as it were, led through the stages and stations of a journey, and the picture of reality which it reveals is like a panoramic survey, not a one-sided, unified representation, dominated by a single point of view. In painting it is the "continuous" method which is favoured; the drama tries to make the episodes as complete as possible and prefers, instead of the concentration of the action in a few decisive situations, frequent changes of scene, of the characters and the motifs. The important thing in Gothic art is not the subjective viewpoint, not the creative, formative will expressed in the mastering of the material, but the thematic material itself, of which both artists and public can never see enough. Gothic art leads the onlooker from one detail to another and causes him, as has been well said, to "unravel" the successive parts of the work one after the other. . . .[24]

The trope of leading anchors this passage, appearing at the beginning and the end. Hauser aims here to convey medieval art's distinctive eschewal of the "subjective viewpoint" that characterizes modernity's understanding of artistic creation and the perceiver's encounter with it. But Hauser's description also elucidates an experiential process of *ductus*. It is the process of being led through the work that organizes the apprehension of that work's episodic nature or relations among stylistic details; in this way, form presents itself as experience. In addition, *ductus* draws the participant's perspective into the constitution of the form. The onlooker's work of "unravel[ing]" plays a role in defining what he experiences as the form of the artifact.

What Hauser calls "unravel[ing]," his source, Dagobert Frey, expresses as the rolling (*rollt*) of a film, and Frey's account further insists upon a formal experience in which the viewer participates.[25] He specifies that while

---

dichotomies (7). On the New Critical privileging of unity and synthesis, as well as its continuing influence despite critical and political denigrations of these practices, see, for instance, Paul H. Fry, *Theory of Literature* (New Haven: Yale University Press, 2011), 56, 70.

24. Arnold Hauser, *The Social History of Art*, vol. 1 (New York: Alfred A. Knopf, 1951), 272–73.

25. Dagobert Frey, *Gotik und Renaissance als Grundlagen der modernen Weltanschauung* (Augsberg: B. Filser, 1929), 38.

Gothic visual perception is like the act of watching a movie as it rolls serially before the viewer, the Gothic perceptual mode depends not on the external instruments of film and camera but rather upon the shaping movement of the viewer's own mind.[26] The metaphor of watching a film communicates the experiential process as constituted by the perceiver as much as by the object perceived. Hauser aims in his section to contrast the Gothic with the Renaissance, the latter of which (in the phrase immediately following the passage quoted above) "forces [the viewer] rather to grasp all the parts at one and the same time."[27] Even in his construction of this epochal distinction, Hauser's rhetoric continues to assert the fundamental sense of interactivity between art and viewer that Frey's metaphor established. In the Middle Ages, the form of art leads, the onlooker unravels; in the Renaissance, the form of art forces, the viewer grasps.[28] Thus the template for Muscatine's comparison between arts reveals itself to be an experience of *ductus* in which the participation of the audience both operates as an integral part of the experience and relies upon an immersive, "panoramic" mode of encounter.

But what this history of formalist criticism has cast as a comparison between expressive media—the procession of a cycle drama and a "procession" of stories, for example—holds the potential to expose instead, through *ductus*, a different structure of relation between them. Avowing that Hauser's understanding of Gothic visual art's form probably reflects "no thought of Chaucer," Muscatine calls Hauser's model a "deep-seated general form for the ordering of experience [that] takes on specific symbolic meaning in its particular manifestations."[29] Thus, Muscatine identifies an ideal sense of order that influences the formal character of any individual artistic manifestation. As Carruthers has noted, however, "medieval aesthetic is not much pleased by simples and 'purities,' or by artifacts that address only

26. Thanks to Stefan Uhlig for assistance with the German. An English excerpt also appears as "Gothic and Renaissance," in *Art History: An Anthology of Modern Criticism*, ed. Wylie Sypher (New York: Vintage, 1963), 154–72.

27. Hauser, 273. Hauser's narrative is invested in temporal passage throughout in that it tracks the movement toward capitalist modernity, beginning with the Stone Age and ending with the Film Age. On early critiques of Hauser and their suspicion of Marxism as inadequately suited to art historical analysis, see Michael R. Orwicz, "Critical Discourse in the Formation of a Social History of Art: Anglo-American Response to Arnold Hauser," *Oxford Art Journal* 8.2 (1985): 53.

28. For recent accounts of this kind of "cooperative interaction" (xxxvii) as characteristic of premodern encounters between viewers and art, see the essays in Blick et al., eds., *Push Me, Pull You*.

29. Muscatine, 167–68.

one sense at a time."[30] It seems possible to ask, consequently, whether artifacts that appear to engage primarily one category of sensory response in fact engage many. *Ductus*, I will suggest in what follows, accommodates a medieval experience in which apprehensional practices established in encounters with various nonverbal media play a defining role in an audience's formal experience of poetic text. The structure of relation *ductus* implies, therefore, is less the comparison between arts evoking a "general form" than the ability of one medium's perceptual habits to inflect the experience that another medium offers.

To argue for this model requires an underlying warrant: that habits of perception or decoding constructed in one arena can affect others. Katharine Breen has discussed medieval reading practice's foundations of habituated skill. She proposes a model of "vernacular *habitus*" that provides a "crucial conceptual framework" for reading experience.[31] Her invocation of *habitus* draws upon not only Bourdieu's location of *habitus* within an almost preconscious body, but also medieval thinkers' approaches to this concept as a conscious pursuit of practice. In this particular case, Latin grammar and other learned constructs inform the vernacular reading habits of a lay public.[32] Within the framework of habituation to reading practice as at once deeply internalized and at the same time an object of self-aware inquiry, we might consider other ways that medieval subjects are habituated to different kinds of literate practice. The introduction referred to Rebecca Krug's argument that "textual engagement" in the Middle Ages is shaped by the social structures and forces surrounding scenes of reading. This claim draws upon anthropological work that understands literacy itself to be a diverse and shifting set of practices constituted by a range of social practices and ideologies.[33] Furthermore, while some aspects of literate practice might thus reflect social formations, others draw attention to more sensory instruments of habituation. Maura Nolan argues, for example, that another means to discern the constitution of habit in reading practice presents itself in the visual and material features of the manuscript. *Mise-en-page*, catchwords, even the size and weight of a book—these features both dictate

30. Carruthers, *Experience*, 48.

31. Katharine Breen, *Imagining an English Reading Public, 1150–1400* (Cambridge: Cambridge University Press, 2010), 5.

32. Ibid., 6–8. See also the distinction Breen draws between *habitus* and *consuetudo*, the latter of which refers to "practices that gain their authority from simple iteration" (46).

33. Krug, 5–6.

and reflect habits of textual encounter.[34] Lara Farina, finally, suggests that the expectations conditioned by dance can negotiate affective responses to a text's tactility. She argues that the "paradoxical feeling" of the dancers in Robert Mannyng's *Handlyng Synne*, moving but still, is the "affective state" that this text "aims to reproduce for its readers and listeners" in their various ways of handling it.[35]

As a corollary to these formulations, and as part of the overall warrant, we might consider as well how cultural practices outside the realm of poetic reading help to construct habits of what we would call formalist reading as a particular kind of textual encounter. D. Vance Smith proposes that medieval supposition theory approximates a sense of medieval formalist reading practice; indeed, he suggests, the rules of supposition theory foster an aesthetic attention even more elaborate than what we tend to associate with close reading.[36] Such a model conceives of the analysis of literary form as predicated upon a reflective relationship between formal characteristics and intellectual imperatives at work elsewhere in the culture.

But while grammar, *mise-en-page*, and supposition theory all represent habits contributing to both literate practices in general and poetic formalist response in particular, they do not derive from performance or spectacle, and a book about dance and poetic form needs especially to attend to the work of the performance-based arena. Claire Sponsler's account of "habits of literacy" focuses on the way that performance settings shape literate practice, uniting the work of visual and material cues with those originating in socially interactive structures. She notes that the kinds of practices "we tend to associate solely with words on a page could extend to other media" in the late Middle Ages. For Sponsler, this dynamic results in a poem's "presentational versatility" as read, heard, or watched in different "scen[es] of

34. Maura Nolan, "Medieval Habit, Modern Sensation: Reading Manuscripts in the Digital Age," *Chaucer Review* 47.4 (2013): 466–69.

35. Lara Farina, "Get a Grip? The Tactile Object of *Handlyng Synne*," in *Feeling Things: Objects and Emotions through History*, ed. Stephanie Downes, Sally Holloway, and Sarah Randles (Oxford: Oxford University Press, 2018), 111.

36. D. Vance Smith, "Medieval *Forma*: The Logic of the Work," in *Reading for Form*, ed. Susan J. Wolfson and Marshall Brown (Seattle: University of Washington Press, 2006), 72–73. This is a reading of *forma tractatus* and *forma tractandi* as manifestations of formal practice. On *forma tractatus* as invention—the content drawn into coherence—and *forma tractandi* as the process of shaping, see Mary Carruthers, *The Book of Memory*, 2nd ed. (Cambridge: Cambridge University Press, 2008), 250.

reading."[37] Her analysis suggests that poetry's situadedness in other medial settings draws the habits of performance spectatorship into the decoding processes of the poetic encounter (further emphasizing the complexity of literacy's meaning in the Middle Ages). Jessica Brantley argues that some texts produce within themselves a performative dynamic that speaks to the nature of reading.[38] In this instance, the habits of performance experience internalize themselves within reading practice. These different models explore textual reception as responsive to habits produced within a crucible of multiple shaping influences—learned, philosophical, social, tactile, visual, performance-based. Within this context, it is plausible to envision a situation in which a self-aware and sophisticated engagement with medieval dance establishes an apprehensional mode deployed in the encounter with poetry.

With this warrant in place, *ductus* provides the means by which the bridge between dance and poetry constructs itself. Paul Crossley's analysis of Chartres Cathedral will help to make this point. Crossley asks about the extent to which *ductus*, as a model for understanding textual and rhetorical process, might affect the rationales that underlie the design of a visual and material site like a cathedral. While *ductus* emerges as most strongly associated with textual and rhetorical tradition, it is, Crossley notes, "essentially about performance." It relies on the conjuration of visually apprehended movement and procession to formulate its textual concept.[39] Within this context emerges an actual "cathedral *ductus*," an apprehensional process of nonverbal art that focuses primarily not on the ideal or absolute but on accessible experience.[40] One way to understand "cathedral *ductus*" is as the possibility that the conventions associated with textual *ductus* might have "consequences for . . . actual buildings." Although it would be "hazardous," Crossley argues, to plot a causal trajectory between rhetorical theory and the "artistic policy" underlying a cathedral's construction, it seems that *ductus*, as a rhetorical and textual mode of thought, bears a relationship for

37. Claire Sponsler, *The Queen's Dumbshows: John Lydgate and the Making of Early Theater* (Philadelphia: University of Pennsylvania Press, 2014), 87.

38. Jessica Brantley, *Reading in the Wilderness: Private Devotion and Public Performance in Late Medieval England* (Chicago: University of Chicago Press, 2007), 2–3, 305, and *passim*.

39. Paul Crossley, "*Ductus* and *Memoria*: Chartres Cathedral and the Workings of Rhetoric," in *Rhetoric beyond Words*, 215. Carruthers places the formation of *ductus* as a "phenomenon of rhetorical art" early in the Middle Ages ("Concept," 195).

40. Crossley, 214, 216. "Cathedral *ductus*" operates, in part, through the exterior imagery's role as "preparation" for the imagery, spatial configuration, and even performance within; this anticipatory function of the imagery dictates sequences of imagery (often repeating) that form paths through the church for audiences (216–18).

medieval audiences to the experience that the physical, kinetic, visually stimulating journey through a cathedral offers.[41] In this case, the habits of textual encounter that *ductus* establishes can shape the experience of a physical building.

The nature of the cathedral suggests that "cathedral *ductus*" is potentially even more complex, with perceptual practices wielding their influence not only from text to object but also among different visual and auditory media as well as from the apprehension of multimedia spectacle to the encounter with language. As a process that leads the audience through different media within in the cathedral—visual, architetural, sonic, embodied—*ductus* orchestrates networks of commerce among those diverse medial components. Crossley identifies an "open" and "creative" interaction among verbal, material, and kinetic components in the audience's ductile experience of the cathedral.[42] Viewers might experience visual and verbal stimuli in terms of each other as they take in simultaneously, for instance, the language of the liturgy and the images on the portals through which entrance processions pass; in Crossley's terms, "the living poetry of the hymns and the mute imagery of the portals join to reenact Christ's *adventus*."[43] At once a symbolic and kinetic act of being led, *ductus* as an experience of the site enables liturgical language and visual imagery to "conspir[e]" within a set of complicated sequences.[44]

While this ductile dynamic is read—by Crossley and others—as analogical, we might also specify it further: it is a situation of multiple and intersecting media in which the process of being led is also a process of applying habits of decoding and perception across medial categories.[45] Margot Fassler conveys this experience in her description of twelfth-century entry processions in Chartres Cathedral: "Just as the texts and music of the introits with their tropes are alive with multiple depictions of history, with prophets crying and clerics singing, all of the coming of Christ and of the coming of his vicar into the cathedral, so too is the portal. It is not a static work of art, but a vivid tableau, which forces our eyes to travel from

41. Ibid., 230.

42. Ibid., 242.

43. Ibid., 227–28. See also Margot Fassler, "Liturgy and Sacred History in the Twelfth-Century Tympana at Chartres," *The Art Bulletin* 75.3 (1993): 500: "arts associated with [ceremonial entrance], whether they worked directly in concert or not, could be concerned with manifesting the power of this symbolic event."

44. Crossley, 228, 215.

45. On analogy, see ibid., 242. Stephen Murray uses the related concept of *plot* to identify the "correlation of storytelling and the actual business of building." The ductile activity of "pull[ing] the reader forward" correlates the experiences of different expressive modes ranging from the material to the textual. *Plotting Gothic*, 8–9, 11.

left to right to center and back again" in order to understand it.[46] While her language is, again, analogical ("just as . . . so too"), the effect she describes is more complex. The viewer's awareness of sonic and kinetic elements in the liturgy reconstitutes his perception of architecture itself as something animate and temporally engaged. Fassler notes that the West Portal could evoke this response whether or not the liturgical material in question was sung at the moment of procession through it (though in the twelfth century it often was).[47] That point emphasizes that it is the perceptual practice associated with a familiar liturgical performance that enables the reinterpration of the architecture in the cathedral's ductile experience.

This example illuminates *ductus*'s potential as a perceptual bridge between one medium and another rather than as a point of correlation between them. The case studies will elaborate in detail upon how this process operates in networks that interweave verse with visual, material, and other dance-based media. But for the moment, I will proceed through my account of poetic form by offering *ductus* as a process that brings diverse perceptual habits into contact with diverse media and as a result configures the experience of each medium in potentially unexpected ways. In many instances, the model of an ideal form realized in particular medial instances shapes explicit discourses concerning art and its reception. At another level, however, the element of ductile process reveals a different perspective upon form, one that is experiential and that engages perceptual practices forged in encounters with multiple media.

What I describe here is yet another "black box": a perceptual experience not fully accessible or demonstrable to us. But as an agent's process of being led through an environment to engage the perceptual habits associated with multiple media—visual and verbal, kinetic and static—*ductus* allows us to reenact an experiential possibility for form. In drawing parallels that ultimately position media as separate from each other, analogy responds to what W. J. T. Mitchell names "the impulse to purify media" as "one of the central utopian gestures of modernity."[48] But perhaps it is largely that: a gesture of modernity. The space of investigation between the medieval and the modern provides an opportunity to question the interpretive practices reified in histories of formalist criticism. In answer, *ductus* will help us to reenact throughout this study a different kind of formalism.

46. Fassler, "Liturgy," 517.

47. Ibid., 500.

48. W. J. T. Mitchell, *Picture Theory: Essays on Verbal and Visual Representation* (Chicago: University of Chicago Press, 1994), 5. Mitchell asserts that "all media are mixed media."

VIRTUAL BONAVENTURE

The prologue to St. Bonaventure's *Breviloquium*, a treatise on the formal reading of scripture, demonstrates that the model of *ductus* outlined above has some unexpected implications for our understanding of medieval textual form. This text, it should be clarified from the outset, does not deal explicitly with poetry, dance, or visual art. It does not reveal an experience of poetic form constituted by dance-based elements. It is instead a treatise on the reading of scripture preoccupied with motifs of structure and the creative interweaving of different components of scriptural source to produce analysis. It is thus useful to the present discussion because it articulates something we might recognize as a formalist reading practice in a medieval context. But most importantly, as a model of formalist reading, the *Breviloquium* supplements its ductile processes with the generation of virtuality.

Bonaventure's approach exemplifies some characteristics of *ductus* we have already seen: specifically, it finds useful the mechanism of leading; it considers the reader's participation in this process; and it appears to employ an analogy between a three-dimensional, material construction and a text to articulate the ductile process. First, the *Breviloquium* situates itself with a larger context of Bonaventurean writing that explores the symbolic work of journey and impulsion. An example is the mystical journey of the *Itinerarium mentis ad Deum*. In this work, as Karnes has shown, ascent and leading (to God) structure the cognitive project.[49] Second, Bonaventure's prologue to the *Breviloquium* illustrates scriptural reading as a process that acknowledges the agency of both the reader and scripture itself; it recognizes the engagement of the reader that is associated with *ductus*.[50] Finally, in the *Breviloquium*, scriptural text seems to mimic the properties of physical structures and spaces: breadth, length, height, and depth. Scripture manifests its agency by leading the reader through each of these dimensions. The reader of scripture must cut through a forest ("quod per sacrarum Scripturarum silvam quis secure incidendo et exponendo incedat").[51] Scripture is in breadth like the widest river ("similis latissimo fluvio"), increasing by the incorporation of more and more waters ("ex concursu multarum aquarum

---

49. Michelle Karnes, *Imagination, Meditation, and Cognition in the Middle Ages* (Chicago: University of Chicago Press, 2011), 75–77, 99, 126–27.

50. Carruthers, "Concept," 204–5.

51. S. Bonaventura, *Breviloquium*, in *Opera omnia*, vol. 5, *Opuscula varia theologica*, ed. Studio et cura PP Collegii a S. Bonventura (Quaracchi, Florence: Typographia Collegii S. Bonaventurae, 1891), 208.

aggregatur magis ac magis").[52] In addition, Bonaventure presents the arresting image of scripture in the form of an apprehensible and comprehensible
(*intelligibilis*) cross ("sub forma cuiusdam crucis intelligibilis").[53] Through
the shape it takes on, the whole machine (*machina*) of the universe is visible by means of the light of the mind ("in qua describi habet et quodam
modo videri lumine mentis tota machina universi").[54] This last figure suggests that scripture's form conflates interior and exterior placement, perception, and experience. But in all cases—scripture like the limitless forest surrounding the mind, the engulfing river, and the infinite cross filling
out the mind and shaping the light that the mind casts—the interpretive
strategy is comparative. Thus, when Bonaventure evokes terms of spatial
dimension in his discussion of scripture—*latitudo, longitudo, altitudo*, and
profunditas—we might understand these to signal an implicit comparison
to an edifice, a subtle analogy of text to material spectacle.[55] He amplifies
this resonance by speaking of Christ in the building-related terms *funda-
mentum* (foundation) and *ianua* (gate or door).[56]

At the same time, however, this account exists alongside other work
where Bonaventure explores cognitive and analytical methods capable of
moving past the mechanism of comparison. For example, on the surface,
the *Itinerarium* seems to function analogically, comparing the functions of
Christ with those of species (which Karnes defines as "cognitive representations that convey sensory and intellectual data about an object").[57] And
yet, Karnes notes that from here "Bonaventure advances to his most ambi-
tious claim, which is that Christ *is* species."[58] Bonaventure's meditations
on Christ emphasize the importance of access to the divine *through* Christ's
suffering. While he does not advocate the manufacture of physical suffering,
he does see meditation as what Karnes terms an "extension" of such experience, a process in which one uses imagination to take on Christ's suffering

52. Bonaventura, 203.

53. Ibid., 208.

54. Ibid. This image recalls the light-wreathed cross stretched across the universe inside
the dreamer's mind in the Old English *Dream of the Rood*. This cross similarly complicates
categories of interiority and exteriority. See my "Vestigial Signs: Inscription, Performance, and
the *Dream of the Rood*," *PMLA* 125.1 (2010): 48–72.

55. Bonaventure first uses these terms to refer to scripture's description of the whole universe
("describit totum universum," 201) but proceeds to apply them to the aspects of scripture itself:
its many parts, its depiction of time and age, its depiction of hierarchical order, and its depth of
meaning (202).

56. Ibid., 201.

57. Karnes, *Imagination*, 92.

58. Ibid., 99, emphasis in original.

emotionally as part of the trajectory toward "heavenly delights." In this way Bonaventure privileges meditative experiences of participation and interaction rather than the comparison of divinity to sensory data.[59] Another perspective on this idea would be that understanding the mediating processes that occur between different realms and modes of reality is central to Bonaventure. For Karnes, imagination plays a particularly important role in such processes, providing a "bridge" between the senses and cognition.[60]

Bonaventure's text leads the reader through an exposure to scriptural form. But within the larger context of his work, we might characterize that ductile process more specifically as one that does not simply compare the visual to the verbal or the material to the conceptual. Bonaventure's prose form functions as a set of material patterns that evoke certain visually-based perceptual habits; these become a means to experience the form of scriptural text. In the *Breviloquium*, the placement of spatial terms constitutes an apprehensible spatial structure on the page. The reader's engagement in the space and time of those words' arrangement on the page makes the *ductus* of reading and physical *ductus* not comparable but interdependent in the formal experience. Before proceeding sequentially through the coordinates of *latitudo, longitudo, altitudo,* and *profunditas,* Bonaventure clusters references to these directional markers close together.[61] He does so near the opening, in a paragraph about the development of the scriptures; again at the end of this same paragraph; and at the close of this opening section, before the first main section, on breadth, begins.[62] Through this technique, he guides the reader into an encompassing view of the whole, where all the directional labels are containable by the reading eye at once. Only after the reader apprehends this cluster within a short span of physical space and time does Bonaventure change his structuring technique. He moves to a longer explanatory sequence of the terms that requires apprehension of the parts progressively. Here the syntax of his prose introduces distance between the orientational terms that had been compressed. Bonaventure's narration thus compels the reader to keep reshaping and reconstituting the object of perception in visible space. In shifting these positions, the language of the prologue also illuminates the variety of temporal pacings offered in the apprehension of scripture. The temporal experience of the reader—the sense of rapidity or slowness of the intervals between each component as

59. Ibid., 92, 129.
60. Ibid., 91.
61. Bonaventura, 202.
62. Ibid., 201, 201–2, 202.

the reader encounters it—becomes another vehicle for articulating the relationships among these components. Bonaventure's prose form asks the reader to apprehend material configurations in space and time in order to experience scriptural concepts formally.

In addition to harnessing the perceptual habits applied to patterns in physical space, and sensible time, to produce a formal experience of scripture, Bonaventure's text explores another aspect of *ductus*: its generation of virtuality. Further on in the *Breviloquium*, Bonaventure conveys an interest in the kind of ontological ambiguity we have elsewhere associated with virtality. In part 2, chapter 5, Bonaventure (alluding to Aristotle) characterizes the threefold natures of the "machina mundialis" (world machine) as *luminosum, opacum,* and *pervia.*[63] While luminosity and opaqueness are comprehensible enough as ends of a spectrum from intangible light to material substance, *pervia* occupies an indeterminate and suggestive middle position. Sometimes rendered as "translucent," the word etymologically conveys the sense of movement through.[64] In articulating a set of theories concerning different natures in the world, Bonaventure's language sustains the possibility of something intermediary, something that contains the force of potential to move through and be moved through, something that is not solid but is not cordoned off entirely in the category of immaterial light. In the modern terms that my last chapter laid out, *pervia* qualifies as something virtual and suggests that Bonaventure's thought accommodates the possibility of this category.

The *Breviloquium* generates a virtual supplement in the grammar of its references to movement, references that enable the ductile process.[65] As terms like *virtus sermonis,* as well as Middle English *vertu,* have shown us, the apprehension of virtuality's dynamic force does not limit itself to danced environments; this sense of force obtains more broadly in the Middle Ages. The *Breviloquium*'s language registers its supplementary presence. In the

---

63. Ibid., 219, 223.

64. See Dominic V. Monti, trans., *Works of St. Bonaventure: Breviloquium* (St. Bonaventure, NY: Franciscan Institute Publications, 2005), 74–75, for the "translucent" translation.

65. Elsewhere, Bonaventure is known for his invocation of *circumcessio* as a central term to depict the communion of love as the movement of divine figures around each other. This Latin word is closely associated with Greek *perichoresis,* which also conveys movement, turning, and "divine dance." Dănut Mănăstireanu, "Perichoresis and the Early Christian Doctrine of God," *Archaeus* 11–12 (2007–2008): 62–63. This association results from a conflated etymology, or a deliberate "play on words," between *chorein,* "to contain," and *choreu/perichoreu,* "to dance around" (Mănăstireanu, 63). Through his use of *circumcessio,* Bonaventure establishes that he is interested in the form that manifests itself through the motion of bodies or other performing agents.

prologue, Bonaventure's term *modus* (a term related to movement) appears
in a section on scripture's way of proceeding: *modus procedendi*.[66] Within
this section, Bonaventure has frequent recourse to both the noun *modus* and
the verb *movere*. Here, the four construction-related attributes—breadth,
length, height, depth—are reclustered in the text to introduce a way of proceeding through scriptural authority.[67] The "affectus" "magis movetur . . .
ad exempla quam ad argumenta" [is moved more by examples than by argu-
ments]; if someone ["quis"] "non movetur ad praecepta et prohibita, saltem
moveatur per exempla narrata; si quis non per haec movetur, moveatur per
beneficia sibi ostensa" [is not moved by precepts and prohibitions, he might
at least be moved by the examples narrated; if he is not moved by these, he
might be moved by the benefits shown to himself].[68] Bonaventure repeats
this construction, juxtaposing *movetur* and *moveatur*, once more immediately following the passage cited here. If the agent is not, in this present
reality, moved by one thing, then he might potentially be, in another reality,
by another thing. In these statements, Bonaventure's prose generates virtuality through grammar, alternating between the reality of the indicative
(*movetur*) and the *irrealis* of the subjunctive (*moveatur*).[69] As Bonaventure
leads the reader through the text with a shuttling movement between the
reality of the indicative and the ontological alterity of the subjunctive, the
reader experiences what my last chapter described as a virtual element.

The pair of conjugations *movetur* and *moveatur* represents less a shift
between literal and metaphoric movement than one between different modes
of being expressed as different grammatical moods. Once more, it appears on
the surface that Bonaventure draws attention to the metaphoric potential of
movement, and in a sense this is true. According to a metaphoric model, we
would track the different uses of movement as follows: Movement through
the text is spatial in some material sense, as we saw. That movement then
informs the metaphoric register into which Bonaventure shades, where
emotional or spiritual change within the individual is expressed as movement. But again, what seems like comparative construction is actually
more complicated. Within movement's metaphoric evocation of spiritual
change, Bonaventure introduces the additional pivot between *movetur* and

66. On *modus* as movement, see Carruthers, "Concept," 204–5.

67. Bonaventura, 206.

68. Ibid., 206–7.

69. On "irrealis" as a grammatical category, and its relationship to the subjunctive, see,
for instance, Jackie Nordström, *Modality and Subordinators* (Philadelphia: John Benjamins,
2010), 33–35. Bonaventure continues: "si quis nec per haec movetur, moveatur per monitiones
sagaces. . . ." (Bonaventura, 207).

moveatur. As a dichotomy of indicative and subjunctive moods, the two terms represent a crossing of realms different from from the literal and figurative axes upon which *movere* might initially appear to have plotted itself. Bonaventure capitalizes on the interpretive potential of conditionality or subjunctivity elsewhere as well. Karnes reads a passage from the *Lignum vitae* as similarly dependent upon a "series of contrary-to-fact conditionals" to create the possibility of "imagined presence," an ambiguous ontology.[70] In the *Breviloquium*'s alternation of *movetur* and *moveatur*, movement as metaphor does not remain statically in its figurative category; rather, it uses shift in mood to explore other kinds of ontological dichotomies and thus constructs a virtual environment.

In the *Breviloquium*'s ductile process, the sensory experience of spatio-temporal elements dictates the experience of scriptural form; that ductile process generates, as a supplement to itself, an environment of virtuality. In the *Breviloquium*'s account, the very act of moving—the force that drives *ductus*—oscillates between real and unreal states. As we proceed into the case studies, the contrasts among different media in the ductile experience of form will become more apparent than they are here. In Bonaventure, we deal with the expansion and contraction of words inscribed in physical space and apprehensible time as this inscriptional medium relates to linguistic expression. To distinguish inscription from language in terms of media is complicated, to say the least, whereas the medial distinction between, say, dance and poetry might seem easier to grasp.[71] But in a sense, Bonaventure's take on the relation of media to virtuality is more radical than what modernity constructs in its dependence on literal multimediacies. That is, contemporary aesthetic criticism locates virtuality in what it terms the "intermedial" environments of different art forms' communications with each other. By Daniel Albright's definition, for example, an intermedial artwork is produced in an opera performance, which combines different components like music, text, and visual decor. The intermedial object is more than the sum of these parts, a "virtual entity brought into being by the superimposition" of these components.[72] Bonaventure, however, employs his textual medium to lead the reader through the apprehension of material patterns and brings this perceptual practice to bear upon a formal experience

70. Karnes, *Imagination*, 133.

71. Chapter 3 will examine the application of visual practices, distinct from what we would call reading, to words.

72. Daniel Albright, *Panaesthetics: On the Unity and Diversity of the Arts* (New Haven: Yale University Press, 2014), 209.

of scriptural language. In that network, and not a more concrete multimediacy, the virtual supplement emerges as the ambiguous force of ductile
motion.

A STRUMPET LEADS US FURTHER

The virtual supplement to Bonaventure's formalist prose has implications
for vernacular English poetry. The Middle English carol "Ladd Y the daunce"
reveals these implications, elucidating medieval poetic form as an experience whose virtuality produces untimeliness and spatial estrangement.
"Ladd Y the daunce" features a female lyric speaker narrating her experience
leading and participating in a round dance—to which I shall refer as a *carole*—
that ultimately puts her in a compromising position with a young clerk. (This
use of dance as a frame for sex, rape, and pregnancy is conventional.)[73] As she
speaks the ductile process of the *carole* from within her perceptual experience of it, she narrates the strangeness of medieval poetic form as an experience dynamically constituted in dance. In what follows I shall describe this
formal experience as it is constituted in the dance-based perceptual practices
that the reader brings to bear upon the poem.

> Alas, ales, the wyle!
> Thouht Y on no gyle,
> > So haue Y god chaunce.
> Ala[s], ales, the wyle
> > That euer Y cowde daunce!

> Ladd Y the daunce a Myssomur Day;
> Y made small trippus, soth for to say.
> Jak, oure haly-watur cle[r]k com by the way,
> And he lokede me vpon; he thout that he was gay.
> > Thout yc on ne gyle.

> Jak, oure haly-watur clerk, the yonge strippelyng,
> For the chesoun of me he com to the ryng,

---

73. Fletcher, "Lyric in the Sermon," *Companion*, 198–99. See Carissa Harris, "Tokens,
Tarses, and Naked Arses: The Politics of Body/Bawdy Talk in Late Medieval Britain," PhD diss.,
Northwestern University, 2012, 114–17, for a survey of the scholarship of pregnancy laments.

And he trippede on my to *and* made a twynkelyng;
Euer he cam ner; he sparet for no thynge.
      Thout Y on [no gyle.]

Jak, ic wot, preyede in my fayre face,
He thout me ful werly, so haue Y god grace;
As we turndun owre daunc[e] in a narw place,
Jak bed me the mouth; a cussynge ther was
      Thout Y on no g[yle.]

Jak tho began to rowne in myn ere:
"Loke that thou by priuey, *and* graunte that thou the bere;
A peyre wyth glouus ic ha to thyn were."
"Gramercy, Jacke!" that was myn answere.
      Thoute yc [on no gyle.]

Sone aftur euensong Jak me mette:
"Com hom aftur thy glouus that yc the byhette."
Wan ic to his chambre com, doun he me sette:
From hym mytte Y nat go wan [we] were mette.
      Thout Y [on no gyle.]

Schetus *and* chalonus, ic wot, a were yspredde;
Forsothe tho Jak *and* yc wenten to bedde;
He prikede, *and* he pransede; nolde he neuer lynne;
Yt was the murgust nyt that euer Y cam ynne.
      Thout Y [on no gyle.]

Wan Jak had don, tho he rong the bell;
Al nyght ther he made me to dwelle;
Of y trewe we haddun yserued the reaggeth deuel of helle;
Of othur smale burdus kep Y nout to telle.
      Thout Y [on no gyle.]

The other day at prime Y com hom, as ic wene;
Meth Y my dame, coppud *and* kene:
"Sey, thou stronge strumpeth, ware hastu bene?
Thy trippyng *and* thy dauncyng, wel it wol be sene."
      Thout Y [on no gyle.]

Eu*er* bi on *and* by on my damme reched me clot;
Eu*er* Y ber it pr*iu*ey wyle th*a*t Y mouth,
Tyl my gurdul aros, my wombe wax out;
Euel yspu*nn*e yern, eu*er* it wole out.
        Thout Y [on no gyle.][74]

While it is possible that this text functioned as a dance accompaniment, that is far from certain, and the poem's multiple complexities invite us to ask what other functions it might fulfill. This text appears in the fifteenth-century Cambridge, Gonville and Caius College MS 383/603.[75] Its arch blend of folksiness and wit bespeaks the clerical influence sometimes attributed to later carols, as does the use of the name Jack, related to Jankyn, which is conventionally applied to clever and clerical young seducers.[76] R. L. Greene compares the carol to an admonitory sermon and sets it in the tradition of lyrics and other texts where Christ compares his bloodied and restrained hands to the gloved and outstretched ones with which sinners lead dances.[77] But the poem's function seems more multivalent than its moralizing, for, as Judith Bennett observes, the text sends a mixed message about the speaker's willingness to follow Jack's lead.[78] Sarah McNamer additionally points out that while female-voiced carols like this have traditionally been perceived as "genuinely popular in origin, reflecting an oral tradition," in fact many such carols are ironic and "manipulate[e] the lyric voice in such a way as to satirize the speaker."[79] Carissa Harris takes a different approach, placing "Ladd Y the daunce" among a set of female-voiced lyrics that negotiate considerable complication around the issues of female consent and sexual knowledge.[80] While these readings treat the poems' attitudes toward their

---

74. *EEC* no. 453, 276–77.

75. Butterfield suggests that this manuscript was an "Oxford student's notebook." "Why Medieval Lyric?" *ELH* 82.2 (2015): 331.

76. Reichl, 169.

77. *EEC*, 489–90.

78. Judith Bennett, "Ventriloquisms: When Maidens Speak in English Songs, c. 1300–1550," in *Medieval Woman's Song: Cross-Cultural Approaches*, ed. Anne L. Klinck and Ann Marie Rasmussen (Philadelphia: University of Pennsylvania Press, 2001), 187–204. See also Neil Cartlidge, "'Alas, I go with chylde': Representations of Extra-Marital Pregnancy in the Middle English Lyric," *English Studies* 79.5 (1998): 409.

79. Sarah McNamer, "Lyrics and Romances," in *The Cambridge Companion to Medieval Women's Writing*, ed. Carolyn Dinshaw and David Wallace (New York: Cambridge University Press, 2003), 196.

80. Harris, 118-19.

female speakers—and thus their tone—differently, together they suggest that these texts display an array of self-reflexive impulses. Within these contexts, "Ladd Y the daunce" potentially asserts self-awareness. In this capacity, it could employ the device of leading a dance not only to explore morality and female subjectivity but also to comment upon its own lyric identity and form.

One way to characterize the form of "Ladd Y the daunce" might be to compare the carol's stanzaic structure to the image of the dance to which it alludes. The carol's "ryng" and the speaker's "turn[ing]" with Jack suggest round dance. The speaker's self-designation as a leader, and the promise Jack makes to give her white gloves, which Greene speculatively associates with leading *caroles*, possibly constitute round dance references as well.[81] These points encourage us to see a correspondence of dance and lyric: whether or not we take the poem literally to accompany a dance, the text can still map its regular alternation of stanza and burden onto the idea of ductile dance practice in which a leader sings the stanzas while the company moves in a round, punctuated by their stopping to sing the burden.[82] This poem refers to that transition from stanza to burden by employing an identical line that ends each stanza and signals the advent of the burden. In response to this feature, we might conceive of the poem as a concatenated structure: circular, with decorative hinges or clasps to overlap the material of the stanza and burden. Such a structure would reinforce a sense of formal order in the communion of dance and text. We might even enjoy the irony of juxtaposing this structure, reminiscent of heavenly maidens' terpsichorean practice, with a more worldly, less spotless set of outcomes.[83] What we would construe as a contrast of form and content Neil Cartlidge understands as a version of "pride before a fall": the dancer's "elegant steps" preceding a traumatic consequence.[84]

And yet, because the speaker is the dance leader, she narrates a different kind of ductile experience, one that conveys perceptual practices from inside the spectacle. She draws attention to trajectories of looking that do not necessarily follow the main circle of the dance. She looks, for instance,

81. *EEC*, 489–90.

82. Reichl, 158.

83. In addition to the dancing maidens of *Hali Meiðhad*, see, for instance, the visionary *carole* near the conclusion of St. Dunstan's *vita*, consisting of virgins "in choro gyranti" (Michael Winterbottom and Michael Lapidge, ed. and trans., *The Early Lives of St Dunstan* [Oxford: Clarendon Press, 2012], 100).

84. Cartlidge, 409.

at Jack, and notices him looking at her, throughout the process of the dance; there is no way to correlate the direction of these gazing trajectories with the arcs of the dance. She is also aware of her own feet, casting another perceptual vector orthogonally to the shape of the choreography. And as the poem thus shifts the focus to pedal concerns, it confronts us with further questions. In one sense, Jack's stepping on her toe is simply a late-medieval version of a timeless flirting technique, as seen in the thirteenth-century *Art d'amours*'s recommendation that the lover "marchier sus le pié" during a *carole*.[85] But it also poses a question integral to the ductile experience of the dance: How does this overlapping of toes map onto the experience of the dance, for instance the overlapping transition between stanza and burden, or the stopping and starting within the dance? Is there a neat correlation here, or has something less orderly occurred?

These perceptual details from within the dance open a window onto the virtual traces and forces that exist in the *carole* and that do not necessarily align with the lineaments of the circle as regarded from outside. Albeit flirtatious, Jack's anticipatory placement of his toe in a space before it should be there makes evident what we have discussed in the perception and experience of dance: the forces and energies that are traced ahead of or behind the dance's ostensibly regular rhythmic movement. In addition, the speaker tells us that she is looking down, looking around, looking at faces, features, limbs, and bodies (the "strippelyng"). She participates in generating, as she gazes, the interstitial and transitional forces implicit to the ductile process of the dance. She observes Jack not as a static entity but in dynamic processes of approach. In addition to watching him drawing closer to her, she also uses the two parts of a line to stage a transition from the anticipatory energy of profferring the mouth to the actual kiss: "Jak bed me the mouth; a cussynge ther was." In these ways, the speaker conveys the attunement to the forces between kinetic agents, what Susanne Langer and Darcey Bussell conceived of as the energy created between danced gestures and between dancers. The poem thus narrates a perceptual practice for dance that acknowledges forces supplementary to the choreography and existing beyond its regular beats and uniform spaces.

In illuminating those forces, the speaker's words further suggest that dance's pereptual habits play a role in the apprehension of the poem: she reveals the poem's experience of form as a virtual manifestation. I shall make this case by suggesting that the ductile transit through the poem's

---

85. *L'Art d'amours* I.80, cited in Mullally, *Carole*, 49.

alternation of stanza and burden produces, for the dance-attuned reader, an oscillation between real and unreal dance (the *movetur* and *moveatur* of Bonaventure). In that suspension between real and unreal emerge the proleptic and lagging forces that characterize virtuality's untimeliness.

To read this text is to encounter two dances that must exist in different realities.[86] The stanza-and-burden sequence leads the reader through the structure of a *carole*, thereby compelling the imagination of such a dance. Alongside that imagined dance, indexed to the poem's structure, is another: the *carole* that the female speaking character describes herself as having led. Because the narrative is set in the past, and because its progression extends beyond the time and space of its represented dance (into Jack's bedroom and then the speaker's home), the two possible dances necessarily differ. The narrative does not self-reflexively describe an event in progress, nor could it line precisely up as a past event identical to an imagined present dance scene. This seems obvious, but I lay it out because the two dances' respective realities in relation to each other are complicated. If a reader allows himself to imagine a dance performed in accompaniment to the lyrics, the dance described in the lyrics must situate itself separately from that image of embodied performance. The more fully a medieval reader wishes to imagine a familiar embodied dance accompanying these lyrics, the less situated in that reality the represented dance (of seduction) becomes. Conversely, we might consider the dance represented in the song to suggest embodied practice more powerfully, partly because of the detailed attention it draws to the speaker's body, but also because that representation proceeds into a world beyond the dance and into a set of material consequences. But the more the reader invests in that dance as reality represented, the looser his hold on the dance hypothetically accompanying the stanzas. If, that is, the primary function of these stanzas is to chronicle past seduction, that chronicle potentially dilutes the reader's attention to the dance that the poem's accompaniment-based structure might imaginatively conjure in the present time. To be led by the speaker through the stanzas of this carol, then, is to acknowledge two round dances that coexist even as they cannot.

To be led through the poem as a reader accustomed to the spectatorship of dance is to recognize the strange virtuality hovering between these two circles in their ambiguous coordination with each other. The poem's

---

86. Bennett calls it a "doubled performance" (188). I place the poem in a scene of reading because I find it somewhat less likely that it served as actual accompaniment, given the length and complexity of its stanzas. But even if we do posit it in performance, the mutual exclusivity of the two dances' realities obtains.

reference to the narrow place in which the speaker turns with Jack emblematizes this ambiguity. When the speaker says that "we turndun owre
daunc[e] in a narw place" after Jack approaches the "ryng," it is difficult
to know the spatial relation of this compressed flirtation to the *carole* as
a whole. One might conjecture that she and Jack are at the center of the
carole's larger circle.[87] But if that is the case, in what sense, exactly, is their
place narrow?[88] How are they placed relative to the *carole*?[89] Does their
narrow circle stay where it is? Is it part of the main circle? Are the two
circles internally tangent? Externally tangent? Interlocking? Disconnected?
Or does she refer to a symbolic dance revolving within a physical one? In
one sense, this ambiguity is simply another example of how the speaker's
experience from within the dance contains possible asymmetries and asyn-
chronies. But in making that point, the narrow place also characterizes the
relation of the two circles of real and *irrealis* motion that the carol sustains.
The image within the poem emphasizes not only the two possible circles
themselves, but also that the forces between them, whatever holds them
together or pulls them apart, delineate a configuration more complex than
straightforward concentricity. Those forces must accommodate the stanzas' casting forth of the speaker from the dance and her impulsion through
seduction and pregnancy, even as the ductile progression of stanzas tries to
espouse a more hermetic and self-resolving impulse. Describing the narrow place in ambiguous relation to the *carole*, the speaker narrates formal
experience as conditioned by the perceptual practices of dance. In the progression through the stanzas, the reader perceives not only the ambiguous
relation of two circles of dance but also the expression of that ambiguity in
forces of virtuality that heighten spatial complexity.

In progressing from one burden to the next, the poem also elucidates a
temporal dimension of virtuality, one that further negotiates between what
is real and unreal, expressed and anticipated.

87. Joseph Bédier, for instance, conjectured the presence of mimed performance in the midst
of earlier round dance. "Les plus anciennes danses françaises," *Revue des deux mondes* 5 (1906):
401–13.

88. See Greene's reference to a line spoken by Christ in a lyric in Oxford, Bodleian Library
MS Bodley 416: "whan thou daucest narwe" (*EEC*, 489).

89. Eustace and King discuss a speculation based on surviving French folk dance concerning
the process of the round dance, which begins with the dancers holding hands in a circle to
habituate themselves to the tempo and then proceeds to the dancers' breaking into couples that
move around the circle at a greater distance from the singer (55–56).

> *Alas, ales, the wyle!*
> *Thouht Y on no gyle,*
>   *So haue Y god chaunce.*
> *Ala[s], ales, the wyle*
>   *That euer Y cowde daunce!*

The burden acknowledges time (*wyle*) from its opening; but in addition, the expression of regret in this burden complicates the temporal structure of the carol as a whole. In terms of the carol's didactic function, Harris sees in the burden a looking back and looking forward: she calls it "lament and instruction."[90] From within the speaker's experience, the burden intensifies this structure, countermanding the possibility of a straightforward arc from action to consequence. As Sarah Kathryn Moore suggests, the burden creates deictic complexity, reflecting "the constant flux of stasis and change" in the speaker's body and experience.[91] We might specify this effect's temporal implications further. A dance-based perspective upon this poem is both attuned to the virtualities of dance and aware of *ductus* not as one linear trajectory but instead as a dynamic and multidimensional network. From such a perspective, the periodic intonation of the burden across the poem's narrative expresses a ruefulness that in each instance is at once proleptic and nostalgic relative to the narrative. The quality of remorseful pang interspersed with the stanzas causes the words of the burden to be always anticipating and reproaching at once. And while we perceived orderly and even anticipation in the use of the tag, which enabled the comparison of the poem to a circling chain, the affective complex in the burden's relation to the stanzas deregularizes this effect. The dread of unwanted consequence and the nostalgia for the prelapsarian moment without awareness of "gyle" both introduce a drag in time: these forces potentially hover and pull in untimely adjacency to the stanzas' uniform progression.[92]

The burden further complicates its position in time by shifting between an indicative standpoint and a more conjectural one. The burden first states factually that the leader thought there was no evil in what she was doing, but it then shades into something more provisional: a lamentation that she

---

90. Harris, 130.

91. Sarah Kathryn Moore, "*Beste of bon and blod*: Embodiment in Middle English Lyric," PhD diss., University of Washington, 2015, 151.

92. On nostalgia's manipulation and slowing of time, see, for instance, Svetlana Boym, *The Future of Nostalgia* (New York: Basic Books, 2001), xv.

knew how to dance, which implies a wish for an alternate world in which she never did. In time as well as in space, then, moving through the poem means fluctuating between Bonaventure's moods of *movetur* and *moveatur*. By means of its repeating burden, the carol suggests that to lead and be led within it is to oscillate in tense and mood. In this capacity, the poem offers a temporal experience that does not precisely align with the stanzas' ostensibly evenly alternating progress with the burden. Through the perceptual conditioning of dance, the reader apprehends the poem's oscillation between an indicative reality and a subjunctive otherworld as the syncopated time of virtuality's force.

We could harness this model of formal experience in the service of a particular interpretive end, which would be to intervene into critical discussions of the poem's tone. Martha Bayless suggests that generic features of this and other poetic pregnancy narratives might go so far as to render their effect comic, while Neil Cartlidge sees them as more solemnly conveying the difficulties of such situations.[93] Moore, meanwhile, notes that no single tonal possibility on this spectrum sufficiently acknowledges the poems' actual complexity.[94] To some degree, investigating tone involves attempting to inhabit the subject position of the poem. But even if we were to locate some interiority for that poetic "I," this would still not fix tone, because tone in this case depends on how we construe the very relation of the speaker as lyric voice and as character. Bayless's detection of a comic stance, for instance, might imply a speaker involved in some species of ventriloquism, creating an ironic distance that makes room for satire and parody. The poem thus seems to resist any modern impulse to characterize tone.

"Ladd Y the daunce"'s formal experience illuminates a different approach, one that foregoes the application of tonal categories in favor of an empathetic engagement that the *ductus* of dance makes possible and that accommodates the ambiguities of the subject's position. *Ductus*, as we have seen, can generate untimely and asymmetrical virtualities. Vijay Iyer argues that when an audience perceives the normative time and rhythm of performance to shift into something more contingent, arrhythmic, and unpredictable, those moments heighten the empathy between audience and performer.[95] His formulation suggests a means for empathy to exist in the reader's par-

93. Martha Bayless, "The Text and the Body in Middle English Seduction Lyrics," *Neophilologus* 93 (2009): 172; Cartlidge, 399.

94. Moore, 166. See also 180–85.

95. Vijay Iyer, "Improvisation, Action Understanding, and Music Cognition with and without Bodies," in *The Oxford Handbook of Critical Improvisation Studies*, vol. 1, ed. George E. Lewis and Benjamin Piekut (New York: Oxford University Press, 2016), 80. Iyer refers specifically

ticipatory and dance-based *ductus*. That is, when the reader formally experiences virituality's divergence from periodicity and symmetry, that very strangeness clarifies the speaker's position in all its disorienting fluctuations of space and time.[96] If a reader of this poem wishes to apprehend the range and subtlety of the speaker's subject position, that opportunity exists not in tonal taxonomy but rather in the empathy that the poem's formal experience of virtuality encourages though a medievally-situated *ductus*.

At the same time that I suggest this hermeneutic possibility, I wish to land only lightly on it, declining to explore it exhaustively, in order to maintain our focus upon the methodological component of my intervention—to reenact experiences of form—which could engender numerous interpretations. "Ladd Y the daunce" refines, in the late-medieval vernacular terms of dance and poetry, the model that Bonaventure instantiates of formalist reading as a ductile experience of virtuality. Invoking the perceptual habits of dance, the carol specifies the asymmetries and orthogonalities that emerge in dance's virtual supplements. In doing so, the poem reminds us as modern readers that the models of circular dance and circular poem in the Middle Ages do not sufficiently explicate either one's form. Instead, "Ladd Y the daunce" shows how those modes of perception to which dance habituates audiences intervene into and participate in constituting form as a ductile experience of strange time and space: the irresolvable real and *irrealis* of the burden's repetition as well as the poem's impossible state of suspension between embodied and imagined dances. In this way "Ladd Y the daunce" outlines a theory of medieval poetic form as experience, an experience produced by reading poetry in terms of the perceptual practices dictated by dance.

WHY DANCE IN SILENCE?

A final qualification is in order. Music would seem to be a crucial component in this theory of poetic form. And yet, music is not a major area of focus in this study. Before proceeding I shall briefly clarify the motivations underlying this methodological choice. First, it must be acknowledged that while this book does not intend to intervene into studies of music and musicology, the critical practices of musicologists working in many periods have fundamentally influenced my thinking about theoretical approaches to

to moments of improvisation here, but the effect of changing the ostensible spatial and temporal parameters of the spectacle is relevant to the present discussion.

96. This idea takes on additional resonance in light of Bennett's suggestion that women might have performed this song (199).

medieval performance, in particular Richard Taruskin's insights concerning reenactment.[97] And medieval musicology in particular contributes important insights to my method. For example, Emma Dillon's goal of "restor[ing] to music a lost interlocutor: a world captured in words, images and music, in which sounds of all kinds shaped human experience, and which also shaped musical listening" speaks to my interest in form as constituted in perceptions of multimediacy.[98] Furthermore, if Dillon wishes to "call on the living to help explain the sounding past," I employ living dances to understand vanished spectatorial effects.[99] Marisa Galvez's focus on the interaction of musical artists and listeners in the formation of poetic culture influences my privileging of networks of perceptual interaction in both dance and poetic form.[100] Elizabeth Randell Upton's suggestion that we attend to different traces of experience and performance than those on which our scholarly forbears relied also motivates my investigation.[101] Holsinger's analysis of music in culture additionally addresses the central topic of experience. His "musicology of the flesh" refers to a dynamic circuit between the body and music, an internalization of each by the other that countermands conventional notions of music as entirely exterior to the body and dictates that a person might "construct abstract concepts (such as a philosophy of music, for example) out of experiences in the flesh."[102] The idea that a medieval agent might derive an aesthetic theory through an experience with performance practice plays a crucial role in my argument. Anna Zayaruznaya, finally, models an innovative formalist approach in order to argue that "the entire musico-poetic complex of a motet can take monstrous shape."[103] Her conception of medieval musical expression as fragmented, divided, hybrid, and chimerical speaks to the strangeness I identify in dance and its inter-

97. Richard Taruskin, *Text & Act: Essays on Music and Performance* (New York: Oxford University Press, 1995), 5. Taruskin points out that "What we had been accustomed to regard as historically authentic performances . . . embodied a whole wish list of modern(ist) values, validated in the academy and the marketplace alike by an eclectic, opportunistic reading of historical evidence."

98. Dillon, 8.

99. Ibid., 4.

100. Marisa Galvez, *Songbook: How Lyrics Became Poetry in Medieval Europe* (Chicago: University of Chicago Press, 2012).

101. Elizabeth Randell Upton, *Music and Performance in the Later Middle Ages* (New York: Palgrave Macmillan, 2013), esp. 45–65.

102. Holsinger, *Music,* 12.

103. Anna Zayaruznaya, *The Monstrous New Art: Divided Forms in the Late Medieval World* (New York: Cambridge University Press, 2015), 14.

section with poetry. Thus *Strange Footing* takes account of contemporary musicological methods throughout its conceptual structure even though it does not explicitly analyze medieval music.

At the same time, my argument's very omission of music as an object of analysis equally advances the project's conceptual stakes as I articulate these. In offering a theory of medieval poetic form, *Strange Footing* acknowledges the increasingly complex relationship of music to poetry in the later Middle Ages' own poetics. Eustache Deschamps's fourteenth-century formulation of "natural music" as poetic language's musical quality distinct from its sonic accompaniment or setting, for instance, speaks to an important stage in the West's developing conception of poetry and poetic form.[104] While critics have rightly questioned Roger Dragonetti's claim that Deschamps marked a turning point that undid the lyric's collaboration of words and music, the poet's theory speaks to an inspired, instinctive musical quality within poetic language itself.[105] This is one reason I have sought to create an experimental environment that subtracts the musical element. But there is another as well. If medieval dance has any accompaniment in my analysis, it is the modern performance with which I juxtapose it. This strategy has allowed me to hear some things about medieval poetry and see some things about medieval dance that would otherwise have been hidden from my perusal. Chapter 5 will address this interpretive mode explicitly, proposing that the deliberate removal of certain medial components in their sensory capacity can uncover important insights. But the basic principle—that considering these objects in analytical silence might have certain unique benefits—is implicit throughout. At the same time, I would be the first to agree that my archive and my readings could benefit in other ways, and yield other insights, from examination through the lenses of music history and musicology. To give just one instance, Elizabeth Eva Leach

104. Deschamps, 60–66.

105. As Elizabeth Eva Leach notes, Deschamps's distinction between natural and artificial (that which is generated by mechanical instruments) music does not constitute an uncomplicated "divorce" of words and music. Leach, *Sung Birds: Music, Nature, and Poetry in the Later Middle Ages* (Ithaca: Cornell University Press, 2007), 57. See also James I. Wimsatt, "Natural Music in Middle French Verse and Chaucer," in *Essays on the Art of Chaucer's Verse*, ed. Alan T. Gaylord (New York: Routledge, 2001), 237; I. S. Laurie, "Deschamps and the Lyric as Natural Music," *Modern Language Review* 59.4 (1964): 561–70; Glending Olson, "Deschamps' *Art de dictier* and Chaucer's Literary Environment," *Speculum* 48.5 (1973): 716–17; and Roger Dragonetti, "'La poésie . . . ceste musique naturele': Essai d'exégèse d'un passage de *L'Art de dictier* d'Eustache Deschamps," in *Fin du moyen âge et renaissance: Mélanges de philologie française offerts à Robert Guiette* (Anvers: Nederlandsche Boekhandel, 1961), 49–64.

shows how sung performance depends upon its own set of collaborations and creative interactions among media, artists, and memory, creating space for further reciprocities beyond the medial interlocutions of dance and poetry I explore.[106] I hope that my argument's life beyond my articulation of it will enjoy further interaction with such work.

106. Elizabeth Eva Leach, "Nature's Forge and Mechanical Production: Writing, Reading, and Performing Song," in *Rhetoric beyond Words*, 72.

PART II

CHAPTER THREE

"A Certain Slant of Light":
Reenacting *Danse macabre* as Dance

Strange Footing's first case study is *danse macabre,* a late-medieval tradition that combines visual art, architecture, poetry, and other media.[1] Featuring skeletons interspersed with human dancers from a broad spectrum of social estates, *danse macabre* is preternatural in many senses and thus might not appear to us as dance in the sense of a physically enacted movement tradition. And yet, I shall argue, *danse macabre*'s incorporation of a virtual supplement makes it danced spectacle to its medieval audiences. To illuminate this virtual supplement, I engage in the narrative reenactment method I described in chapter 1, reading *danse macabre* in terms of Lucinda Childs's iconic *Dance* (1979), a choreographic work that, like *danse macabre,* introduces multiple media into a dance-based spectacle and generates virtual forces in that network.[2] By identifying the virtual forces in *danse macabre* installation, this chapter will elucidate *danse macabre*'s impact upon its medieval audiences. While to us *danse macabre*'s predictable seriality might undermine its potential to terrify or shock, medieval audiences experience in *danse macabre*'s multiple virtualities the disorientation of multiple rates and types of temporal passage occurring simultaneously. My reading locates an experience of *danse macabre* in the space between the postmodern spectatorial practices we bring to *Dance* and the

---

1. *Danse macabre* is not the only medieval artistic tradition that integrates dance-based imagery with other media, in particular poetic inscription. Discussing the Lorenzetti *Buon governo* frescoes, which include both dance imagery and written inscription, Quentin Skinner mentions Giotto's *Justice* fresco, which shows three dancers directly above a short Latin poetic text. "Ambrogio Lorenzetti's *Buon governo* Frescoes: Two Old Questions, Two New Answers," *Journal of the Warburg and Courtauld Institutes* 62 (1999): 17, 25.

2. See my "*Danse macabre* and the Virtual Churchyard," *postmedieval* 3 (2012): 7–26, for an earlier argument about virtuality in the *danse macabre* installation.

medieval *danse macabre* archive. In narratively reenacting this experience, the present chapter describes a perceptual practice for *dance macabre*. The next chapter will argue that this perceptual practice dictates the medieval audience's engagement with *danse macabre* poetry and their experience of its form.

THE PROBLEM: *DANSE MACABRE* AND DANCE

In one sense, *danse macabre* is obviously dance. Its surviving manifestations depict choreographic gesture and blocking in detail. In addition, certain forms of evidence obliquely suggest that the idiom of *danse macabre* bears some relationship to performance practice, whether its aesthetic might inform components of sermons, plays, or other occasions of embodied and kinetic spectacle. When we try to consider the dance-based component of *danse macabre* specifically as dance, however, we tend to do so in conceptual rather than embodied terms. If medieval dance often finds itself tipping into symbolic realms, *danse macabre* seems to initiate its existence suffused with symbolic resonance rather than material identity. In this section, I will discuss why, despite various forms of evidence linking *danse macabre* to embodied movement tradition, it has been difficult to discern any actual, rather than symbolic, relationship to dance that it might have.

The extant representations of *danse macabre* seem to reflect a few basic conventions pertaining to a dance vocabulary.[3] Often *danse macabre* features loping, gesticulating skeletons parading in alternation with live figures representing descending degrees of social estate: popes, kings, empresses, knights, lawyers, and so on. In their representation of danced movement, it has often been noted, the skeletons appear more animatedly agile than their human counterparts, moving in a way that looks to us like dancing.[4] The skeletons also sometimes carry musical instruments to reinforce the terpsichorean nature of the activity being depicted.[5] These features of *danse macabre* appear in a variety of static media, including stained glass, wood-

3. For reproductions of intact Continental pictorial *danse macabre* examples, see Elina Gertsman, *The Dance of Death in the Middle Ages: Image, Text, Performance* (Turnhout: Brepols, 2010); and Ashby Kinch, *Imago Mortis: Mediating Images of Death in Late Medieval Culture* (Leiden: Brill, 2013), 17–19.

4. See, for instance, David A. Fein, trans., *The Danse Macabre: Printed by Guyot Marchant, 1485* (Tempe, AZ: ACMRS, 2013), 3.

5. On skeletons carrying musical instruments, see Kathi Meyer-Baer, *Music of the Spheres and the Dance of Death* (Princeton: Princeton University Press, 1970), 300.

cuts, and tapestry, in addition to book illustration and wall painting.[6] Notable examples of wall paintings survive in Reval, Berlin (badly damaged), Stratford-upon-Avon (badly damaged and subsequently covered), Inkoo, Brittany, and elsewhere. Recent work, particularly that of Elina Gertsman, Sophie Oosterwijk, and Ashby Kinch, has provided thorough surveys of the extant visual tradition's range of possibilities as well as the social and political functions its iconographic programs fulfill.[7]

Some important examples of *danse macabre* art, including influential *danse macabre* churchyard installations in London and Paris, have not endured beyond the early modern period, but various forms of indirect evidence provide a sense of these installations. The Pardon Churchyard in London once contained what appears to have been a well-known set of wall paintings containing *danse macabre* images and poetry.[8] Paris's Cemetery of the Holy Innocents' *dance macabre*, the inspiration for the Pardon Churchyard, is known to have been a mural running underneath the cemetery's *charniers*, whose open skylights left their human bones visible to the public.[9] The entrance portal to the church there contained a Three Living

6. For an account of the existing evidence relating to *danse macabre* art in various media, see Sophie Oosterwijk, "Of Corpses, Constables, and Kings: The *Danse Macabre* in Late-Medieval and Renaissance Culture," *Journal of the British Archaeological Association* 157 (2004): 61–90, esp. 70–71. Léonard Paul Kürtz, *The Dance of Death and the Macabre Spirit in European Literature* (Geneva: Slatkine, 1975), 145, enumerates different manifestations of this tradition, including a nineteenth-century account of a tapestry in the Tower of London. See also Francis Douce, *The Dance of Death in a Series of Engravings on Wood from Designs Attributed to Hans Holbein* . . . (London: George Bell & Sons, 1902), 44–47, for a brief survey of English examples. David Dymond and Clive Paine, *The Spoil of Melford Church: The Reformation of a Suffolk Parish* (Ipswich: Salient, 1989), 23, list, in the inventory of Holy Trinity Church of Long Melford for 1529, "Three long cloths hanging before the rood loft, stained, or painted with the Dawnce of Powlis." See also Jennifer Floyd, "Writing on the Wall: John Lydgate's Architectural Verse," PhD dissertation, Stanford University, 2008, 34n10 for a discussion of the references to these cloths.

7. See, for instance, Elina Gertsman, "Death and the Miniaturized City: Nostalgia, Authority, Idyll," *Essays in Medieval Studies* 24 (2007): 43–52; as well as *Dance*; Sophie Oosterwijk, "'For no man mai fro dethes stroke fle': Death and *Danse Macabre* Iconography in Memorial Art," *Church Monuments* 23 (2008): 62–87, 166–68; Oosterwijk, "Dance, Dialogue and Duality: Fatal Encounters in the Medieval *Danse Macabre*," in *Mixed Metaphors*, 9–42; Oosterwijk, "Of Dead Kings, Dukes, and Constables: The Historical Context of the *Danse Macabre* in Late Medieval Paris," *Journal of the British Archaeological Association* 161.1 (2008): 131–62; and Kinch, 185–260.

8. On the destruction of this site within a critical narrative concerning Lydgate and vernacular literary production, and the status of the poem as a "perfectly representative artifact of a 'reformist' culture" (62), see James Simpson, *The Oxford English Literary History, Volume 2, 1350–1547: Reform and Cultural Revolution* (New York: Oxford University Press, 2002), 34–62.

9. Vanessa Harding, *The Dead and the Living in Paris and London, 1500–1670* (Cambridge: Cambridge University Press, 2002), 101–2; the mural itself was painted along the ten arcades of the south wall, the Charnier des Lingères (102). See also Guillebert de Metz's fifteenth-century

and Three Dead sculpture, which contributed to the imagery of the painted *danse macabre* installation by providing another idiom of confrontation between the living and the dead.[10] Associated with this early-fifteenth-century installation is a series of woodcuts first published by Guyot Marchant in 1485, which bear some relation to the Paris installation, as well as the mural's verse dialogues, here printed in 1490 with Latin text (figure 2).[11] This imagery, if conjectured to resemble the wall installations at Paris and at London, replicates the basic conventions of the alternating parade members, the skeletons, the variously gesticulative poses, and other components. Thus, even though a significant portion of *danse macabre* art is fragmentary or conjectural, certain general commonalities shaping an image of a processional dance seem identifiable across it.

Danse macabre also makes use of partner configurations and engages these in visual play with the surrounding architectural elements. As partnered movement, *danse macabre* recalls to some the fifteenth-century idiom of *basse danse*, a sedate, decorous, and in some instances partnered tradition that gained popularity in the fifteenth century. Eustace and King consider the ways that the visual imagery of *danse macabre* resonates with specific features of dance practice potentially relevant to processional dance or *basse danse*: the choosing of partners, the holding of hands or garments, and the empathetic mirroring of couples.[12] *Basse danse* also reminds us that while modernity might separate the categories of dance and procession, they over-

---

description, which records that the Holy Innocents cemetery contains "paintures notables de la danse macabre et autres, avec escriptures pour esmouvoir les gens à devotion." Le Roux de Lincy, ed., *Description de la ville de Paris au XVe siècle par Guillebert de Metz* (Paris: Auguste Aubry, 1855), 63–64.

10. Robert W. Berger, *Public Access to Art in Paris: A Documentary History from the Middle Ages to 1800* (University Park, PA: Pennsylvania State University Press, 1999), 29–30. The etiological relationship between these artistic traditions is uncertain, because while they both portray conversations between the dead and the living, they also differ in the social levels of the doomed people they portray (Christine Kralik, "Dialogue and Violence in Medieval Illuminations of the Three Living and the Three Dead," in *Mixed Metaphors*, 133–34). But as two visual motifs they were juxtaposed in late-medieval France (Marco Piccat, "Mixed Encounters: The Three Living and the Three Dead in Italian Art," in *Mixed Metaphors*, 155). And their conceptual relationship was suggestive; Paul Binski, for instance, points out that *danse macabre* and the Three Living and Three Dead both create a *mise-en-abyme* between the living and the dead. *Medieval Death: Ritual and Representation* (Ithaca: Cornell University Press, 1996), 54, 138.

11. Gertsman, *Dance*, 4–5, sees the woodcuts as preserving the mural's images, but Amy Appleford cautions that this relationship is conjectural. Appleford, "The Dance of Death in London: John Carpenter, John Lydgate, and the *Daunce of Poulys*," *JMEMS* 38.2 (2008): 287.

12. Eustace with King, 56–70. For a discussion of *basse danse* that summarizes twentieth-century dance history's major claims about it, see my "Proleptic Steps: Rethinking Historical Period in the Fifteenth-Century Dance Manual," *Dance Research Journal* 44.2 (2012): 29–47.

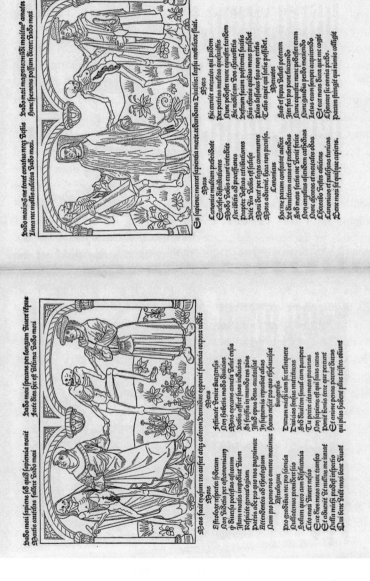

Fig. 2. Guyot Marchant, *The Dance of Death* (Latin text), woodcut edition (1490). Death, the Astrologer, the Bourgeois, the Canon, the Merchant. Photograph: Rosenwald Collection, Rare Book and Special Collections Division of the Library of Congress, Washington, DC.

lap in the arena of medieval dance. Partnered procession might most effectively characterize what seems consistently depicted in *danse macabre* as
a dance idiom, though its procession seems oriented somewhat differently
from *basse danse*. Furthermore, as the Marchant example indicates (figure 2),
danse macabre embellishes upon that choreography of partnering by using architectural elements both to frame and to lend dimension to bodily
configurations of pairing in the procession.[13]

Despite the fact that *danse macabre* is thus recognizable in certain
ways as dance, however, we remain limited in our understanding of the
visual idiom's relationship to embodied dance practice. Instead, we find
ourselves focusing on the material context of *danse macabre* in order to
speculate about the bodily movement this tradition might have involved.
The Pardon Churchyard offers one example. That installation came about
after John Lydgate translated the Holy Innocents verse inscriptions around
1426; his English verses were then inscribed on what was probably a similar
painting executed on wooden boards and hung along the walls of the Pardon
Churchyard at St. Paul's Cathedral in London.[14] Because the early modern
historiographer John Stow discusses this installation, a narrative account
of it is available to us. Stow refers to both the Pardon Churchyard and the
Holy Innocents cemetery as "cloisters," aligning them with each other and
thereby allowing a measure of conjecture about their similarity in appearance and structure as a series of paintings presumably running along one or
more walls of a cloister arcade.[15] Other details about various contexts for
the London *danse macabre* paintings exist as well. For example, early in
its history, the Pardon Churchyard was a burying ground for plague victims
but later became a cemetery for the socially elite.[16] According to Amy Appleford, the churchyard's name suggests that those buried there would be
pardoned for their sins even if interred without proper ceremony. In addition, Thomas More's construction of the Pardon Churchyard's surround-

---

13. Eustace with King, 57–64, 67–70.

14. Caroline M. Barron and Marie-Hélène Rousseau, "Cathedral, City, and State, 1300–1540,"
in *St. Paul's: The Cathedral Church of London, 604–2004*, 33–44, ed. Derek Keene, Arthur Burns,
and Andrew Saint (New Haven: Yale University Press, 2004), 36, cite John Stow describing the
murals as a sequence of painted boards, paid for by John Carpenter around 1430.

15. Warren and White, xxii. On the construction of the Holy Innocents installation in the
longer history of that site's development, see William M. Ivins, Jr., ed., *The Dance of Death
Printed at Paris in 1490: A Reproduction Made from the Copy in the Lessing J. Rosenwald
Collection, Library of Congress* (Washington, DC: Library of Congress, 1945), vi–viii.

16. Barron and Rousseau, 35.

ing cloister in the 1420s was accompanied by his renovation within the churchyard of a chapel to St. Thomas à Becket and his mother St. Anne.[17]

Such specificities of historical and material context indicate something important about the installation's setting, which is that it included bodies in motion responding to the painted dancers. As a site of interest to a wealthy clientele, and containing a chapel to an important English martyr, the Pardon Churchyard almost certainly incorporated into its overall spectacle the presence of embodied spectators performing a kind of *de facto* procession as they walked along the walls of the cloister to peruse the art and accompanying inscriptional verse. Gertsman describes this effect of *danse macabre* images in their installation contexts as fostering "complex relationships between visual and performative arts in the Middle Ages, and their reception by a spectator."[18] She develops her analysis by positing that a dance of death installation could "induce the beholder to participate in a particular practice of viewing, and the impetus to do so is provided by the dancing itself: the movement of the painted figures is echoed in the movement of the viewer who must advance to take in the entire piece."[19] Thus, the paintings set the viewers in a motion parallel and responsive to them.

In contributing an additional medium to the installation, the walking body encourages the perception of still other types of movement in the installation. Exploring premodern perambulation, Paul Strohm has contended that the medieval walker is never an aimless wanderer—a Baudelairean *flâneur*—because he is always interacting with the "symbolic character of late-medieval space." The areas through which he moves are "densely marked" symbolically, and those physical terrains offer experiences of dynamic time and space. To walk through the medieval city is to sustain simultaneously a perception of static pattern and, at the same time, the enrichment and complication of such pattern by "invisible lines of force," animated trajectories of alternative space and time existing in relation to the material body.[20] *Danse macabre* localizes this concept by suggesting the possibility of such animated trajectories within it. Reinforcing this idea is Gertsman's further observation that live viewers would stroll in the

17. Amy Appleford, *Learning to Die in London, 1380–1540* (Philadelphia: University of Pennsylvania Press, 2015), 84.

18. Gertsman, *Dance*, 98.

19. Ibid., 124.

20. Paul Strohm, *Theory and the Premodern Text* (Minneapolis: University of Minnesota Press, 2000), 3–6.

opposite direction from the characters in the paintings to read the poetic inscriptions.[21] Walking along the installation is thus a choreographic activity, an orchestrated pattern that introduces conflicting experiences of directionality, motion, and time. Interacting with the imagery on the walls, the body can, while moving in one direction, draw to a perceptual surface the painting's impulse of movement in the other direction. These forces, reactions, and interactions between the body in motion and the symbolically laden site give visible shape to the concept Strohm posits. In doing so, they reveal the kinetic force in the *danse macabre* itself, beyond the embodied gestures of its spectators. The processional quality of the spectator's embodied movement, in other words, generates a multimedia spectacle of kinesis from a painting of a procession. Later, I will elaborate in more detail upon the virtual motion generated across specific aspects of the installation, but for now this account outlines the installation's overall spectatorial effect.

Danse macabre installation art connects to embodied movement in other ways as well. First, beyond the ambulatory spectatorship of its friezes, *danse macabre* art is conjectured to have engendered choreographed and consciously performed movement. Pearsall, for example, speculates concerning sermon-related performance in the Cemetery of the Holy Innocents. He posits the cemetery as a backdrop that might have affected the components of the sermons taking place in front of it. The image of a preacher in the pulpit at the end of a dance of death mural from Metnitz intriguingly evokes such a scheme.[22] Pearsall suggests the incorporation of "dramatic impersonation" into a *memento mori* sermon, a performance employing a moving figure to remind the congregation of death's approach. He wonders if a performer costumed as death might glide amidst the congregation during the sermon's delivery.[23] This performer could emphasize the power of the *danse macabre* imagery by foregrounding, through his movement, the bodily excess that the congregation should avoid and that the *danse* betokens in the background.[24] The audience's experience of a dancer creeping among them, in concert with the art, could also inspire a creeping dread of

21. Gertsman, *Dance*, 123, on the Reval dance of death.

22. See Sophie Oosterwijk, "'Fro Paris to Inglond'? The *Danse macabre* in Text and Image in Late-Medieval England," PhD diss., Leiden University, 2009, 113.

23. Derek Pearsall, "Signs of Life in Lydgate's *Danse Macabre*," *Zeit, Tod und Ewigkeit in der Renaissance Literatur*, vol. 3, ed. J. Hogg (Salzburg: Institut für Anglistik und Amerikanstik, 1987), 61.

24. Michael Freeman, "The Dance of the Living beyond the Macabre in Fifteenth-Century France," in *Sur quel pied danser! Danse et littérature, Actes du colloque organisé par Hélène Stafford, Michael Freeman et Edward Nye . . .* , ed. Edward Nye (Amsterdam: Rodopi, 2005), 18, 29.

Judgment.[25] The mechanics of relation between the representational art and the performer's activity are important here because they offer another way to characterize the relationship between the art and the moving body.[26] Like the ambulatory spectators, the performing figure responds in bodily and gestural terms to the visual imagery of the *danse macabre* figures (as well as the churchyard's open charnel houses). But the specific engine driving this response differs from the one generated by the audience walking along the churchyard walls. The processional movement of the spectators generates a pattern that results from the kinesis required of the object's perusal. Pearsall's speculation, by contrast, posits a performer who intends deliberately to enhance and develop the visual art through a choreographed program of embodied spectacle. This difference intimates the breadth of the possible spectrum accommodating *danse macabre's* kinetic components.

Other examples of performance might reflect the features of *danse macabre* imagery even beyond the installation setting. These possibilities range from dancers, costumed as skeletons performing ritualistic dances, to dramas, or other performance occasions, structured around what we might call death dancing. Gertsman describes a fifteenth-century Corpus Christi procession featuring a figure costumed as a skeleton, who tries to touch everyone in the procession with his scythe.[27] She also cites evidence of the Burgundian court's commission in 1449 of a "certain jeu, histoire et moralité sur le fait de la danse macabre."[28] Eustace and King offer Spanish and English texts that take the form of dance songs and allude to themes reminiscent of

---

25. Pearsall, "Signs," 61. See also Gertsman's comment that "In the Dance of Death, the Preacher becomes one with the image he comments on, and the procession of Death transforms the Preacher's words into flesh, so to speak" (*Dance*, 85).

26. The more general possibility that a performance would include both kinetic spectacle and static representation was familiar to late-medieval culture. Pamela Sheingorn offers another version of this embodiment/representation nexus in medieval performance, depicting medieval drama as combining static *tableaux* with animated scenes. "The Visual Language of Drama: Principles of Composition," in *Contexts for Early English Drama*, ed. Marianne G. Briscoe and John C. Coldewey (Bloomington: Indiana University Press, 1989), 185. Sheingorn cites a review that she and Theresa Coletti wrote of a 1982 Carmina Burana *Greater Passion Play* production at the Cloisters, which performed the hypothesis about *tableaux vivants* by playing "many scenes" as "frozen for somewhat less than a minute, so that the play progressed as a series of tableaux." Coletti and Sheingorn, "The Carmina Burana Greater Passion Play at the Cloisters," *RORD* 25 (1982): 143. These representational moments might thus appear as juxtaposed with the dramatic activity that precedes and follows them, a scene "cut out . . . from the flow of events" (Otto Pächt quoted in Sheingorn, 185).

27. Gertsman, *Dance*, 79.

28. Cited in ibid., 268n17.

danse macabre.[29] In a more speculative vein, Robert Eisler has pointed out that images of *danse macabre* skeletons regularly carry the equipment of grave diggers, and also that they sometimes are manifestly not skeletons but figures wearing skeleton costumes. He therefore suggests that the iconography of *danse macabre* reflects a folk ritual involving gravediggers pantomiming and possibly dancing.[30] James M. Clark mentions a dance of death "masque" performed as part of a wedding in Jedburgh in 1285, citing a description in John of Fordun's *Scotichronicon* of a performer "of whom it might almost be doubted whether he was a man or a phantom."[31] E. K. Chambers also refers to speculation that *danse macabre* originated as a "quasi-dramatic ceremony, in which a priest pronounced [lines] from a pulpit, while appropriately clad figures, led by Death, passed to a tomb in the nave of the Church."[32] For David A. Fein, *danse macabre* "reflects important aspects of the farce" or "suggest[s] a theatrical tableau."[33] Fein's characterization illustrates in particular how attested dramatic conventions—like farce—give shape to a possible scene of dance. In these different ways, then, scholars have made constructive use of evidence that is somewhat thin on the ground to posit dance-related spectacles that may have borne some relationship to *danse macabre* imagery.

Fein's comment about farce gives us another way to consider *danse macabre* as an artistic tradition with a life in dramatic, kinetic performance. Specific performance idioms, including but not limited to farce, are themselves more stable in their evidence than performed *danse macabre*. Such traditions might have incorporated danced scenes reflecting in some way the painted imagery of *danse macabre*. For instance, Jane H. M. Taylor sees in the *Jeu d'Adam*'s devils, as well as in the *branle* of the *Mystère de Sainte Barbe*, some ties to the visual *danse macabre* idiom.[34] Clark speculates

29. Eustace with King, 51–52.

30. Robert Eisler, "Danse Macabre," *Traditio* 6 (1948): 217–24; see also Meyer-Baer, 310.

31. James M. Clark, *The Dance of Death in the Middle Ages and the Renaissance* (Glasgow: Jackson, 1950), 93.

32. E. K. Chambers, *English Literature at the Close of the Middle Ages* (Oxford: Oxford University Press, 1947), 52–53. See also Brian J. Levy, *The Comic Text: Patterns and Images in the Old French Fabliaux* (Amsterdam: Rodopi, 2000), 119, on *fabliaux* with scenes that indicate a format comparable to a dance of death.

33. Fein, *Danse*, 8.

34. Jane H. M. Taylor, "Que signifiait *danse* au quinzième siècle? Danser la Danse macabré," *Fifteenth-Century Studies* 18 (1991): 269–70. On the incorporation of dance into dramas originating in the Middle Ages, see Katherine Steele Brokaw's discussion of the Digby *Mary Magdalene* and *Wisdom*. *Staging Harmony: Music and Religious Change in Late Medieval and Early Modern English Drama* (Ithaca: Cornell University Press, 2016), 26–32.

that the *danse macabre* mural in Paris shared with other early versions at Lübeck and in Spain a common origin in drama, a "chorea Machabaeorum" performed during the fifteenth century. Although specific references to these performances do not date earlier than the middle of the century, Clark and Gertsman point out that fifteenth-century dramatic texts such as the *Pride of Life*, *Everyman*, and parts of the N-Town cycle depict death in ways that draw upon the *danse macabre*'s conventions.[35] For instance, we might note that while the character of Death vanishes from the stage before the substance of Everyman's reckoning begins (l. 180), Everyman queries whether no one will "lede" him from life (l. 156), and the play emphasizes sequential structure in its character interactions. [36] These features leave room either for speculation about *macabresque* choreography embellishing the play or simply for the sense that *Everyman*'s framework echoes the *danse macabre*'s idiom.

This survey of possibilities, however, only foregrounds the original problem, which is that the correlation between the visual art and the spectrum of performance possibilities pertaining to movement practice remains opaque. The examples above suggest movement-based practices somehow reflecting the imagery of *danse macabre* art. Missing, though, is an attested choreographic tradition that either inspires the art in the first place or responds to those images.[37] The surviving textual and visual witnesses to

35. Clark, 91–92; Gertsman, *Dance*, 80, 95.

36. David Bevington, ed., *Everyman*, in *Medieval Drama* (Boston: Houghton Mifflin, 1975), 944–45.

37. Clark's citation (92) of a glossary of medieval Latin that contains an entry for "machabaeorum chorea" refers to a mid-eighteenth-century record of a reference to a 1453 dance of death (my translations follow): "Sexcallus solvat D. Johanni Caletì matriculario S. Joannis quatuor simasias vini per dictum matricularium exhibitas illis, qui choream Machabaeorum fecerunt 10 Julii (1453) nuper lapsa hora missae in Ecclesia S. Joannis Evangelistae propter capitulum provinciale Fratrum Minorum." Domino du Cange et al., eds., *Glossarium Mediae et Infimae Latinitatis*, dig. G. A. L. Henschel, vol. 4 (Paris: Firmin Didot, 1845), 168. [The seneschal paid John of Calais, registrar of St. John's, four units of wine to said registrar, to be furnished to those people who made a *danse macabre* on July 10, 1453, shortly after the hour of mass in the church of St. John the Evangelist, on behalf of the provincial chapter of the friars minor.] On the one hand, this text seems to indicate a performance, given that those who have been paid for it appear to have "made" (*fecerunt*) the *danse macabre* at a specific hour, a designation that would more easily imply a performance occasion than the creation of a painting or other artifact. On the other hand, it is the glossary itself leading its readers into a performance-based notion of *danse macabre*, not specific medieval evidence. The glossary editor calls it a "ritus" and describes how its participants lead themselves ludically to death ("Ludicra quaedam ceremonia ab ecclesiasticis pie instituta, qua omnium dignitatum, tam ecclesiae quam imperii personae choream simul ducendo . . . evanescebant. . . .") [a ludic ceremony piously established by ecclesiastics, by which people of every rank, as much of the church as of the empire, disappeared alike in leading the dance], but this is not a passage

performances do not specify that their choreographic conventions actually correlate with the processional mode that the artistic tradition of *danse ma-cabre* represents. As Gertsman rightly notes, many elements of *danse ma-cabre* painting indicate an impulse toward performance. To argue that "the Dance was meant to be performed, its words pronounced, and its move-ment enacted" is the only way to acknowledge fully its gestural, dramatic, and dialogic nature.[38] But to try to reconstruct performance that in any way alludes to *danse macabre* requires depending on several speculations and untestable assumptions. Some challenging questions would include: How exactly were the partners arranged and where were the points of contact between and among them? Did they always process in a line? How did such procession configure itself when incorporated into plays, sermons, or other performance occasions? What do the differing orientations of performers in the paintings tell us about the use of directional change? How would such a dance end and still sustain its *memento mori* agenda? Were poetic texts in-corporated into the performers' actions?

Ultimately, questions like these destabilize the very meaning of the word *dance* in *danse macabre*. Some critics treat the dance element of *danse macabre* as metaphoric rather than literal. While it is certainly the case that dance could do a great deal of symbolic work in the Middle Ages, one also has to wonder if this critical strategy responds to a situation of unreconstructability. Jane Taylor, for instance, answers the question "Que signifiait *danse*?" in the term *danse macabre* by considering its meaning metaphorically. Distinctions among particular qualities of movement, such as decorous reserve or lubricious animation, that is, are indexed to moral, spiritual, and social difference.[39] Taylor points out the tendency of death dances to make their audiences feel grimly compelled to join in (the theme of compulsory dancing is familiar from the story of the cursed carolers of Kölbek, doomed to turn in a circle for a year as punishment for inappropri-ate churchyard dancing).[40] This theme of compulsion, constraint, and sub-

---

from the medieval text. In addition, the example following the John the Evangelist reference seems to concern what is almost certainly the painting at the Holy Innocents, based on its date of 1424. To what degree has Clark superimposed the modern editorializing of the glossary upon the fifteenth-century payment record? The nature of whatever performance occurred is unspecified in the version of the medieval record itself.

38. Gertsman, *Dance*, 81.

39. Taylor, "Que," 265.

40. On the dance in Mannyng's version of this story, see Mark Miller, "Displaced Souls, Idle Talk, Spectacular Scenes: *Handlyng Synne* and the Perspective of Agency," *Speculum* 71

jugation to command allows dance to stand in as a metaphor for the fact of death itself.[41] This reading indicates that to ask what dance signifies in *danse macabre* cannot be a question primarily concerning what choreographic practices, or spectatorial experiences, are designated in the titular reference to dance. No matter the direction from which we approach *danse macabre*, a reconstructive protocol for such an approach will eventually confront us with *danse macabre*'s obscurity as danced practice. In this situation, one recourse is to empty embodied kinetic performance from the idiom's dance reference. But defanging the dance of *danse macabre* does not entirely sit right with us either, because it elides this tradition's strong affiliation with choreographically-based imagery. Thus, we have tended to respond by envisioning spectacles like some of those listed above, which place it in the general category of performance but do not confront the experience it offers as dance.

A SOLUTION: *DANSE MACABRE* AND *DANCE*

This section responds to that problem by narratively reenacting a spectatorial experience of *danse macabre* through its juxtaposition with a postmodern counterpart. Using this approach to *danse macabre*, I will argue for its identity as medieval dance by bringing to light the virtual forces that we have detected supplementing other medieval dance-based scenes thus far. To locate the virtuality of *dance macabre*, I read it alongside Lucinda Childs's 1979 *Dance*, a visionary integration of dancing bodies, film, music, and light. In the experience of watching *Dance*, the audience perceives virtual forces both between bodily movements and among media. Through the process of narrative reenactment, *Dance* will reveal *danse macabre* to be dance by virtue of its premodern virtuality. We shall begin by examining the experience of spectating *Dance* and then turn to the Middle Ages, considering its perceptual experiences in light of *Dance*'s, and, finally, reenacting the experience of *danse macabre*.

Subsequent to her work with Philip Glass on *Einstein on the Beach* (1976), Childs premiered *Dance*, featuring music by Glass and film by the artist Sol LeWitt. In this multipart work, dancers perform highly structured choreography, involving phrases that are repeated and varied in complex patterns.

(1996): 606–32; my "Choreographing *Mouvance*: The Case of the English Carol," *Philological Quarterly* 87.1/2 (2008): 83–86; and Farina, 97–113.

41. Taylor, "Que," 266–69.

Childs draws upon a repertoire of classical steps—*glissades, saut de basque* turns, *pirouettes en attitude, sautés*—but presents them in a manner stylized at the levels of both gesture and configuration. The effect of the whole is that of an understated perpetual-motion machine driven by enormous underlying energy. As the live dancers perform, a translucent scrim hung downstage displays LeWitt's films of the same dance being performed by the piece's original 1979 dancers. The filmed dancers are sometimes larger, sometimes the same size as the live dancers, and the film images occupy the projection space in inventive and unexpected ways, appearing sometimes above the dancers, sometimes to one side, and sometimes superimposed directly upon them (figure 3 and plate 1).[42] In the latter instance, the translucency of the projected images creates the effect of live and filmed dancers crossing and moving through each other. Caitlin Scranton, a dancer in Childs's company, sees the piece as having "harnessed the ideal of mixing . . . media."[43]

Dance is a particularly appropriate object of analysis here because it uses different media to delineate a space between past and present experience. In the Childs company's recent revivals, the filmed dancers in the piece have been those who performed it originally in the late 1970s.[44] This means that while its premiere featured the same dancers on the screen and on the stage, these revivals have necessarily introduced a new disjunction, whereby the dancers on stage are not the same as the ones in the film. Many viewers have remarked upon the differences in movement quality between the 1979 dancers and the present ones, despite the fact that the choreography is the same and is being set on the dancers by the same living choreographer.[45] In fewer than fifty years, innumerable considerations

42. All images are of the 2009 Bard SummerScape performance of *Dance*, produced by Pomegranate Arts (Linda Brumbach, Director). This reconstruction was commissioned by the Richard B. Fisher Center for the Performing Arts, Bard College, with additional support from The Yard, a colony for performing artists on Martha's Vineyard; Wendy Taucher; and the National Endowment for the Arts' "American Masterpieces: Dance" Initiative, administered by the New England Foundation for the Arts.

43. Interview with Caitlin Scranton, 28 January 2017.

44. The Lyon Opera Ballet's 2016 revival of this piece, however, features new films of the current dancers, made by Marie-Hélène Rebois; this version aligns film and performers in a manner different from what Childs's company has been performing.

45. See, for instance, "Dancing Perfectly Free: Past Meets Present in Lucinda Childs' 'Dance,'" http://dancingperfectlyfree.com/2009/10/12/past-meets-present-in-lucinda-childs-Dance/. Deborah Jowitt comments on the changes in footwear and technical training as well as the appeal of the earlier performers' less ballet-based aesthetic: "I prefer the fluid, free-flowing arms of the dancers in the film to the more precise positions their onstage doubles etch." "Lucinda Childs, Philip Glass, and

Fig. 3. Lucinda Childs, *Dance* (1979), with music by Philip Glass, film by Sol LeWitt, lighting by Beverly Emmons, and original costume design by A. Christina Giannini. The Lucinda Childs Dance Company, Bard SummerScape Festival. Annandale-on-Hudson, New York, 2009. Photograph: Sally Cohn © 2009.

of training, context, aesthetic principles, and material accoutrements (like footwear) make the work different.[46] Furthermore, Scranton explains that in working with more recent generations of dancers, Childs has not simply directed them to mimic the style of the film's original dancers. Rather, Childs teaches the original choreography while also invoking a classical vocabulary ("arms in second, arms in first"); what the audience perceives is her company's original style juxtaposed with the "classic clean line" of

Sol LeWitt 'Dance' at Bard's Summerscape," *Village Voice*, 15 July 2009, http://www.villagevoice .com/arts/lucinda-childs-philip-glass-and-sol-lewitt-dance-at-bards-summerscape-7133919.

46. Scranton notes a difference in "base technique" between the 1979 dancers and her contemporaries: "Lucinda Childs' DANCE (1979) Revival (2009)," http://www.youtube.com /watch?v=cE0RmY2e2vI&feature=related.

many contemporary professionals.[47] Revivals of the piece thus make visible
a juxtaposition of past and present experience. In that sense, *Dance* enacts
visually what I construct verbally as narrative reenactment.

Its juxtaposition of dancers and filmed representations shapes *Dance*'s
identity as a performance in another way as well. Specifically, the representation of the dance contributes integrally to—and thus even becomes—the
performance of the dance for its spectators. While Childs's and LeWitt's idea
that "The décor becomes the dancers" might seem to suggest that the films
function as a backdrop to the live performers, the statement is also intriguingly ambiguous.[48] It leaves unspecified, as do the interweaving mechanics
of the spectacle, which dancers are the decor and which the performers at
any given moment. What we apprehend as the integral performance therefore relies on all these components. In its effects of chasing and crossing, the
installation posits the filmed and live dancers as interacting with each other.
The disembodied representations shift into the category of present performance and indeed interrogate the very distinction between the dancing body
and the representation of dance. *Dance* elaborates on Philip Auslander's
theory of "liveness," which troubles ingrained distinctions between live and
technologically mediated performances because of the extent to which even
"live" performance is itself deeply mediated through the material conditions
of the spectacle.[49]

This category destabilization does not occur simply by reconceiving of
representation as performance; it occurs also because the spaces between
the filmed and live dancers have a mobile and surprising life of their own,
through which they assert themselves as part of the danced spectacle. Su-
perimposing or otherwise interweaving the bodies and filmed dancers emphasizes, in the spectator's experience, the presence and shape of the moving spaces between them. Still images make this effect somewhat apparent
(plate 2). More successfully communicative of this experiential occurrence
is video of the performance.[50] Like the dancers themselves, these interstices

47. Scranton interview. On Childs's interest in working with new generations of young
dancers, see Jessica Gelt, "Lucinda Childs's First New Dance for Her Company in 16 Years Comes
with an Arcade Fire Connection," *LA Times*, 4 November 2016.

48. Julie Caniglia, "Past & Present: An Interview with Lucinda Childs," Walker Art Center,
Fourth Wall, 17 February 2011.

49. Philip Auslander, *Liveness: Performance in a Mediatized Culture*, 2nd ed. (London:
Routledge, 2008), 10–11 and *passim*. See also Auslander, "Live and Technologically Mediated
Performance," in *The Cambridge Companion to Performance Studies*, ed. Tracy C. Davis
(Cambridge: Cambridge University Press, 2008), 108–11.

50. Some exemplary instances appear from 2:30–2:40 at https://www.youtube.com/watch
?v=B_uHPXMsuX8.

Fig. 4. Lucinda Childs, *Dance* (1979), with music by Philip Glass, film by Sol LeWitt, lighting by Beverly Emmons, and original costume design by A. Christina Giannini. The Lucinda Childs Dance Company, Bard SummerScape Festival. Annandale-on-Hudson, New York, 2009. Photograph: Sally Cohn © 2009.

perpetually shift in configuration. Sometimes the live and filmed danc-ers create parallelograms. At other times, their gestures and orientations produce more complex relations, less easy to categorize as pure symme-try (figure 4). It is perhaps in these latter instances that space in the dance becomes most compellingly animate and energized. These moments that challenge expectations of straightforward alignment emphasize the dyna-mism of the space between moving figures in the visual intersection of live and filmed dance.

In those animate spaces between live and filmed dancers, *Dance* makes visible a theory of danced virtuality with which we are already familiar. This theory of virtuality underlies Susanne K. Langer's characterization of dance (see chapter 1) as inhering not in the muscles and movements of dancers but rather in the "interacting forces" that these create in the specta-tor's perception.[51] Elsewhere she elaborates upon this perceptual experience of dance:

51. Langer, "Dynamic," 78.

. . . one does not see *people running around*; one sees the dance driving this way, drawn that way, gathering here, spreading there—fleeing, resting, rising, and so forth; and all the motion seems to spring from powers beyond the performers. In a *pas de deux* the two dancers appear to magnetize each other; the relation between them is more than a spatial one, it is a relation of forces; but the forces they exercise, that seem to be as physical as those which orient the compass needle toward its pole, really do not exist physically at all. They are dance forces, virtual powers.[52]

According to Langer, the motion of which an audience is aware locates itself not within the dancer's body itself but rather in the spaces that danced performance creates between, around, and beyond physical bodies and limbs. Langer calls these forces "virtual." As chapter 1 suggested, such virtual forces are ontologically indeterminate; they may not occupy a material realm, but like the magnetism to which Langer analogizes dance's virtual powers, they interact with and manifest themselves through material elements. By incorporating a filmed component into the performance, *Dance* illustrates this description of choreography's impact on the viewer as located in the interstitial forces between movements rather than emanating from the movements themselves. In specifying these forces as virtual, Langer's theory suggests that *Dance* consists of a virtual component not in the plain unreality of its filmed dancers but rather in the more subtly shaded sense of virtuality that we have discussed. The piece uses the space between its material and immaterial components to make visible forces of kinesis and potential that surround, link, and move through any particular bodily articulation.

Dance further defines dance by locating the constitution of the virtual supplement in the collaboration of dance and spectator. Childs's title invites speculation as to whether the piece intends to explain what dance means, or what dance is. Indeed, what has often been characterized as its minimalist and stylized nature suggests this kind of aim, a presentation of something that is, in a sense, purely dance. Sally Banes notes that in Childs's "dances of the 1970s it is the very structure of the dance that supplies divergent points of view. Phrases and fields of movement are stated, broken down, and reconstructed."[53] Childs experimented within a context

---

52. Susanne K. Langer, *Feeling and Form: A Theory of Art* (New York: Scribner's, 1953), 175–76, emphasis in original.

53. Sally Banes, *Terpsichore in Sneakers: Post-Modern Dance* (Boston, Houghton Mifflin, 1980), 136. Elsewhere, Banes comments that "The work of both Glass and Childs is characterized

of choreographic work in the 1970s and 1980s that "shunned fiction and drew our attention to structure and process," according to Deborah Jowitt.[54] In both its own features and the aesthetics influencing it, then, *Dance* appears to designate, in its title, a sense of what dance means by presenting its most stripped-down incarnation. But Banes adds another important point to her discussion. For Childs, Banes notes, "the collaborative work functions didactically, turning attention to modes of perception . . . the act of dancing provokes a conscious act of seeing."[55] Childs's work thus invites us to consider the mechanics and results of perceptual experience as crucial to danced performance. What occurs in the audience's perceptual interaction with dance shapes dance's definition. In the case of *Dance*, the perceptual intervention of the audience identifies the virtual forces between the live and filmed dancers. *Dance* is dance, then, in its incorporation of Langer's virtual forces and in its location of their production not only between the dancers' moving gestures but also between the audience and the work. Self-defining in its eponymy, *Dance* tells its audience that it is dance in part because of the virtualities it creates in its spectatorial experience.

These virtualities derive from what we have called the *ductus* of dance. For LeWitt's films carefully lead the audience's sightlines within the piece. LeWitt frequently changes the camera's perspective on the dancers being filmed as well as the placement of the filmed dancers in relation to the live ones, so that while we must watch the live dancers from a static position in the audience, the film draws our visual perspective over, under, around, and through them.[56] Thus, even if they cannot move from their seats to follow a structured process, the audience's gaze is conducted through space in highly specific ways. The films allow the piece as a whole to loosen the distinction between audience and participant by creating visual trajectories that originate from various points around the dance, not just from the audience's proscenium-dictated position. From this perspectival position, it is

---

by repetition and accretion of simple sounds and movements." *Subversive Expectations: Performance Art and Paratheater in New York, 1976–85* (Ann Arbor: University of Michigan Press, 1998), 24.

54. Deborah Jowitt, "Beyond Description: Writing beneath the Surface," in *Moving History/ Dancing Cultures: A Dance History Reader*, ed. Ann Dils and Ann Cooper Albright (Middletown, CT: Wesleyan University Press, 2001), 9.

55. Banes, *Terpsichore*, 145.

56. Scranton points out that the space in which the dancers were filmed was much "tight[er]" than the stage space upon which performances take place, so in that sense as well the films set the audience into a different spatial relationship with the choreography (Scranton interview).

ductus, a leading of the audience's perceptual acts, that makes visible the interstitial forces of motion and intent as these emerge between real and represented dancers. *Dance* creates for the viewer an experience of being moved around, placed, and led through different spatial and perspectival configurations within the dance, and this experience shapes the virtual spaces and forces that we see in the performance.

This characterization of *Dance* casts into relief *danse macabre*'s virtual effects: *Dance* illuminates some experiential possibilities for *danse macabre* that would not be detectable in a reconstructive study of its archival evidence alone. *Dance*'s integration of representational and embodied components reflects the installation-based situation of *danse macabre*. In *Dance*'s positing of representational components as integral to danced performance, this work foregrounds that possibility for *danse macabre*. As a two-dimensional manifestation, *danse macabre* imagery can suggest—even on its own—the possibility of virtual forces in its interstices. But ultimately, to reenact the experience of *danse macabre* as three-dimensional spectacle, its juxtaposition with *Dance* becomes necessary. This reenactment process will show that the audience's ductile experience of *danse macabre*'s media generates the kinetic virtualities that define this medieval tradition as dance.

One prominent feature of *danse macabre* as a visual tradition is its elaborate use of interstitial space in the processional configuration. A ca. 1491 French book image provides a useful illustrative example because its layout, Gertsman argues, aims to preserve the effect of continuity found in the churchyard murals (plate 3).[57] The printer and bookseller associated with this image, Anthoine Vérard, also produced a number of printed play scripts at the close of the fifteenth century; this image thus exists within a textual environment interested in the conversion of performance occasion to book perusal.[58] The precise relationship of this image to the lost churchyard paintings in Paris and London is, of course, impossible to determine. But the illustration's elements bear some relationship to those manifestations, particularly in its incorporation of architectural elements into the painting. In displaying the different kinds of space possible in the *danse macabre* as visual tradition, this image draws attention to the complex interstitialities of the skeletons. Along with the spaces between each moribund couple, the painting encourages the perception of seriality across the skeletons themselves, not only through their similar appearance but also through the ways

57. Gertsman, *Dance*, 174.
58. Weigert, *French*, 11.

their gestures and gazes hail each other. In one sense, a viewer might not register the space between the skeletons because a living unfortunate fills that space. But looked at another way, the series of skeletons highlights the area between them beyond simply the interposition of the living interlocutor. Indeed, one critical tradition sees the skeletons not as individual revenants arising one by one but rather as serial representations of a universal Death figure.[59] The interstitial dynamics of the image reinforce this idea, offering not only the possibility of one couple replacing another in the process of the dance, but also the possibility of engineering continuity among all the skeletons so that they become one figure seen over time.[60] The *danse macabre* thus creates a sense of play among different possible borders for the serial interstices the viewer perceives—between the arcades, between the living figures and the skeletons, between the skeletons as individual agents, and between the skeletons as serial manifestations of a single entity.

Interstitial space appears in numerous guises across medieval artistic traditions, and it seems to evoke dynamic modes of seeing. Art historical scholarship draws upon theoretical discourses around liminality to consider the work that interstitial space does for medieval viewers of art. Corine Schleif, for instance, returns to Victor Turner and Arnold Gennep's constructs of liminality to explore how the interstitial spaces of donor art signify for viewers. She points out that depictions of donors sometimes appear in marginal spaces as part of a piece's visual program. Through images' placement in such loci, she argues, they can experiment with the testing and reinforcement of rules.[61] Schleif's reading of the donor figure in the margins implies that such conventions habituate medieval viewers to detect important representational or conceptual work in interstitial spaces. Other readings suggest that what such viewers detect is a transformative and transitional dynamic. In Michael Camille's analysis, page margins, an "extra-textual space" of liminality, provide "a site of artistic elaboration" in the transition from one visual focus to another.[62] Speaking back to Bakhtinian theory, marginal

59. Ernst M. Manasse, "The Dance Motive of the Latin Dance of Death," *Medievalia et Humanistica* 4 (1946): 83–84.

60. For Manasse, the seriality of *danse macabre* speaks to the nature of death in this tradition. That is to say, while on the one hand this art form might suggest that the repeating visual motif of dancing corpses represents a plurality of individuals, on the other hand we cannot we rule out the presence of a Death figure as master piper compelling his followers, one figure seen many times in the process of compulsion (96–98).

61. Corine Schleif, "Kneeling on the Threshold: Donors Negotiating Realms Betwixt and Between," in *Thresholds*, 206–7.

62. Michael Camille, *Image on the Edge: The Margins of Medieval Art* (London: Reaktion Books, 2003), 16–18.

images and the spaces containing them perpetually generate more than themselves and strain against their boundaries.[63]

As a still medieval image that negotiates transition and interstice, *danse macabre* art potentially responds to these habits of seeing by presenting more than just its static self to its viewers. For in addition to their attention to liminal space, audiences of medieval art appear to discern motion in stillness, detecting animate stirrings while looking, for instance, at the painted likeness of a holy figure.[64] While such effects often occur in devotional images, Gwenfair Adams specifies that the kinesis of eucharistic visions depends less upon the devout attitude of the viewer than upon the act of looking itself.[65] Medieval looking, then, can seem ready to see movement not materially there. Sarah Stanbury wonders, for instance, if Lollard polemic against "dead images" reflects "a fear that images will come to life."[66] Hans Belting, meanwhile, has discussed the interaction between the narrative and iconic qualities of images, suggesting that these qualities can merge within particular images (rather than existing as qualifying categories of image) to endow the static image, again, with "liveliness."[67] The gesturing figures that appear in devotional imagery, Belting argues, do not originate exclusively in private worship but rather engage in a reciprocal relationship with cultic practices, rituals, or plays that comprise "the staging of the cult."[68] In this sense as well, the medieval image communicates movement to its viewer, sometimes even a genuinely interactive "display gesture" that involves the viewer.[69] If the apprehension of kinesis is thus possible in static imagery, *danse*

63. Ibid., 54.

64. Sponsler, *Queen's*, 71–2.

65. Gwenfair Walters Adams, *Visions in Late-Medieval England: Lay Spirituality and Sacred Glimpses of the Hidden Worlds of Faith* (Boston: Brill, 2007), 152–154.

66. Sarah Stanbury, *The Visual Object of Desire in Late Medieval England* (Philadelphia: University of Pennsylvania Press, 2008), 26. Stanbury attributes the late-medieval devotional image's ability to "violate natural boundaries delineating object, body, and spirit" to its "troubled links to capital" (31). Stanbury also argues that in Nicholas Love's *Mirror of the Blessed Life of Christ*, "images take on life as scenes of participatory spectatorship" (179), and they invite the real spectator to replicate the stance of the spectator within the kind of visual representation he would frequently have encountered (180).

67. Hans Belting, *The Image and its Public in the Middle Ages: Form and Function of Early Paintings of the Passion*, trans. Mark Bartusis and Ramond Meyer (New Rochelle, NY: Aristide D. Caratzas, 1990), 46.

68. Ibid., 189, 90.

69. Ibid., 189. Also relevant here is P. A. Skantze, *Stillness in Motion in the Seventeenth-Century Theatre* (New York: Routledge, 2003), which questions assumptions about the stasis of early printed material, noting that such material requires an "effort to reanimate kinesthetic exchange in time and space" (6), in both its performance and its circulation contexts, to be accurately understood (6–10).

macabre's networks of transitional force, its skeletons' tending into each other's frames, identities, and spaces, might enable with particular effectiveness a perceptual experience of motion.

In *danse macabre*'s potential to contain such motion and force—supplementary to, yet born of, the concrete visible image—lies its virtuality. Indeed, a closer look at those skeletons shows us that they, in particular, present a visual experience of what we have been calling virtuality. In the Marchant woodcuts, Eustace and King posit energies within the interstices on which we have focused; for them, these energies manifest themselves as the resistance that the skeletons' human counterparts exert against them, forces made visible in folds of clothing pulled in either direction.[70] In addition, the skeleton images themselves interiorize liminality and transformation through their translucent, perpetually progressive state between life and death. Embodying transformative mechanisms, and therefore demanding that the viewer supply perceptions of movement within them, the skeletons position themselves to conjure, in the perceiver's eyes, potential movement in the spaces between them. In this way, the features of *danse macabre* as visual image produce the dynamics of virtuality as I have defined these: the forces of potential motion and energy that are animated within but also supplement what is tangible or unambiguously apprehensible.

Another discourse that can helpfully characterize virtual movement in *danse macabre* exists in the study of early serial imagery. Richard Brilliant's work on Etruscan and Roman art, for instance, acknowledges the serial image's dual effect as both caught in narrative momentum and contained within itself. On the one hand, Brilliant sees in serial images the possibility of apprehending an entire scene at once by combining all the elements of the series. The viewer's eye "may track the line of temporal succession in unbroken continuity as it moves stage by stage."[71] As Otto Pächt argued before Brilliant, "It is the very essence of continuous narrative to render changes visible by means of comparing the same person in different moments or states."[72] On the other hand, Brilliant also considers what happens when the premodern eye rests in one place, both acknowledging the single point and, at the same time, working against the sense of discontinuity created by the frame around the image. This dynamic usefully describes

---

70. Eustace with King, 63.

71. Richard Brilliant, *Visual Narratives: Storytelling in Etruscan and Roman Art* (Ithaca: Cornell University Press, 1984), 18–19.

72. Otto Pächt, *The Rise of Pictorial Narrative in Twelfth-Century England* (Oxford: Oxford University Press, 1962), 8n1.

a possible experience of looking at the *danse macabre* scene above, with its directional momentum in constant play with the frames that hold each image in discrete place.[73] Such a model offers an additional way to locate the *danse macabre*'s forces of potential suspended across it. It further specifies how the still artistic image of *danse macabre* presents itself in virtual motion through certain conventions of premodern seeing.[74]

One might even say that *danse macabre*'s interstitial virtual motion profits from modern theories of the comic book "gutter" as a site of movement. Scott McCloud refers to the gutter as a "limbo" where human perspective and "imagination" intervene to run two separate images together and lend them narrative cohesion.[75] Colin Milburn elaborates on this point by naming movement as an ingredient in this process: "The comics medium compels us to suture internal gaps with assumptions of spatial and temporal movement." The comic engages us in play, asking us to "fill in the blanks with imaginary moving parts, connecting and reconnecting, animating stories on the fly."[76] Given the context informing the medieval viewer's experience, one that habituates him to the possibility of motion within static images and to activity within the interstitial space, we might conceive of such a viewer performing an operation analogous to what Milburn describes. In the gap between one skeleton and another, behind the intervening live figures, exist such "imaginary moving parts," particularly if one considers the skeletons to represent a continuous identity rather than a set of discrete ones.

Comparing *danse macabre* to comic book art also exposes, however, what this reading of the skeletal imagery does not take into account: the three-dimensionality of *danse macabre* in its architectural settings and, con-

---

73. My student Jillian Kern thus articulated this feature of the *danse macabre* painting during a seminar meeting (2014). See also Gertsman on the potential of *danse macabre* to register as both integral and processional (*Dance*, 33).

74. When a nineteenth-century playwright sets a scene before a *danse macabre* painting in the cathedral at Grüssau, he imagines the skeletons becoming animate, leaving their two-dimensional confinement, sitting down at a banquet table, and dancing. Their gestures then mimic and "moc[k]" those of the scene's living characters. Thomas Lovell Beddoes, *Death's Jest-Book; or, The Fool's Tragedy* (London: William Pickering, 1850), 153–55. While not a medieval example, the scene suggests *danse macabre*'s invitation to its audiences to envision it in interactive motion.

75. Scott McCloud, *Understanding Comics: The Invisible Art* (New York: HarperCollins, 1994), 19.

76. Colin Milburn, *Mondo Nano: Fun and Games in the World of Digital Matter* (Durham, NC: Duke University Press, 2015), 143.

sequently, its greater complexity of space and interstice. The late fifteenth-century *danse macabre* at Chaise-Dieu, for instance, is painted on an expanse of wall divided by piers. These piers structurally interrupt the flat space of the painting, and some of them also contain alternative imagery. Gertsman argues that through their structure and imagery the piers disturb the "spell" that the *danse macabre* casts on viewers even as the whole installation produces another kind of experience for its viewers by interweaving its iconographies. In this configuration, the piers manipulate the viewer's experience by introducing another dimensional coordinate into the experience of the spectacle: they "jut out . . . dramatically."[77] Chaise-Dieu emphasizes that the spatial dimensionality of architectural features lends to *danse macabre* installations a complexity beyond that of a gutter or separator on the two-dimensional page.

To continue our reenactment we must therefore take that architectural element into account, and the surviving evidence has by chance left us with a tool to with which to do so, one perhaps even more useful than an integral extant *danse macabre* churchyard. This is Simon Marmion's fifteenth-century depiction of a French cloister, which portrays both a dance of death mural and its spectators. The foreground of this section of the altarpiece depicts St. Bertin receiving Winnoc and his brothers at the monastery, one of the altarpiece's scenes of his life. Behind them is a *danse macabre* cloister.[78] This painting might have been inspired by the dance of death in the city of Amiens, of which Marmion was a native (plate 4 and figure 5).[79] The painting endows us with a significant advantage for reenactment—and for the detection of virtual force in the installation—because it not only features the distinctive imagery of the *danse macabre* itself but also provides a window onto the perceptual situations of medieval spectators engaging with the installation.

The altarpiece treats movement, its representation, its spectatorship, and its setting as integral components of the *danse macabre* spectacle. As a painting of a painting of a dance, it foregrounds both representing and viewing

---

77. Gertsman, *Dance*, 134; see also 130–31 and 159.

78. The altarpiece's depiction of the *danse macabre* appears have undergone alteration. From the underdrawing, it appears the alterations render the *danse macabre* both more visible and more accessible to the figures in the scene. Rainald Grosshans, "Simon Marmion and the Saint Bertin Altarpiece: Notes on the Genesis of the Painting," in *Margaret of York, Simon Marmion, and "The Visions of Tondal,"* ed. Thomas Kren (Malibu, CA: The J. Paul Getty Museum, 1992), 240.

79. Clark, 85.

Fig. 5. Simon Marmion, *Scenes from the Life of St. Bertin* (1459). Right wing of the Altarpiece formerly at Saint-Omer. Photograph: bpk Bildagentur / Gemaeldegalerie, Staatliche Museen, Berlin / Joerg P. Anders / Art Resource, New York.

dance-based imagery. Another painting attributed to Marmion seems similarly interested in the project of representing motion in all its complex contexts (figure 6). Sandra Hindman notes that this breviary miniature depicts scenes from the marriage of the Wise Virgins to Christ (Common of the Virgins).[80] The left border scene, which appears to involve the virgins' choreographed movement in a circle, draws attention to its interactions with other bodily modes of motion and stasis, as well as with architecture, in the painting. Hindman sees a number of "figural" and "architectural" correspondences between this work and the St. Bertin altarpiece.[81] Together, the two paintings make the point that for Marmion, kinetic spectacle in its integrity includes the activities and structures adjacent to it in both space and time. The holy virgins' depiction in the breviary miniature encourages us to understand the *dance macabre*'s constitution of animate spectacle in the fullness of its multiple components. For example, in Marmion's *danse macabre*, the spectatorship of the installation is a major preoccupation. And while the painting's viewer—medieval or modern—cannot precisely inhabit the experiences of the spectators in the painting (most of whom face it from angles not possible for that of the painting's viewer to replicate), the viewer as spectator of the painting is brought into collusion with the spectators within the painting. The experience of the viewer looking at the paint-

80. Sandra Hindman, "Two Leaves from an Unknown Breviary: The Case for Simon Marmion," in *Margaret of York*, 224.

81. Ibid., 226–27.

Fig. 6. Simon Marmion (attributed), *The Holy Virgins Greeted by Christ as They Enter the Gates of Paradise* (ca. 1467–70). Credit: Metropolitan Museum of Art, Robert Lehman Collection (1975.1.2477).

ing enters the network of spectatorship spun by the painted figures walking through the architecture as they gaze within the scene.

In this scene of site-specific spectatorship, *danse macabre*'s interstitial dynamics exist in three dimensions. In embedding the processional mural within the scene, Marmion draws upon the effect we have already seen in the visual image of the procession, whereby a transition or transformation asserts itself in the space between one skeleton's gestural articulation and another's. As in the case of the book page (plate 3), the depiction of the mural weaves different categories of liminality together, not only the space between skeletons but also the space between partners. But both the architectural frame itself and the perspective in which Marmion places the viewer multiply the dimensionality and complexity of the interstices. Looking at the churchyard through the various architectural elements and at a slight angle, the viewer perceives the archways and other structures not only to frame the dance images (as on the manuscript page) but also to produce other kinds of interstitial space. In Marmion's presentation of depth, arches and pillars overlap, crossing into each other's space, and thereby draw visual attention to an increased range of interstitial shapes between different medial components.

To reenact the experience of this three-dimensionality and its interstices in *danse macabre* installation, we must turn back to *Dance*, for Childs's work can illuminate the virtual forces in *danse macabre*'s multiple dimensions and multiple media. In *Dance*, the spectator apprehends virtual force and motion in the spaces between different medial components. As I suggested earlier, these spaces can animate themselves most powerfully in moments of complicated angling or skewing. This dynamic helps us to read the painting's interstices and its material figures. Like the viewers within the painting, the viewer of the painting cannot apprehend the cloister scene in a simply centered or symmetrical way. The left-hand colonnade creates one kind of directional conduit in the parallel angle of the line of columns and the wall containing the painting; there, the columns do not interrupt the view of the painting because of the perspectival angle. On the right, however, something different occurs, with the empty space in front of the painting traced as a weaving trajectory interrupted by the stone columns and other elements. In *Dance*, the perception of asymmetries in space becomes an important means for the spectator to trace virtual force in the spectacle's interstices. Within this context, we might consider how the generation of small perspectival asymmetries in the *danse macabre* (between, for instance, its left and right sides) enhances the viewer's awareness of the mobile potential of those spaces, the forces to which they give rise. *Dance* can thus help us to read the spectatorial experience that Marmion conveys, one in which the scene of *danse macabre* incorporates not only stone, paint, and bodies but also the energies animating the spaces where these media cross in the architectural setting.

Dance furthermore reveals *ductus*'s investment of the *danse macabre*'s interstices with a sense of movement. As we saw in *Dance*, forces emerge in a ductile process of multiple trajectories, created in the film, its interaction with the live dancers, and the spectator's participatory perspectival work. Looking at Marmion's painting in these terms, we can see that it engages its viewer in a *ductus* that layers the interstitial force of the skeletal procession with the viewer's additional sense of being tipped around stone corners and drawn through columned archways. In this way, the painting's different virtual forces—in its interstices both within the mural and along the arcades—draw out and interact with each other as the viewer participates in the ductile process, his perspective led through different points as is the spectator of *Dance*'s. At one level, painted cloisters like this will always reflect Erwin Panofsky's sense of medieval architecture's fractal unity, its orderliness gesturing toward the realm of the ideal. But at another, the experience of the *danse macabre* churchyard produces a supplement to this ordered effect through the "mental habit" of apprehending it.[82] In Marmion's painting, we might reenact a medieval viewer's experience of a ductile momentum, one that makes apprehensible the layers of virtual motion in the interacting media of *danse macabre*'s three dimensions and the dynamically irregular spaces between them.

Reading Marmion by means of *Dance* thus reenacts the experience of *danse macabre* spectatorship specifically as dance-based. This reenactment illuminates something we could not see before: that what seemed a general performance dynamic associated with the visual tradition can be more specifically choreographic because of its virtual supplements. In juxtaposition with each other, Childs and Marmion mutually reinforce the spectator's role as not only participatory but also as engaged in the perceptual practice that dance encourages: one that is led through multiple directions of looking to encounter the strange forces of virtuality in spaces that diverge from what is parallel or regular. *Dance*'s film incorporates into itself the audience's shifting spectatorial perspectives on the choreography. Marmion's depiction, meanwhile, emphasizes the participatory capacity of the audience by positioning its internal and external viewers as variously oriented

---

82. Erwin Panofsky, *Gothic Architecture and Scholasticism* (London: Thames and Hudson, 1957), 28, 43, 21.

toward the mural, facing it at different angles and situating their bodies in different ways. Their combined presence suggests multiplicity of perspective—even originating within the single spectator—as a component of the encounter with this installation. Marmion's painting thus enables a reenactment of *danse macabre* as a ductile experience of virtual forces and their layered, skewed, multidirectional trajectories. The presence of these virtual forces in the participatory spectatorship of *danse macabre* defines its experience as dance.

VIRTUALITY AND TEMPORAL EXPERIENCE IN *DANSE MACABRE*

The dance-based experience of *danse macabre* affects perceptions of both space and time. For the virtualities of *danse macabre* produce, I will argue in this final section, an experience for the viewer that layers several temporal rates of passage at once. Making this case will require shifting our perspectival axis from the horizontal one along which we have been considering this processional tradition to a vertical one from which to notice different aspects of its kinesis and virtuality. *Danse macabre*'s horizontal momentum speaks to its thematics of relentless seriality, a traditional view of this idiom.[83] But in both Childs's *Dance* and *danse macabre*, virtual and actual motion plot themselves on vertical as well as horizontal axes. Continuing to juxtapose *Dance* with *danse macabre*, this section will illustrate how *danse macabre* uses vertical orientation to dictate the viewer's experience of time. Casting its forces of motion along both vertical and horizontal axes, *danse macabre* makes the confrontation with death a disorienting experience of multiple rates of temporal passage in simultaneous operation. As Isabel Davis has noted, medieval audiences were in many ways accustomed to highly complex temporal models.[84] *Danse macabre*'s reenactment as dance-based experience reveals its species of temporal strangeness.

To continue this reenactment, we must note that *Dance* organizes itself on vertical as well as horizontal axes and that its virtual supplements appear along both. Certain moments in *Dance* emphasize a vertically configured

83. On the *danse macabre* as expressing compulsion in its impulse to repetition, see Taylor, "Que," above, as well as R. H. Bowers, "Iconography in Lydgate's 'Dance of Death,'" *Southern Folklore Quarterly* 12.2 (1948): 118 (discussing Manasse).

84. Isabel Davis, "Cutaneous Time in the Late-Medieval Literary Imagination," in *Reading Skin in Medieval Literature and Culture*, ed. Katie L. Walter (New York: Palgrave Macmillan, 2013), 100.

Fig. 7. Lucinda Childs, *Dance* (1979), with music by Philip Glass, film by Sol LeWitt, lighting by Beverly Emmons, and original costume design by A. Christina Giannini. The Lucinda Childs Dance Company, Bard SummerScape Festival. Annandale-on-Hudson, New York, 2009. Photograph: Sally Cohn © 2009.

relationship between the live and filmed dancers (figure 7). There are also instances in *Dance* when LeWitt shifts the angle of the camera so that the filmed dancers appear on a plane above the live dancers, sometimes with the image of the filmed dance space's floor visually separating them (figure 8).[85] In one sense, the effect of moving shapes and forces between live and filmed dancers is the same whether articulated on a horizontal or a vertical axis. In both cases, as figure 8 shows, the piece makes visible the same range we see horizontally, from coordination between the two media, on the one hand, to

85. See, for example, https://www.youtube.com/watch?v=B_uHPXMsuX8 at 1:33, 2:20, and 2:30 for such moments.

Fig. 8. Lucinda Childs, *Dance* (1979), with music by Philip Glass, film by Sol LeWitt,
lighting by Beverly Emmons, and original costume design by A. Christina Giannini.
The Lucinda Childs Dance Company, Bard SummerScape Festival. Annandale-
on-Hudson, New York, 2009. Photograph: Sally Cohn © 2009.

something more skewed, on the other. The vertical axis offers another way
of detecting dynamic force between and around physical bodies.

There is also, however, an important difference: the vertical juxtapositions of live and filmed media confront the spectator with different kinds of
temporal passage. Considered on a horizontal axis, both live and filmed dancers similarly follow Childs's processional aesthetic, sharing the same general
quality of momentum to get the across the stage. On the vertical axis, however, the juxtaposition of different media elucidates different modes of temporal passage simultaneously. Looking at the piece on a vertical axis can challenge our sense of live and filmed performers dancing together, causing them
inhabit more deeply distinct categories of motion. In those instances, asyn-

chrony results from the way that a lived and filmed dancer must each occupy a different medial time. The filmed dancers' luminous indistinction compels them to move through the music at a subtly different pace from the time that a live body in motion appears to inhabit. The live dancers' more sharply outlined bodies, as well as the purposiveness with which their material limbs imbue their gestures, prevent them from replicating fully the rhythms of the hazier filmed bodies. If we earlier identified gestural character to distinguish live and filmed dancers, here we discern a more fundamental difference, established in the nature of the media, concerning the time of the dance. On the vertical axis, the spaces between the real and filmed dancers allow the viewer to register a sense of time as variously inhabited by different media.

These spaces in *Dance* manifest our sense of virtuality as untimeliness, time that does not quite follow the order of the material world and is ahead of or behind itself. That untimeliness becomes further evident when we understand that the two medial components' responses to light produce their differing relations to time. The influence of light on visual effect becomes particularly clear (if the spectator is focusing on the vertical axis) when the filmed dancers appear as larger in scale than the live dancers, dancing above as well as around the live dancers (plate 1). The way that each medium—bodily and filmed—reflects light reinforces its distinct temporal quality. The live bodies become more precise as their angles are illuminated, enhancing the viewer's sense that they are cutting through musically marked time. But for the magnified films in particular, light operates as a diffusing mechanism that countermands this momentum. Attending to the spectator's perception of light thus further specifies the sense of temporal difference we might perceive in the spaces between live and filmed dancers.

Dance foregrounds medieval *danse macabre*'s presentation along its own vertical axis. The fragmentary wall paintings on the north wall of the Guild Chapel in Stratford-upon-Avon (possibly commissioned at the end of the fifteenth century) will illustrate this claim. This *danse macabre* mural was subject to early-modern whitewashing and possible subsequent wall painting.[86] Wooden paneling has covered the north and south walls throughout

---

86. Wilfrid Puddephat, "The Mural Paintings of the Dance of Death in the Guild Chapel of Stratford-upon-Avon," *Birmingham Archaeological Society Transactions* 76 (1960): 30–31. Clifford Davidson, *The Guild Chapel Wall Paintings at Stratford-upon-Avon* (New York: AMS, 1988), 10–11, 33; see also Davidson on a nineteenth-century restoration and drawings (11–13). Puddephat dates the paintings to the early sixteenth century (29). On the figures and colors in the paintings:

> The sixty participants in the dance were arranged in pairs, each consisting of a sprightly cadaver with a reluctant victim in its grasp. There were two pairs of characters in each

Fig. 9. Guild Chapel, Stratford-upon-Avon (2016). Interior north wall.
Photograph: Michael Brooks / Alamy Stock Photo.

much of the chapel's modern configuration (figure 9), although at this writing a project has been undertaken, involving the removal of some paneling, to conserve certain of the chapel's wall paintings.[87] In the 1950s, Wilfrid Puddephat removed the panels then in place to study the painting (figures 10, 11). Unlike the French book illustration or Marmion's painting, this *danse macabre* survival presents serious obstacles to our present apprehension of it. Even in its nearly illegible state, however, the Guild Chapel installation makes clear its dramatic use of vertical orientation in its visual program.

---

compartment. The figures were lighter in tone than the rich scarlet background against which they were represented in attitudes which suggested that they were moving to the left along a floor paved with vermilion and black tiles, which formed a chequered pattern of squares in the upper tier but of lozenge shapes in the lower. (Puddephat, 32)

Davidson notes, however, the tenuousness of some of Puddephat's records (50). On early-modern whitewash and the dynamics of erasure and preservation, see Juliet Fleming, "Whitewash and the Scene of Writing," *Shakespeare Studies* 28 (2000): 133–38.

87. Project supervised by Trevor Edwards, AABC Conservation Architect. What has thus far been uncovered of the dance of death is highly degraded, but it is possible that future work might yield more revealing results regarding this painting. (E-mail conversation with Cate Statham, project manager, July 2017.)

Fig. 10. Guild Chapel, Stratford-upon-Avon (1955–62). Restoration work.
Photograph: Wilfrid Puddephat by kind permission of the
Shakespeare Birthplace Trust (DR409_6_24).

Fig. 11. Guild Chapel, Stratford-upon-Avon (1955–62). Restoration work.
Photograph: Wilfrid Puddephat by kind permission of the
Shakespeare Birthplace Trust (DR409_6_26).

With Puddephat's removal of the wooden paneling, a contrast appears between the horizontal trajectory that the mural impels and the verticality of
the tall windows in the nave. This nave, a bequest of Hugh Clopton, reflects
the late-Gothic building style known as Perpendicular.[88] As the name implies, this architectural idiom emphasizes vertical lines; its features respond to what John Harvey calls the "demand for vertical emphasis."[89] The
building's Perpendicular style suggests that the tall windows held special
significance in the visual and aesthetic program of the architecture, declar-
ing their distinction from the horizontality of the mural.[90]

88. Puddephat, 29, 31.
89. John Harvey, *The Perpendicular Style 1330–1485* (London: B. T. Batsford, Ltd., 1978), 68.
90. Harvey suggests that in the Perpendicular tradition, the use of ogee-shaped cusping in
windows was meant to "ad[d] to the impression of verticality" (58). He continues, "Windows
were enlarged to reach their practical limits, stretching from buttress to buttress and eliminating
wall-space. Their verticality of effect was emphasized, not only by Perpendicular detail and other
tricks of design, but by actual height . . ." (67). Gail McMurray Gibson discusses the proliferation
of churches in this style in East Anglia, where they often resulted from the profitable wool trade.
The Theater of Devotion: East Anglian Drama and Society in the Late Middle Ages (Chicago:
University of Chicago Press, 1989), 26. On the device of "vertical reading" in the De Lisle

Plate 1. Lucinda Childs, *Dance* (1979), with music by Philip Glass, film by Sol LeWitt, lighting by Beverly Emmons, and original costume design by A. Christina Giannini. The Lucinda Childs Dance Company, Bard SummerScape Festival. Annandale-on-Hudson, New York, 2009. Photograph: Sally Cohn © 2009.

Plate 2. Lucinda Childs, *Dance* (1979), with music by Philip Glass, film by Sol LeWitt, lighting by Beverly Emmons, and original costume design by A. Christina Giannini. The Lucinda Childs Dance Company, Bard SummerScape Festival. Annandale-on-Hudson, New York, 2009. Photograph: Sally Cohn © 2009.

Plate 3. Detail of the Archbishop, the Knight, the Bishop, the Squire, the Cordelier (Franciscan), the Child, the Cleric, and the Hermit. From *La danse macabre* (Paris: Pierre le Rouge for Anthoine Vérard, ca. 1491–92). BnF, Réserve Te-8-Fol, page 3. Photograph: Bibliothèque nationale de France.

Plate 4. Simon Marmion, *Scenes from the Life of St. Bertin* (1459) (detail). Right wing of the Altarpiece formerly at Saint-Omer. Gemaeldegalerie, Staatliche Museen, Berlin. Photograph: bpk Bildagentur / Gemaeldegalerie, Staatliche Museen, Berlin / Joerg P. Anders / Art Resource, New York.

Plate 5. William Blake, "The Goblin," Milton's *L'Allegro ed il Penseroso* (ca. 1816–1820). The Morgan Library and Museum (1949.4:5). Purchased with the assistance of the Fellows with the special support of Mrs. Landon K. Thorne and Mr. Paul Mellon. Photograph: The Pierpont Morgan Library, New York.

Plate 6. Mark Morris, *L'Allegro, il Penseroso ed il Moderato* (1988). Mark Morris Dance Group with the English National Opera. London Coliseum, London, England, 2000. Photograph: Bill Cooper/ArenaPAL.

Plate 7. Mark Morris, *L'Allegro, il Penseroso ed il Moderato* (1988). Mark Morris Dance Group, Lincoln Center for the Perfoming Arts—White Light Festival. David H. Koch Theater, New York, 2013. Photograph: Costas.

Plate 8. The Bodleian Libraries, The University of Oxford, MS Bodley 264, f. 181v (1338–44). Photograph: Bodleian Libraries, Oxford.

Plate 9. The Bodleian Libraries, The University of Oxford, MS Douce 195,
f. 7r (late fifteenth century). Photograph: Bodleian Libraries, Oxford.

Plate 10. The Bodleian Libraries, The University of Oxford, MS Rawlinson D.913,
now recto (fourteenth century) (detail). Photograph: Bodleian Libraries, Oxford.

Given the site's obfuscation of the original *danse macabre* mural, we are fortunate to have in the Digital Guild Chapel a means to reenact this installation (figure 12).[91] Restoring the painting, this digital site shows what the actual site cannot. But it accomplishes more as well, using virtual reality to reenact, according to chapter 1's definition, rather than merely to reconstruct. The Digital Guild Chapel introduces virtuality as a force in time to our encounter with this setting. It does so by setting the wall paintings in motion, conveying their different states over time as well as the conjectural nature of their placement. While virtual technologies that aim to reconstruct sites sometimes reify their components, the Digital Guild Chapel uses the virtual platform to do the opposite. The creators use the digital platform to convey the lack of critical consensus around the church paintings' placement, to suggest thematic as well as structural connections between them, and, perhaps most importantly, to avoid a false impression of stability by depicting the building as existing in states of change.[92] The Digital Guild Chapel provides different perspectives on the chapel over time by presenting it as a site in virtual motion. This project harnesses the indeterminate time of virtuality (see chapter 1) in order to present an unstable past.

The Digital Guild Chapel is especially useful because in concert with *Dance*, it makes evident the original installation's use of different media to experiment with horizontal and vertical forces. While the *danse macabre*

Psalter's illustrated "three living and three dead" material, see Susanna Greer Fein, "Life and Death, Reader and Page: Mirrors of Mortality in English Manuscripts," *Mosaic* 35.1 (2002): 86.

91. This project is located at "The Digital Guild Chapel," http://intarch.ac.uk/journal /issue32/1/GuildChapelInterface3.html. See also Kate Giles and Jonathan Clark, "The Archaeology of the Guild Buildings of Shakespeare's Stratford-upon-Avon," in *The Guild and Guild Buildings of Shakespeare's Stratford: Society, Religion, School, and Stage*, ed. J. R. Mulryne (New York: Routledge, 2016), esp. 164.

92. For example, Giles et al. have pointed out that the Guild Chapel *danse macabre*'s incorporation of Seven Deadly Sin imagery resonates with the Doom painting above the chancel—this connection potentially constitutes another form of kinesis in the still images, one that the virtual chapel can emphasize. As these critics also note, "within the digital heritage field there has been increasing concern about the use of virtual models in this rather uncritical way. Scholars have pointed out that the creation of 'a' virtual model inadvertently closes down alternative and multiple interpretations of the same evidence." Giles, Anthony Masinston, and Geoff Arnott, "Visualising the Guild Chapel, Stratford-upon-Avon: Digital Models as Research Tools in Historical Archaeology," *Internet Archaeology Journal* 32 (2012). See also the discussion of the limitations of "virtual heritage" in terms of its spatial fixity and oculocentrism in Erik Champion, "History and Cultural Heritage in Virtual Environments," in *Oxford Handbook of Virtuality*, 271–72.

Fig. 12. Guild Chapel, Stratford-upon-Avon. North wall of the nave. Digital model reconstruction by Anthony Masinton and Geoff Arnott (2008). Still image by Geoff Arnott (2017).

Fig. 13. Guild Chapel, Stratford-upon-Avon. Dance of death, north wall. Credit: Wilfrid Puddephat by kind permission of the Shakespeare Birthplace Trust (DR399_1_3_GC_G51).

painting generates processional, lateral momentum (emphasized by the mural's depictions of the horizontal *gisant* and banner), the windows express vertical impulses. The Guild Chapel's relations among media thus emerge as an interaction of horizontal and vertical vectors.[93] In addition to the soaring height of the windows, the vertical aesthetic of the wall behind and above the mural might receive even further emphasis in what Puddephat speculates were tall figures in the alcoves above the *danse macabre* (figure 13). These figures between the windows intensify the focus on verticality by introducing proportional play in the installation as well, offering human bodies much enlarged, along a vertical axis, beyond their counterparts in the procession. In an evocative reminder of the imagery of Childs's *Dance* (figure 7), the Guild Chapel *danse macabre* (in Puddephat's conjecture) offers its audience, within a predominantly interstitial structural aesthetic, a towering expanse along a vertical axis while also asking the eye to follow the progression of its horizontal one. And like *Dance*, this *danse macabre* plays with scalar enlargement and diminishment along these horizontal and vertical axes. *Dance* casts into relief the dynamic quality of Guild Chapel's horizontal and vertical impulses as they structure its medial relations.

The installation also enhances its conceptual resonances by subverting its own alignment of direction with medium (glass : vertical :: mural : horizontal). It introduces verticalities into the ostensibly horizontal mural. The Guild Chapel painting is arranged in a double layer, soliciting attunement to the dynamics of both vertical and horizontal space as its viewers look up and down as well as across to follow its visual program. We might ascribe the Guild Chapel's visual layout purely to the happenstance of architectural constraint introduced by a single interior wall rather than by a square churchyard. But the result still encourages the viewer's attention to the various directions, including vertical, in which his perceptual acts cast themselves in the apprehension of the spectacle. Locating the play of horizontal and vertical tendencies within the mural itself enters the mural's configuration into dialogue with its sociopolitical meaning. Amy Appleford has seen the lateral nature of the *danse macabre* as

---

93. Scholarship of *danse macabre* suggests that it is an aesthetic tradition particularly invested in the dynamics of interactivity as multimedia conditions establish them. These occur, for instance, not only between author and reader (Oosterwijk, "Dance," 21) but also in the introduction of *macabre* imagery into other decorative programs (Kristiane Lemé-Hébuterne, "Places for Reflection: Death Imagery in Medieval Choir Stalls," in *Mixed Metaphors*, 271).

a departure from a more traditional, vertically-oriented hierarchy, producing a "community organized along horizontal or lateral lines," representative of what David Wallace has termed an "associational ideology" for the city of London.[94] The directional complexity in the *danse macabre*'s media accommodates the conceptual dichotomy of hierarchy and association.

But besides elucidating this type of social thematic, attention to the verticality of the *danse macabre* installation also alerts us to another medium, one that is mobile itself and also produces the appearance of moving forces: that medium is light. In particular, the painting would have received illumination from the south windows across from it. Viewers contemplating the *danse macabre* for any length of time would also be aware of the shifting angles, qualities, and intensities of light from the chapel's windows. Light in fact comprises an important factor in medieval church architecture, in terms not only of its Sugerian symbolism but also of its role in the mechanics of viewing experience.[95] Simon Roffey, for instance, suggests that English chantry chapel design took into account the directional vectors of incoming light in order to highlight certain architectural features of the structure, like altars or tombs.[96] The placement of the painting under and across from a set of perpendicular windows suggests this kind of intentional interaction between the site of the artwork and the sources of light (fig-

94. Appleford, *Learning*, 96. See also Wallace, *Chaucerian Polity: Absolutist Lineages and Associational Forms in England and Italy* (Stanford: Stanford University Press, 1997), 65–82. The play of lateral movement and vertically-configured placement within the mural potentially foregrounds the mural's political intervention. That is, the mural's capitalization on vertical and horizontal lines of sight—made obvious in the media interaction of glass and paint but then further articulated within the mural itself—becomes ideologically revelatory. For other arguments that deal with visual detail's relationship to sociopolitical content, see Sophie Oosterwijk, "Death, Memory, and Commemoration: John Lydgate and 'Macabrees daunce' at Old St. Paul's Cathedral, London," in *Memory and Commemoration in Medieval England*, ed. Caroline M. Barron and Clive Burgess (Harlaxton: Harlaxton Symposium Proceedings, 2010), 185–201; and Kinch, 198–99.

95. See, for instance, the references to light in the poetic inscriptions for Saint-Denis that Suger records. *Oeuvres*, vol. 1, ed. and trans. Françoise Gasparri (Paris: Les belles lettres, 1996), 116, 120.

96. Simon Roffey, *The Medieval Chantry Chapel: An Archeology* (Woodridge: Boydell, 2007), 64, 134. See also Roffey, "Reconstructing English Medieval Parish Church Chantries and Chapels: An Archaeological Approach," *Church Archaeology* 5/6 (2004): 63–66 on the importance of orchestrating sightlines and vision in medieval chantry chapels and the use of view-shed analysis. Roffey also discusses the architectural feature of chapel squints, another means by which such architecture emphasized its integration of dynamic sightlines. *Chantry*, 57–59.

ure 9).[97] In such an arrangement, moving light maps itself onto the vertical and horizontal axes of motion in the *danse macabre*. As the installation leads its ambulatory spectators along a horizontal space, they see and pass through another kind of motion in the shifting of the sun through the vertical windows. Light has its own animate quality, migrating over time as it pours through a window. But in addition, Kate Giles posits that "light and architecture could be used to structure a belief in the power of images to look back and affect the observer."[98] In this way light's own migration in actual space might engage the imagery of the mural in another kind of virtual motion, catching the skeletons' weird translucencies in diverse ways.

In another sense, *danse macabre* contrasts the ontological strangeness of the procession's virtual momentum with light's more conventionally apprehensible motion; *Dance* can help us to see how complex and suggestive this contrast is. In *danse macabre*, the passage of time in the shifting of light, measurable in a worldly and predictable sense, exists at odds with the stranger time of the processional figures' virtual motion across their interstices. The Guild Chapel installation thus incorporates a light-based mode of temporal pacing along its vertical axis that is in a sense irresolvable with the temporal experience that its horizontal trajectory creates. Comparing this effect to what occurs in *Dance* magnifies the strangeness of *danse macabre*. When I asked Scranton about the relationship between her performing and spectating experience, she noted that the precision of *Dance*'s music and choreography requires the dancers to train their focus "very much on the down. . . . We're constantly almost pulling our vertical down . . . and that's . . . where we are, down, down, down. . . . Knowing that as a dancer and then watching it from the outside, I can appreciate . . . as a spectator . . . how important it is to have this vertical draw [in the films] in order not to make the dance so heavy. . . . The film takes something that's so rhythmic and gives an

---

97. C. Pamela Graves revises conventional architectural historical approaches to "capture" instead "the way in which light and human sight worked within the churches." *The Form and Fabric of Belief: An Archaeology of the Lay Experience of Religion in Medieval Norfolk and Devon* (Oxford: Hadrian Books, 2000), 1. See, for instance, her account of the play of light, shadow, and movement as the viewer experienced these in an early church at Ingworth: "on entering the original church, the lay person would have experienced a lofty, narrow space, with an overhanging gallery at the west end, lit from windows in the tower behind. Their attention would be drawn to the smaller, penumbral space of the chancel by the movements of the priest himself" (83).

98. Giles, "Seeing," 115.

ethereal . . . vibe to it."[99] In integrating participatory and spectating perspectives, Scranton sees in *Dance* a vertically oriented contrast between the temporal quality of the embodied dance and another less palpable ingredient that the films offer. "Down" pertains to both direction and the beat of time in dance: the "rhythmic." In this characterization, the embodied dance seems to inhabit a worldly time, located in the performing body's moment-by-moment experience of intense focus upon the choreography. The film as "ethereal," however, capitalizes on light and lightness to create an alternative to that temporal experience; it is the stranger time and space for the audience to experience in an upward impulse. This contrast foregrounds how surprising *danse macabre*'s temporal contrast is. In the medieval example, light becomes the worldlier manifestation of temporal passage, its sunlit source marking time on the vertical axis in a manner that grounds itself in physical and natural law. It is the force of virtual motion generated in the ambulatory spectator's encounter with the painting that occupies time in a more inscrutable manner. What might be the "down" of the embodied *danse macabre* spectator rhythmically treading his own processional choreography subjects itself to multiple other trajectories of desynchronizing force in the dance-inflected encounter with the installation.

This account indicates an experience of multiple modes of temporal passage at once.[100] I noted above that *Dance*'s animate spaces between live and filmed dancers on the vertical axis express virtuality as untimeliness and asynchrony. In this way, *Dance* provides a guide with which to specify the different and conflicting temporal structures produced in *danse macabre*'s negotiations of horizontal and vertical space, of material and immaterial media. It has often been remarked that the movement quality of the skeletons appears to differ from that of the live characters, being more animated and gesticulative, a difference generally attributed to social marking or a reminder of the chaos of death.[101] But perhaps this difference in movement quality emblematizes something about the experience of the entire installation: the presence not only of different motion but also of different and misaligned markings of time cast across the work.

99. Scranton interview.

100. As Dinshaw points out, Aristotle's strategy to approach to time's measuring capacities by means of "experience" can "ope[n] up the question of temporality," accommodating its ambiguity and heterogeneity (10).

101. Taylor, "Que," 265; Gertsman, *Dance*, 65–67.

The passage of light through the windows marks one only kind of time. There are other, stranger, time signatures to be experienced in the perception of those virtual forces emerging from *danse macabre*'s manifold and multidimensional interstices. These temporal experiences find themselves further multiplied by the virtual forces that present themselves to the eye while the sun, tracing its quotidian arc, directly illuminates the installation's marvelous, liminal figures. In one sense, *danse macabre* offers some obvious temporal trajectories that the speaker might inhabit, particularly intending forward to the possibility of death. But reenacting *danse macabre* in terms of its danced virtuality locates experiences of time in a more multivectored *ductus*.

That multiplicity of simultaneous temporal modes, at base apprehensible through the perceptual habits of dance, is not a neutral effect; it seems likely to disorient or overwhelm a viewer. In this way *danse macabre* communicates the terror of death's encounter. The popularity of this idiom at the end of the Middle Ages suggests that something about it was profoundly effective, but it is hard for us to discern this when on the surface *danse macabre* seems to espouse a predictable, repetitive message concerning death's inevitability, violence, and power. Claire M. Waters has argued that earlier in the Middle Ages, narratives of medieval encounters with death establish themselves to be far more didactically elaborate and complex than the eliciting of visceral fear they might seem superficially to involve.[102] Within this context, we might wonder if something more conceptually and aesthetically adventurous, or even surprising and estranging, might be at stake in the *danse macabre*'s program. A reenacted *danse macabre* responds to this question by revealing the disorientation and confusion that the installation's virtual environment has the potential to create. The space between *Dance* and *danse macabre* demarcates the medieval agent's experience: led through a network of multiply overlapping axes and trajectories in space, he perceives the forces that intend in animate bodies, representational media, and the interstices among all those elements. That dance-based perceptual practice coerces him to inhabit a daunting array of temporal modes at once. In this manner, *danse macabre* produces a temporal experience neither blandly and conventionally serial nor simplistically visceral. Rather, through an intricate aesthetic experience, *danse macabre* destabilizes its

102. Claire M. Waters, *Translating Clergie: Status, Education, and Salvation in Thirteenth-Century Vernacular Texts* (Philadelphia: University of Pennsylvania Press, 2016), 62.

audience to cause a sense of estrangement at a level as deep as their sense of time.

I conclude with a brief reference to a familiar Emily Dickinson poem, which describes the "certain slant of light" that titles this chapter. In addition to being preoccupied with representing subtle and distinct experience, Dickinson also shifts our focus to poetry:

> There's a certain Slant of light,
> Winter Afternoons–
> That oppresses, like the Heft
> Of Cathedral Tunes–

Oren Izenberg sees Dickinson as centrally concerned with the experiential, "the epistemological problem of third-person access to first person states." The imagery of this poem, he suggests, privileges itself as idiosyncratic experience rather than subsuming itself to abstract concept or metaphor.[103] Dickinson's reference to light emblematizes the dynamic of perceptual experience we have negotiated in our medieval example.

> When it comes, the Landscape listens–
> Shadows—hold their breath–
> When it goes, 'tis like the Distance
> On the look of Death–[104]

For Dickinson, *Dance*, and *danse macabre*, light wanes, angles to indirection, suspends itself agitatedly (causing a kind of held breath) between bodies and pictures, and is otherwise contingent in the way that premodern experience necessarily is to us. But at the same time, experiences of illumination make reenactment possible in that space between the Middle Ages and modernity. Light in Childs's *Dance* attunes us to dance's accommodation of different ontological categories of motion as well as different systems of temporal marking. In this way, *Dance* reveals some possibilities in the ductile experience of *danse macabre* that its archives alone, necessarily alienated from its dance-based identity, would not be able to convey. The next chapter will consider how the dance-based *ductus* of multimedia

---

103. Oren Izenberg, "Poems Out of Our Heads," *PMLA* 123.1 (2008): 220, 221.

104. R. W. Franklin, ed., *The Poems of Emily Dickinson* (Cambridge: Harvard University Press, 1999), 142–43.

danse macabre establishes an experience of poetic form in *danse macabre* verse. Through these means, *ductus* forms a bridge between dance and poetry that is built from habits of perceptual experience, uncovering different—and stranger—experiences of poetic form than might otherwise be available to us.

CHAPTER FOUR

"Dredful Fotyng":
Reenacting *Danse macabre*'s Poetic Form

W e now arrive at the second part of the *danse macabre* case study. Here, the apprehensional practices forged in the experience of *danse macabre* installations produce both authorial and readerly experiences of *danse macabre* as a poetic tradition. *Danses macabres* often contain stanzaic verse dialogues between the painting's figures. In English, this poetic material originates mainly with the fifteenth-century author John Lydgate, who translated and adapted a Parisian version he encountered. The matter of Lydgate's poem compelled audiences within and beyond the fifteenth century: several of its manuscript copies reflect a highly engaged and participatory relationship with the text past Lydgate's own lifetime. As late as the seventeenth century, recusants continued to revisit this poetic idiom.[1] This continued appeal is unsurprising, for it appears to reflect a premodern and early modern interest in *memento mori* conventions.

I would argue, however, that the experience of *danse macabre* poetry's *form*, as produced collaboratively between text and reader, more comprehensively explains the impact of this poetic tradition. Because Lydgate attests to having seen the French *danse macabre*, his English version offers an opportunity to consider how his perceptual experience of the visual installation inflects the choices he makes in translating and producing text. Lydgate's *danse macabre* poem represents an instance in which the perceptual practices of *danse macabre* installation internalize themselves to his version of the poem, shaping the reader's experience through the poem and by interacting with the reader's own sense of the visual tradition. From

---

1. See the poem at ff. 15–16 of London, British Library MS Additional 15225, transcribed in Douglas Gray, "Two Songs of Death," *Neuphilologische Mitteilungen* 64.1 (1963): 64–69. On sixteenth-century references to the "dance of Paul's," see Oosterwijk, "Death," 196.

authorial as well as readerly perspectives conditioned by *danse macabre*'s disorienting and multifarious temporalities, the apparent regularity of the poem's *huitain* stanzaic form emerges as something different: an untimely and irregular experience. I shall make this case in three stages. First, I will show how the poem's imagery indicates Lydgate's attunement as an author to *danse macabre*'s virtual supplement. Second, both the incidental and deliberate choices that make up scribal variation across the poem's versions will enable a reenactment of the reader's ductile experience in the encounter with the poem. Third, setting Lydgate's perspective in collaboration with the reader's, I will reenact this text's experience of poetic form as the strange footing of the virtual supplement.

READING AND SEEING:
POETIC INSCRIPTION IN A MULTIMEDIA SETTING

To reenact *danse macabre*'s poetic form, it is necessary first to establish that in a multimedia spectacle, audiences experience a *ductus* that integrates textual encounter with other kinds of perceptual practice. Because the features of the installation exist on a continuum from verbal to nonverbal, *danse macabre* as a whole requires us to articulate a relationship between the activities of reading and other kinds of semiotic processing. The following section will briefly describe the Lydgate dance of death poem and then survey some different ways that the poetic text interacts with *danse macabre*'s other media. In this interaction, the *danse macabre* churchyard hosts the model of ductile experience I proposed in chapter 2. This *ductus* builds a bridge between poetry and nonverbal art by bringing the perceptual habits of one to bear upon the other.

Danse macabre establishes a complicated relationship between its art and its text, raising questions about whether specific versions were destined for specific media formats. In several *danse macabre* installations, vernacular poetic text visibly collaborates with the spectacle's other media of paint, architecture, and moving bodies, appearing as verse dialogues inscribed under the painted sets of partners. Lydgate's ca. 1426 translation of a French *danse macabre* poem, thus inscribed at the Cemetery of the Holy Innocents in Paris, provides the main source of the English poetic tradition.[2] Lydgate's text appears to have been included on the painted boards

2. See, for instance, Fein, *Danse*, 16.

of the *danse macabre* installation at the Pardon Churchyard in London.[3] Versions of Lydgate's texts are incorporated into other English *danse macabre* installations, including the wall painting at the Guild Chapel as well as a site (now destroyed) referred to in London, British Library MS Cotton Vespasian A.XXV, as "the chapel of Wortley at Wortley Hall." English *danse macabre* text survives in several medieval and early modern manuscripts as well. The poem's early-twentieth-century editor, Florence Warren, categorizes these as belonging to A and B groups; the distinctions are sometimes thought to reflect the different versions either required for the wall installation format or suitable to be copied into books.[4] This categorization, however, is complicated. While, on the one hand, the A group's inclusion of a translator's prologue might render it less appropriate for a wall inscription than for a book copy, on the other hand it is possible that material from the *verba translatoris* stanzas appeared in the installation context.[5] Establishing universally how textual versions aligned with wall installations is challenging. We might instead characterize the situation as follows: in many instances, the dance of death poem presents us with a continuum of possibilities for readerly encounter, one that runs between confrontation with a physical installation and an awareness of the possibility of such a multimedia object even in its absence.

Lydgate's dance of death poem occurs within a larger context of Lydgatean poetry appearing as inscription in, or bearing some relation to, architecture. Jennifer E. Floyd demonstrates this occurrence in a study of Lydgate's "architectural verse." Floyd considers the relationship between the "literary and the decorative" as an important component of the audience's reception of text in the Middle Ages.[6] As she notes, "The Lydgate verses at Long Melford," for example, "offer a rare opportunity to trace the concrete relationships that existed between literary and other forms of cultural patronage in late-medieval England."[7] In different ways, examples of Lydgate's

---

3. On Lydgate as a translator who wished to "'perform' as an English poet mediating the French verbo-visual text," see Kinch, 203. See chapter 3, as well as Barron and Rousseau, 36.

4. Warren and White, xxiv–xxv.

5. On the A group prologue's "doubtful pertinence" to wall painting, see Appleford, *Learning*, 89–90. Puddephat states that the text he found at the Guild Chapel included "the first and third verses in the group of five contained in the *Verba translatoris*" (33). Davidson believes that elements of both A and B texts existed in the Guild Chapel version but cautions that Puddephat's notes seem to depend on manuscript sources (7, 50, 53–55). Conservation underway might expand our knowledge of this painting's contents (see chapter 3, note 87).

6. Floyd, 1.

7. Ibid., 33.

poetry potentially highlight acts of collaboration between the inscriptional and the architectural.

The appearance of Lydgate's verse in architectural settings pertains also to a conflict between the efficacy of words and of images, though they seem to reflect Lydgate's general tendency toward language's superiority. Shannon Gayk has argued that Lydgate stages "interventions in the contemporary debates about the proper use of visual images" in order ultimately to argue for the primacy of engagement with textual material.[8] In addition, Gayk suggests that as it appears in other material and architectural contexts, Lydgate's poetry continues to develop its messages concerning visuality. The excerpting of "Quis dabit meo" and the *Testament* at Long Melford, for instance, reflects "a more typical example of the period's visual and affective piety" than what Lydgate's own poetic project might endorse. In their gestures toward the architectural structure, the verses at Long Melford in particular solicit "emotional response" from the viewer, fostering an alignment with affective piety about which Lydgate himself would hesitate.[9] These examples suggest that approaching the question of material or site-specific inscription reveals Lydgate's privileging—if somewhat complicated—of the written word.

Underlying this question about word and image lies another concerning the signifying nature of the verses inscribed in settings like these. To what extent, that is, do the stanzas encourage apprehension as decorative and visual objects, and to what extent do they respond to verbal literacy? Floyd characterizes the spectrum of possible responses to inscription as existing between "technical" literacy, on the one hand, and literacies that, on the other, address nonverbal spectacle or decoration.[10] She sees Lydgate's verses as accomplishing both textual and decorative ends, reading architectural verses as "simultaneously textual and visual objects encountered within a specific, built environment."[11] In a discussion of Lydgatean "tapestry poems," Claire Sponsler similarly articulates the possible categories of reception as "legible texts" and "written text as a constitutive feature of the design."[12] The tapestries, like other inscriptional verse, suggest a reading

8. Shannon Gayk, *Image, Text, and Religious Reform in Fifteenth-Century England* (Cambridge: Cambridge University Press, 2010), 87.

9. Ibid., 118.

10. Floyd, 15.

11. Ibid., 18.

12. Claire Sponsler, "Text and Textiles: Lydgate's Tapestry Poems," in *Medieval Fabrications*, ed. E. Jane Burns (New York: Palgrave Macmillan, 2004), 22. Elsewhere, Sponsler, building upon Anne Lancashire's work, considers that in architectural settings, Lydgate's inscriptional verse

situation that accommodates both verbal and visual decoding. Gayk understands this question as presenting itself in Lydgate's mind as a fulcrum between "seeing and reading."[13] Lydgate's frequent explicit references to material inscription, printing, and engraving throughout his poetry reflect his preoccupation with the relationship between the two.

If "seeing" represents one end of a spectrum of modes of engagement with Lydgatean poetic inscription, *danse macabre* rewards this perceptual mode by allowing the poetry to exist as a visual object in its setting. Indeed, *danse macabre*'s visual incorporation of poetry is potentially distinctive if, as Sponsler suggests, some of Lydgate's poems for other mural sites might simply have been read aloud at the site rather than inscribed into it.[14] Sponsler also notes that the B version of the *danse macabre* poem draws attention to visuality as part of a "range of sensory perception."[15] Furthermore, when Simon Marmion includes black lines in his painting to indicate the poetic inscription accompanying the Amiens mural, he depicts poetic stanzas registered in visual collaboration with other media, including paint and stone (plate 4). The text becomes part of a visual program—in Floyd's terms, decorative—through its rendering as illegible. While Marmion depicts figures reading the words, they are not legible to the painting's viewer. Rather, the regular blocks of writing contribute to the visual patterning of the installation's multimedia program, constituting a frieze to border the processional painting. The *danse macabre* installation at Chaise-Dieu indicates a similar effect. In this instance, ruled lines appear under the painting, suggesting that verses would eventually be inserted as further embellishment to the site. Léonard Kürtz speculates that the painter ran out of time to inscribe the words, leaving the placeholding lines to indicate the visual rationale by which text would be incorporated into painting, imagery, and architecture.[16] The visibility of this step in the construction process of the

provided an interactive backdrop to "live performance" (*Queen's*, 85; see also 93–95). Laura Weigert argues that tapestries exist in intriguing relation to performance genres, noting that tapestries could convey dynamics of participatory spectatorship. "'Theatricality' in Tapestries and Mystery Plays and its Afterlife in Painting," *Art History* 33.2 (2010): 230. See also Christine Sciacca, "Raising the Curtain on the Use of Textiles in Manuscripts," in *Weaving, Veiling, and Dressing: Textiles and Their Metaphors in the Late Middle Ages*, ed. Kathryn M. Rudy and Barbara Baert (Turnhout: Brepols, 2007), 161, on textiles' "role in mediating the medieval reader's experience of text and image."

13. Gayk, 89.

14. Sponsler, "Text," 28.

15. Sponsler, *Queen's*, 78. Sponsler goes on to suggest that this version's "concluding verses reframe this sensorily engaged and active participation as *reading*" (78, emphasis in original).

16. Kürtz, 81.

installation makes evident that one important role of the poetic material is to contribute to the spatial patterning of the work in concert with other visual elements.

While this focus on decorative pattern might seem to efface the poem's legible textuality, *danse macabre* imagery equally exhorts its audience to consider the poem's legibility. Introducing the French *danse macabre* wood-cuts associated with the Paris installation is an image of the poem's "acteur" reading while surrounded by numerous other books (figure 14).[17] The place-ment of this illustration makes the reading of text a structuring activity for the presentation of the *danse macabre*; this concept could obtain whether or not such an image appeared in any particular installation. The Pardon Churchyard, meanwhile, connects reading practice to the spectacle of the *danse macabre* in its own way. Following John Stow's description of the Pardon Churchyard is his comment that during the mid-fifteenth century, a library existed above the cloister where the *danse macabre* paintings appeared:

There was also one great cloister, on the north side of this church, envi-roning a plot of ground, of old time called Pardon churchyard; whereof Thomas More, dean of Paules, was either the first builder, or a most espe-cial benefactor, and was buried there. About this cloister was artificially and richly painted the Dance of Machabray, or Dance of Death, com-monly called the Dance of Paul's; the like whereof was painted about St. Innocent's cloister at Paris, in France. The metres, or poesy of this dance, were translated out of French into English by John Lidgate, monk of Bury, and with the picture of death leading all estates, painted about the cloister, at the special request and at the dispence of Jenken Carpenter, in the reign of Henry VI. In this cloister were buried many persons, some of worship, and others of honour; the monuments of whom, in number and curious workmanship, passed all other that were in that church.

Over the east quadrant of this cloister was a fair library, built at the costs and charges of Walter Sherington, chancellor of the duchy of Lan-caster, in the reign of Henry VI., which hath been well furnished with fair written books in vellum, but few of them now do remain there.[18]

---

17. This *danse macabre* also ends with the image of the "acteur."

18. John Stow, *A Survey of London, Written in the Year 1598*, ed. William J. Thomas (London: Whitaker and Co., 1842), 122. Walter Sherrington was the prebendary from 1440–49 (Barron and Rousseau, 42); "by 1500 St Paul's had an impressive collection of books and an exceptionally well-ordered archive" (Barron and Rousseau, 42).

Fig. 14. Guyot Marchant, *The Dance of Death* (Latin text), woodcut edition (1490). The "Acteur." Photograph: Rosenwald Collection, Rare Book and Special Collections Division of the Library of Congress, Washington, DC.

A Londoner's reporting of this information, subsequent to the churchyard's destruction, suggests awareness, originating in the fifteenth century and potent enough to last beyond it, of a configuration that sets a textual repository atop a dance-based art installation. Situated within this informational complex, the inscribed *danse macabre* poem reflects a more multivalent contribution than that of a decorative frieze. Rather, the "metres" and "poesy" of the *danse macabre* text occupy an apprehensional space that includes the library structure.[19] Both the architectural space of the library and the illustrative frame of the woodcuts' initial page prevent the *danse macabre*'s inscriptional accompaniments from presenting themselves as a medium visual but not textual. These different frames draw attention to legibility and acts of reading.

This account renders chapter 2's model of ductile experience relevant to the premodern encounter with multimedia *danse macabre*. That chapter draws upon Paul Crossley's reading of *ductus*, which construes medieval agents as being led through various media programs at once in certain built environments: seeing iconography and architecture, for instance, while hearing liturgical language. While other critics tend to see the resulting mental process as analogical—medieval viewers, that is, might compare the structures of different media they encounter—I posit a different possibility. I propose that settings containing diverse media bring diverse perceptual habits to bear on the interpretive process, and specifically, that the habits of visual encounter can play a role in the audience's response to verbal and textual material. My account of the *danse macabre* churchyard as one that integrates literate encounters, or the consciousness of reading, into other acts of visual perception suggests its potential to produce that kind of ductile experience. Within that frame, we might now seek evidence that these habits of perception affect both writers and readers of *danse macabre* poetry.

THE MIRROR AS VIRTUAL *SURPLUSAGE*

Does Lydgate's poem signal awareness of such a multimedia *ductus*, one where reading is inflected with other kinds of apprehensional work? This question is possible to ask because Lydgate seems to refer to seeing at least one *danse macabre* installation, the Holy Innocents, as part of the process of composing his translation: "the exawmple / which that at Parise / I fownde depicte / ones on a walle."[20] This section will argue that Lydgate uses the motif of the mirror to name the process of apprehending multiple media, as well as the virtual forces this perceptual act produces, as integral

19. In Stow's time *poesy* designated not only poetry but also "a skill to speak and write harmonically." Frank Wigham and Wayne A. Rebhorn, ed., *The Art of English Poesy, by George Puttenham: A Critical Edition* (Ithaca: Cornell University Press, 2007), 154, II.i.53.

20. Except in cases where I transcribe, I will cite Warren and White's *Dance of Death* edition, indicating "E" for Ellesmere and "L" for Lansdowne along with line numbers. E19–20.

to the apprehension of poetic language. While the mirror is a conventional component of this poem, appearing in the French version as well, Lydgate expands upon it in his prologue.[21] Lydgate's mirror motif indicates how the perceptual habits brought into play in the apprehension of a visual, material, performance-based, and virtual installation shape his poetic engagement with language.

Lydgate's A version of the poem opens with a *verba translatoris* section that, on the surface, appears to dissociate the textual component of the *danse macabre* from its visual element, thereby privileging its legible textuality. In general, a translator's explanation might seem to draw attention away from the visual and material component of *danse macabre* in order to emphasize instead its language as the object of translation. The speaker narrates the creation of the poem thus:

> . . . I obeyed / vnto her [the French clerks'] requeste
> Ther of to make /a pleyne translacioun
> In Inglisshe tunge / of entencioun
> That prowde folks which that ben stoute & bolde
> As in a myrrowre / to-forn yn her reason
> Her owgly fyn / may clierli ther be-holde.
>
> By exaumple / that thei yn her ententis
> A-mende her life / in eueri maner age
> The whiche daunce / at seint Innocentis
> Portreied is /with al the surplu[s]age
> To schewe this worlde / is but a pilgrimage
> ʒeuen vn-to vs / owre lyues to correcte
> And to declare / the fyne of owre passage
> Ryght a-noon / my stile I wille directe.

(E27–40)

As indicated above, analyses of Lydgate's work often identify a hierarchy or conflict between verbal and visual possibilities for expression. Appleford reads the *danse macabre* as a poem that ultimately privileges private read-

---

21. Mirrors also figure in carved choir-stall depictions of death (Lemé-Hébuterne, 281–85). Josette A. Wisman discusses the mirror of Guyot Marchant's *danse macabre* as an instrument to resolve contradictions and one that emphasizes present, transitory, material life. "La Symbolique du miroir dans les 'danses macabres' de Guyot Marchant," *Romanische Forschungen* 103.2/3 (1991): 158, 159.

ing, so that the element of spectacle is less instrumental to the reader's understanding than is the text.[22] For this reason, Lydgate's term *surplusage* in the second stanza above can suggest to modern readers the sense of "surplus," "remainder," or "superfluity" as characterizing the visual component. The lines of the *verba translatoris* would thus draw a distinction between the French version—with its paint, sculpture, and architecture—and Lydgate's textual rendering of the poem in English, where the former's visual and material components represent excess or superfluity. Along these lines, Ashby Kinch understands the phrase "al the surplusage" to "sugges[t] that the image stands as a remainder, or even an excess, of the verbal text," a set of medial components that can be left behind without affecting the meaning or efficacy of the poem, even as the poem refers to those conditions of remediation.[23]

The word *surplusage*, however, potentially enables Lydgate to entertain a more complicated relationship between the visual and verbal elements of the installation, one that approximates the Derridean supplementarity to which I refer in chapters 1 and 2. For Lydgate, *surplusage* does not always denote "excess"; its meaning can be more expansive. The *MED* reads the word to signify "embellishments" in the *Fall of Princes* and "trappings" in *Guy of Warwick*: "Lyk a prynce with al the surplusage, They took hym vp and leyd hym in his grave" (l. 549).[24] In this last instance, *surplusage* seems, for Lydgate, to convey something not exactly extraneous, but rather integral while still on a different order from the mundane: the trappings are necessary to indicate princely condition but at the same time occupy a plane distinct from the earthly setting of the gravebound body. In this sense, *surplusage* approximates the work of what I have previously called the supplement: it is ancillary and integral at once. Lydgate's use of *surplusage* might thus indicate a broader action of supplementarity: the production of some other entity in the integrated perceptual practice of art and text and not simply material embellishment itself. Despite his interest elsewhere in ekphrastic description of multimedia spectacles (such as Hector's memorial in the *Troy*

---

22. Appleford, *Learning*, 88–89.

23. Kinch, 204–5.

24. *MED* s.v. *surplusage*. "He be wisdam kauhte the auauntage In his mateeres, with al the surplusage That myhte auaile onto his partie" (*FP* 6.3113). (For Lydgate, *surplus* covers a slightly different spectrum between "excess" and "remainder" or "unused portion"; *surplusage* might thus carry some additional resonances for Lydgate semantically. *MED* s.v. *surplus*.) Lydgate, *Fall of Princes* Book VI, ed. Henry Bergen, 4 vols., EETS e.s. 123 (London: Oxford University Press, 1924–27); *Guy of Warwick*, in *The Minor Poems of John Lydgate*, ed. H. N. MacCracken, vol. 2, EETS 192 (London: Oxford University Press, 1934).

Book), Lydgate does not apply the term *surplusage* to any specific visual or material component of the installation in the *verba translatoris*; perhaps what he detects as *surplusage* is more ineffable than we realize.[25]

Lydgate's opening connects the *surplusage* of the Holy Innocents with the motif of the mirror, which he introduces to explain the *danse macabre*'s function; we might thus investigate the resonances of the mirror to understand *surplusage* in more detail. The *verba translatoris* indicate that the Holy Innocents, with its *surplusage*, portrays a dance that functions as an example by which those viewing it might change their ways. For Lydgate, this exemplary dynamic operates in a "translacioun" into English that is posited as a mirror placed before the minds of the proud, where they might see their dreadful end:

> . . . I obeyed / vnto her [the French clerks'] requeste
> Ther of to make / a pleyne translacioun
> In Inglisshe tunge / of entencioun
> That prowde folks whiche that ben stoute & bolde
> As in a myrrowre / to-forn yn her reasoun
> Her owgly fyn / may clierli ther be-holde.
>
> > (E27–32)

Lydgate repeats the reference to the mirror in the second stanza of the poem proper, where "In this myrrow[r]e" every man may find that it behooves him to participate in this dance (E49–50), a translation of the French original that appears in A and B versions.[26] The source poem thus establishes the mirror motif's connection to the *danse macabre*, but its use in the *verba translatoris* is particular to Lydgate. In one sense, poetic mirrors are unremarkable in their conventionality, from the mirror for princes to Hoccleve's *Series*.[27] In another, however, the mirror denotes for its medieval audiences a realm that is preternatural or ambiguously real. What Donald Maddox calls the literary "specular encounter" involves, for instance, a confrontation with the "mirror of the past," a relationship between the informant

25. John Lydgate, *The Troy Book*, ed. H. Bergen, EETS e.s. 103, 106 (London: Kegan Paul, Trench, Trübner, 1908), 3.5615–73.

26. In Ellesmere, this reference is in the *verba auctoris*, while in Lansdowne, the Angelus speaks it (Warren and White, 6–7).

27. An early printed version of Lydgate's *danse macabre* poem appears following his *Fall of Princes* in Richard Tottel's folio edition (Warren and White, 107).

from an earlier time and the addressee who looks to a utopian future.[28] The "Three Living and Three Dead" is a familiar literary idiom that renders mirroring as supernatural, portraying a gaze between those in this world and those out of it.[29] In evoking the mirror—particularly in a scene of living skeletons—*danse macabre* poetry emphasizes the uncanniness of that reflective device. *Danse macabre* also, however, elaborates further upon the mirror image's impact by setting it in danced motion. The mirror expresses the exemplary function of the installation's *surplusage*, but it also draws out the uncanny and animate forces cast across that multimedia site.

As a motif for a realm of otherness, the mirror can figure literary tropes as well as the reading process itself. Anna Torti categorizes the mirror's function as metaphoric in an array of late-medieval uses, evocative of a "fundamental analogy" whereby "God, mirror of all Creation, creates Man in his image and likeness." As man is like and unlike God, so mirror images elucidate likeness and difference, real and ideal.[30] In this reading, the mirror is a metaphor for genre or mode, such as allegory. It also figures specific tropes like chiasmus and even the literary text itself.[31] In the *danse macabre* and the "Three Living and Three Dead" tradition, the mirror is related not only to textuality but also to reading practice.[32] Susanna Fein's interpretation of Oxford, Bodleian Library MS Douce 302's "Three Living and Three Dead" text builds on Paul Binski's analysis of this tradition in its textual manifestation; both see the mirror image therein as "ternary." For Binski, this term suggests the presence of a "third-party viewer" rather than simply the duality of two reflected images. For Fein, the mirror image in the "Three Living and Three Dead" reveals that to the medieval audience, "reading can be like viewing oneself in a mirror," not metaphorically but as "descriptive of actual experience."[33] Lydgate's lines above produce a related dynamic. In this account, his readers exist as one perceptual point; his literary depiction of the dancers occupies another position and fulfills a function analogous to the presence and activity of a physical mirror; and the interior zone of

28. Donald Maddox, *Fictions of Identity in Medieval France* (Cambridge: Cambridge University Press, 2004), 191.

29. Susanna Greer Fein, "Life and Death, Reader and Page: Mirrors of Mortality in English Manuscripts," *Mosaic* 35.1 (2002): 69–71.

30. Anna Torti, *The Glass of Form: Mirroring Structures from Chaucer to Skelton* (Cambridge: D. S. Brewer, 1991), 1, 23.

31. Ibid., 2–3, 29.

32. For a survey of this tradition, including John Audelay's interpretation of it, as well as its relationship to *danse macabre*, see Kinch, 109–181.

33. Fein, "Life," 71, 91. Binski, 138.

readers' minds—their "reasoun"—becomes the reflective (so to speak) other space, separate from material reality, that accommodates the recognition of the image as well as the changes that come about in response to the readerly encounter with the characters depicted.

Like Susanna Fein's argument, which explores verbal and visual relations, readings of the mirror in *danse macabre* also address the mirror's role in the medial networks surrounding the textual encounter. When David A. Fein suggests that Guyot Marchant's French *danse macabre* speaks to a mirroring relation of image and text, he gestures explicitly to a multimedia dynamic.[34] He sees the interactions of word and image in *danse macabre* as complex and even "contrapuntal" in their mirroring.[35] Furthermore, ekphrastic traditions enhance the language for the way the mirror arbitrates among media. Bissera V. Pentcheva examines mirroring motifs in early medieval ekphrastic writing and the architectural and other material spaces with which these resonate. Of Prudentius's poetic commentary on the baptistery of St. Peter's, she notes: "The poem builds an image of fusion where the surface of water takes on the glitter of the gold mosaic above." In this representation, the mirror brings about "a fusion and transformation of matter."[36] Thus, even as the mirror elucidates certain mechanics of reading practice, it also enables negotiation among other media to the point of their transformative interaction.

Lydgate's mirror expresses the virtual motion discernible in the *danse macabre* installation's multimedia *ductus*. When Lydgate says that he translates the poem so that readers might see their end as in a mirror held up before their minds, he refers to a structure of some spatial convolution. The phrase's prepositional use intimates this complexity: "As in a myrrowre / toforn yn her reasoun / Her owgly fine / may clierli ther be-holde" (E30–31). Through the clustering of *in, before, in,* the image of the mirror becomes at once an entity externally apprehensible to readers and at the same time something interior to them, located in their "reasoun." Lydgate's phrasing

---

34. David A. Fein, "Guyot Marchant's *Danse macabre*: The Relationship between Image and Text," *Mirator Elokuu* (2000): 7, 10. Elsewhere, Fein develops the mirror metaphor, recognizing "the reflection of the conflict between the two modes of discourse present in the book—one associated with the Church, incarnated in the figure of the *Acteur*, the other associated with the theater, incarnated in the corpse figures, which appear in various ludic poses." Fein, *Danse*, 14.

35. Fein, "Guyot," 7.

36. Bissera V. Pentcheva, "The Power of Glittering Materiality: Mirror Reflections between Poetry and Architecture in Greek and Arabic Medieval Culture," in *Istanbul and Water*, ed. Paul Magdalino and Nina Ergin (Bristol, CT: Peeters, 2015), 253–54.

recalls Foucault's account of the movement through the mirror space as real and unreal: "From this gaze which in a sense heads toward me, from the ground of that virtual space which is on the other side of the mirror, I return to me. . . ."[37] By setting in motion these forces that intend and suspend between the real and the unreal, the body and the image, Lydgate's mirror evokes the dynamic of interstitial virtual motion we have discerned across the *danse macabre* site. Furthermore, in this passage, Lydgate calls upon light as the means to produce that virtual motion. Modifying the act of looking with "clierli," Lydgate involves the element of light: while he ostensibly uses this word to mean "keenly" or "readily visible," the lexeme is also frequently attested throughout the Middle Ages to refer to light and brightness (*MED* s.v. *cler* 1a, 1b). Light, chapter 3 suggested, is central to the *danse macabre*'s ductile experience, enabling and intensifying the virtual forces cast among the installation's different media by means of its own motion. Lydgate's language in his presentation of the mirror image thus expresses the perception of ambiguously real motion across media, the forces of virtual *surplusage*.

Lydgate's presentation of the mirror performs a further function as well: it communicates the act of reading his text in terms of the *surplusage* of virtual motion. In using the word *reasoun* in the mirror passage, Lydgate specifies how the perceptual work forged in the installation's multimedia context shapes the encounter with language. *Reasoun*, as it functions in his passage, is a space that originates from the body but also seems to exist on some other plane that is both apprehensible and unreal: the space that, in Foucault's terms, accommodates the motion of virtual force in the encounter with the mirror. In this capacity, *reasoun* would seem to encompass "mind," or "intellectual faculty" (*MED* s.v. *resoun* 1a). But *reasoun* also means "inscribed verse" (*MED* s.v. *resoun* 9a; attested in the *Fall of Princes*), in particular language of a proverbial character (9a). This latter definition would not easily make literal sense of the sentence. It is, however, relevant to the text at hand, for the *danse macabre* poem is reliably proverbial, closing many of its stanzas, as Lydgate takes care to preserve from the French, with such aphoristic utterances.[38] In the phrase "to-forn yn her reasoun," *reasoun* calls forth a perceptual practice for the visualized, virtual space of the mind but also sets within that space the proverbial dialogues that equally pertain to the readers. Paul Zumthor ascribes to the medieval proverb a unique signaling force as text, manipulating tense and

37. See chapter 1.
38. See note 83 below.

syntax to universalize its recognition.[39] To confront the space of *reasoun* into which the mirror image is cast is thus to adopt a perceptual mode by which to confront the textuality of *danse macabre* at its most intense or concentrated.[40] *Reasoun* locates a specific point at which a perceptual practice born of the site's multimediacy and virtuality contacts its language.

Lydgate's opening image indicates his sense of a spectating mode that informs the apprehension of the text. His figure of the mirror, and the reflective spaces it generates, names the *danse macabre*'s apprehensional experience and the ways that the text participates in and is conditioned by the perception of the virtual supplement. As his text makes plain, he does not simply indicate his awareness of the installation by describing its features. In fact, at an explicit level, the visual component as a purely material *surplusage* is potentially vexed in status for him. But the language of the opening, which details the reader's encounter with his text, encompasses Lydgate's deeper and more subtle response. Lydgate's imagery acknowledges that textual encounter occurs in terms of a ductile experience in a multimedia and virtually kinetic setting.

EXPERIENCING UNTIMELINESS

In the reading above, the mirror identifies Lydgate's sensitivity to the perceptual habits *danse macabre* fosters. In what follows, I shall turn to the experience of the *danse macabre* poem's reader and audience. This shift between Lydgate and his readers intends ultimately to reenact the experience of poetic form as a collaboration between the artist's work and the audience's perception, a collaboration that characterizes the ductile process. The present section will suggest that the perception of multimedia *danse macabre*'s temporal disorientation dictates readers' interventions into the poem and that this dynamic becomes visible to us in the poem's complex network of versions. Modern readers are usually alerted to the high level of variance in the *danse macabre* poem through its changes in character order as well as omissions from and additions to the list of personages. But a look at changes on a smaller scale reveals a different sensitivity at work, one that reacts specifically to a problematic sense of time. This readerly experience

39. Paul Zumthor, *Essai de poétique médiévale* (Paris: Éditions du seuil, 1972), 78.

40. David Fein identifies a mirroring effect in the French text's language: two instances of the same rhyming word (such as *mainne* [lead] in the Pope's stanza) create distorted reflections of each other. "Text and Image Mirror Play in Guyot Marchant's 1485 *Danse Macabre*," *Neophilologus* 98 (2014): 228–29. Lydgate does not reproduce this technique throughout, though he does include *lede* in this stanza.

of the poem, to which the manuscripts' variation testifies, emerges from the habits of perception that the visual installation establishes.

Lydgate's *danse macabre* poem invites us to reenact medieval reading experience by explicitly asking its readers to intervene in its content. One such call appears at the end of the poem's A version in the form of an "envoye de translatoure" that Lydgate appends to the French original:

> O ȝe my lordes / and maistres al in fere
> Of a-venture / that shal this daunce [r]ede
> Loweli I preye / with al myn herte entere
> To correcte / where as ȝe see nede. . . .
>
> (E657–60)

Pearsall speculates that the network of this text's revisions was so complicated that "[i]t would be difficult . . . to talk about stages in a process of revision." James Simpson makes the more extreme case that Lydgate himself is merely "a point across which this poem traverses in its path from Paris to London."[41] If the existence of the two manuscript groups indicates revisions made in response to John Carpenter's 1430 request to inscribe the walls with the poem, then others besides Lydgate, Pearsall notes, might have contributed to the poem.[42] The manuscripts' copious instances of change, both across groups and within a particular group, offer some patterns by which to discern readerly responses, confusions, and objections. As Daniel Wakelin argues, scribal and readerly correction "witne[ss] processes of thinking consciously about language and texts."[43] Wakelin's study makes a case for deliberate acts of intervention reflected in scribal practices, whereas the scribal work that this chapter will discuss indicates what is perhaps a less fully self-aware response to an effect born in the application of spectacle-based perception to text. But the two claims share a basis in locating cognitive processes within manuscript copying practices and recognizing that the presence of such changes might indicate the apprehensional experiences of medieval audiences.

To reenact such experience, I employ two manuscripts from what Warren identifies as the "B" group of witnesses, London, British Library MS

---

41. Simpson, *Reform and Cultural Revolution*, 59.

42. Pearsall, "Signs," 62–63. See also E. P. Hammond, "The Texts of Lydgate's *Danse Macabre*," *MLN* 36 (1921): 250.

43. Daniel Wakelin, *Scribal Correction and Literary Craft: English Manuscripts 1375–1510* (Cambridge: Cambridge University Press, 2014), 4.

Lansdowne 699 (fifteenth century) and London, British Library MS Cotton Vespasian A.XXV (sixteenth century).[44] Their differences would be attributable not to significantly divergent manuscript traditions (as would be the case in examining an A group manuscript against a B group one) but rather to more subtle acts of adjustment reflecting reactions to the poem's iterations within a group. Lansdowne 699 also offers a useful comparison to Cotton Vespasian A.XXV as the former seems in Warren's estimation to be the most stable and comprehensive of the B versions, standing as the exemplary B version in her edition.[45] Cotton Vespasian A.XXV, meanwhile, is a much-corrected and incomplete text whose features make visible a negotiation between poetry as written on the page and as inscribed on a wall. Because the variants in both manuscript families are so complicated, it would probably not be judicious simply to treat Cotton Vespasian A.XXV as representative of the genre of wall-copy (figure 15), and Lansdowne 699 as representative of book-copy (figure 16). But for the purposes of creating a method and setting up a series of readings, it seems legitimate to consider Cotton Vespasian A.XXV and Lansdowne 699 as indicative of certain traits that might unfold from a wall- or book-based situation, respectively.

Cotton Vespasian A.XXV numbers among the copies of this poem that refer to the *danse macabre* as a visual installation, but it differs in appearance from those other copies. Explicitly signaling its relationship to the installation tradition, Cotton Vespasian A.XXV's initial folio for the *danse macabre* begins: "An history and daunce of deathe of all estatte and degres writen in the cappell of Wortley of Wortley Hall." Vespasian is not the only version to refer to an installation; Oxford, Bodleian Library MS Bodley 686 and Oxford, Corpus Christi College MS 237, for example, title themselves "The Daunce of Poules," alluding to the Pardon Churchyard; Cambridge, Trinity College MS R.3.21 refers to this title and additionally contains an explanatory note concerning the translation as well as the fact that the poem has been painted at the Pardon Churchyard cloister.[46] Cotton Vespasian

---

44. Lansdowne 699 contains works mostly by Lydgate, while Cotton Vespasian A.XXV contains works from various sources, including some carol texts, a *Rule of St. Benedict*, a ballad, and a hymn by Richard de Caistre. On the manuscript's recusant character, see Arthur F. Marotti, *Manuscript, Print, and the English Renaissance Lyric* (Ithaca: Cornell University Press, 1995), 44; and Peter J. Seng, ed., *Tudor Songs and Ballads from MS Cotton Vespasian A-25* (Cambridge, MA: Harvard University Press, 1978), xiv and *passim*.

45. Warren and White, xxviii.

46. Warren and White xxvi–xxvii. Trinity College R.3.21 was produced by well-known scribes: the "Trinity Anthologies Scribe" working with the "Hammond Scribe." See Margaret Connolly, "Mapping Manuscripts and Readers of *Contemplations of the Dread and Love of God*," in *Design and Distribution of Late Medieval Manuscripts in England*, ed. Margaret Con-

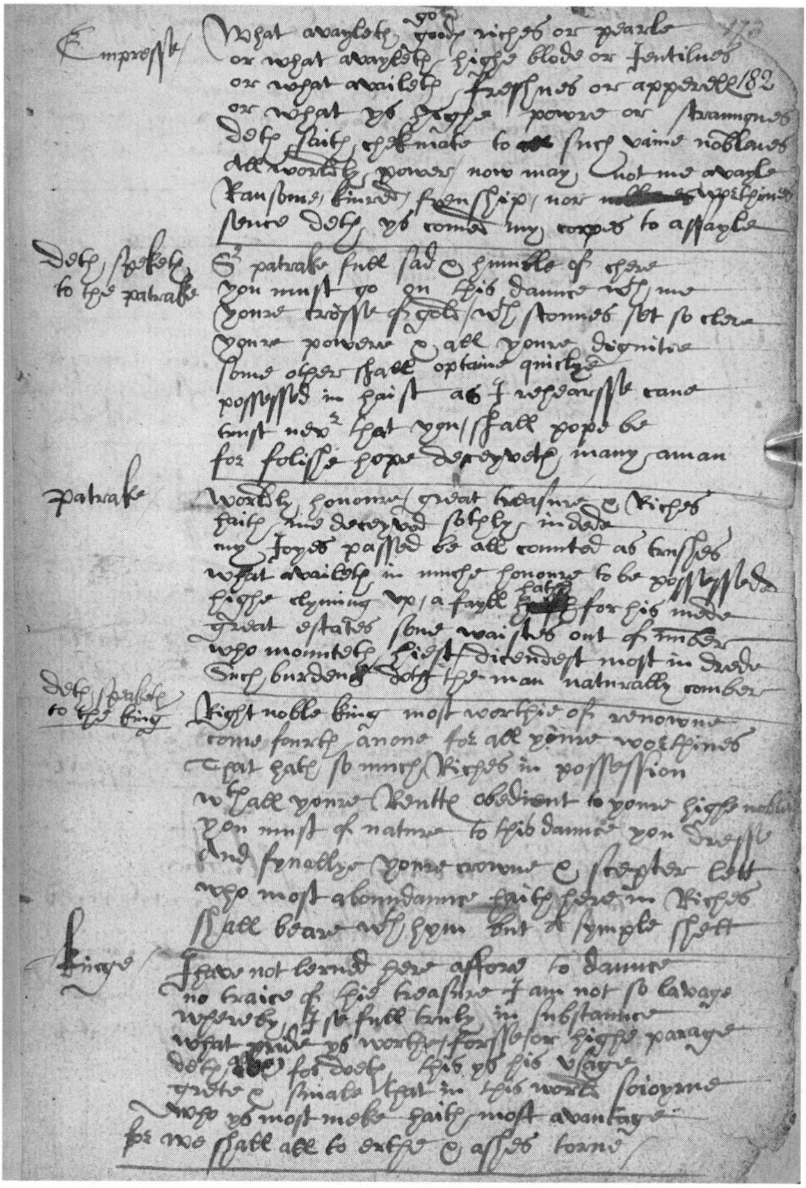

Fig. 15. British Library MS Cotton Vespasian A.XXV, f. 172r (sixteenth century).
Credit: © The British Library Board.

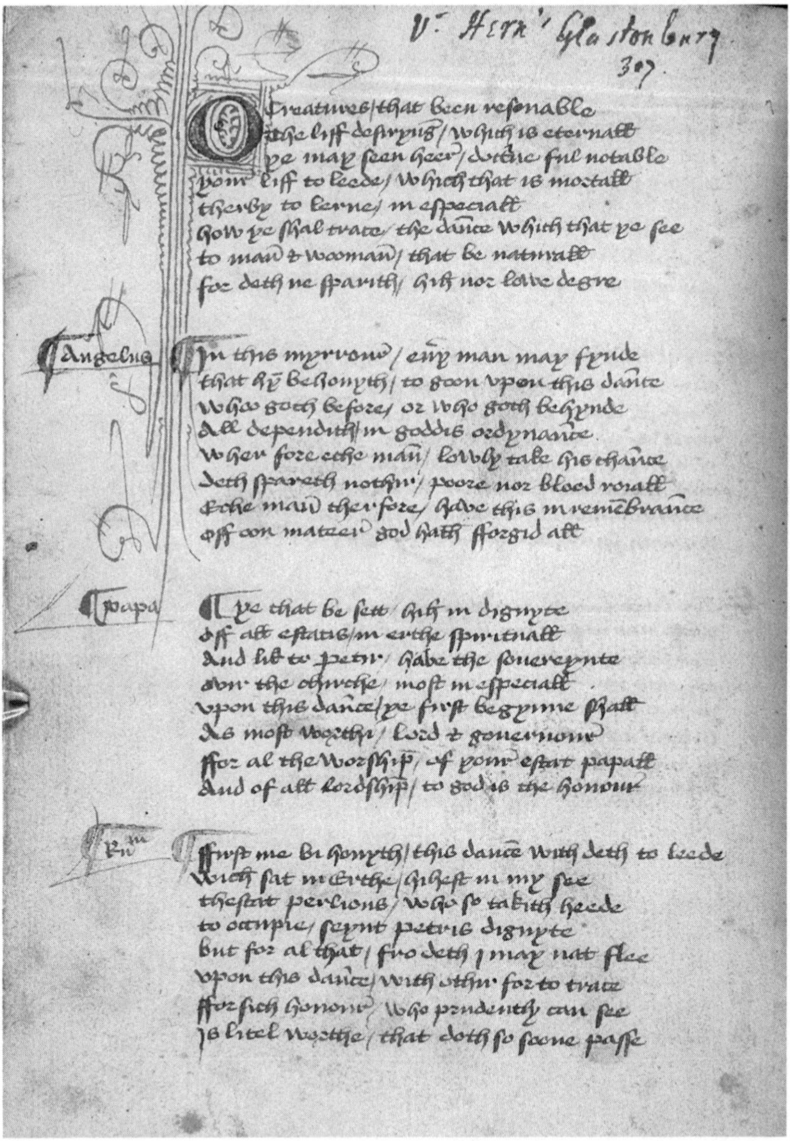

O Creatures / that been resonable
The liff desiryng / which is eternall
Ye may seen heer / doctrine ful notable
Your liff to leede / which that is mortall
Therby to lerne / in especiall
How ye shal trace / the daunce which that ye see
To man & woman / that be naturall
For deth ne sparith / high nor lowe degre

Auctor

In this myrrour / eury man may fynde
That hym behovyth / to goon vpon this daunce
Who goth before / or who goth behynde
All dependith / in goddis ordynaunce
Wherfore eche man / lowly take his chaunce
Deth sparith nothyng / poore nor blood roiall
Eche man therfore / have this in remembraunce
Off oon matere / god hath fforgid all

Papa

Ye that be sett / high in dignyte
Off all estatis / in erthe spirituall
And lik to petir / have the souereynte
Don the otheresse / most in especiall
Vpon this daunce / ye first begynne shall
As most worthi / lord & gouernour
Ffor al the worship / of your estat papall
And of all lordship / to god is the honour

Rex

Ffyrst me bihovyth / this daunce with deth to leede
Which sat in erthe / chiefest in my see
The stat perilous / who so takith heede
To ocupie / seynt petris dignyte
But for al that / fro deth I may natt flee
Vpon this daunce / with other for to trace
Ffor siche honour / who prudently can see
Is litel worthe / that doth so soone passe

Fig. 16. British Library MS Lansdowne 699, f. 41v (second half of the fifteenth century).
Credit: © The British Library Board.

A.XXV's intriguing instability, however, seems, in a manner unlike the others, to make apparent its relationship to some species of encounter with an installation. This is a difficult manuscript; as Peter Seng notes, in the section containing the *danse macabre* "it is impossible to be certain about anything regarding the physical construction."[47] There are different hands, pens, and types of paper. The *danse macabre* stanzas, themselves an interpolation, are out of order and incomplete.

One way to narrate Cotton Vespasian A.XXV's aspect would be as conjuring a particular kind of reading scene, where a spectator negotiates between confronting the manifestation on the wall and performing the task of recording it on a page. Appleford speculates that Cotton Vespsian A.XXV directly transcribes a wall painting.[48] When other manuscripts title the poem "The Daunce of Poulys," they refer to the Pardon Churchyard but do not seem to suggest, as does Cotton Vespasian A.XXV's opening inscription, an act of direct copying. Whereas "The Daunce of Poulys" simply conscripts St. Paul's into the formation of a title, the Vespasian annotation appears to convey a more specific relation between the scribe's encounter with the wall installation and the production of the manuscript copy. Cotton Vespasian A.XXV seems further to indicate that this apprehensional act might not have occurred in a straight line. Its strikethroughs, corrections, changes in stanzaic order, and lacunae might indicate that if the poem was translated from one medium to another during, or as a result of, an act of perambulating through the installation, this tour would entail the retrospection, retrograde motion, reconsideration, and correction that we could envision in such an ambulatory encounter, one that doubles back or even returns later. The manuscript plots a contingent, recursive, nonlinear experience, which we have seen the *ductus* of *danse macabre* to engender.

Cotton Vespasian A.XXV's Sergeant of the Law suggests that the experience of the installation shapes the reader's interaction with the poetic text. The Sergeant of the Law's stanza is bordered by images of daggers (figure 17). These images are distinctive in the section of the manuscript containing

---

nolly and Linne R. Mooney (Woodbridge: Boydell and York Medieval Press, 2008), 268. This manuscript specifies that these were "words paynted in the cloystar." See Sponsler, "Text," 28. Another annotation before the rubricated opening of the poem on f. 278v also indicates that the *danse macabre* was "depeyntyd" at the Holy Innocents (http://trin-sites-pub.trin.cam.ac.uk /manuscripts/R_3_21/manuscript.php?fullpage=1&startingpage=1).

47. Seng, xvi.
48. *Learning*, 90.

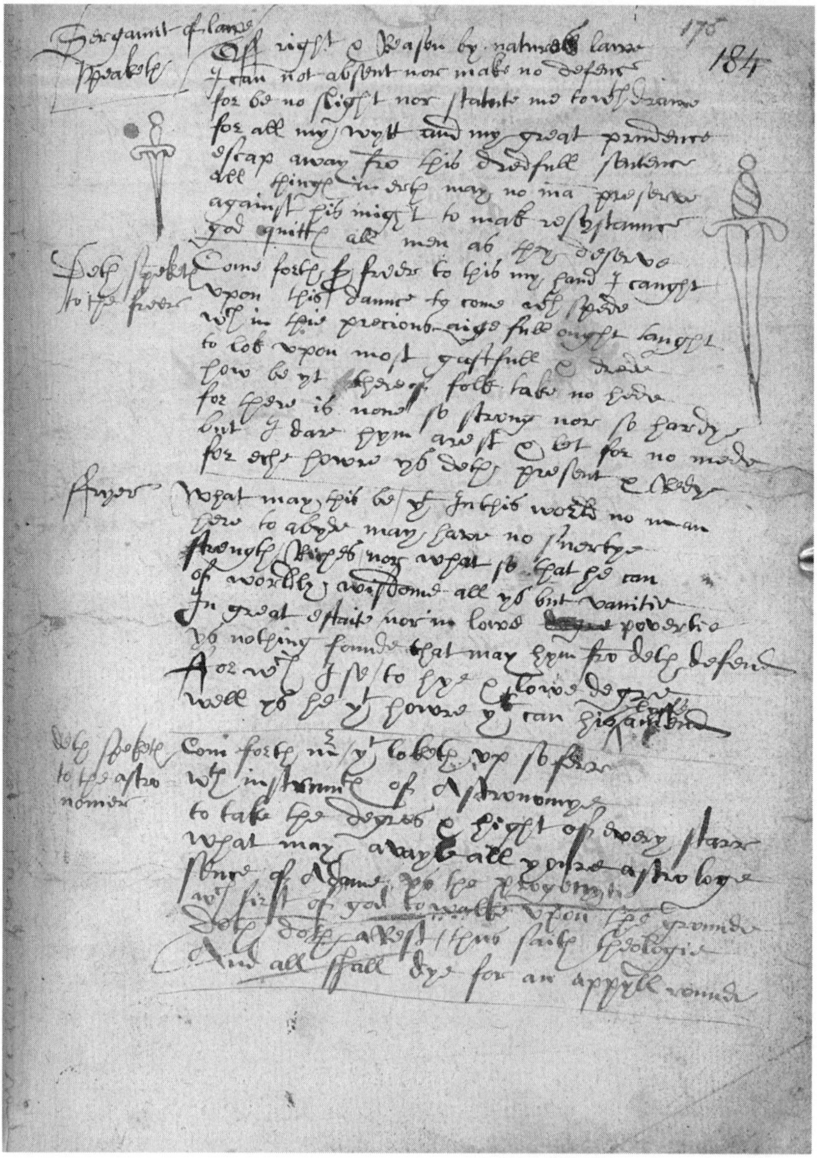

the *danse macabre*.[49] Whoever made these early doodles (in a different ink) could be intimating their readerly relationship to the *danse macabre* as a visual object, an awareness communicated as marginalia that reflect accoutrements associable with the paintings.[50] Such a reader brings not only specific visual images but also, potentially, a set of visually-based perceptual habits to bear upon the textual encounter. We might detect these perceptual habits in the daggers' verticality, which becomes notable specifically in light of chapter 3's discussion of horizontal and vertical play in the installation. The daggers' perpendicularity to the poetic lines hints at the play of directional force we observed in the *danse macabre* as multimedia installation.

Within this general framework appears a more specific possibility: the *danse macabre*'s tendency to cross and multiply perceptual vectors dictates not only the interaction of text and visual medium but also the interaction among textual versions. In this way, what begins as a perceptual practice associated with the installation emerges as a shaping force for textual response. This possibility reveals itself in a confusion surrounding the Sergeant of the Law. Other versions of this poem contain not only a Sergeant of the Law but also a Sergeant. The latter speaks of his policing role, while the former is a barrister.[51] The Sergeant is missing from the Wortley Hall copy, but does this copy indicate an encounter that recognizes a trace of that Sergeant? The language of each character's stanzas is, at certain points, reminiscent of the other's. Where Death says to the Sergeant: "Make no deffence / nor no rebellion" (L402), Vespasian's Sergeant of the Law says, "I can not absent nor make no defence" (other B versions also use the word "defense"). Vespasian's Sergeant of the Law is also a point at which the folio ordering of Cotton Vespasian A.XXV problematizes the ordering of the poem, separating the Sergeant of the Law's two dialogue stanzas. The image above, at f. 175r, shows the lawyer's response to Death, but Death's initiating stanza

49. There are two manicules at f. 172v. Seng delineates the section as ff. 127–79, containing the recusant carols, ballads, and other lyrics (xvi–xvii). Either the daggers were introduced before the *danse macabre* was interpolated, or a reader of the section included such marginalia only here.

50. The ink used to draw the daggers differs from that of the text, and this whole leaf shows a different ink and pen from the rest of the poem. (E-mail conversation with Megan Cook, June 2017.)

51. The *MED* records multiple examples of this designation as referring, in the late Middle Ages, to the occupations of "barrister" (s.v. *sergeaunt* 4) and "soldier" or armed officer, sometimes bearing a mace (s.v. *sergeaunt* 2). The phrase "sergeant-at-law" to refer to an attorney is attested through the nineteenth century, according to the *OED*. Sponsler and Appleford understand the presence of the Sergeant of the Law in the B versions to reflect an impulse to foreground certain civic dynamics of London. Sponsler, *Queen's*, 77, and Appleford, *Learning*, 90.

appears at f. 177v, on a damaged page where it is the only complete stanza.[52] On the recto of this folio appear the stanzas for the Chartreux; while in B texts this character precedes the Sergeant of the Law, in A texts he precedes the Sergeant.[53] In this space of disordering, however it might have been created in the manuscript, it is possible that the Sergeant exists as a virtual supplement to what is present in the text. The daggers' placement seems specific to the stanza on the Sergeant of the Law, but they would be more relevant to the missing Sergeant. In addition to carrying a "stately mace," the Sergeant also conveys a beefy belligerence in his stanzas ("How darst thou dethe / set on me arreste?" [L409]). The Sergeant of Law, in contrast, bookishly alludes to his training in specialized discourse ("For be no slight nor statute me to with drawe" [Vespasian 347]), and Death refers to his "subtill wyttines" (Vespasian 341) rather than any physical weaponry. Perhaps the casual encounter with the word "sergeant" prompted these drawings. But "Sergeant of the Law" was still a familiar term in this period; perhaps some other set of associations is being traced here. Do the daggers signal the apprehension of a virtual Sergeant in the recollection of some other textual manifestation? Megan Cook speculates that this scribe's correctional practices might indicate his access to other versions of the poem.[54] In considering the encounter with this text as conditioned by the installation's virtualities and multimediacies, we might specify the nature of such interaction between a reader and a possible multiplicity of texts. Through its very difficulty, that is, the Wortley Hall copy tenders a reader who engages a textual network by means of a perceptual sensitivity to the crossing of actual and virtual elements in the visual tradition.

In these negotiations, readers experience the time of the text differently depending upon its medial setting. Our manuscripts suggest these differing experiences because certain episodes from Cotton Vespasian A.XXV appear in the present, while Lansdowne 699 (the copy that seems more indicative of a book-based encounter) narrates those corresponding moments in the past tense. In Lansdowne 699, Death refers to the king as someone who "somtyme had so gret possession":

---

52. The single stanza on f. 177v is followed by an underline and then additional text, including the phrase "The rest you shall fynde before the beginning of this daunce of dethe."

53. The torn folio onto which text was copied in Cotton Vespasian A.XXV indicates that the Chartreux directly precedes the first stanza of the Sergeant of the Law dialogue. Lansdowne 699, f. 46v (B) shows Chartreux/Sergeant in Law, and British Library MS Harley 116, ff. 135r–135v (A) shows Monk of the Charterhouse [Chartreux]/Sergeant.

54. E-mail conversation with Megan Cook, June 2017.

Right noble king / most worthi of renon
Cum forth anon / for al your worthynesse
That somtyme had / so gret possession
Remys obeyng / vn to youre hih noblesse
Ye most of nature / to this daunce yow dresse
And fynally your crounne / & sceptre leete
For who so most / haboundith in gret rychesse
Shal bere with hym / but a sengle sheete.[55]

In Cotton Vespasian A.XXV, however, the king "hath so much riches in possession" (figure 15):

Right noble king most worthie of renoune
Come fourthe anone for all youre worthines
That hath so much Riches in possession
With all youre Renttes obedient to your highe noblesse
You must of nature to this daunce you dresse
And fynally youre crowne & scepter lett
Who most aboundance haith here in Riches
Shal beare with hym but a symple shett.

Cotton Vespasian A.XXV appears to be the only B group version that changes the verb tense here. Lansdowne 699's pastness asserts itself not only in its verb but also in the distancing adverb "somtyme," which appears as "whilom" in other B group versions; there is no corresponding adverb in Cotton Vespasian A.XXV. We might suppose that this difference in tense reflects the distinct natures of these two medial experiences, although the Guild Chapel's wall version—a B stanza—also sets this statement in the past.[56] Perhaps a distinctive temporal complexity is made manifest in Cotton Vespasian A.XXV: the act of spectating an image of the king painted on the wall either is integrated into reading (or listening to) the words of Death's statement to this character or is integrated into the copying of the text onto paper. Death thus refers to riches evident in the visual image at which an audience or copyist gazes in that present moment. In Lansdowne 699, meanwhile, the unillustrated book medium casts the utterance's location

---

55. The following transcriptions combine Warren and White's readings (15, 17, 19) with mine. Megan Cook and Elizaveta Strakhov are, at this writing, preparing a new edition of the dance of death poem for TEAMS that will include manuscripts not covered in Warren and White.
56. Davidson, 52.

into a narrative past. Unconfronted by the image of the rich king, the reader experiences narrative time expanding in the reading process. In this temporal structure, Death conjures a past of riches. In other settings as well, adjustments to the grammar and syntax of Lydgatean text potentially reflect a response to architectural, rather than book-based, setting. Matthew Evan Davis makes this case about the *Testament* at Long Melford, which substitutes "we" for "I" to acknowledge the communal and public dynamic of the Clopton chapel.[57] In the case of Cotton Vespasian A.XXV, tense difference correspondingly indicates a reader's response to, and participation in, that text's medial environment.

This difference poses more questions than it answers. As intimated above: Does the wall copy at Wortley Hall Chapel itself reflect these present-tense constructions, having edited these from whatever text was used as the basis to produce this installation? Did the scribe of the Cotton Vespasian A.XXV *danse macabre* introduce these changes himself, perhaps semi-consciously reflecting a sense of presence in the encounter with the installation? More broadly, at what point on the complex chain linking copies did this tense adjustment occur? While these questions may not be answerable, the fact of the tense difference allows us to reenact an experiential component at work in the reception of this poem, a reaction to the different temporalities that different media stipulate in the process of apprehending the text.

In the multimedia installation, temporal ambiguity exists not exclusively in the difference between one medium's time and another; rather, their interactions multiply those instabilities of time. The manuscripts seem to express not just temporal difference itself but also disorientation around those differences, suggesting again a perceptual experience inflected by the installation. Death's dialogue with the Prince illustrates this point. In the Prince's speech, Lansdowne 699's "My purpos *was* [emphasis mine] & myn entention" becomes "My purposse & myn intention / *Ys* [emphasis mine] . . ." in Cotton Vespasian A.XXV. Cotton Vespasian A.XXV appears to be the only B-group manuscript to make this change. As in the case of the rich king, the character's speech reflects through tense the immediate nature of visual encounter with him.[58] In Lansdowne 699, the Prince's lan-

57. Matthew Evan Davis, "Lydgate at Long Melford: Reassessing the *Testament* and 'Quis Dabit Meo Capiti Fontem Lacrimarum' in their Local Context," *Journal of Medieval Religious Cultures* 43.1 (2017): 85–86.

58. Other examples of parallel tense shift occur as well. Compare Lansdowne "my thank also devised" (171) to Vespasian "my thanke ys ey devised" (171) [tense change in Vespasian only]. And compare Lansdowne "Com forth sir Mayr / which had gou*er*nance / Bi pollicie to rewle this cite" to Vespasian "Com forth sir Mayr /w*h*ich have gouernance / We purposse now to rule this

guage offers a narratively created past housing his purpose, while the Wortley Hall text contains a declaration coinciding with the time and space of a
visual encounter with him. But a more complicated wrinkle in time occurs
in Death's address to the Prince. Lansdowne 699's Death asks, concerning
Charlemagne and Arthur, "What did ther platis / ther armor or their maile /
Ther strong corage / there sheelds defensable / ageyns deth / whan he hem
dide assaile."

> Right myhty prynce / be rith well certeyn
> This daunce to yow / is mysschevable
> For more myhty / than euer was Carlemayn
> Or worthy Arhtour / of prowes ful notable
> With al his knyhtes / at the rounde table
> What did ther platis / ther armor or their maile
> Ther strong corage / ther sheelds defensable
> Ageyns deth / whan he hem dide assaile.

In Cotton Vespasian A.XXV, however, Death asks of Arthur's knights:
"what *might* there plate . . . when deth *ys comed* his corpes to assaile
[emphases mine]." Cotton Vespasian A.XXV's question superficially parallels
Lansdowne 699's, given that indicative *may* can conjugate as *might* in the
past tense and that the use of *is* as an auxiliary verb can simply place the
main verb *to come* in the past tense as well: *What were those implements
able to do when death came?* And yet Cotton Vespasian A.XXV's is a somewhat oddly phrased query, one more straightforwardly expressed in other
versions. Oxford, Bodleian Library MS Bodley 686, another B copy, shifts
the question into a hypothetical present, asking what good are the implements when death "doth hem assaile."[59] The fact that the tense construction changes in another version reinforces the sense that the phrase presents
some temporal indeterminacy to its readers. That its migration across versions blurs this question's tense seems to indicate the text's conjuration
of a temporal situation more equivocating than simply a distinction between past and present. The temporal ambiguity in the Wortley Hall copy

---

cyte" (257–58) [tense change in Vespasian only]. Compare, in the Mayor's response, Lansdowne's
"thestat in which I stood" to Vespasian's "the staite that y in stande" (265) [present tense appears
also in Corpus Christi]. Compare Lansdowne "Lat see your hand / sir chanon Regular / Som-tyme
[y]sworn / to religion" to Vespasian "Lat see . . . While I am shorne into religion" (273–74) [tense
change in Vespasian only; change between *shorn* and *sworn* appears in other manuscripts].

59. Warren and White, 17.

could be understood as a readerly encounter constituted in the perceptual experience of ambiguous and even disorienting time that we saw at work in the installation.

To elaborate on the indeterminacy of this temporal situation, we must first consider a more material indeterminacy for us as modern readers: that of Wortley Chapel's whereabouts. The Wortley Hall named before the poem's opening has often been assigned a location in Gloucestershire.[60] Early criticism of the poem tends not to explain this association. It is, however, the case that in this section of the manuscript, both the *danse macabre* poem and a sermon are early interpolations, and the sermon is inscribed as originating "at glocetere 1558."[61] It might also be possible to attribute a Cotswolds location to certain dialect features of the *danse macabre* poem. The manuscript's frequent use of an "ai" spelling where other dialects use "a," for example, is recorded as characteristic of the Cotswolds, and the conjugation "comed," although not as a past participle, also appears in colloquial speech in that region.[62]

A closer examination, however, suggests that the *danse macabre* might be identified with much of the rest of the manuscript's northern location. The manuscript's opening inscription "Henry Sauill" ties it to Yorkshire.[63] LALME lists folios preceding the *danse macabre*'s section (the *Rule of St. Benedict*, ff. 66r–124v) as exemplifying a fifteenth-century West Yorkshire dialect. In addition, Seng associates this late manuscript's Catholic character with a distinctive recusant culture in northern England.[64] In terms of the *danse macabre* itself, while both it and the sermon located at "glocetere" are interpolated, the sermon seems to be a different hand

60. In the mid-nineteenth century, a death figure is mentioned in relation to a no-longer extant Wortley Hall in Gloucestershire; see "The Dance of Death," *St. James Magazine* 14 (1865): 440. County records for Gloucestershire mention a Wortley chapel, "repaired in 1506," but not the mural. See Thomas Dudley Fosbrooke, ed., *Abstracts of Records and Manuscripts Respecting the County of Gloucestershire*, vol. 1 (Gloucester: Jos. Harris, 1807), 479. Subsequent studies of the *danse macabre* allude again to the Gloucester location. See, for instance, Douce, 53; Charles Isaac Elton, *William Shakespeare: His Family and Friends*, ed. Hamilton Thompson (London: John Murray, 1904), 88; and John Aberth, *From the Brink of the Apocalypse: Confronting Famine, War, Plague, and Death in the Later Middle Ages*, 2nd ed. (New York: Routledge, 2010), 235.

61. Seng, xvi–xvii.

62. On the "ai" spelling, see Richard Webster Huntley, *A Glossary of the Cotswold (Gloucestershire) Dialect* (London: John Russell Smith, 1868), 5. On "comed" as a past tense conjugation, see J. Drummond Robertson, *A Glossary of Dialect & Archaic Words Used in the County of Gloucester* (London: Kegan Paul, Trench, Trübner, & Co., 1890), 212.

63. Seng, xiii.

64. Ibid., xviii. M. Benskin, M. Laing, V. Karaiskos, and K. Williamson, "An Electronic Version of *A Linguistic Atlas of Late Mediaeval English*" [http://www.lel.ed.ac.uk/ihd/elalme/elalme .html] (Edinburgh: © 2013, The Authors and The University of Edinburgh), Index of Sources by County, Yorkshire (LP 0).

from that of the *danse macabre* poem, suggesting an independent origin.[65] Furthermore, the Yorkshire-based ballads and songs elsewhere in this section of the manuscript display an orthography that shares certain spelling characteristics with the *danse macabre* text. Ballad 39 contains an inscription, "T Richeson," that Seng associates with Yorkshire. We might compare "raire" in this ballad's epigraph to the *danse macabre*'s "spaire" at lines 8 and 14; "graice" at line 39 of the ballad with "graice" at line 301 of the *danse macabre*; and their common use of "haith" for "hath." "Haith" also appears in Number 36 (line 26), which is "maid in May at Yorke."[66] Number 44, a Christmas carol, renders "us" as "hus" (stanza 3), as does Number 36 (line 33); this spelling appears in the opening of the *danse macabre* also (line 16). Number 44 addresses "Master Wortly," a reference Seng attaches to the Wortley Hall of the *danse macabre*, and the Yorkshire Wortleys, within the context of aristocratic recusant presence in the north.[67] The information concerning the Yorkshire Wortley Hall indicates the existence of a medieval chapel of ease associated with the main seat of the Wortley family.[68] The chapel in Gloucestershire appears to have been a chantry chapel.[69] A chapel of ease, sited for the convenience of the manor house residents, might align itself more closely with the inscription's designation of a "chapel of Wortley of Wortley Hall" than would a chantry chapel. Thus, while the history of *danse macabre* criticism has perpetuated a Gloucestershire location for the poem, cross-referencing it with the ballads of Cotton Vespasian A.XXV introduces a possible Yorkshire location for the *danse macabre* installation.

The possible relocation of the *danse macabre* matters in part because Northern England is shown to have experimented with emerging progressive forms of verbal conjugation, a complex way of expressing time and tense. David Crystal claims that the rise of the progressive form, which

65. In particular, the *danse macabre* scribe has a characteristic "h" that the sermon scribe by and large does not share; in addition, the density of the script, overall legibility of the hand, and directional slope of the lines vary between the two texts.

66. Seng, 78, 84–87.

67. Ibid., 110–11. On recusancy in Yorkshire among "families of discretion and property," see Frances E. Dolan, *Whores of Babylon: Catholicism, Gender, and Seventeenth-Century Print Culture* (Ithaca: Cornell University Press, 1999), 5.

68. This information derives from a lecture to a local historical society at the end of the nineteenth century and does not make clear its sources or research protocols. Alfred Gatty, *Wortley and the Wortleys: A Lecture* (Sheffield: Thomas Rogers, 1877), 5, 8. The fifteenth-century head of the family, Thomas Wortley, was, according to this lecture, a colorful and somewhat profligate character, partial to entertaining and hunting (10–12).

69. Fosbrooke mentions the chantry priest's wages paid in 1514 (479). He also mentions a chapel founded in Wortley, Gloucestershire, by Edward III in honor of John the Baptist (476).

occurred at the end of the Middle Ages, is most frequently apparent in northern examples.[70] "She was sat," in these dialects, could indicate—and in some instances still does—"she was sitting."[71] The northern use of "to be" as an auxiliary verb would thus not necessarily create a past tense but rather indicate more diverse temporal settings. Within this context, Cotton Vespasian A.XXV's "is comed" might reflect a locus of tense-related experiment and development, drawing out further the temporal ambiguity of the stanza as a whole.

This excursus is, of course, speculative; its main purpose is to cast into relief the effect of shifting conjugations across the manuscripts and their intimation of a reading practice affected by the multimedia and dance-centered experience of the installation. The possible northern location simply emphasizes a temporal situation at work in the poem regardless of location. *Might*, for its part, could wield the force of conditionality or even of the *irrealis*, the ambiguous ontology of the subjunctive. Bodley 686, in also emending to *myght*, offers a verbal configuration that solidifies this possibility: *What might they do when death assails?*[72] With this resonance in mind, we might hear whispered behind *might* as indicative past in Cotton Vespasian A.XXV another question: *What could possibly have been done*—what, that is, in an alternate time or space? Nothing, of course, in the face of death, but the question's phrasing implies some different temporal conditions from those in Lansdowne 699, which asks a simpler rhetorical question.[73] The tense difference reflects not only a change in the audience's temporal placement on a spectrum from past to present, as in the example of the rich king, but also the possibility of an entirely different kind of temporal setting that occupies this very spectrum ambiguously. The textual situation of the poem positions it to ask: "*What might/could those implements do at the moment when death is arrived/is arriving/will have arrived?*" as a question of significant temporal multivalence. The interactions between versions display readers' creation of a distinct but ambiguous temporal environment that is not now or then. This effect undermines the singular linearity of temporal passage and replaces it with the force of potential or inverted time, the *virtus* of anticipation, progression stretched and held,

---

70. David Crystal, *Cambridge Encyclopedia of the English Language*, 2nd ed. (New York: Cambridge University Press, 2003), 45.

71. See David Graddol, Dick Leith, and Joan Swann, eds., *English: History, Diversity, and Change* (New York: Routledge, 2003), 236, on the northern construction "she was sat."

72. Warren and White, 17.

73. The A group of manuscripts cleaves to the question "What geyneth armes . . . ?" (Warren and White, 16).

and *irrealis*. In this way as well, changes in the text reflect a perceptual mode conditioned in a dance-based installation tradition.

Placing a temporally complex *danse macabre* in a northern recusant setting potentially contributes to our understanding of historical recusancy. Specifically, the Wortley Hall *danse macabre* lends dimension to the retrospective force of the recusant environment. Chapter 3's reenactment of the *danse macabre* installation as dance uncovered a drag in time between different medial components. This effect of held or estranged time in the spectacle could intersect with a sense of nostalgia, temporal drag, or untimeliness created by a vestigial Catholicism whose media were being destroyed. Indeed, M. C. Seymour speculates that the scribe copied the Vespasian text in response to the 1549 destruction of the installation in London.[74] A dance-based apprehension of text might even turn itself back onto encounters with spectacle. The Yorkshire-based lyrics and carols in Cotton Vespasian A.XXV imply recusant performance practices, tendencies, or desires. We might consider such performances to be mediated through a perceptual mode sensitized to temporal strangeness in *danse macabre* tradition, awakening those temporal instabilities in the encounter with text, and, finally, bringing them back to bear on the nostalgic experience of performance emphatically out of its own time.[75] Alexandra Walsham has argued that early modern space organizes "the task of remembering" and that the "trajectory" of reform and revolution was not "linear in any simple sense."[76] As an untimely experience in its interaction with visual culture, *danse macabre* poetry holds the potential to theorize and give aesthetic structure to the quality of nostalgia and sense of loss that the threat to Catholic artifacts and practices prompted. This is a historically-oriented interpretation on which I briefly alight and do not treat exhaustively. In part, I make this choice because the Yorkshire location is speculative, but more saliently, I aim to maintain focus on the mechanics of the apprehensional experience itself. My supposition does, however, gesture toward a different category of approach to the past that might benefit from the reenactment method my study constructs.

74. M. C. Seymour, "Some Lydgate Manuscripts: *Lives of SS. Edmund and Fremund* and *Danse Macabre*," *Edinburgh Bibliographical Society Transactions* 5.4 (1983–4; 1984–5): 23.

75. On sixteenth- and seventeenth-century English nostalgia for the Catholic past, and the desire to "trace out [its] sites," see Margaret Aston, "English Ruins and English History: The Dissolution and the Sense of the Past," *Journal of the Warburg and Courtauld Institutes* 36 (1973): 247, 255.

76. Alexandra Walsham, *The Reformation of the Landscape: Religion, Identity, and Memory in Early Modern Britain and Ireland* (New York: Oxford University Press, 2011), 7, 11.

Readerly interventions into the *danse macabre* text convey an experience of the text constituted in the temporal dynamics of the installation tradition. Chapter 3 laid out an apprehensional experience for viewers in which the *danse macabre* installation relied upon the manipulation of vertical and horizontal trajectories to generate the virtual movement in its interstitial spaces and ultimately to create its effect of a fearsome, hydra-headed time, looming with many different modes of temporal passage and direction at once. In considering the reader's experience of the attendant poem, we might find it difficult to envision a situation in which the poem's audience deliberately analogizes the installation to the text in order to attribute such qualities of temporal disorientation to it. A more tenable structure of relation would be a reader's habituation to an experience of time forged in the *ductus* of the installation, an experience that in turn informs—at a self-aware level or not—the means by which such a reader responds to the poetic text. The different adjustments made to this text express uncertainty and disorientation around time, or else simply the possibility of complicated temporal trajectories. These moments potentially represent traces of a reading experience produced in the habits of encounter with the installation's untimeliness.

I conclude this section by asserting that what Lydgate articulates as mirror and *surplusage*, early readers of this poem experience as the virtuality of untimeliness. If we were to imagine the copying act from which Cotton Vespasian A.XXV results as one-dimensional and straightforward, we might construe the poem as an idealized entity statically inhabiting the space between two media, the wall and the page. Somewhat in the spirit of old-fashioned Lachmannian manuscript study, we might see it as a hypothetically stable presence in the interstice between particular manifestations that reflect change and intervention of various kinds.[77] But the perceptual atmosphere dictated by the visual installation explains why the poem seems, in its variants, to register as hovering between normatively delineated spaces or temporal settings. If the manuscripts display evidence of a kind of *mouvance*, it is a perceptual *mouvance* dependent upon the shaping consciousness of the visual installation. Judson Boyce Allen has argued that "the serial experience of the poem is its meaning"; in this case seriality must be recognized for the plural dimensionality with which the *danse ma-*

---

77. Lachmann's method of privileging an *ur*-text as a stable original synthesized ideas current when he was active. See Sebastiano Timpanaro, *The Genesis of Lachmann's Method*, trans. Glenn W. Most (Chicago: University of Chicago Press, 2006), ch. 5. See also Zumthor's discussion in *Essai*, ch. 2. And see my "Choreographing," 78–81, for a summary of these traditions and debates.

cabre's environment invests it.[78] The forces of prolepsis and recursion, the ambiguous mood of the *irrealis*, the use of physical *ductus* to orchestrate the immaterial vectors readers might cast between versions: together these produce, in the audience's experience, the virtual forces whose strange time and space dictate the reading experience.

THE FORMAL EXPERIENCE OF LYDGATE'S *DANSE MACABRE*

We have seen *surplusage* and the mirror communicate Lydgate's perception of the installation's complex medial engagements and thus its environment of ambiguous space and time. And we have detected the readerly apprehension of these untimely effects in details of the poem's manuscript copies. The final section of this chapter will reenact the experience of the *danse macabre* poem's *form*. I will argue that the formal experience of this poem consists in the apprehension of a virtual supplement, one expressing the untimeliness and asymmetry that the regularity of the *huitain* stanza cannot. As Susanne Warda has shown, aspects of the *danse macabre* tradition beyond England manifest themes of disorder and inversion through their content, such as upside-down instruments or complexities of social ordering.[79] The symmetry of the *huitain* poses a question about how the formal experience of the poem can accommodate this element. An answer lies in the ductile experience that brings the apprehension of dance to bear on the encounter with poetry, for in this process emerges a virtual supplement to accommodate the strange time and space that the *huitain* on its own does not.

In making these claims, I invoke the critical tendency to incorporate a medieval text's various physical aspects, including its inscriptional identity, into the discussion of its form; I extend this idea to consider what other media might equally be at stake in the constitution of poetic formal identity. Leah Price has argued that formalists have perennially "defined their object of study as 'the words on the page.' The problem was that the second half of the phrase rarely rose above the metaphorical; it remained for book history to upstage the text (a sequence of 'words') by its tangible form (the 'page')."[80] Medieval scholarship has long offered suggestive formal

78. Judson Boyce Allen, "Grammar, Poetic Form, and the Lyric Ego: A Medieval *A Priori*," in *Vernacular Poetics in the Middle Ages*, ed. Lois Ebin (Kalamazoo, MI: Medieval Institute Publications, 1984), 213.

79. Susanne Warda, "Dance, Music, and Inversion: The Reversal of the Natural Order in the Medieval *Danse Macabre*," in *Mixed Metaphors*, 76–78, 86–87.

80. Leah Price, "Introduction: Reading Matter," *PMLA* 121.1 (2006): 11.

analyses that integrate form's textual and material aspects, as Seth Lerer has discussed.[81] Recently, Arthur Bahr has argued that literary form can present itself in the analysis of the physical dynamics of the manuscript.[82] What follows will concern itelf less with the visual form of a particular *mise-en-page* than with the manuscript tradition's foregrounding of variance. Such inscribed variances will ultimately indicate a specifically formal experience of virtuality.

To investigate the formal experience of Lydgate's poetry requires acknowledging his preoccupations with what we would understand as poetic form. As briefly observed above, Lydgate wishes in his translation to preserve the French original's structural habit of ending stanzas with proverbial statements.[83] Thus, for instance, "Mort nespargne petit ne grant" becomes Ellesmere's "For dethe ne spareth hye ne lowe degre," and "Aussy tot meurt jeune que vielx" becomes "As sone dyeth a ȝounge man as an olde."[84] Walter F. Schirmer observes that Lydgate's commitment to this proverbial structure regulates the poem's rhyme scheme and stanzaic structure according to the French model.[85] The structure of the stanza and the proportions of its different elements thus matter to Lydgate in his process of translation and composition. Maura Nolan has argued that in *The Serpent of Division*, Lydgate experiments with duration through form. Rather than constructing a "simple narration of the falls of evil men," "Lydgate relies upon formal cues—the length and order of his examplars, for example—to signal to audiences that an act of interpretation is required." In Nolan's reading, this strategy constitutes a "stylistic" means of "produc[ing] semiotic complexity."[86] It indicates, in a different way, Lydgate's sense of the

81. Seth Lerer, "The Endurance of Formalism in Middle English Studies," *Literature Compass* 1 (2003): 10–12.

82. Arthur Bahr, *Fragments and Assemblages: Forming Compilations of Medieval London* (Chicago: University of Chicago Press, 2013), 4.

83. Walter F. Schirmer, *John Lydgate: A Study in the Culture of the XVth Century*, trans. Ann E. Keep (Westport, CT: Greenwood, 1979), 128. See also David A. Fein's comment that the proverbial endings to the French stanzas in Guyot Marchant's printing "enri[ch] the tonality of the work by adding another voice, complementing the voices of the living and the dead that sustain the extended dialogue, validating the message of the text by linking it to popular wisdom" (*Danse*, 11). They additionally reinforce the poem's didactic character (12). Zumthor's discussion of the proverb's textuality extends to its formal features and style (*Essai*, 78–79).

84. Warren and White, 79, 6, 94, 70.

85. Lydgate's "desire to retain the proverbial line with which each stanza terminates in the French text led him to take over much of the French rhyme-scheme" (Schirmer, 128).

86. Maura Nolan, *John Lydgate and the Making of Public Culture* (Cambridge: Cambridge University Press, 2005), 139–40.

reader's awareness of the proportions generated, and the pace of the unfold-
ing process, as formal elements crucial to the semiotic viability of the work.

Additionally, in the *danse macabre* A group's final appeal to the audience for intervention and collaboration, there exists a concern with what
we would consider formal attributes. A *Lenvoye de translatoure* closes the
translator's frame at the poem's end; the last stanza reads:

> Owte of the frensshe / I drowe hit of entent
> Not worde be worde / but folwyng the substaunce
> And fro Paris / to Inglond hit sent
> Oneli of purpose / ȝow to do plesaunce
> Rude of langage / y was not borne yn fraunce
> Haue me excused / my name is Jon Lidgate
> Of her tunge / I haue no suffisaunce
> Her corious metris / in Inglissh to translate. Amen.

(E663–72)

In extending this invitation to shape the poem collaboratively, Lydgate
might, in his self-professed inexpertise in French, initially appear concerned
with issues of content. As he puts it, his project aims all along to translate
"not worde be worde" but rather "folwynge the substaunce." At the same
time, in his self-characterization as lacking "suffisaunce" to translate poetry from French, Lydgate notes that this lack affects the activity of "Her
[the French language's] corious metris / In Inglissh to translate." *Metris* at
one level designates simply the content-based entity of a line of verse. But
at another, it includes itself in a lexical set conjuring the issues relating to
pattern, structure (*MED* s.v. *metre* 1), and temporality (*MED* s.v. *metrik*)
that underlie medieval compositional discourses of form.

Turning to readerly response to this poem, meanwhile, we might note
that Cotton Vespasian A.XXV's interventions and changes also specify a
focus on form. Elsewhere, in the second stanza of the poem proper of both
the A and B groups, the narrator declares (in the B group):

> In this myrrour / euery man may fynde
> That hym behouyth / to goon vpon this daunce
> Whoo goth before / or who goth behynde
> All dependith / in goddis ordynaunce
> Where-fore eche man / lowly take his chaunce
> Deth spareth nothir / poore nor blood roiall

Eche man ther-fore / haue this in remembraunce
Of oon mateer / god hathe Forgid all.

(L9–16)

Wortley Hall, however, offers a unique variant for this stanza, substituting
"substance" for "matier" and "formed" for "forgid": "Of one substaunce god
haith formed hus all." The other versions, in their use of "forgid," follow
the French "Tout est forgie dune matere" (l. 16). The literal sense of *formed*
in Cotton Vespasian A.XXV, referring to the constitution of the people addressed in the poem, is clear. But the adjustment potentially also indicates
a response to a more complicated set of concepts. *Forgen* is a technical or
artisanal term applying to a single medium in a process of construction (the
forging of metal, the creation of structures, or the counterfeiting of coins).
Form, however, evokes another set of questions and a less instrumental,
more abstract language, one that would gesture toward and accommodate a
multiplicity of media in a way that "forgid" might not so readily, thus specifying form as a concept (bolstered by the use of "substaunce").

   As chapter 2 discussed, thinking about form as a manifestation of an ideal
concept often implies thinking about a formal attribute that expresses or approaches it; in this case, such an attribute would be the poem's *huitain* stanzas
(ABABBCBC). The *huitain*'s characteristics of managed progression and pro-
portionality become particularly evident when we engage in the traditional
formalist practice of deploying analogy to describe this verse form.[87] With their
alternating and interlocking rhyme scheme, for example, the stanzas comprise
alternating and interlocking dialogues between Death and the living, creating
the effect of microcosmic structure replicating a macrocosmic operation. David Fein additionally conveys the symmetrical nature of the *huitain* by invoking the comparison to the mirror.[88] Another effect that the *huitain* employs is
the pivot, given how its center swings it from one rhyme scheme into another
(ABAB to BCBC). The pivot encourages further analogy, an angular turn paral-
leling the ambulatory encounter with the installation: two linear processions
periodically rounding a corner. As a mirror, a pivot, or a fractal, the *huitain*
appears to generate a formal experience of measure and boundedness.

   And yet, for a modern reader considering the *huitain* as formal attribute,
what might at first seem affirming regularity deepens into obfuscation as
the poem's dialogue between Death and the living interlocutors unfurls in

---

87. We have seen these terms inflect the concept of medieval form in both philosophical and
literary senses. See chapter 2.

88. Fein, *Danse*, 10.

such an extremely predictable and formulaic manner.[89] The *huitains*, that is, progress with resolutely impenetrable banality. Perhaps this is simply another version of fifteenth-century dullness, but the overall effect does somewhat hinder us as modern readers. We can perceive how the repetitive stanzas might have communicated death's relentlessness and inevitability through the singularity of its rhythm: a particular kind of memory work for the *memento mori*. But their character makes it difficult to see beyond this. The analogical discourse deployed around their interweaving line structure ultimately limits our attempts to recognize what might be most intriguing or unexpected about them. We might trust that they fall into a formal category to which Cannon alludes, where what is interesting about a particular Middle English textual form "often tends to appear as tediousness . . . or ineptitude."[90] And we are mindful of Rosemary Woolf's assertion, regarding medieval death poetry, that "the simplicity is on the surface, and beneath is a strong foundation of serious and subtle thought."[91] But we are not always sure how to uncover this interesting potential when form is so formulaic.

This response occurs in part because the protocols of modern and contemporary formalist analysis have internalized procedures that privilege breaks in regularity as sites of formal revelation. These modes of reading assume contemporary readers to have evolved beyond Kenneth Burke's condition of "gratifi[cation] by the sequence" that poetic forms might bring about.[92] Modern formalism instead values ruptures in expected sequences, and that valuation has its own critical history. For instance, Michael Riffaterre's structuralist theory of "ungrammaticalities," points at which a poem's interpretive matrix appears, depends on the reader's awareness of textual irregularity, his recognition of "stumbling blocks."[93] Harold Bloom sees the "breaking of form," the struggle and subversion in a text, as both a structural and a psychological manifestation of the text's agenda. "The lustres of poetic meaning," as he puts it, are found in "the breaking apart of form"; for him gratification derives not only from the disruption of sequence but also from the revelation of form as a "place of invention."[94]

89. Zumthor ascribes to *danse macabre* a "structure litanique" (*Essai*, 135).

90. Cannon, "Form," 178. Cannon refers here specifically to Middle English forms that have a puzzling uniqueness in the absence of other vernacular models.

91. Rosemary Woolf, *The English Religious Lyric in the Middle Ages* (Oxford: Clarendon, 1968), 370. She does, however, critique Lydgate's verse as "lacking" "ironic tautness" (367)

92. Kenneth Burke, *Counter-Statement* (Berkeley: University of California Press, 1968), 124.

93. Michael Riffaterre, *The Semiotics of Poetry* (Bloomington: Indiana University Press, 1978), 2, 6.

94. Bloom, "Breaking," 275–76.

While most contemporary formalist readers may not incorporate these thought structures explicitly into their practices, we continue to depend on a text's ability to show us difficulties, surprises of self-awareness, and flaws in the poetic textile. Yopie Prins, for example, returns to the discourse of "breaking" in her discussion of Tennyson, Robert Browning, and Elizabeth Barrett Browning, using this term to consider the denormalizing of poetic voice through its history. In this instance as well, breaking as disjunction and instability—the "disarticulation of voice by meter"—offers a privileged site at which to produce interpretation.[95]

We arrive, thus, at the dilemma: while on the one hand, certain aspects of contemporary formalist methodology might yield useful insights about this poem, on the other hand, a deeper resonance of formalist reading for medieval studies—the analogical impulse we saw in, for instance, Muscatine—occludes this poetic structure's asymmetries and strangeness. This is not to say, of course, that as modern readers of medieval literature we lack attunement to its disruptions at the level of narrative or sociopolitical engagement. As Elizabeth Scala has argued, for instance, the *Canterbury Tales* make clear to us their "power of disruption," their "dissonance."[96] But it can be challenging to account for such qualities in the specific operations of verse form.

I respond to this dilemma by understanding *danse macabre* poetry's form not as an attribute but rather as an experience, one conditioned by the perceptual habits instilled by the *danse macabre* installation. This approach alters the text's formal identity. We have seen how the installation's *ductus* shapes, in the apprehension of the poem, the untimeliness and spatial skewing of the virtual supplement. In what remains of this chapter, I will suggest that this virtual supplement accommodates the irregularity, asymmetry, and breaking that the *huitain* cannot. As a medium collusive with the installation's other components in the generation of virtuality, the *danse macabre* poem can sustain much stranger footing in its *ductus* than what the *huitain* might seem to dictate as formal attribute. Jane Gilbert has noted that medieval constructs of death-in-life and life-in-death destabilize

---

95. Prins, "'What,'" 28.

96. Elizabeth Scala, *Desire in the Canterbury Tales* (Columbus, OH: Ohio State University Press, 2015), 3. For Scala, formal features like stanzaic structure draw attention to the work of the signifier in its Lacanian sense as well as—more problematically, for her, in the reification of the historical—a "means to . . . knowledge of a signified: those historical meanings, associations, and resonances we hope to glean from Chaucer's poetry" (16).

norms and productively disorient.[97] *Danse macabre* emblematizes those oscillating dynamics of life and death; it additionally reveals how poetic form as an experience can articulate that destabilization.

To illustrate this point, I turn to the A group's stanzas on the Minstrel, whose response to Death conveys an obsession with the strange time of his dance.

> This newe daunce / is to me so straunge
> Wonder dyuerse and passyngli contrarie
> The dredful fotyng / doth so ofte chaunge
> And the mesures / so ofte sithes varie
> Which now to me / is no thyng necessarie
> ȝif hit were so / that I myght asterte
> But many a man / ȝif I shal not tarie
> Ofte daunceth / but no thyng of herte.[98]

(E505–12)

The B group also has a Minstrel, but his language refers less specifically than does the A group's to issues of temporal measurement and placement: "newe," "ofte," "mesures," "sithes," "now," and "tarie." Lydgate's proliferation of such terms in this stanza might appear merely to suggest the obvious, which is that to engage in the dance requires alertness to the mechanics of time's passage.[99] Indeed, the musician is a character especially attuned to this kind of demand. And yet, this alertness is a source of disorientation

---

97. Jane Gilbert, *Living Death in Medieval French and English Literature* (Cambridge: Cambridge University Press, 2011), 5–6. See also J. H. M. Taylor's point that the *danse macabre* "places itself at that moment of equilibrium between life and death." "Danse macabré and *Bande dessiné*: A Question of Reading," *Forum for Modern Language Studies* 25.4 (1989): 365.

98. The meaning of the last two lines is somewhat obscure. Does it suggest dancing when one's heart is not in it? This seems possible, but the awkward text appears to betray some befuddlement on encountering the French text. The French version reads: "Tel danse a quy au cuer nen tient" (l. 408), which seems related to Lydgate's line, though the content of the rest of that stanza seems to correspond more closely to the B version.

99. The poem alludes elsewhere to the concept of pace; Lydgate uses versions of Middle English *passen/pace* (a word designating temporal unit [*MED* s.v. *passen* 4]) throughout. While this word does not denote rate and speed as consistently as it does in Modern English, it sometimes conveys this sense for Lydgate, as two examples from the *OED* indicate (s.v. *pace*, n. 1, 5a). The Pope comments that "For sich honour / who prudently can see / Is litel worthe / that doth so soone passe" (L32–33) ["pace" in Ellesmere and other A-group manuscripts]. Passing away is accelerated by "soone" and also rhymes with "trace" in line 30, a word associated with danced steps that introduces the resonance of pacing into passing.

and stress because the tempo of the dance's measures is so unstable: these measures are "straunge," "dyuerse," "contrarie," and often "chaunge" and "varie." The "fotyng" is "dredful" and strange to the speaker for reasons of time and measure.

This stanza indicates the effect of the perceptual practices forged in the visual installation upon the poem, an effect potentially carried through Lydgate to the poem's readers.[100] In other words, the Minstrel's lament bears out the ductile model I have proposed, whereby to understand the poem's language is to respond to and be influenced by the experience of being led through a dance-based installation with all its own temporal complexity. The dance's dreadfulness of time, the Minstrel suggests, stems from its insistence upon occupying several different temporal registers at once. For in bemoaning temporal confusion, the Minstrel also subtly indicates the presence of multiple temporal registers in his description of the dance as "passyngli contrarie." This phrase conveys not only the sense of adversity or recalcitrance but also the effect of opposing forces exerted simultaneously (*MED* s.v. *contrarie* 1, 2a, 3, 5). Within this context, what seems a compulsive proliferation of differing time-related words ("mesures" vs. "sithes," for instance) reinforces this sense that a network of different—and conflicting—temporal qualities, rates, and values produces the anxiety the Minstrel expresses. While we might recognize this poetic effect as one conditioned by features of the installation, it is important to ask as well how to understand that bridge from spectacle to poetry in light of the A version's possibly more attenuated association with the installation.[101] I would suggest that the language of the A stanza bears witness to the impact of the installation's *ductus* upon the writer's conception of the poetry. In this capacity, the poem's language introduces those conditions of temporal disorientation into readerly experience, no matter where any particular reader might stand on the spectrum of possible relations to the physical media of the installation.

    100. This interpretation of Lydgate's text recalls Caroline Levine's reading of Elizabeth Barrett Browning's prosodic creation of disunified temporalities. But whereas for Levine, this account of form intends to describe poetry's participation in a social world—"the patterns of state and family," etc., I am interested in isolating this effect in Lydgate to explain why Lydgate's poem seems to offer such a disquieting experience to its audience. Levine, 99.
    101. This stanza revises the French version Lydgate might have seen, which desultorily names some musical instruments and mainly concerns itself with the Minstrel's unwillingness, and then resignation, to dance (similarly to the B-version stanza). The French version speaks not about the dance's strangeness but rather the reluctance to participate: "De danser ainsy neusse cure, / Certes tres enuis je men melle." Warren and White, 92, ll. 401–2.

The formal problem lies in the fact that the Minstrel is constrained to express all that temporal trouble within the attribute of the *huitain*. To only a limited extent can the rhyme pattern of the *huitain* convey these effects on its own. The stanza can, it should be acknowledged, speak to the simultaneity of opposing temporal forces in that its structure borrows a rhyme from its first half into its second half and reverses that rhyme's order of presentation. So, where the word "varie" functions as the resolution of the first quatrain pattern, its rhyme sound then becomes the initiating value for the second quatrain, meaning that its equally important rhyme, "tarie," cannot resolve the second quatrain. It instead launches a rhyme pattern it does not close. In this sense, the reader attuned to structure and progression experiences this rhyme as, alternately, both the ending and the beginning of a trajectory, allowing that displacement to complicate linear temporal progression. In addition, the importation of sound from the first half of the stanza into the second half reinforces the sense of simultaneous occurrence rather than a progression that changes continuously as it advances. Ultimately, however, the *huitain* is an entity of evenness, embracing closure and balance. As a formal attribute, it cannot fully respond to or participate in either the Minstrel's dismaying account of his experience or the tipped axes we saw in the viewer's ductile encounter with the installation. The *huitain*'s perfect octogonality obliges it to return to normative temporal marking and balance even as it might strain toward other temporal experiences.

To address this problem, the poem produces a formal experience of virtuality that supplements the formal attribute of the *huitain*. The reader has access to this experience of virtuality through the mirror of virtual *surplusage* that the poem establishes at the outset. In positing the Minstrel—like all the characters—as a reflection of the reader who apprehends him, the text makes the Minstrel's experience the reader's. The Minstrel's words thus narrate a readerly experience of temporal dislocation and disorientation. While the *huitain* cannot accommodate this disorientation on its own, the mirror as Foucauldian virtual environment can in the reader's process of being led through the stanza. The reader apprehends the mirror space as one of temporally complex kinesis, encountering that textual image in the ductile terms of the installation's crossing, anticipatory, and syncopated forces.

In this *ductus*, virtuality's untimeliness supplements the temporal regularity of the stanza's rhyme scheme. This experience of form accommodates the profound and essential strangeness of *danse macabre*, which is in the end the strangeness of dance. Even as the recurring rhyme leads the reader in the expectation of periodicity—*strange, contrary, change, vary*—that reader conditioned to dance-based perception apprehends those rhyming words to cast from themselves the forces of the very asymmetry and untimeliness they name. Depicting not only the dance but also the participant's experience of it, this stanza's language makes explicit the formal experience of the whole poem. In the *danse macabre* poem's ductile process, strange forces project themselves forth from the *huitain*'s symmetrical rhymes, away from the syntactic hominess of the proverb. These forces are limited only by the multifarious untimeliness of the installation itself. This reading suggests that the difficulties of tense and time that we saw illustrated in manuscript variance potentially indicate temporal disorientation not only between media but also in the experience of the poem's form. The *huitain*, in other words, is not the fullness of the poem's form. That form is the experience of the *huitain* casting from itself other forces that interact but also misalign with it, tracing the time of the *danse macabre* that the Minstrel finds so terrifying. Without this temporal irregularity and rupture, the formal experience of the poem is incomplete.

This reenactment of medieval poetic formal experience in *danse macabre* both positions itself within the modern languages of formalism to which we are accustomed and, at the same time, shows us something of the alterity of medieval poetic formal character. The off-putting regularity of the poem makes it appear unavailable to the interpretive subtlety of the formalist discourses on which we rely, namely those that privilege breaking and disrupting patterns. Reenacting medieval poetic form experientially, however, and in terms of dance's virtual supplements, provides a different access to form. Here, the medieval conception of poetic form responds through its associated medial networks to the modern interest in what breaks, trips, and misaligns in time or space. That medial network offers us a means to exercise our impulse to seek what more a poem's structure can accomplish beneath a formulaic surface.

It is important to stress that we have elicited medieval poetic form's experience from a culturally specific *surplusage* generated in experiences of medieval dance; this element leavens or even challenges the inevitable weight of modern interpretive method upon us as we read this poem. It is in this sense that I reenact formal experience, positioning it between premodern and postmodern poles. From that position, reenactment speaks to Butterfield's description of medieval poetic form as something caught on and off the page, in and out of history.[102] Her characterization encourages

102. Butterfield, "Why," 339.

specific accounts of how such a version of poetic form might operate, and the reenactment of strange footing offers a methodology for generating such accounts. At the same time, reenactment allows the medieval to speak back to and complicate modernity. In *danse macabre*, medieval poetic form is an experience that depends upon perceptual practices shaped by multimediacy. This model exerts force against what is often a more restricted modern sense of poetic form and of where and how its breaking can occur. *Danse macabre* is able to expose premodern poetry's form as experience because it foregrounds medial complexity and dance-based virtuality. It is in this sense that *danse macabre* and its poetry possess what Douglas Gray once characterized as "strange force."[103]

103. Gray, "Two Songs," 64.

PART III

CHAPTER FIVE

The *Carole*'s Virtual Circles

My second case study focuses on the round dance often referred to as *carole* and its relationship to the English poetic carol text. This chapter establishes a set of perceptual practices at work in the participatory spectatorship of the *carole*, practices that I will later suggest are crucial to the poetic tradition of carol. The capacious category of medieval round dance exists as an embodied practice in many arenas, performed indoors or outdoors by a variety of social classes, and accompanied by sung verse.[1] Silen suggests that *carole* has the advantage of "portability," the capacity to be performed independently of any particular site or facility, and that this characteristic contributes to its popularity.[2] As a dance, this chapter will argue, the *carole* shares with *danse macabre* the presence of a virtual supplement. Woven into the bodily *ductus* of the *carole* is always another circular dance that is perceptible but ambiguous in its ontology. If virtuality enables a particular temporal experience in the *danse macabre*, it underlies a strange but characteristic use of space in the *carole*. In visual representations of the *carole*, light, emptiness, and the complicated spaces between bodies generate arcs of force that may or may not describe a closed circle. These forces challenge the apparent symmetry and periodicity of the dance. In order to reenact the experience of this virtual supplement to the *carole*, I will juxtapose it to a modern performance, Mark Morris's *L'Allegro, Il Penseroso ed il Moderato* (1988), which offers various and suggestive manifestations of choreography in the round.

As spectacles, *danse macabre* and *carole* differ in the kind of hermeneutic activity to which they give rise. *Danse macabre* builds itself around a

---

1. On the contrast between courtly and country round dancing, see Howard, *Politics*, 11–13.
2. Silen, "Dance," 72.

specific category of conceptual and narrative content: the encounter with
death. Thus, when I contend that *danse macabre*'s untimeliness informs
the reader's disorientation in the encounter with death, I make an argument
that rests on the foundation of this tradition's thematics. The *carole*, conversely, is a generic dance format that could apply itself to many possible
themes or narratives. Ring dances are among the oldest dance forms, crossing civilizations from European to indigenous American, and their designation as *carole* reflects some of this breadth of association. Trevisa translates
Latin *chorea*, a term connoting not only dance but also broader conceptions
of movement (planetary, musical), as "carol," emphasizing the universality
of this category of dance. Because of its breadth of conceptual affiliation—in
particular as relative to the defined agenda of *danse macabre*—the danced
carole and poetic carol together do not offer one interpretive claim, but
rather emphasize the range of interventions that my method of reading
might accommodate.

THE UNRECONSTRUCTABLE *CAROLE*

Because the *carole* aligns itself, more readily than does *danse macabre*,
with our modern understanding of what dance means, it presents itself as
reasonably available to reconstruction. As this section will show, however,
the *carole* calls for theoretical and speculative reenactment, perhaps even
more urgently than does *danse macabre*, in order to see what its evidence
does not make obvious to us. Because the *carole* is more likely than *danse
macabre* to reassure us that it is a dance in terms that we recognize, we risk
passing over the features constituted in its alterity.

Whereas the possibility of a performed *danse macabre*—in the sense that
postmodernity might understand a mainstream category of danced performance—is murky, the *carole* represents what we might consider an actual
dance tradition for the Middle Ages. The evidence is often Continental and
secular, with references to the *carole* appearing in not only the thirteenth-
century *Roman de la Violette*, and the late-thirteenth-century *Châtelain
de Coucy*, but also, perhaps most famously, the *Roman de la rose*, with its
carol to the god of love illustrated in a number of manuscripts.[3] Medieval
English texts speak of danced *carole* as well. Greene speculates that these

---

3. See Mullally, *Carole*, 113 on Trevisa and 41–47 on additional French textual sources.
Some descriptions are religious, emphasizing celestial harmony; see, for instance, *La Court de
Paradis*, in Étienne Barbazan and Dominique Martin Méon, eds., *Fabliaux et contes des poètes
françois. . .*, vol. 3 (Paris: B. Warée, 1808), 128–48.

dances were imported into England shortly after the Norman Conquest and that they endured as a familiar dance-song idiom throughout the English Middle Ages.[4] Several English authors refer to the *carole* as a dance or as the sung accompaniment to a dance. In Gower's *Confessio Amantis*, for instance, the daughter of Jephtha "waiteth upon [her father's] cominge / With dansinge and with carolinge." *Sir Gawain and the Green Knight*'s aristocratic characters "daunsed ful dreȝly wyth dere carolez."[5] In instances like these, the word *carole* appears as a dance-song indexed to a movement practice that late-medieval audiences know.

In addition, the medieval *carole* sometimes involves specific measures and steps that align it with what we might think of as choreography. The *carole* seems to involve either a ring or a line of dancers often linked by fingers or hands, with a leader singing the stanzas and the rest of the company singing the burden, or external refrain (a refrain distinct in terms of rhyme, structure, or content from the stanza), also sung at the beginning of the carol.[6] Dancers generally step to the left as they mark the leader's singing of the stanzas, following which everyone stops and sings the burden.[7] Men lead *caroles*, but so do women, as indicated by Chaucer's female leader Gladnesse, who "couthe ynow of sich doyng / As longeth unto karolyng, / For she was wont in every place / To syngen first" in the *Romaunt of the Rose* (A.753–56). This basic structure is not necessarily comprehensive; Eustace and King, for instance, discuss speculation concerning a process by which the *carole* would start as a linked circle but then break into pairs traveling in a circle; one implication of this possibility, they note, is that the visual images of *caroles* familiar to us capture one initiating moment in the dance, not its entire character.[8]

Other medieval evidence additionally expands our perspectives on what *caroles* are and how to understand their movement. Kathleen Palti's work on English carols (possibly both danced and sung), for instance, opens up

4. *EEC*, xlvii–xlviii.

5. John Gower, *Confessio Amantis*, in *The Complete Works of John Gower*, ed. G. C. Macaulay (Oxford: Clarendon Press, 1899–1902, repr. Grosse Pointe, MI: Scholarly Press, 1968), IV.1529–30; Malcolm Andrew and Ronald Waldron eds., *The Poems of the "Pearl" Manuscript*, 3rd ed. (Exeter: University of Exter Press, 1996), 246, l. 1026.

6. Reichl, 158. In a paper presented at ICMS, Kalamazoo, 2016, Kathryn Dickason noted that in some secular late-medieval dances, adjacent performers held opposite ends of a handkerchief to create the link between them; see, for instance, the dance depiction on Bibliothèque Municipale de Dijon MS 527, f. 1r.

7. *EEC*, xlv–xlvi.

8. Eustace with King, 56. Jean-Michel Guilcher's discussion of Breton folk dance raises some related possibilities. *La Tradition populaire de danse en Basse-Bretagne* (Paris, 1963), 414, 448.

our sense of these dance songs by looking into the relationship between lullabies and carols. She shows first how the carol negotiates between popular and clerical cultures (in, for example, Marian lullabies) and, second, suggests that carols indicate that women played a more significant role in the composition of lyrics than has hitherto been supposed.[9] Furthermore, the movement practice of the *carole* potentially has multiple homes, whether church procession or what Palti elsewhere describes as "crossing a shifting border between ritual and revel."[10] Arguments such as this contribute further to our sense of what the *carole* was, revealing an interweaving of traditions—dance, song, text, sacred, secular, vernacular, Latin, pastoral, liturgical. While this information does not refine the dance's choreographic features, it provides context and rationale to suggest what the movement practice means within a given culture.

The *carole* also seems recognizable and even recoverable to us as dance practice because its form as a linked circle and its measured steps encourage a moral discourse ranging from virtuous concord to sinful abandon; it participates in a familiar assignation of moral values to bodily activity. On the one hand, early dance is an art perceived to enact ideals of order and harmony. This understanding of dance has a powerful medieval iteration in, as the introduction mentioned, visions of heavenly round dances, but also reflects origins in classical culture. On the other hand, the round dance emblematizes dance's suspect potential as licentious, excessive, or otherwise immoral. This perspective also has a long history. As early as the sixth century, Caesarius of Arles criticized the ring dancing and "pantomiming in a devilish fashion" of celebrants who came to church on the feast days of martyrs.[11] In the late Middle Ages, Gower censoriously specifies dancing in general as exhibitionist behavior. Because Jephtha's daughter "wolde be tofore / Al other" (*CA* IV.1531–32), she becomes the first person Jephtha sees upon his victorious return from battle and therefore the one he must sacrifice to keep a promise he had earlier made to God. This moral doubt about dance does not exist in thematic isolation. Chaucer's *Physician's Tale*, which resonates with Gower's parable of filicide, also mentions "daunces" (VI.65) as

9. Kathleen Palti, "Singing Women: Lullabies and Carols in Medieval England," *Journal of English and Germanic Philology* 110.3 (2011): 365–68, 373.

10. On the *carole* and procession, see Rossell Hope Robbins, "Middle English Carols as Processional Hymms," *Studies in Philology* 56.4 (1959): 560. Kathleen Palti, "Representations of Voices in Middle English Lyrics," in *Citation, Intertextuality and Memory in the Middle Ages and Renaissance*, vol. 1, ed. Yolanda Plumley et al. (Exeter: University of Exeter Press, 2011), 146.

11. Mary Magdalene Mueller, trans., *Saint Caesarius of Arles, Sermons*, vol. 1 (Washington, DC: Catholic University Press, 2004), 271.

one of the activities the virtuous Virginia takes pains to avoid as leading to just the kind of "booldnesse" (VI.71) that undoes Jephtha's daughter. The realm of moralizing literature offers Robert Mannyng's versions of the story, in *Handlyng Synne*, of the cursed carolers of Kölbek, doomed to repeat their *carole* ceaselessly after they blaspheme by performing it in a churchyard on a holy day.[12] In addition, Richard Rolle inserts "To lede Carols" into a list of sins between "To hald the office that we suffice nogth tille" and "To bryng vp new gyses."[13] Thus the *carole* as dance signifies in a manner that correlates with ingrained notions of the body's uses and meanings, hovering between its potential for perfection and its troubling immoderation. Theorizing the dance's moral meaning in this manner makes the *carole* seems familiar and translatable.

And yet, the more closely we consider the evidence, the more problematic the exercise of reconstructing the *carole* reveals itself to be. This is perhaps nowhere more apparent than in the medieval use of the term *carole* itself. The word has semantically broad range, and dance historians have understood it in different ways. Robert Mullally contends, for instance, that *carole* designates round dance more commonly than it does dancing in a line, and that it requires its dancers to step to the left with each person's feet meeting each other between those steps.[14] Others, meanwhile, have queried whether the *carole* is exclusively round, for example in the earlier criticism of Margit R. Sahlin, who proposed it as a "cortège" of people walking two by two or three by three.[15] The linearity or roundness of the *carole* also concerns the nature of its couple configurations, with some critics seeing it as couples in a line or lines and others interpreting the couple pattern as a way to create gender alternation in the group's circular figure. Paul Falk rebuts Sahlin's proposal of a procession of couples, noting that they could easily have taken their places in a circle as couples.[16] Mullally's discussion of the term *carole* addresses as well its further ambiguities. He proposes that certain dance names are interchangeable because aspects of the different dances they might designate are similar. One example appears in Mullally's

12. Robert Mannyng, *Robert of Brunne's Handlyng Synne*, ed. Frederick J. Furnivall, EETS o.s. 119 (London: K. Paul, Trench, and Trübner, 1901–1903), ll. 9015–260.

13. Hope Emily Allen, ed., *The English Writings of Richard Rolle, Hermit of Hampole* (Oxford: Clarendon, 1931), 98. See also Reichl, 152.

14. Mullally, *Carole*, 45, 83.

15. Margit Sahlin, *Étude sur la carole médiévale: L'origine du mot et ses rapports avec l'Église* (Uppsala: Almqvist & Wiksells, 1940), 25; Silen, "Dance," 72.

16. Paul Falk, review of Sahlin, *Étude*, *Studia Neophilologica* 13 (1940/41): 137.

analysis of the terms *carole* and *tresche*. He suggests that their terminologi-
cal interchangeability (even though the latter seems to refer more often to a
line dance) reflects a premodern perception of the dances' interchangeability, sharing features of handholding and movement to the left despite their
different configurations.[17] The details of the *carole*'s choreography seem at
once precise and indeterminate, reasonably clear from a distance but increasingly obfuscated as we approach the dance more closely or try to assign
it stable characteristics. Greene's description, as noted above, traces itself
to Jeanroy (along with Bédier after him). But Jeanroy also allows that the
dance is rarely directly described in these terms; the evidence does not leave
us with a totalizing fixity for every aspect of every *carole* as performance.[18]

The evidence represented in poems whose verse structure reflects the
dance is similarly ambiguous. On the one hand, the very existence of such
coordinating poetry makes aspects of the *carole*'s performance appear clear
to us. For example, as in chapter 2's "Ladd Y the daunce," some written carols structure their stanzas to contain transitional lines between stanza and
burden, a vestigial reminder to the performer or listener of the impending
burden.[19] This poetic phenomenon conjures for us the scenario of a round-
dancing chorus listening to the tag line of the leader's stanza, using it as a
cue to recall the rhyming line of the burden. Such a textual structure might
possibly give us a sense of a performance protocol, a window onto the dance's
transitional scenarios in performance. On the other hand, certain aspects of
the steps and their coordination with music and lyrics are less specific and
clear. Variations on the basic choreographic format might have existed, such
as movement occurring during the singing of the burden rather than the stanzas.[20] Thus, while in one sense the stanza-and-burden structure seems to

17. Mullally, *Carole*, 60–61.

18. Alfred Jeanroy, *Les Origines de la poésie lyrique en France au moyen âge: études de
littérature française et comparée, suivies de textes inédits* (Paris: H. Champion, 1904), 392. Jeanroy is one of the earliest modern critics to propose a structure for the French *carole*. He describes
this dance as involving a singer (or perhaps sometimes singers) performing the stanzas alternating
with a chorus singing the refrain. See in addition Bédier, 398, on the form of the dance as an open
or closed chain. The fact that *caroles* were sometimes performed around objects, as the dancers
in the *Legend of Good Women* make clear, circling the honored daisy (G.200), might reinforce the
possibility of circular configuration. The *carole* is sometimes compared to the Renaissance *branle*
as well, which involves three steps to the left and a pause.

19. On the tag as a textual manifestation of a bodily impulse toward anticipation in dance,
see my "Choreographing," 88–89.

20. Dronke enumerates some of the different possibilities regarding when the chorus moved
and when it stood still: "The circular movement in the dance can coincide with the strophe, or
with the refrain, or again with an instrumental or vocal *reprise* between them—depending on

communicate a dance form with assuredness, many details of this dance blur upon the deployment of more microscopic focus.

In naming further aspects of its indeterminacy, we might also take into account how the *carole*—as dance or text—tends to transfer itself into new settings and contexts. One way in which this trait becomes apparent is in the conversion of secular carol texts into sacred counterparts. This occurs in the practice of composing Latin *contrafacta* meant to fit the tunes of *caroles* while substituting lyrics more appropriate and devout than what their vernacular counterparts presumably discussed. A series of such *contrafacta* appears in the fourteenth-century *Red Book of Ossory*, a collection of bureaucratic documents and other items by the Franciscan bishop Richard de Ledrede. The original template of a round dance lyric could thus dictate a new iteration in a different time, space, and context. Another kind of transferability is apparent in the refrains that migrate across medieval lyrics.[21] Manuscript witnesses display various instances of burdens being reincorporated into different songs, or perhaps new songs being built around old burdens. We might wonder how this verbal situation interacts with the potential of danced *caroles* to be self-transferring and translatable. An old song might be fitted to a new choreography, or a newly composed song might be danced to a formation whose details include archaic elements.[22] The international status of this dance, existing in versions across Europe, additionally suggests the possible play of regionally specific choreographic elements against various language traditions. These possibilities make the *carole* an intriguing object temporally and geospatially but also further complicate the reconstruction project.

Finally, complexity exists in the terminology of the round dance's associated musical genres as well as their specific applications to dance. There

---

the rhythm, nature and content of the particular song" (189–90). See also Sahlin, 36; and Silen, "Dance," 72.

21. On the incorporation of existing refrains into new songs, and other forms of intertextuality in refrain lyric, see Jennifer Saltzstein, *The Refrain and the Rise of the Vernacular in Medieval French Music and Poetry* (Cambridge: D. S. Brewer, 2013), 3–6, 13–16, 37–43, and *passim*; see Ardis Butterfield, *Poetry and Music in Medieval France: From Jean Renart to Guillaume de Machaut* (Cambridge: Cambridge University Press, 2002), 75–102, on refrains' connecting function both across and within genres (79).

22. This conjectural phenomenon in early dance is somewhat more reliably documentable through the tradition of fifteenth-century *basse danse* and *bassadanza*, for with these genres the textual tradition of dance manuals was born in Western Europe. On the possibility that French, Italian, early, and late components of this dance tradition might all have been perceptible to performers and audiences within the enactment of a dance, see my "Proleptic."

was, from the thirteenth century, a French verse refrain form classified as the *rondet de carole*. In Butterfield's analysis of the refrain in the dance-song *rondet de carole*, the generative presence of independent refrains, in romances that narrate dance, hovers on a complex spectrum between the notion that the refrain accompaniment might convey something about actual dance, on the one hand, and authorial intervention, stylization, and mediation that comments upon performance, on the other.[23] On song terms for dance accompaniment, Mullally notes that while there are *rondets de carole*, "there is no piece of music called a *carole*" in French.[24] Lyric and musical forms with different names were danced to, or otherwise associated with, choreography in the round. In a miniature from Paris, Bibliothèque nationale MS Fr. 1586's *Remede de Fortune*, Sylvia Huot remarks, the lover "joins the [circular] carol next to his lady and sings a virelay (f. 51)."[25] Mullally suggests, in a discussion of the thirteenth-century Johannes de Grocheio, that song in *virelai* form came to replace the *rondeau* as an accompaniment to *carole*, though he also conjectures that the two might have continued to coexist as dance accompaniment.[26] Leach speculates that the idea of the round *carole* could figure the absorbing "centripetal" quality of Fortune in the conclusion to Machaut's *Voir Dit*, which includes a *rondeau*.[27] Peraino makes a case for the Machauvian *virelai*'s ambiguity in regard to its danced association, ultimately seeing it as a "mixed register" that incorporates social performance and the personal.[28] Finally, the refrain structure of the *virelai*, to which Machaut refers as *chanson baladée* to designate its dance func-

---

23. Butterfield, *Poetry*, 45–63. On the *rondet de carole*, see also Judith A. Peraino, *Giving Voice to Love: Song and Self-Expression from the Troubadours to Guillaume de Machaut* (New York: Oxford University Press, 2011), 248; and Mark Everist, *French Motets in the Thirteenth Century: Music, Poetry and Genre* (Cambridge: Cambridge University Press, 1994), 92–94.

24. Mullally, *Carole*, 79.

25. Sylvia Huot, *From Song to Book: The Poetics of Writing in Old French Lyric and Lyrical Narrative Poetry* (Ithaca: Cornell University Press, 1987), 256. The *virelai* in the text of that folio is "Dame a vous sans retollir." While she concludes that their identity is more "literary" than performance-based, Huot proposes that the *lais* inserted in Fr. 1586's *Remede de Fortune* imitate, in their alternation of male and female voices and their positioning of "miniature and marginalia," "the format of the carol." Huot conjectures a version of a *carole* in which "a male and female singer could perform a pair of songs, each alternately standing to one side to sing while the one on whom the song focused assumed 'center stage,' perhaps executing some simple dance steps" (Huot, 272–73).

26. Mullally, "'Musica Vulgaris,'" 10–11; see this discussion's relation of *virelai* and *ductia*.

27. Elizabeth Eva Leach, *Guillaume de Machaut: Secretary, Poet, Musician* (Ithaca: Cornell University Press, 2014), 241.

28. Peraino, 245.

tion, can differ from that of the "balade" (G 202) that Chaucer describes as danced "carol-wyse" (G 201) in the *Legend of Good Women*.[29] The different musical entities would thus produce somewhat different dance experiences.

The question of the dance's metrical relationship to music also presents an array of possibilities. While 6/8 time would allow for a duple meter that would accommodate the two steps to the left, the precise mechanics of this accompaniment—the way that time was marked and measured in the music as one danced—is difficult to know with certainty, especially if certain types of variation, like anacrusis, might also have existed.[30] In the cases of individual vs. choral singing, as well as instrumentation, the evidence also seems to indicate various possibilities.[31] Concerning the ambiguity of musical accompaniment to medieval dance, Taruskin notes that "All the questions raised by those lovely, pesky miniatures remain open after all"; this caveat is important to keep in mind.[32]

Though its reasons for doing so differ, the *carole* might welcome alternative methods of approach as much as did *danse macabre*. The *carole* appears, from our modern perspective, to offer a great deal more detail with which to work. In part this is because it is a recognizably embodied movement tradition that we would think of as "dance" in a way that *danse macabre* is not. The sense of relatively abundant guidance also derives from the presence of musical and lyric poetic evidence that intersects with the practice of medieval round dancing. But when one attempts to paint a complete picture of any one dance from these details, one inevitably must leave certain spots on the canvas untinctured due to incertitudes about the many choreographic and other performance-based aspects that would comprise a *carole* in full. We might recall here chapter 1's discussion of Richard Schechner and his

29. Peraino distinguishes between Machaut's *virelai* and *ballade* refrains (236). Both these forms exhibit more independent refrains than the earlier *rondet de carole*. While *ballade* appears etymologically linked to dancing, it does not appear frequently as the name of a dance-song. Exceptions, however, include Chaucer's reference as well as a *ballade* meant to accompany a *carole* dance in *Le Romans de la Dame à la Licorne* (Mullally, *Carole*, 76–77). See also Lawrence Earp, "Lyrics for Reading and Lyrics for Singing in Late Medieval France: The Development of the Dance Lyric from Adam de la Halle to Guillaume de Machaut," in *The Union of Words and Music in Medieval Poetry*, ed. Rebecca A. Baltzer et al. (Austin: University of Texas Press, 1991), 113–15, on the idea that "Machaut was quite self-consciously preserving the [*virelai*] genre for the dance." On the sources of Chaucer's *balade*, see Nelson, 134–37.

30. Mullally, *Carole*, 82–83.

31. Ibid., 86–87, 88–90.

32. Richard Taruskin, *Music from the Earliest Notations to the Sixteenth Century*, rev. ed. (New York: Oxford University Press, 2009), 133.

critique of reconstructed Shaker dance. As Schechner points out, a reconstruction purporting to be "authentic" invites the expectation of a high degree of specificity—which particular dance, what dancers, what rhythm,
what relevant situational elements? To reconstruct a given *carole* in this manner would require a comprehensive sheaf of evidence rarely available in the
medieval archive.

VIRTUAL CIRCLES: MARK MORRIS'S *L'ALLEGRO,*
IL PENSEROSO ED IL MODERATO

As with *danse macabre*, one solution is to consider round dance's experiential effects in the collaboration of the audience and the spectacle. To work
toward this solution, I will subject the *carole* to the same strategy that I
brought to *danse macabre*, seeking an understanding of premodern dance
in the space between its historical occurrence and our modern access to
dance's experiential effects. This section will identify in Morris's *L'Allegro,
Il Penseroso ed Il Moderato* a tool for reenacting medieval round dance.[33]
Morris's piece contains several round dances, and as this section will argue,
the gazes of dancers and spectators during these sections produce circular
impulses of force that exist in multiple, unexpected, and not always symmetrical relation to the embodied circle dance itself.

The medial interplay of *L'Allegro*, this section will further suggest, reminds us of multimediacy's role in generating the virtual forces of dance.
The dancers' and spectators' attention negotiates among the piece's different medial components, not only bodies but also sung poetry and visual
art. The most evident form of medial relation in this piece lies in Morris's
integration of dance and poetic text. The piece is set to Charles Jennens's
arrangement of George Frideric Handel's musical composition for sections
from John Milton's poems. *L'Allegro*'s choreography uses cues from these
texts to bind together series of performed scenes ranging from abstract geo-
metric patterns to narrative representation. The dancers do not sing the
verses, of course, but Morris's choreography acknowledges the attributes
and content of the poetry and requires throughout that the audience take its
relationship to the dance into account. Less obvious, but equally important,

---

33. This piece has received treatment at the hands of the literary scholar Stephen Greenblatt
in a symposium on the occasion of *L'Allegro*'s 1994 West Coast premiere. Greenblatt's approach,
framed with biographical narrative of Milton, and preoccupied with the poem's narrative ability
to transform the textual and abstract to the bodily, does not engage the question of form. Wendy
Lesser, Greenblatt, Nicholas McGegan, Joan Acocella, and Alastair Macauley, "A Mark Morris
Symposium," *Threepenny Review* 61 (1995): 20–21.

is the fact that *L'Allegro* alludes to William Blake's illustrations of the Miltonic works.[34] The paintings do not appear in the sets, but their influence is evident in an array of visual elements, from gestural patterns to formations on stage. In different ways, these components inform the audience's and the performers' spectatorial experience, their shared network of gazing.

One might well ask why I have selected *L'Allegro*: whereas *Dance* is, as Scranton put it, an unusual "ideal" of medial engagement and therefore an especially apt interlocutor with *danse macabre*, round dance and variations upon it exist in numerous contemporary instances. One reason is *L'Allegro*'s own historical consciousness, a subject to which I shall return. Another involves experiential response. I chose this piece not only based on my spectatorship of contemporary dance but also after canvassing teachers, former professionals, and current dance students. Morris consistently surfaced as the contemporary choreographer whom the members of these communities associated with round dance. While obviously anecdotal, this information speaks to the experiences of those with participatory relationships to dance. Although *L'Allegro* contains many configurations and patterns, the round dances were especially memorable and suggestive to a group with various investments in dance. To some extent, this effect might derive from Morris's interest in folk and social dance tradition. I mention this not because Morris necessarily aims to create an overt choreographic continuum between premodernity and his own work, but rather because this affiliation infuses the choreography with a deeply participatory sense, one that—even in the proscenium structure—undermines the divide between audience and performer. For all these reasons, *L'Allegro* provides a useful means by which to reenact the subtly elusive medieval round dance.

A short scene fairly early in *L'Allegro* will illustrate its use of its different media. This scene appears in the section known as "The Diet Dances."[35] The libretto for this dance is drawn from the "pensive nun" section of *Il Penseroso*:

Accompagnato
There held in holy passion still,
Forget thyself to marble, till

---

34. On Blake's influence upon Morris in this work, see Alastair Macauley, "Still Tingling Spines after 25 Years: 'L'Allegro,' Mark Morris's Renowned Masterwork, Returns," *New York Times*, 10 November 2013, AR8.

35. Jeffrey Escoffier and Matthew Lore, eds., *Mark Morris' "L'Allegro, il Penseroso ed il Moderato": A Celebration* (New York: Marlowe, 2001), 48.

With a sad leaden downward cast
Thou fix them on the earth as fast.
Arioso
And join with thee calm Peace and Quiet,
Spare Fast, that oft with gods doth diet,
And hears the Muses in a ring
Round about Jove's altar sing.
Chorus
Join with thee calm Peace and Quiet,
Spare Fast, that oft with gods doth diet.[36]

As Joan Acocella notes, throughout *L'Allegro* the choreography moves alternately toward and away from the text: in some places it "sticks . . . close"
to the poetry's content, while elsewhere "the imitative logic is indirect."[37]
Certain gestures in "The Diet Dances" refer to the libretto's image of Muses
singing, perhaps most noticeably the dancers' periodic wide opening of the
mouth, often with fingers pointed toward their faces (figure 18). But what
begins as a seemingly straightforward enactment of the poem's reference to
singing diverts itself onto another path. For as the gesture is repeated, its exaggerated quality becomes increasingly disturbing.[38] The movement begins
to metamorphose from the imitation of singing to something more like the
gaping face of death, darkly alluded to in the poem's phrase "Forget thyself
to marble." Acocella reads the gesture similarly: "their mouths don't seem
to be singing; they look as though they're screaming. . . . I would call this
the Greek principle: no beauty without a note of terror."[39] Here we might
see text and dance responding to and embellishing each other.

Introducing *L'Allegro*'s invisible medium of painting into this reading
lends additional dimension to our understanding of this gesture. An illustration of "The Goblin," from Blake's watercolor accompaniments to the
poem, seems particularly relevant to this scene (plate 5).[40] Choreography

36. Libretto for Morris's work appears at http://markmorrisdancegroup.org/documents
/LAllegro-Libretto.pdf.
37. Joan Acocella, *Mark Morris* (New York: Farrar Straus Giroux, 1993), 242.
38. Teatro Real recording, PBS, 19:23–45, as well as, for example, 19:52–53, 21:29–31.
39. Joan Acocella, "A Silvered World," in *L'Allegro*, 18.
40. This Goblin refers to the Puck-like figure at ll. 100 ff. of *L'Allegro*, immediately following
the poem's "spicy nut-brown ale" reference. Roy Flannagan, ed., *The Riverside Milton* (Boston:
Houghton Mifflin, 1998) 69–70. Other illustrations that make similar use of this translucent
effect include "The Wandering Moon" (a phrase reflected in the dance beginning at 30:36) and
"Milton in his Old Age."

Fig. 18. Mark Morris, *L'Allegro, il Penseroso ed il Moderato* (1988).
Mark Morris Dance Group, Luminato Festival. Sony Centre,
Toronto, Canada, 2013. Photograph: David Leyes

throughout the "Diet Dances"' phrase pictured at right recalls both the shape
of the arms and the unsettling nature of the open-mouthed expression in
the painting. Through gesture, Blake's illustration thus suggests the contribution of the paintings to *L'Allegro*'s medial conversation. David Leventhal,
a retired member (1997–2011) of the Mark Morris Dance Group, confirms
this connection in a conversation about the experience of performing
L'Allegro. He notes that the paintings play a crucial role in Morris's choreography and that many of the "gestural motifs come directly from Blake."[41]
While the painting is not visible in the dance, it can still introduce itself into
the circuit between dance and text, intervening into the subtly disquieting
atmosphere of the performance at this moment.

This triangulation has implications for both the creation and the spectatorship of the piece. Leventhal identifies the network of dance-text-painting
as integral to the piece's process of choreographic construction, stating that
"Mark draws directly from . . . the text, in terms of taking a word and making
up his own gesture to it, as well as from an image from Blake, as well as from

41. Interview with David Leventhal, 29 January 2016.

both. So, a textual reference [is] supported by an image that Blake painted, and then that manifests itself in the choreography. . . ."[42] From the audience's perspective, that medial circuit in "The Diet Dances" occurs along those same points but in a different way: Hearing described the orderly and affirming circle of Muses in the text, we simultaneously perceive the danced gesture to tease Acocella's classical, tragic horror out from under it. The Goblin's spectrality, in turn, offers the ambient possibility—even if unseen—of an outlined, diaphanous shape for the inchoate shadow of terror lying beneath the meditative and orderly mood of the dance and its solid bodies.

In the collaboration of media underlying *L'Allegro*, then, lies the nascent suggestion of a virtual supplement to the dance. The painting undermines what at first appears to be the "imitative logic" whereby the dance simply mimics an image in the poem: a verse describing a ring of singers intended to correspond to a ring onstage appearing to sing. Instead, Blake's painting illuminates a different kind of trajectory. In dance and text's interaction exclusively with each other, we find the possibilities of warm, living movement as well as a kind of frozen death, communicated in the still maw of the dancers as well as the poetic image of amnesiac marble. Dance, text, and painting together, however, impel us along an arc of medial categories running from bodily performance, to the cold stasis of alabaster oblivion, to an image ambiguously material in its translucency. Blake's painting extends the scene's imagery to introduce a presence that inhabits living and otherworldly realms at once in its diaphanousness and its adumbrated role as a medium in the performance. The painting traces the possibility of a half-seen, partially present figure gesturally shadowing *L'Allegro*'s embodied performers. It gives shape to the ontologically indeterminate forces that we have labeled as virtuality in dance.

But how would an audience perceive such a virtual component given that Blake's paintings do not hover visibly over the stage? Answering this question requires us to understand what work occurs in the piece as a set of perceptual encounters, a network of gazing both at the piece and within it. As Alastair Macauley points out, sight and gazing comprise an important theme in *L'Allegro*. He mentions that the dance's gestures and its poetic accompaniment (as well as Milton's original poems) refer throughout to acts of seeing. For example, early in the libretto, we find a spectrum of gazing vectors in the lines "With a sad leaden downward cast / Thou fix them on the earth as fast," which continue the poem's earlier reference to Melan-

42. Ibid.

choly's "looks commercing with the skies, / Thy rapt soul sitting in thine eyes." In addition, the final air of the dance concerns Orpheus, a story that emphasizes many conceptual resonances of sight. Macauley describes the dynamic of this scene as one in which "we see Orpheus *seeing* Eurydice."[43] As this formulation suggests, gazing finds its operative power not simply in the audience's gaze at the work, but rather in the more elaborate networks created between and among dancers and spectators. In discussing the foundations of *L'Allegro*, Morris refers to his longstanding interest in folk and ethnic dance (including circle dances), noting that the dynamism of social dance lies largely in the interactions among participants rather than entirely in "what it looks like" from the outside, or in the proscenium theater setting.[44] A model of networked gazing, which includes the dancers' engagements with each other, thus offers an important point of departure from which to characterize the experience of *L'Allegro* and what will be revealed as its virtualities.

In *L'Allegro*'s round dance, gazing produces forces and presences that originate from the body but do not precisely align themselves with it. The first part of "The Diet Dances," for instance, involves several small circles of women. In the course of this section, the women tend to look directly at each other when in the process of forming their circles (as when the two initial groups each draw their third member onto the stage to form the two circles), or when the circle is still (as when the three recline on the ground and acknowledge each other by directing their arms and faces into the center of the circle, toward each other). But when the circles are moving, the women often send their gazes elsewhere (plate 6). Discussing his experience of the round dances in *L'Allegro*, Leventhal characterizes the distinct categories of gaze as the "aesthetically aware" focus of the dancer moving in the circle, on the one hand, and the "pragmatic, practical focus," on the other, of the dancer helping to engineer the circle's change or expansion as others join it.[45] What Leventhal calls the "aesthetically informed focus of looking in the line of direction of the circle" creates a complex effect for the audience of "The Diet Dances," because the women move in a circle while maintaining a straight trajectory of gaze. This means that their focus seems at times to cast itself outward and beyond the circle.[46] Their gazes thus

43. "Morris Symposium," 23.

44. "The Art of Mark Morris: *L'Allegro, Il Penseroso ed Il Moderato*," https://www.youtube .com/watch?v=bPakF1dNcs8.

45. Leventhal interview.

46. Leventhal's further description of dancing in a circle helps to clarify this subtle spatial dissonance. As he puts it, "the step travels in the line of direction of the circle, but there's a twist

bring attention to spatial elements of the spectacle that are not the embodied circle itself. In doing so, they destabilize any sense of hermetic closure
that the circular shapes might otherwise produce, prompting us to ask what
else is there in that negative space. While the text progressively shifts in
perspectival position between sky and earth, the dancers use their eyes both
to strengthen and to complicate the circular chains articulated in gesture,
movement, and blocking. When the audience watches the sightlines of the
dancers as they move through circular formations, they are prompted to ask:
What is traced in these dancers' gazes? What entities immaterial or ambiguously seen?

"The Diet Dances"' staging acknowledges the relevance of these questions by incorporating a scrim, which creates the effect of immaterial elements
interacting with the dancers' and audience's gazes. Morris places a translucent scrim between the downstage circle of three women and an upstage circle of another three women. That upstage circle multiplies into more circles
that eventually join to form a large circle turning in the shadows behind the
more unambiguously visible downstage round dance. Macauley states that
the scrim in this dance "makes us sense another world beyond this one, or at
least the denizens of this world addressing or conceiving those of another."[47]
This comment addresses the scrim's ability to represent different modes of
reality.[48] In *L'Allegro*, the lighting and the translucent barrier together create
the illusion that the upstage dancers are not quite ontologically the same
as the trio downstage. Within the context of this difference, the dancers behind
the scrim intermittently become the objects of the downstage dancers' gazes,
offering a focal point for what the main trio sees beyond the circle in which
it moves (plate 7). The dancers behind the scrim, in other words, become immaterial presences at which their more solid companions sometimes gaze. In
addition, the upstage dancers move in and out of temporal synchrony with
the downstage dancers, shifting between the temporal delay of echo, on the

---

in the body. . . . You start out with everybody standing facing into the circle, and then you take a
quarter turn in your lower body to the left, but you have to leave your back arm reaching to the
person next to you, so there's a little bit of a twist in the body" (Leventhal interview). Thus, the
body traveling in a circle is not exactly uniform in its vectors of eyes, feet, and torso; these must all
be oriented in slightly different directions in order to enable the circular movement.

47. "Morris Symposium," 23.

48. The scrim is often acknowledged to enable this effect in concert dance. Jack Anderson
notes that in ballet "a scrim makes it possible to see two scenic realities simultaneously." "Looking at Mirrors, Peering through Scrims (review of Siegel, *Mirrors and Scrims*)," *Dance Chronicle*
34 (2011): 290.

one hand, and mirroring, on the other hand, without such delay. In this way, the upstage dancers render indeterminate their relationship not only to the space of the downstage group but also to its time. Thus, by means of the scrim, we and the downstage dancers are looking at something spatiotemporally other.

Morris's exploration of the round dance in "The Diet Dances" further suggests that a circle of dancers not only sees but also, in seeing, projects other circles with its revolving and multidirectional gazes. We might recall Macauley's characterization of the worldly dancers as "conceiving" the others. To render this description in more specific terms: the gazes of the downstage dancers, flung outward and around the stage, seem to call the other circles into being. An example of this effect appears beginning at 21:10. As the group of three downstage dancers moves in the circle, their gazes rest in turn on the dancers on the other side of the scrim (rather than on each other). As this occurs, those three upstage circles expand outward into one large circle, with the step employed in that circle responding directly to the one the three downstage figures dance. From the audience's perspective, the choreography creates an effect whereby the gazing vectors emanating from the downstage circle seem to bring about and orchestrate the larger circle upstage.

To understand what occurs here in "The Diet Dances," we must turn to a round dance further along in *L'Allegro*. In the section titled "The Ladies' Dance" (1:12:40), the viewing experience of round dance involves a set of circular traceries that hover between bodies and syncopated forces; such forces are now familiar to us as the virtuality of dance.[49] This section of *L'Allegro* resonates gesturally with "The Diet Dances" through its repetition of the open-mouthed motif, the covering of the mouth, and a similar use of arms. The ensemble's final pose features what we might call the "goblin arms" of Blake's painting. This section's open mouth also coincides with its libretto's reference to Lydian airs:

Air
And ever against eating cares,
Lap me in soft Lydian airs;
Soothe me with immortal verse,
Such as the meeting soul may pierce
In notes, with many a winding bout

49. Escoffier and Lore, 96.

Of linkèd sweetness long drawn out;
With wanton heed, and giddy cunning,
The melting voice through mazes running,
Untwisting all the chains that tie
The hidden soul of harmony.

While the imagery of this verse preoccupies itself with sound more than sight, the discourse of winding, links, twisting, and chains emphasizes the concatenated gazing of the circle formation. To articulate these circles, the choreography enacts a species of spontaneous generation. The piece opens with a single circle that quickly transforms into concentric circles: alternating women in the circle propel themselves toward and away from the center with an energetic arm-swinging gesture, using force and momentum to separate a single circle into two, one inside another. The visual theme of concentricity continues throughout this section, with the dancers moving themselves, by means of various gestures, out of one circle and into two. The movement dynamics underlying this pattern speak to Langer's theory of dance existing in the forces and spaces between embodied gestures, the "relation of forces" that comprises the spectatorial experience of dance.[50] "The Ladies' Dance" involves formations that present the viewer with different bodily circles in relation to each other: high and low (figure 19) as well as concentric (figure 20). In addition to the circles made in the limbs' arrangement, the spectator is aware of circular spaces and forces between the bodily circles as the latter move toward and away from each other. By thus foregrounding propulsive and potential force, "The Ladies' Dance" lends further precision to the perceptual effect of the round dance in "The Diet Dances." In both cases, the bodily occurrence of round dance projects other circles—virtual circles—of ambiguous materiality ancillary to itself. These are easier to discern in "The Ladies' Dance" because the choreography there keeps the embodied circles and the dynamic interstices between them close together. That effect, however, allows us to see that in "The Diet Dances," acts of gazing other circles into being, and of apprehending circles that seem to occupy different ontological planes, equally launch virtual arcs of force in the spaces between, around, and within the embodied circles. Some of these forces function with closed circularity; others are more ambiguously unresolved, arcs of energy manifested as a circle takes or leaves its shape.

---

50. This phrase is cited in chapter 3; see also chapter 1 for a general discussion of Langer.

Fig. 19. Mark Morris, *L'Allegro, il Penseroso ed il Moderato*. Mark Morris Dance Group. Teatro Real, Madrid, Spain, 2014. Photograph: Javier del Real.

Fig. 20. Mark Morris, *L'Allegro, il Penseroso ed il Moderato*. Mark Morris Dance Group, Spring Dance (presented by Askonas Holt, Raymond Gubbay, and Sadler's Wells). London Coliseum, London, England, 2010. Photograph: Elaine Mayson.

We might now understand how the virtuality intimated by the painted medium of *L'Allegro* finds expression even when that medial element is not present in the performance. The possibility of the virtual supplement establishes itself in the piece's negotiation among its painted, textual, and gestural components, the translucent Goblin who hovers in the dance's conception and the dancers' knowledge of that. The paintings are crucial in endowing *L'Allegro* with its distinctive strangeness as dance. That strange virtuality manifests itself, however, in the spectatorial experience of the dance, the networks of gazing—across both dancers and audience—that produce virtual circles. "The Diet Dances" and "The Ladies' Dance" use different aspects of round dance choreography to create an experience of virtual circles as forces cast alongside, inside, and outside the main dance. Whereas "The Diet Dances" imagine circles generated from the main circle and existing adjacent to and behind it, "The Ladies' Dance" produces circles within and without each other and directly interacting with each other. All these circles, like other virtual supplements we have identified in dance, are ambiguously situated in reality, estranging in their space and time. They are apprehensible and fundamental to the spectatorial experience but not tangible, shadowing, like the Goblin, bodily gestures. And like the virtual effects we have seen elsewhere, their generation relies on a collaborative network of gazes that travel in many directions and originate at many sources, from audience member to dancer.

Morris's *L'Allegro* produces insights about danced virtuality that will play an important role in reenacting medieval dance. First, it elucidates the locus of such force not only in bodily movement but also in the sometimes undetectable interactions among the spectacle's different media. Second, the round dance choreography of *L'Allegro* reveals a virtual supplement that other circular formations could also generate through their gazing networks. In a further treatment of *L'Allegro*, Acocella comments that "The minute one pattern is formed, the next is born within it. You can't keep track of the thing. It blooms and blooms, never stopping."[51] In terms of the participant's experience, David Leventhal notes a similarly proleptic sense in the performance of the dance.[52] Virtuality—especially as dance theory understands it—gives a name to that sense of dance anticipated, the nascent but not quite mate-

---

51. "Morris Symposium," 21–22.

52. As Leventhal describes it, "You never really feel that sense of settling in it; it's constantly breaking open and re-forming itself, and so you always have to be aware and conscious of the pattern that you're creating on the floor because you have to . . . maintain the integrity of the shape as a large group, but you also have to get where you're going. . . . You're always looking ahead [to the next pattern]." Leventhal interview.

rial gesture within and around what is tangible. As Langer has suggested, the spectator apprehends such virtual force in any danced performance; Acocella's response to *L'Allegro* thus taxonomizes a feature essential to all dance. But her metaphor of blooming, the radiation outward of the bud, reflects the intensity with which round dance in particular foregrounds this effect. The spectacle's orchestrated gazing patterns conspire with material bodies to trace ancillary arcs that reorganize our experience of the spectacle.

REENACTING THE *CAROLE'S* VIRTUAL CIRCLES

L'Allegro's virtual circles, imminent within, and casting themselves around and beside, the actual circles of dance, offer a useful tool with which to reenact the medieval *carole*. In part, what was interpretive in the last section becomes methodological here. As we saw, in *L'Allegro* one medium of the multimedia spectacle (painting) plays a role in establishing virtuality's presence even as it operates undetected in the piece's spectatorship. In fact, its invisibility in the spectacle might cast *L'Allegro's* uncanny virtual forces into clearer relief than would otherwise be the case as they unspool from experiences of watching and dancing. *L'Allegro* thus suggests a methodological strategy: to *remove* certain relevant media from the spectacle's analysis, rather than capitalizing on their multiplicity of interlocution, as we did with *danse macabre*. At the end of chapter 2, I acknowledged that my study does not focus on music despite the fact that it was clearly an essential medial component of many dance traditions. My reenactment of the *carole* builds from the premise offered there that by removing music from the spectacle, we might more fully reveal certain visual dynamics that characterize the experience of this medieval dance. This method results, this section will demonstrate, in a reenacted medieval round dance layered with virtual circularities within, without, and beyond the embodied circles of dancers.

Before initiating the process of reenactment, let us acknowledge *L'Allegro's* actual and perceived limitations as a means to read medieval culture. First, *L'Allegro* is, of course, unconcerned with reconstructing the specific bodily experience of a premodern dancer. While Morris is informed about the history of Western European dance, he does not attempt to reconstruct the medieval *carole* or other ring dances with a goal of historical accuracy.[53] In chapter 3, *Dance* provided a reminder of the very contingency of such historical agents—differences in dance training and style at different historical moments—

53. Acocella sees Thracian line dance and Balkan folk dance among the work's major influences ("Morris Symposium," 22).

and that bodily contingency insists upon itself here as well. For example, the modern techniques and training underlying the Mark Morris Dance Group's movement style habituate the dancers to incorporating release work and to pushing themselves off their axes.[54] It might be for this reason that the women's propulsion into inner and outer circles as part of "The Ladies' Dance" so emphatically conveys the force of potential. Medieval performers dancing in a circle might have experienced such potential motion within their bodies similarly, but they might equally have experienced movement quite differently, and they were not trained in the modern techniques that attune dancers to that perspective upon movement. Thus, by virtue of reenactment's awareness of the gap between the historical occurrence and our present position, this method cannot attempt to recreate definitively the dancer's bodily status moving through choreography.

One might further judge that *L'Allegro*'s bridging of modernity and the Enlightenment renders it irrelevant to the medieval *carole*. *L'Allegro*'s critical response encourages the perception that this piece's defining aesthetics derive from the seventeenth and eighteenth centuries. Macauley, for instance, refers to the finale as "glowing enlightenment" and to the whole piece as a "musically structured, philosophical analysis of separate impulses in human thought." Its classical structure is much remarked upon, its "Grecian" costumes and "nymphs, goddesses, graces, or muses" who "start to look more like ordinary human beings, though their world, as in Homer, is one they share with deities. And, as these humans form into groups, you see the birth of society."[55] Critics seem committed to narrating Renaissance humanism through the dance. Acocella notes, "As its title indicates, it is a philosophical work. It shows us the mind bending itself not just around its own life, but around human life. For Milton in the seventeenth century, and Handel in the eighteenth, that was a normal stance, indeed the job of art"; Morris's harnessing and interpretation of these elements ultimately show "how much we still wanted to hear an artist talk about human life."[56] Here again, the discourses of humanism and enlightenment philosophy figure in the analysis of this piece.

But to what extent does this humanist association indicate a bias of modern and postmodern critical perspective? We must determine whether the valorization of postmedieval humanism reflects some essential char-

---

54. Acocella names Isadora Duncan and Doris Humphrey, for instance, as influences upon this piece (*Mark Morris*, 249).

55. Macauley, "Creation Myth," in *L'Allegro*, 126–29.

56. Acocella, "Silvered," 19.

acter of *L'Allegro* or whether we as postmodern audiences are conditioned to privilege philosophical rebirth and enlightenment in a piece like Morris's. In a review of Wayne A. Rebhorn's *Decameron* translation, Acocella's choice of rhetoric indicates a particular mode of approach to historical material. She ends her piece:

> I see the Decameron as a picture, with the ten elegant Florentines, in their silk gowns and embroidered doublets, joining hands and dancing their lovely circle dance, the *carola*. And in the middle of the circle are monks and merchants and painters and prostitutes eating dinner and having sex and kicking one another into ditches. In other words, we see the Renaissance embraced by the Middle Ages, like a planet orbited by its moons. It is a beautiful sight, and also strange. We see it from afar.[57]

This is a striking, provocative image of the relationship between the medieval and the early modern, but it is important to note here the extent to which the value of the medieval is construed in terms of its relation to the Renaissance. The *carola*'s cosmically ordered force is honored as medieval. But its function is to attend Ganymede-like upon, and give strange beauty to, the emergent modern. Acocella's simile reflects a pervasive inclination to look for foundational philosophical modernity and humanist subjectivity in works that reach into the distant past. It therefore encourages us to question whether *L'Allegro* really is a piece for post-1500 humanist discourse only or whether critical perception has created the belief that it is exclusively so.

While *L'Allegro* does not explicitly refer to medieval performance or artistic tradition, certain of its features resonate with the experience of the medieval *carole*. Perhaps most obviously, both *L'Allegro* and the *carole* inventively integrate poetic language and dance.[58] Not only are the dancers accompanied by poetry throughout the piece, but also, the nature of alignment between words and dance configures itself in different ways, as we saw above. To some degree, this structure approximates the experience the *carole* afforded, for the texts of medieval carols offered diverse possibilities in their relation to dance. In addition, the temporal complexity of Morris's piece models the temporal complexity of the *carole* tradition. Morris's choice

---

57. Joan Acocella, "Renaissance Man: A New Translation of Boccaccio's *Decameron*," *New Yorker*, 11 November 2013.

58. *L'Allegro* shares with many of Morris's other pieces a commitment to putting dancers into gestural conversation with a verse libretto (examples include *Dido and Aeneas* [1989], *Orfeo ed Euridice* [2007], and *Acis and Galatea* [2014]).

of baroque music fosters an atmosphere of retrospection and even deliberate archaism in the juxtaposition of contemporary choreography with earlier sound.[59] Wendy Lesser notes, "The line back to the seventeenth-century words and the eighteenth-century music feels strong and unbroken, and yet the dancers are performing steps and combinations that seem thoroughly modern."[60] As suggested above, a given *carole* performance might also potentially have contained within itself elements hailing from different temporal moments, deliberate archaisms of its own. While its temporal indeterminacy makes the *carole* on its own less reconstructable, its juxtaposition with *L'Allegro*'s version of chronological multivalence might make the *carole* more reenactable.

Initiating this reenactment process, we might note that *carole* evidence suggests the dance's potential to be construed in virtual terms even without a contemporary heuristic device. This suggestion occurs in the *Restor du paon* section of a fourteenth-century Alexander romance manuscript, Oxford, Bodleian Library MS Bodley 264. Here, a *carole* illustration appears in the left column of f. 181v (plate 8).[61] Attendant upon this folio are others that also refer visually to dancing the *carole* and feasting. A small round dance, for instance, appears at the bottom of f. 172v as well as a group of instrumentalists on the following folio (173r). Regarding f. 181v, Mark Cruse states that few manuscripts combine, as this one does, dance imagery, musical notation, and text on a single folio, and that this is the only such folio in this manuscript. He argues that this page integrates "music's imaginary presence," in the dance imagery and narrative, with actual musical notation in order to create a "proxy performance space."[62] In another study, Cruse, Gabrielle Parussa, and Isabelle Ragnard argue that the inclusion of music, image, and text in the Aix *Jeu de Robin et Marion* manuscript allows the eye to be more "dramatically engaged" than in other copies of this play.[63] The Alexander romance might be seen as sharing with the Aix *Robin et Marion* the ability to provide a spectatorial experience of dance in motion in the "theatrical and multi-media approach to its iconography and layout,"

59. Acocella sees the combination of these various epochs as indicating a belief in "the unity of history," "claiming that what Milton and Handel said is still true" (*Mark Morris*, 245–46).

60. Wendy Lesser, "An Artist for our Time," in *L'Allegro*, 134.

61. The description of this *carole* begins at l. 1159 (Mullally, *Carole*, 48n38).

62. Mark Cruse, *Illuminating the "Roman d'Alexandre": Oxford, Bodleian Library, MS Bodley 264* (Cambridge: D. S. Brewer, 2011), 41, 45.

63. Mark Cruse, Gabrielle Parussa, and Isabelle Ragnard, "The Aix *Jeu de Robin et Marion*: Image, Text, Music," *Studies in Iconography* 25 (2004): 9.

a "dynamic visual complement" to textual description.[64] What Cruse and his coauthors sense to be a "proxy performance space," containing dynamism and allowing active engagement by the eye, fits the parameters of virtuality as articulated in this study. Their reading conveys the possibility of a perceptible but intangible, as well as supplementary (what they call "complement[ary]"), presence that allows the audience to register motion even where none is embodied, an effect we saw in *danse macabre* installation. In short, the page casts the dance as a virtual manifestation for its medieval readers. Furthermore, the folio accomplishes this feat, like the virtual manifestations of *danse macabre*, by taking advantage of the intersections among media, finding animation in the spaces between them.[65]

The *Restor du paon*, then, offers the possibility that a medieval audience might perceive a *carole* as a virtual manifestation. The manuscript page suggests that within its intersecting medial trajectories—text, musical notation, and painting—springs motion of an apprehensible but ontologically distinct sort. Other theories of medieval reading practice reinforce this idea. For example, Cruse et al.'s reading of the folio speaks to Martha Rust's formulation of the "manuscript matrix," "an imagined, virtual dimension" in which text and image, "physical form and linguistic content . . . function together in one overarching, category-crossing metasystem of systems of signs."[66] Perhaps even more specifically, the elements of the *Restor du paon* folio, and the way that they set themselves and each other in motion, resonate with Jessica Brantley's theory of "performative reading," in which the act of reading could produce within the reader a "private and individual" or meditative performance responsive to traditions of public spectacle.[67] Against these analytical backdrops, the *Restor du paon*'s *carole* offers another opportunity to discern the medieval reader's experience of a performance in the perusal of a page; my reenactment method would specify that experience as one consistent with danced virtuality.

But while this scene of viewing facilitates the reenactment exercise by rendering tenable a *carole*'s virtual motion, it focuses primarily on the reader's mental processes rather than on the embodied perceptual experience the *carole* offered and thus can only partially complete the interpretive exercise.

64. Cruse, Parussa, and Ragnard, 30, 34.
65. Keith Busby sees the miniature of the golden eagle as a gesture towards a broader "ekphrastic perspective" in the manuscripts of this text. *Codex and Context: Reading Old French Verse Narrative in Manuscript*, vol. 1 (Amsterdam: Rodopi, 2002), 319.
66. Rust, 9.
67. Brantley, 305.

An interest in the *carole* as dance requires a different approach to the evidence. Placing Morris's contemporary dance beside the *carole* makes visible some components of the experience the *carole* offered to its viewers and participants. While this strategy might appear simply to chase the goal of finer-grained detail, it in fact diverges from that goal in two ways. One is that reenactment concentrates on the experience generated in the dance's multiplicity of perceptual vectors, rather than attempting to achieve a quantitative mastery of the dance's steps. The other is that the juxtaposition of medieval and modern—and in this case a modern example that is itself invested in historical positioning—maintains our necessary sense of the medieval performance's alterity even as we consider the experiences it offered.

The act of *joining* round dance emerges as one of its important experiential components; the comparison of *L'Allegro* to the *carole* augments the visibility of the gazing networks implicit to such acts of joining in the *carole*. To reenact the moment of joining, I read a fifteenth-century *Roman de la rose* illustration through Morris's *L'Allegro* (plate 9). In Oxford, Bodleian Library MS Douce 195, the lover is invited through both gesture and glance to join the circle, reminding us that moving from the nondancing state into the dancing one is an important component of the dance's ductile identity, the process by which one is led through it.[68] The *carole*'s visual and gestural means of invitation recall those moments in "The Diet Dances" when dancers nonverbally solicit their counterparts to enter and complete the two circles on stage. "The Diet Dances" employ a shift in the mode of the gaze when each group of two women brings a third one onstage to create the two initial circles. In Morris's work, a glance of interpersonal acknowledgment among the women draws the third into the circle. This mode of gazing distinguishes itself, as we saw, from the looking that takes place in the circle choreography, in which the women not only face away from each other but also seem to do so in a stylized manner that makes gazing part of a movement pattern, or more specifically an act that brings other patterns into being rather than signaling specific personal recognition. Turning to

68. Other depictions of the *carole* that incorporate the process of joining it exist, such as a scene from *Méraugis de Portlesguez* in which Méraugis "vet caroler" with his shield on his neck (Mullally, *Carole*, 85), passing from a nondanced mode and space into dance. Oxford, Bodleian Library MS Douce 332, f. 9v, also shows the Garden of Deduiz *carole* in the process of forming; at the moment that the illustration captures the participants, the configuration tends toward the linear. See also the *Court de Paradis*, which specifies the moment of invitation in a detailed description of the *carole*: "Tuit cil qui sont enamouraz, / Viengnent danssier, li autre non!" Barbazan, 141, ll. 400–401.

the illustration, we might ask whether this spectrum of different possible gazing modes also obtains here. While it is impossible to say definitively, there seems to exist a difference between the way that Coirtoise and the dancers to her immediate left and right engage the Lover, and the multiply directed gazes of the other dancers, which mostly do not fulfill this function of personal connection but rather communicate the effect of a more abstracted gaze—what Leventhal refers to as an "aesthetically informed focus"—on the part of the dancers turning in a circle.

The image's negotiation among these different types of gaze suggests the presence of the virtual circle that Morris's choreography elucidates. The category of the intersubjective gaze seems clearest, in both *L'Allegro* and the *carole*, in the transitional space and time of the circle's reconfiguration into a new circle. In *L'Allegro*, this variation in gazing mode allows trajectories of looking to appear to bring circles into being. With this idea in mind, we can perceive, even in the painting's stasis, the means by which the existing circle anticipates a new circle in a temporal and spatial phrase that contains the dreamer's gazing interaction with the other dancers. The gaze of invitation and response makes apprehensible the force of potentiality in the forming of a new, not yet actual, circle. In this way, the painting responds to Leventhal's point that if you are a dancer starting offstage, outside the circle, you must "envision the circle you're stepping into before you can even see anyone else in it" in order not to disturb its arcs when you enter it.[69] When a round dance forms or changes, that is, the gazes of its dancers produce a potential circle as supplementary to its actual one. Other types of gaze in the painting also communicate the presence of the spectacle's virtual supplement. Among the onlookers at the window, for instance, appears a musician whose gaze seems to include both the dreamer and the empty space between him and the existing *carole*. His vector of spectatorship reinforces the possibility that the *carole* has generated other apprehensible elements besides its embodied self. The visual mechanics of a round dance experience accessible to us in *L'Allegro* suggest that such experience might include a circle traced but not materially there, a manifestation of force, rather than bodies, that is nevertheless sensible to both audience and participants.

Coirtoise does speak her invitation (ll. 784 ff.), but in attending to the illustration's nonverbal representation of this interaction, different details of the dance's ductile experience become visible. The textual medium of

69. Leventhal interview.

the poem's narrative can perforce represent only a single sequence of gazing. The dreamer in this section of the text, that is, shifts his attention from one dancer to the next in turn, describing the physical aspects and costumes of each. Encountering this dance textually limits access to the dance's full complement of perspectival trajectories, and using the text alone to gloss what other viewing activities the illustration makes possible does not necessarily illuminate anything about the experience of the dance. It makes the *ductus* of the dance appear as a two-dimensional seriality. As has been suggested throughout, however, the ductile experience of dance is quite different. It involves a network of gazes across the inviting performer, the visually reactive audience, and the interstitial agent who hovers between dancing and not dancing. Together, these gazes trace the force and hovering potential of the circle not yet formed.

Reenacting the *carole* suggests that, in addition to the quality of gaze in the act of joining, specific directional vectors of gazing could also structure the dance's appearance and ductile experience. Indeed, not only MS Douce 195 but also other illustrations of *carole* seem preoccupied with conveying the experiential component of dancers' gazes moving in the act of dancing. Perhaps the most interesting orientation of gaze occurs in those representations that turn the dancers outward, away from the circle. Two such configurations occur in a *Roman de la rose* illustration of the *carole* in the Garden of Deduiz from the first half of the fourteenth century (figure 21) and an ivory depiction from approximately the same period of a *carole* scene from another text, the *Chastelaine de Vergi* (figure 22). Regarding the ivory *carole*, Mullally has argued that while "the double line of dancers is undoubtedly intended to represent a circle," the outward-turned orientation of the carolers in the front does not reflect the normal choreography of the *carole*.[70] Mullally's assertion opens some interesting possibilities. Perhaps the dancers' exterior focus in both images indicates the challenge their artists felt to convey movement in the static image. But equally possible is a scenario in which artists employ nonrepresentative or abnormal choreographic depictions to specific thematic or conceptual purpose. As Jonathan J. G. Alexander contends, medieval representations of dance do not appear to strive toward progressively more suc-

70. Mullally, *Carole*, 96. He notes that this carving and the other four ivory caskets that also depict scenes from this text are the only ivory representations of a medieval *carole* (95). While it is possible that these two different representations—ivory and illustration—of this outward-turned choreography indicate its real occurrence in some round dance, we might also keep in mind Richard H. Randall, Jr.'s observation that fourteenth-century ivories engaging romance tropes seem to share certain representational techniques with painting in this period. "Medieval Ivories in the Romance Tradition," *Gesta* 28.1 (1989): 33.

Fig. 21. Koninklijke Bibliotheek MS KB 120 D 13, f. 6v (1300–1350).
Photograph: Koninklijke Bibliotheek, The Hague.

cessful realistic representations.[71] It would thus seem that artistic choices regarding gazing orientation in the round dance do not reflect representational
struggles eventually conquered so much as other issues at stake in perceptions and experiences of round dance.

If we bear *L'Allegro* in mind, we might understand the outward-facing
carolers in the *Roman de la rose* image to trace with their gazes a virtual
supplement concentric to their embodied round dances. As *L'Allegro* demonstrated, engaging in round dance causes dancers to train their eyes on circles not yet articulated, making those circles subtly apprehensible to themselves and audiences. In the medieval representations, the dancers create an
immaterial circle outside their own with their gazes. The orientation of the
dancers in the *carole* depictions indicates its dancers' tendency—as both
performers and spectators—to generate ontologically indeterminate circles,
like the ones *L'Allegro* makes apparent as we watch it, in relation to their

71. Rather, a ninth-century depiction in the Utrecht Psalter, for instance, more effectively
conveys a danced circle than one in the fourteenth-century Luttrell Psalter. And at around the
same time as the stylized and somewhat flattened Luttrell Psalter image was produced, a Sienese
mural successfully captured "dancers interweaving in an illusionistic, three-dimensional space."
Jonathan J. G. Alexander, "Dancing in the Streets," *Journal of the Walters Art Gallery* 54 (1996):
158.

Fig. 22. Scenes from the *Chastelaine de Vergi* (ca. 1326–1350), France. Front left side of casket. Photograph: © Trustees of the British Museum.

own. In the case of the *Roman de la rose* illustration, the consistent pattern by which all the dancers in the *carole* face away from it suggests a circle of gazes all trained outward toward a circular outline outside the dancers' own, a circle of force that, like the one in "The Ladies' Dance," traces a shape outside the bodies. The ivory, for its part, seems to envision something more complex that I will discuss further below. In both cases, however, the orientation of the dancers' gazes casts virtual arcs outward and away from the embodied circle itself.

The concentric forces suggested here in the *Roman de la rose*'s gazing orientation have another home in medieval culture, functioning philosophically in Boethius's *Consolatio*. This text's incarnations evolve over time to articulate their own concentric virtual circles by means of analogies among media. In Boethius's text, Lady Philosophy instructs her listener:

Imagine a set of revolving concentric circles. The inmost one comes closest to the simplicity of the center. . . . The relationship between the ever-changing course of fate and the stable simplicity of providence is like that between . . . that which is coming into being and that which is, between time and eternity, or between the moving circle and the still point in the middle.[72]

Circles turning within and without each other provide a trope to explain the relationship of Boethian fate and providence in time and eternity. The viewer's perception of such immaterial circular manifestations receives additional emphasis in later medieval treatments of the Boethian construct. Anna Zayaruznaya reads Guillaume de Machaut's Motet 12, for instance, as encouraging the visualization of circle images in elaborating upon the Boethian content it musically describes. Machaut capitalizes on the circle not only as sonic structure but also as visual manifestation by asking its auditor, as Zayaruznaya proposes, "to see a circle in his mind's eye while listening to such a piece." The sensory apprehension of an auditory performance could thus foster a circular vision more ambiguously anchored in actuality. The motet implies circles of intangible force and sensible sound radiating outward from each other in the audience's experience. Zayaruznaya places this cognitive technique within the context of a new emphasis on visualization in cognitive process in the first half of the fourteenth century.[73] In a sense, therefore, the reenacted experience of the *carole's* virtual outward circle aligns it with a perceptual practice at work in its surrounding culture: the perception of concentric circles, associated with material manifestations but not on the same plane of being, which explicate a fundamental philosophical principle.

As they develop their relationship of analogy, the vision of the philosophical circles and the sound of the music align not only in hermetic circularity but also in more disorienting kinds of motion. Zayaruznaya elaborates on the comparison of music to philosophical construct by noting that the musical content promoting the imagination of a circle is far more complicated

72. "Nam ut orbium circa eundem cardinem sese uertentium qui est intimus ad simplicitatem medietatis . . . uti est . . . ad id quod est id quod gignitur, ad aeternitatem tempus, ad punctum medium circulus, ita est fati series mobilis ad prouidentiae stabilem simplicitatem." Boethius, *Philosophiae consolationis* IV, ch. 6, in H. F. Stewart et al., eds., *The Theological Tractates and the Consolation of Philosophy* (Cambridge: Harvard University Press, 1973), 342–44, ll. 65–67, 78–82. Victor Watts, trans., *The Consolation of Philosophy* (New York: Penguin, 1969), 136–37.

73. Anna Zayaruznaya, " 'She Has a Wheel that Turns . . .': Crossed and Contradictory Voices in Machaut's Motets," *Early Music History* 28 (2009): 199.

than a simple assertion of symmetry and order. On the contrary, its use of crossed voices also deliberately stages Fortune's vertiginous randomness.[74] As Zayaruznaya argues, voice crossing in the motet creates a sense of "extremes," of "plung[ing]," that *depicts* the precarious "state of flux" experienced by those on Fortune's wheel.[75] The similarity between the media of music and philosophical language foregrounds, in a medieval and modern audience's apprehension, elements of discord, asymmetry, or startling contradiction in the context of the wheeling, circular motion of Fortune.

Zayaruznaya's analysis might suggest that the next logical step would be to consider music and dance as layered together in their creation of virtual circles, but both the exigencies of dance and our modern relationship to it militate against this mode of proceeding. For when we try to consider music and dance's virtual circles as analogous in the manner of music and text, such an activity might occlude, rather than reveal, what is complex, orthogonal, or unexpected about those virtual manifestations. Thinking about how music accompanies medieval dance, we risk being lulled into a sense of accord or symbiosis that obscures from our eyes the more complicated engines of the medieval danced circle's articulation.[76] In part, we might exhibit this tendency simply because dance evidence lacks the detail that Machauvian musical notation provides to be recuperated with such complexity.

But I wonder if there is another reason as well, which is the extent to which some Western dance spectators (and I include myself here) have internalized Balanchinian notions of music's relationship to dance, the idea that choreography is a means to realize music interpretively. Jennifer Homans describes a relation George Balanchine understood between music and dance that has influenced the culture of contemporary concert dance (particularly ballet). In considering the nexus of narrative, dance, and music, she writes, "even when his dances followed a plot . . . they had a visual and musical logic all their own." She goes on to cite a formulation of Balanchine's own: "Stravinsky made time . . . not big grand time—but time that worked with the small parts of how our bodies are made."[77] This language emphasizes the strength of our modern constructs around the relation of

74. Ibid., 194.

75. Ibid.,194–95, emphasis in original.

76. See also Butterfield's point that circularity can be problematic in relating, and regulating, music and the text of "Maiden in the mor lay"; I take up this essay in chapter 6. "Poems without Form? *Maiden in the mor lay* Revisited," in *Readings in Medieval Textuality*, 192.

77. Jennifer Homans, *Apollo's Angels: A History of Ballet* (New York: Random House, 2010), 504, 526.

music and dance, the way that music and the body in motion can articulate each other's meanings in both formal and affective spheres.[78] Certainly, Balanchine and other modern choreographers, whose aesthetics influence what is familiar to many of us in classical and concert dance, do not subscribe to simplistic alignments of music and dance and often work instead in elaborately contrapuntal or oppositional ways. But this latter kind of interaction would be challenging to envision or reconstruct in early examples of round dance, leaving an interpreter to revert to a harmonious analogical model in which music, the dancing body, and the virtual forces it generates mutually affirm effects of resolution, closure, and symmetry.

For these reasons, while the Boethian example offers a relevant model for the tracing of concentric forces, it also casts into relief the importance of isolating from musical accompaniment the perceptual and kinetic mechanism by which such forces of circularity might form in dance. To remove music does, of course, provide an incomplete sense of the experience that the *carole* offers. For—as with the paintings in *L'Allegro*—the medieval performance's array of media all play crucial roles in constituting the experience of the spectacle and its virtual supplement. But in the case of musical accompaniment to vanished dance, it is more difficult to perceive the full spectrum of those effects. Contemplating the dance instead in the kind of unnatural silence I propose diverts us from applying assumptions about the medieval experience of sonic accompaniment forged in our own sense of sound's relationship to dance. It might, that is, leave space for us to discern the complexities of dance's virtual circles; some of these may resemble the crossing and asymmetry that Zayaruznaya detects in music, but some may also operate in distinct ways.

In this strange silence, the ivory *Chastelaine de Vergi carole* exposes an attempt to represent not symmetrical concentricity but rather a less resolving pattern of virtual arcs that participants trace in their gazes and along which they lead each other (figure 22). The three-dimensionality of the medium captures the "twist in the body" that Leventhal characterizes as necessary to round dance. From these variously torqued orientations, the dancers on the casket's surface face the viewer in a general sense, but their specific gazing trajectories are, predictably, more multiply directional. In addition, as delineated by the dancers' orientation, the embodied circle appears as a

78. The influence of this construct, again, largely advanced by George Balanchine, is apparent, as Homans shows, in Balanchinian ballet's entry into American culture in the twentieth century (538–39).

combination of a concave arc and a convex one. If the medieval *carole* generates virtual circularities, then this ivory's composition implies a particular
configuration of such virtuality. Specifically, the dancers' placement as all
facing the viewer would produce the virtual supplement from a set of gazing arcs cast in front of the scene rather than the concentric circle that the
Roman de la rose image suggests, with some of its dancers facing the back.
Perhaps the depth of the bas-relief, absent from the painting, works against a
fuller concentricity, the dimensionality of the dancers blocking the possibility of projecting something behind them to complete the circle.[79]

To reenact the *carole* based on the ivory suggests an array of perceptions
of circular force; it is not entirely symmetrical in three dimensions. The
carving, like other *carole* representations, creates its effects of circularity
by means of an elaborate network of gazing patterns, but these, as mentioned above, may evoke a kind of doubled open arc rather than a closed
circle. Perhaps this reflects the fact that the scene the ivory represents in the
Chastelaine de Vergi concerns not one *carole* but rather what might be more
than one occurring at once ("aus caroles" at lines 703, 722, and 849).[80] This
difference might explain the complexity of the gazing patterns in the ivory.
As an experience of looking, this *carole* is potentially reacting to a great deal
of visual information, not the single *carole* that its dancers both participate
in and watch but rather a multiplicity of circles around them ranging from
embodied presentations to the virtual forces between and among those tangible elements. The ivory's multiple points of focus among the dancers also
remind the viewer that the arcs these carolers generate in space are not experienced in exactly the same way by every viewer. While the front line of dancers creates symmetry in the alternating directions of the glances, the ivory as
a whole, with all the glancing trajectories taken together, renders the *carole*
not as an experience of completely smooth circularity but rather as one that
might bristle with ancillary, crossing, contingent arcs of force. The ivory representation of the *carole* conveys the mechanics of its gaze—the perceptual
arcs cast out from the circle—with a high degree of specificity. But its bodily

79. Other painted representations also employ this configuration, such as Bibliothèque nationale Fr. 12595, f. 10v. The much smaller size of this *carole*, however, makes the projection of
arcs in its sightlines—and indeed the very circularity of the dance itself—a bit more ambiguous
generally.

80. Gaston Raynaud, ed., *La Chastelaine de Vergi, poème de 13e siècle*, 2nd ed. rev. Lucien
Foulet (Paris: Honoré Champion, 1912), 22, 23, 27. This text quotes one stanza from the *chanson*
"A vos, amant, plus k'a nule autre gente." See Butterfield, *Poetry*, 39, for a discussion of this stanza
quotation in the context of the relationship between songs in *chansonniers* and as insertions into
romance narrative.

arrangement also prevents it from offering a symmetrical, resolved sense of concentricity. It therefore broadens, in the reenactment process, the possibilities for understanding the *carole*'s experiential character.

It is perhaps in its very choreographic oddity, its subtle skewing of the concentric impulse, that the ivory casket communicates the bodily and perceptual experience, as well the pivotal role of the gaze itself, that define the medieval *carole* and its virtual supplement. To elaborate upon this experience I turn back momentarily to *L'Allegro*. The casket scene might, for instance, project an incomplete arc radiating around itself. Or its company of dancers might constitute through their gazes a virtual circle that overlaps with the embodied circle, linked with and situated in front of *carole* rather than around it. Or different dancers might generate different perceptual arcs according to their placement in relation to each other and to the other embodied *caroles*, a multiplicity of virtual forces that *L'Allegro* allows us to experience in round dance. The ivory *carole*'s visual program conveys the potential to interlock many circles, traced in bodies, spaces, and light, which *L'Allegro* reveals as fundamental to the experience of round dance.

But can we, finally, hope to ascertain anything of the virtual circles the medieval audience sensed in the black box of their experiences? Not fully; however, in its juxtaposition with Morris's round dances, a fifteenth-century illustration by the Master of the Vienna *Roman de la rose* in Vienna, Austrian National Library MS 2568 intimates the perception of a *carole*'s virtual circle in its complex orientation to the dance (figure 23). Here, the shape traced in the contours of the God of Love's wings (slightly off the center of the image) generates a negative (and not quite complete) ovoid space that reflects, at a ninety-degree twist, the oval shape of the round dance. Some of the dancers' multidirectional gazes in this illustration seem to acknowledge the oval formed by the wings. Reading this image in terms of *L'Allegro*'s visual effects inflects our sense of what it conveys. As noted earlier, "The Diet Dances" employ a scrim to create an apparent distinction between real and otherworldly participants. Another choreographic component contributing to this effect is the use of level change between the upstage and downstage dancers. The blocking in this section creates the effect of a slight difference in vertical level between the upstage and downstage performers (see, for example, 20:00–20:08). This level difference, as generated in the perceptual vectors of *L'Allegro*'s spectators, performs an additional function beyond distinguishing the different circles' relations to material reality. It lends another directional axis to the kinetic interaction of the two circles, multiplying the possibilities by which virtual circles might orient themselves in relation to real ones in the perceptual experience

Fig. 23. Österreichische Nationalbibliothek Cod. 2568, f. 7r (ca. 1425).
Photograph: Austrian National Library, Vienna.

of round dance. This reading of Morris allows us to perceive the effect that the *Roman de la rose* illumination attempts to portray. The empty oval floats above the danced one, and on a vertical rather than a horizontal axis. In its portrayal of not only the oval shape itself but also the other dancers' gazers floating up to it, the scene conveys a perceptual experience for the *carole*'s participating spectators. As they turn in their own circle, collective in participation and spectatorship, their kinetic bodies and gazes manufacture other circular impulses, forces, and environments to perceive.

Rather than blooming outward symmetrically, the virtual circles in the *carole* images discussed here project themselves in orthogonal orientation. They function as suggestively ancillary, floating in the corner of the eye rather than asserting themselves at the center of a mental landscape. They are tangent to the danced circle but also set slightly askew of it. In a sense, the God of Love illustration recalls Zayaruznaya's imagined circle, which figures musical experience as a metaphoric shape floating in the mind's eye to explicate the Boethian content of a listening encounter. Reenacting dance by focusing on its perceptual experiences, however, also casts into relief another spatial characteristic of this virtual circle. It engineers projection, an effect where the circle of air and light originates in, but also hovers as spatially distinct from, the embodied dance.[81] Albert Henrichs proposes the term "choral projection" to describe how the danced performance of the Greek chorus—often a circle—casts itself into other times and spaces during the experience of Hellenic dramatic spectacle. Henrichs notes that choral performance moves across time, between myth and reality, and from the orchestra to the dramatic world onstage; the spectacle, in his account, constantly separates the dancing from the orchestra and resituates it in other times and places.[82] In this more ancient context, then, the virtual other in performance can articulate its operation in the language of projection. The virtual circle of the *Roman de la rose carole*, formed in the collaboration of dancing bodies, the space of the potential circle, and the many gazing trajectories organizing the spectacle, is cast contiguously to the embodied carol, reoriented out of an absolute center and hovering peripherally so as to be different for each dancing viewer and spectator.

This chapter provides a foundation from which to reenact the poetic form of the textual carol in the next chapter. Reenacting the danced *carole* by juxtaposing it with Morris's *L'Allegro* reveals the virtual supplement that the *carole* generates and that seems reflected in certain depictions of this dance. In these, the oddity of representation might sometimes indicate an attempt to convey the familiar strangeness of the virtual circle that the

---

81. This is not to exclude music from participating in this dynamic—on the contrary, it seems likely that one could make an argument about music's relationship to dance that would enhance such orthogonality.

82. Albert Henrichs, "'Why Should I Dance?': Choral Self-Referentiality in Greek Tragedy," *Arion* 3.1 (1994/5): 68, 73; Henrichs, "Dancing in Athens, Dancing in Delos: Some Patterns of Choral Projection in Euripides," *Philologus* 140.1 (1996): 48.

carole's ductile experience generates. To gain access to the surprise and occasional irregularity of these circles, which develop not only concentrically but also contingently, contiguously, incompletely, orthogonally, and asynchronously, the narrative reenactment method has focused on the *carole*'s visual effects by approaching dance in terms other than its music. Moving into the second part of this case study, which investigates the poetic carol, we take with us both the animated diversity of the virtual supplement's placement in the *carole* and an approach to medial relations that does not depend upon materially present multimediacy. Even a nondanced medieval poetic tradition, we shall see, can draw upon the medium of dance in complex ways. In the readings that follow, the virtual supplement of the *carole* guides the strange footing of the carol's poetic form.

CHAPTER SIX

Dance on the Surface, Dance in the Depths: Reenacting Form in the Middle English Carol

A s the second part of the case study on *carole* and carol, this chapter will argue that the spectator's habituation to virtual circles in round dance configures the formal experience of the Middle English poetic carol. In this ductile experience of poetic form, the reader is aware of forces, irregular and uncanny, supplemental to the evident regularity of the lyric's stanzaic pattern. Formalist criticism preoccupied with modernity has—unsurprisingly—limited the potential for the formal interpretation of the Middle English lyric, in particular the carol. Modern lyric theory relies upon the medieval carol's predictability and unselfconscious repetitiveness to stage contrast to the modern and postmodern refrains that incisively trouble such seriality. Reenacting a formal experience conditioned in the *ductus* of dance, however, reveals in the virtual supplement a strangeness of form not conceivable in modern and postmodern contexts and terms.

My model of formal experience is based on a conception of *ductus*, outlined in chapter 2, that addresses the interaction of different media and the possibility that perceptual habits elicited by one medium can inform a spectator's encounter with another. For this reason, it is vital to acknowledge the medial situation of the carol in relation to the multimedia tradition of *danse macabre*. *Danse macabre* as installation construes an audience encountering textual and dance-based media (in the form of bodies or visual art) at once; even its very late copying, as we saw, announces its tie to an installation. For readers not physically immersed in the physical spectacle, *dance macabre* verse positions its author, Lydgate, as a spectator of those dance-based media; he turns to the project of poetic making with a consciousness thus inflected. In this way, the ductile experience of *danse macabre* poetry's form not only negotiates between authorial and readerly habituation to dance-based media but also, in doing so, preserves some manner of engagement with the visual and bodily media even in a book-based situation. Carols also reflect a complicated relationship to dance-based material media but do so within a different narrative: by the late Middle Ages, the intensity of association between poetic carols and dancing varies. Given, as the introduction discussed, that dance enjoyed ubiquitous integration into medieval culture, it seems unlikely that someone reading or hearing a late-medieval carol did so utterly devoid of any awareness of *carole* and other round dance. But the range of possibilities for a poetic audience's contact with dance runs from participation to memory to other associations less explicit and clear than what Lydgate provides by incorporating his encounter with the installation into his poem.

Thus, where *danse macabre* verse profits from a reading method that values a plurality of media and capitalizes on those multifarious interactions, the carol requires some different means to theorize its medial situation. The approach that would attempt to reconstruct the presence or absence of the danced medium in the ambit of any particular poem carries the same limits reconstruction has been shown to possess throughout. This chapter will concern itself instead, therefore, with the extent to which a poem makes evident the possibility of the danced medium, signaling the perceptual habits of that medial setting even if it is not present. Mark B. N. Hansen has argued that the body "preserve[s] within itself" the recognition of media as "self-differing." Embodied experience and response, that is, organize environments of medial heterogeneity that distinguish themselves from the kind of installation that understands individual media as independent and coherent.[1] This formulation buttresses the notion that for a reader, dance can function as a constitutive medium in the encounter with poetry even in its bodily absence. It is the relationship to dance formulated in the reader's body, rather than the presence of dance, that produces the experiential mode affecting the perception of other media. At the same time, the medieval context lends even greater specificity to the dance's capacity as a medium to constitute the poetic carol's formal experience, whether dance is apparent at the lyric's surface or lies, obscured from detection, in the lyric's depths. In the readings that follow, we shall see how a poem's formal experience might, for instance, call attention to the complexity of that experience's relation to what can be embodied as dance. Alternately, the virtual supplement can become a residue of danced *ductus* more apparent in the lyric than dance itself.

---

1. Mark B. N. Hansen, *New Philosophy for New Media* (Cambridge, MA: MIT Press, 2004), 24–25, 30–31. Hansen refers here to the work of Rosalind Krauss.

These medial situations are partly attributable to developments in the carol's fate. For example, the carol's musical identity adjusted itself through the increasing use of polyphony, possibly creating distance from the function of dance accompaniment.[2] At the same time, dances accompanied by carols continued to be performed into the early modern period.[3] Certain carols, meanwhile, seem to exist as nonperformed textual presences only, even as their verse structure and other formal attributes continue to reflect the requirements of the danced idiom. The emergence of singly-authored, or singly-compiled, carol collections in the fifteenth and sixteenth centuries also shifts the carol into a more emphatically textual category. In addition to the late-fifteenth-century carol collection of James Ryman (Cambridge, University Library MS Ee.1.12), as well as the fourteenth-century holograph manuscript of John of Grimestone (Edinburgh, National Library of Scotland MS Advocates 18.7.21), containing numerous carols, we find a sequence of carols appearing to have been planned by the fifteenth-century poet John Audelay in Oxford, Bodleian Library MS Douce 302. E. K. Chambers and F. Sidgwick muse on the possibility of Audelay's Goliardic past, positing through this speculation a connection between the pious carols of the manuscript and the "secular *caroles* or dance-songs from which they must, in some sense, have inherited their name."[4] While this analysis remarks upon the stanzaic similarity between Audelay's poems and those of the dance-song tradition, most critics would at the same time acknowledge the Audeleian carol's physical and conceptual abstraction from any danced situation.[5]

But it would oversimplify the case to plot a trajectory of increasing distance between dance and poetry; the carol often finds itself in a temporal situation involving retrospection, belatedness, and nostalgia concerning dance. Perhaps independently of the carol's status as actual dance accompaniment through the progression of the Middle Ages, it can sometimes convey a sense of wistful relation to dance practice. One might wonder, for instance, about

2. On fifteenth-century carols recorded as "part-songs" for two or three voices in the vellum roll Trinity College MS Cambridge O.3.58, see Chambers, *Close*, 94–95.

3. Frank Llewellyn Harrison, *Music in Medieval Britain* (London: Routledge and Paul, 1958), 416–24; Frank McKay, "The Survival of the Carol in the Seventeenth Century," *Anglia* 100 (1982): 36.

4. E. K. Chambers and F. Sidgwick, "Fifteenth Century Carols by John Audelay," *Modern Language Review* 5.4 (1910): 475.

5. Elsewhere, Chambers questions his speculation concerning Audelay's "Goliardic youth," attributing the poet's critique of his indulgent past to "conventional piety." "On the whole," Chambers notes, "I feel that Awdelay is rather remote from the main tradition of carol development" because his carols tend to concern individual "didactic personality" rather than the "singing throng." *Close*, 93–94.

the extent to which Sir Gawain's danced *carole* emblematizes the retrospective impulses of the whole poem. In addition, as chapter 1 mentions, the Wife of Bath's ring of dancing ladies accompanies her distress over a lost time of greater magic.[6] John Speirs notes that "the English medieval carols may indeed be described as in their essential nature dance-songs, whether or not those that have survived were still being danced to or were simply being sung at the time when they were written down."[7] Although Speirs's statement reflects a temporal shift from dance to song, it also intimates the extent to which the uncoupling of carol from dance is far from chronologically neat or definitive. Mullally sees the word *carole* as an "archaism" in the fifteenth century, something that has ceased to refer to a contemporary choreographic practice but that still recalls a choreographic idiom.[8]

The readings that follow take place, then, within a complex sense of medial engagement, where dance may, in different ways, approach and recede from any given encounter with a poetic text. While the first poem under discussion, "A child is boren," is considered a carol mainly by modern taxonomy, the second, "Maiden in the mor lay," finds itself explicitly referred to as a carol in its immediate late-medieval context. Neither poem, however, conforms entirely compliantly to the formal protocols that the poetic carol seems to impose. And while "A child is boren" is fairly conventional, "Maiden in the mor lay" is the subject of a venerable critical tradition predicated upon its stylistic and atmospheric uniqueness. The choice of the latter example in particular risks appearing to disregard Butterfield's reminder that many medieval lyric texts are, in fact, formulaic and conventional. As she notes, our modern construction of the lyric as a category tends to lead us to exceptional instances in premodern literature, but these exceptions potentially compromise our ability to understand the medieval corpus on its terms.[9] To address this problem, I offer a method for reenacting poetic

---

6. An analogue to this scene emphasizes the role dance plays in attunement to the past. Walter Map records a Celtic tale in which a man sees on three successive nights "choreas feminarum," dancing women who repeatedly sink into the stagnant water as he approaches them, appearing again the following night. Map's anecdotes gesture toward his preoccupation with historical tradition. *De nugis curialium*, ed. M. R. James (Oxford: Clarendon Press, 1914), 72. For Lilla Train, the similarities between the Wife's dancers and those in Map's anecdote suggest that both signal a transition between the worldly and the supernatural. "Chaucer's Ladyes Foure and Twenty," *MLN* 50.2 (1935): 85–87.

7. John Speirs, *Middle English Poetry: The Non-Chaucerian Tradition* (London: Faber, 1971), 51.

8. Mullally, *Carole*, 1.

9. Butterfield, "Why," 325–26. In her terms, "large swathes of verse" from the Middle Ages do not conform to our sense of what lyric should be (325); rather, "the 'lyrical' lyrics are the ex-

formal experience that explains the perceived exceptionality of a lyric to modern readers but does not depend upon that exceptionality to do so. What it does depend upon, instead, is the unexceptionality, familiar in its very strangeness, of the *ductus* of dance.

RELIEVED OF THIS BURDEN

To discuss the formal experience of the medieval carol requires first addressing what we might consider its distinguishing formal attribute: the *burden*.[10] The burden's most important characteristics, from our perspective as modern readers of the carol, are the fact that it repeats regularly throughout the carol and the fact that it differs from other kinds of lyric refrain in its structural independence from the carol's stanzas. This independence can obtain at the level of verse structure, rhyme, or musical setting. In all cases, the burden functions as an independent poetic unit and is not integrated into the stanza as would be the case for other types of refrain. But while such a characterization of the burden seems reasonably value-neutral, this section will demonstrate that our critical taxonomy of repeatability and separability in the carol burden has in fact obstructed our understanding of the full range of formal experience this poetry offered its readers. Considering the problem of New Criticism's identification of short, stanzaic medieval poems as "lyrics," Butterfield has proposed that medieval lyric "was invented as category of medieval writing to satisfy the predilections of 'practical criticism.'"[11] The carol finds itself in an even tighter bind: construed as lyric according to certain modern principles, it is then doomed to fail as an object of productive formal analysis because of the very characteristics that define it.

The *burden* refers to a verse that begins and ends a carol and is repeated after each stanza, but in this usage it is a somewhat vexed term. This sense of *burden* represents postmedieval nomenclature (first attested in the sixteenth century and finding its most famous early modern utterance in Shakespeare's stage directions for Ariel's songs); in the late Middle Ages, the term did not designate a repeating verse between stanzas, but rather a "drone"

---

ceptions that prove the rule that medieval short verse is essentially formulaic, often practical, and, above all, religious" (325). See also Nelson, 6, 18–26 on the problematic nature of the term "lyric" in medieval poetry.

10. There is a degree of predictability to the form of the English carol stanza itself; however, it varies enough to warrant employing the burden's existence as a more consistent defining criterion. For a summary of the carol stanza's structure and variants, see Chambers, *Close*, 100–101; he notes as well that "the refrain is the making of the carol" (101).

11. Butterfield, "Why," 325.

or "undersong," as in the "stif burdoun" that the Summoner bears the Par-
doner in the *Canterbury Tales*.[12] *Refrain*, however, was a term in use in
the period, a point to which I shall return at the end of this section. In the
scholarship of the carol, the term *burden* emerged to signal that the repeated verse in the carol is distinct from other kinds of lyric refrains: removing the burden in the copying of the poem does not affect the integrity of
any individual stanza. In addition, according to the limited evidence of the
English carol tradition, burdens could also be musically distinct from their
surrounding stanzas.[13] Some carols, as we have seen, end their stanzas with
short lines or phrases that signal the impending burden by rhyming with its
first line. The presence of these lines speaks to the carol's danced heritage,
in which the chorus would benefit from the lyrical alert to chime in with
the burden.[14] But in terms of its poetic content and form, the burden is still
structurally separable from individual stanzas even though it is repeated
throughout the carol.

In a medieval context, the effect of formal repetition might be to create
a sense of familiarity and expectation fulfilled. This effect suggests itself
most obviously in a performer's reliance upon the consistent recurrence of
a burden. But it can be reflected in the burden's content as well, particularly
its use of idiomatic and proverbial language, phrasing perforce experienced
as frequently repeated. Taruskin notes that the French refrain's ability to
circulate and reappear in different contexts likens it to a proverb.[15] Certain
English carol burdens, like those of John Audelay, in fact have an overtly
proverbial character. As Greene notes, the burden of a late carol (from Richard Hill's sixteenth-century collection) even begins "An old sawe hath be
fownd trewe."[16] The poem creates familiarity in its repetitions while also
self-consciously gesturing to this very quality of familiarity in the phrase
"old sawe." While Taruskin and Greene's comparisons of the burden's lan-

---

12. William Shakespeare, *The Tempest*, in *The Riverside Shakespeare*, ed. G. Blakemore
Evans et al. (Boston: Houghton Mifflin, 1974), II.i.375–405. *MED* s.v. *burdoun*. Reichl, 157. See
also *CT* I.673. Greene emphasizes this distinction in his carol anthology: "It is hardly necessary
to say that in this work 'burden' is never used in its other and older sense of an under-song, words
to be sung simultaneously with the stanza-text" (*EEC*, clx).

13. Kathleen Rose Palti, "'Synge we now alle and sum': Three Fifteenth-Century Collections
of Communal Song," vol. 1. PhD diss., University College, London, 2008, 142.

14. *EEC*, clxv. Tags can vary from one stanza to the next or be repeated lines themselves.
Greene describes how the *cauda* of a carol's tail-rhyme stanza might rhyme with the burden, in
addition to a structure used by Audelay whereby each stanza has appended to it the same short
line or phrase, which rhymes with the burden.

15. Taruskin, *Earliest*, 120.

16. *EEC*, no. 346, 209; clxx. See also Zumthor, *Essai*, 78, on proverbial language.

guage to proverbs primarily concern transmission, the similarity also speaks
to the proverb's dependence on recognition and the ability to satisfy expectation through the familiarity that accompanies repeated pronouncement.
The repetition of a stanza in a poem builds a sense of expectation around itself through its multiple occurrences within the poem. It might sometimes
even enhance this sense of familiarity in the homespun echo of proverbial
language. Recognition and expectation fulfilled thus seem to be hallmarks
of the medieval burden.

For modern readers, however, the burden's recurrent quality can be more
likely to signal not simply repetition but rather repetition tempered or inflected with variation. A repeating element like a burden, that is, creates an
expectation of periodicity while at the same time subverting and varying
what rises to meet that expectation. Modern theories often perceive such
conscious subversion of expectation in a verse's repetition. This model finds
a foundation in Edgar Allan Poe's essay "The Philosophy of Composition."
Here, Poe (who refers to his construction as a "burden" as well as a refrain)
specifies that variation around a poem's repeated element augments the
pleasure derived from that repetition:

> The pleasure is deduced solely from the sense of identity—of repetition.
> I resolved to diversify, and so vastly heighten, the effect, by adhering,
> in general, to the monotone of sound, while I continually varied that of
> thought: that is to say, I determined to produce continuously novel ef-
> fects, by the variation *of the application* of the *refrain*—the *refrain* itself
> remaining for the most part, unvaried.[17]

Thus, the modern understanding of the repeated burden or refrain in a poem
hinges upon a suggestive conflict between the anticipation of sameness
and the introduction of difference. This conflict characterizes modern constructs concerning the nature of poetic language more broadly. Roman Ja-
kobson's "poetic function," for instance, involves repetition with variation
as well (as in his "I like Ike" example); Jonathan Culler applies this quality
of repetition with *variatio* specifically to poetic rhythm.[18] Poe's location

17. Edgar Allan Poe, "The Philosophy of Composition" (1846), repr. in *Essays and Reviews*,
ed. G. R. Thompson (New York: Library Classics, 1984), 17, emphasis in original.
18. Jonathan Culler, *Theory of the Lyric* (Cambridge, MA: Harvard University Press, 2015),
132. Culler cites Northrop Frye's identification of an "oracular, meditative, irregular, unpredictable, and essentially discontinuous rhythm" in the metrical packaging of *Measure for Measure*'s
iambic pentameter (Culler, 132–33).

of this effect within the poetic refrain emphasizes the refrain's constitutive role in these broader characterizations of poetic language's function. One might say that lyric refrain emblematizes the different kinds of repetitive impulses (list making, alliteration), and their sometimes unexpected effects, that poetry hosts.[19] In all these modern cases, sameness exists in productive tension with difference.

Poe further elaborates on his burden by establishing a requirement that the repeating element of the poem be short and simple to accommodate the oscillation between sameness and difference. Specifically, Poe explains that the actual repeating component in the poem must be as brief as possible in order to enable adjustments to its presentation, context, and the sounds to which it is attached:

> Since its application was to be repeatedly varied it was clear that the *refrain* itself must be brief, for there would have been an insurmountable difficulty in frequent variations of application in any sentence of length. In proportion to the brevity of the sentence would, of course, be the facility of the variation.[20]

Through its brevity, the refrain is thus able, despite its repetitiveness, to "startl[e]" the reader from "*nonchalance.*"[21] In dictating the formal experience of a poem, then, a repeated verse uses its own simplicity and adaptability to manufacture a fulcrum between adage-like familiarity and the suspense of a creatively engineered note of change.

This dichotomy of sameness and difference, as engendered in the formal practice of repetition, would appear to be available to the medieval carol as well: one could presumably read any carol, like any refrain-based poem, as reinflecting the burden with each repetition. Indeed, formalist scholars of medieval literature engage in the general formalist practice that seeks out subtle variations and obtrusions within the structure of a medieval lyric's repeating verses. Cristina Maria Cervone, for example, notes in her discussion of medieval lyrics that "at its best, a refrain also thwarts our expectations when it offers an apt surprise."[22] Readings such as this suggest that we might, as modern readers of medieval lyric, apply our conditioning—which

---

19. On these iterative elements, and the idea that a poem "seduces by lists," see ibid., 178–80.
20. Poe, 17–18, emphasis in original.
21. Ibid., 19, emphasis in original.
22. Cristina Maria Cervone, *Poetics of the Incarnation: Middle English Writing and the Leap of Love* (Philadelphia: University of Pennsylvania Press, 2013), 188.

privileges this kind of surprise or unexpectedness—to our interpretive practices around medieval lyric.

And yet, when we scrutinize the points of intersection between medievalist scholarship and the formalist discourses shaped by modernity, we run
into a problem. Aspects of the burden make it difficult to read in terms of the
modern construct of variation-within-sameness. For one thing, medievalist
scholarship often understands the English carol to showcase conceptual sophistication by means of the very complexity of its burdens. In Greene's
terms, the more substantive a burden, the further removed from the "simplicity" of folk idiom.[23] This type of more detailed burden succeeds, for
Greene, in reflecting "the matter of the stanzas" effectively. Siegfried Wenzel reads "Lovely tear of lovely eye" (1372) as articulating intricate emotion
through its address to Christ's tears; with the stanzas, the burden "reinforces the poem's theme and mood."[24] Such burdens offer more than what
Greene calls an "exclamatory chorus, such as it often is in folk-song, where
its structural importance wholly overshadows its meaning."[25] (This type
of chorus would include onomatopoetic burdens of carol lullabies, which,
with their soporifically reiterated "lully lullays," are associated with infan-
tile "monotony and slightness of idea."[26]) In the medievalist study of carols,
the more elaborate the burden, the greater its potential for hermeneutic or
thematic elaboration. But herein lies the conundrum. This very complexity countermands the simplicity of structure that, for modernity, enables a
valuable formal dynamism and changeability in the refrain's repetition. The
more substantive and intricate the burden—the further it travels from the
"or" sound in Poe's "Nevermore"—the more reified it becomes, and therefore the less susceptible to shadings of variation by its repeated adhesion to
different stanzas. Within the context of an ingrained modern formalist
discourse around refrain repetition, the structural and thematic richness of
the burden itself might restrict the richness produced in the interactions of
the burden with what surrounds it.

If the medieval burden's complexity implicitly limits the interpretive
possibilities in its repetition, then the burden's separability is even more
interpretively confining. The burden's detachability from the stanzas of the

---

23. *EEC*, clxv-clxvii.

24. Siegfried Wenzel, *Preachers, Poets, and the Early English Lyric* (Princeton: Princeton University Press, 1986), 136–37.

25. *EEC*, clxxii.

26. *EEC*, clxix. A different, but perhaps related, articulation of the limits of carol lullabies
appears in Rosemary Woolf's discussion of carols, where she notes that while lullaby carols have
meditative potential, they are "more external," "more fitted for public performance" (386).

carol has allowed modern formalist criticism explicitly to call the medieval lyric conceptually limited in relation to modern poetry. This point rests on another frustrating paradox, because that separability is crucial to understanding the formal nature of the carol. As we saw earlier, Greene defines the carol burden in terms of its separability. He calls the burden "a repeated element which does not form any part of a stanza," in contrast to a refrain, which, in English poetry, "is a member of the stanza" whose removal would alter the rest of the stanzaic structure.[27] But while this distinction might register as a neutral structural taxonomy, it has harmful implications for medieval carol. These become clear in postmodernity's elaborations upon Poe's theory of the refrain. Responding to Poe that reads primarily modern poems, John Hollander characterizes the modern refrain by invoking the issues of both separability and repeatability. Hollander shows how a poem can not only reinflect the refrain in each iteration by means of its relationship to the stanzas, but also sustain a self-aware and thoughtful relationship between stanza and refrain. For the modern poem, in Hollander's view, the refrain provides an opportunity for poetic self-reflexivity in the generation of manifold correspondences between verse and chorus. "For *poetry*, rather than mere verse, to employ a refrain," Hollander notes, "it must thereby, therein, therewith, propound its own parable of the device itself, its etiology or its effect. . . ."[28] The *poetic* refrain cannot separate itself from the rest of the poem but rather must speak to and about the rest of the poem. While it may "remembe[r]" its "distant ancestry" in medieval performance, it also does other sophisticated memory work related to its more recent history as well as its own occurrences throughout the poem.[29]

It seems that for Hollander, the medieval burden does not perform these feats. "*Poetry*" contrasts with "mere verse": medieval and characterized by the burden's independence from the rest of the poem. This independence implies an inability to foster ideational ties between the burden and the rest of the poem, restricting what kinds of formalist insights could attach to the carol. The medieval burden's repetition and separation together render the burden what Hollander calls "a univocal sign (*That was all full of meaning; now meaning stops for a while and we all dance again.*)."[30] The burden

27. *EEC*, clx.

28. John Hollander, "Breaking into Song: Some Notes on Refrain," repr. in *Lyric Poetry*, 87, emphasis in original.

29. Ibid., 77, 80.

30. Ibid., 87, 74–75, emphasis in original. Hollander refers to the burden as "danced-to," locating movement in the intonation of the burden rather than the stanzas.

does not comment upon itself or its relationship to the rest of the poem. For the branch of post–New Critical formalist reading to which Hollander contributes, the detachability of the iterable medieval burden exists in the service of asserting modern poetry's "rhetorical self-consciousness."[31] Hollander concludes with his poem "Refrains," whose own end is "the heavy / Burden of the tune we carry, humming, to the grave."[32] The medieval carol burden is in the modern refrain, but it is death, or it is "how *Greensleeves*, her smock stained from love in the grass, / Outlasts all the boys who had a go at her." It is what "comes back anyway," not the freedom to interpret modernity's refrain in its experimental relationship to the rest of the poem.

Underlying an influential tradition of modern formalist analysis, then, is a sense of the medieval burden's structural detachability as limiting its relationship to the rest of the carol, therefore limiting the interpretive potential of the carol as a whole. While medievalists would at least recognize the hermeneutic value of the burden as a contained and unvarying unit, as demonstrated in Greene's praise of the burden's "sum[ming] up the matter of the stanzas," scholarship that privileges the modern denies the burden even this capacity. These comments do not intend to make Hollander a straw man any more than Muscatine was in chapter 2; rather, Hollander, like Muscatine, makes explicit some critical tendencies deeply ingrained in our casual, everyday formalist reading practices even if no longer named as such. Because such tendencies can seem to disparage premodern poetic culture, it might behoove us as medievalists not to replicate them when we do formalist work.

This is a tall order, though, because even the medieval manuscript appears to confirm this impulse to overlook the burden for its redundancy and lack of interesting relation to the rest of the poem. Premodern copyists frequently either abbreviate the burden, indicating its presence with a single line or phrase, or omit the burden from the body of the poem once copied at the poem's head.[33] Given the critical context above, in which burdens work against the protocols for seeking provocative and unexpected variations, we might well interpret medieval scribal choice as reflecting a sense we develop that the burden's formal contribution to the carol is limited. Modern editing of the carol has reinforced this idea. Greene's edition of Middle English carols similarly reproduces the burden only at the head of the carol, not between stanzas, indicating in notes whether and how a given manuscript includes the

31. Ibid., 75.
32. Ibid., 89.
33. Palti distinguishes between burden repetition for the reader and the singer of the lyric. "Synge," vol. 1, 142.

burden.[34] The regularity of the burden's repetition, one might say, creates a version of familiarity breeding contempt. This effect has come to inform not only our editing of these texts but also our understanding of manuscripts as indicating the medieval reader's experience of burdens in poetic texts.

It should be noted that French medieval lyric traditions, and the criticism examining them, have sustained a different attitude toward the French refrain as both a repeating and a separable component. Greene argues that the English burden and the French *refrain* are more comparable than the English refrain and burden, in that the French *refrain* also has an "intrinsic interest" not dependent on its relationship to the rest of the *chanson*.[35] And yet scholarship has treated the English burden and the French *refrain* somewhat differently. In addition to certain structural divergences between the two, touched upon below, this difference in approach rests partly on the fact that, as Butterfield points out, French medieval lyrics were collected, generically codified, and aesthetically theorized at a much earlier medieval stage than were English lyrics.[36] Furthermore, because of French medieval practices for recording lyrics, the phenomenon of a refrain's repetition across a tradition of lyrics, in addition to within a single one, has provided particularly productive points of focus.[37] This mode of tracking can lead to important insights about networks of transmission and the very nature of dissemination in written and performance-based contexts. Such studies exist for the English lyric, and these involve some especially intriguing examples.[38] But repeatability as a theme or aesthetic seems somewhat less worked out overall across the English tradition as opposed to the French; as Palti notes, "the movement of English carol burdens is not as extensive as that of the French *refrains*."[39]

Scholarship of the French lyric has also suggestively complicated the detachability of the refrain, both within individual texts and across related

---

34. John C. Hirsh's more recent edition of medieval lyrics, containing some carols, indicates the insertion of the burden between carol stanzas with an italicized initial phrase, encouraging the reader to reintone the burden mentally as part of the reading process. *Medieval Lyric: Middle English Lyrics, Ballads, and Carols* (Malden, MA: Blackwell, 2005), for example 81–82, 89–90.

35. *EEC*, clx.

36. Butterfield, "Why," 326. While French writers were naming and thinking about lyric genres in the thirteenth century, English carol and other lyric collections, such as those found in London, British Library MS Sloane 2593, Oxford, Bodleian Library MS Eng. poet. e. 1., and the carol sequence of John Audelay in Oxford, Bodleian Library MS Douce 302, did not appear until at least the fifteenth century. Richard Hill's collection of carols, mentioned above, was produced in the sixteenth century.

37. Saltzstein, 3.

38. Butterfield, "Why," 332–35.

39. Palti, "'Synge,'" 142.

ones. Butterfield, for instance, demonstrates that in the French *rondet de carole*, the refrain may repeat in a specific instance but is not the primarily repetitive component of that song tradition. On the contrary, those refrains exhibit variation across the tradition while the strophes—the unrepeated narrative element within a particular song—are themselves limited in content and appear similarly across different songs.[40] Meanwhile, the complexity of separability as a structural quality is more fully acknowledged in Butterfield's discussion of the *rondet de carole* than it often is in the English carol. Butterfield continues that while "the form of a *rondet* does appear to encase a refrain in a way which makes the refrain more integral to the song than if the refrain were an independent burden recurring at the end of successive stanzas," this structure at the same time indicates the *rondet de carole*'s dependence upon on the refrain as an "autonomous" unit, and not, as might be assumed, vice versa.[41] The *rondet de carole*'s refrain can thus exist autonomously even as it displays a more complex kind of structural incorporation into the ground of the poetic narrative, enabling an account of formal sophistication not so consistently available to the English carol burden. Zumthor conveys the audience's experience of such complexity in the French tradition in his comment that the refrain's etymological basis in breaking manifests itself in the breaking (*briser, rupture*) of the "déroulement de la chanson et y introduit un facteur supplémentaire de rythme."[42] Here the concept of the supplement applies to poetic rhythm.

This brief survey suggests that reenacting the formal experience of the carol will require adjusting our perspective on the burden and its relationship to the carol. One means to accomplish this aim is to relieve ourselves of the term *burden*, at least internally. It seems especially self-sabotaging for us as medievalists to borrow a shadow-casting word from Shakespeare's lexicon to delineate the function of a distinctive medieval poetic feature. The word *refrain*, by contrast, is attested as a Chaucerian term during the late Middle Ages, translating its French counterpart as an element of the *carole*:

This folk, of which I telle you soo,
Upon a karole wenten thoo.
A lady karolede hem that hyghte

---

40. Butterfield, *Poetry*, 48–49.

41. Ibid., 49–50. See also her later comment that French refrains "at once imply a context while possessing a certain autonomy" (62).

42. Zumthor, *Essai*, 247. "The refrain thus breaks the unrolling of the song and introduces there a supplementary rhythmic factor."

Gladnesse, [the] blissful and the lighte;
Wel coude she synge and lustyly,
Noon half so wel and semely,
And make in song sich refreynynge:
It sat hir wonder wel to synge. (*RR* 743–50)[43]

As Hollander points out, the etymological root of *refrain*, *re-frangere*, signals the idea of re-breaking.[44] It is a break in the rest of the poem, an object
that might break internally (like Poe's little shard of sound), or an element
that might produce other kinds of formal breaking across the poem as it in-
terlocutes with the poem's stanzas. A good deal of the complexity Hollander
ascribes to the modern refrain emerges from this term's access to ideas of
breaking. Chaucer recognizes the relevance of *refreyn* to the specific category of danced *carole* and the carol text accompanying it. I propose that we
think of the carol burden as a refrain in order to afford this verse component
the sophistication so privileged in the modern refrain. To advocate changing this terminology would of course create insoluble taxonomic confusion,
especially given the French context as well as the use of *refrain* to designate
other specific verse phenomena in both English and French traditions. What
I suggest, then, is not a renaming but rather, in reenacting the carol's formal experience, a mindfulness of the conceptual—rather than structural—
associations of *refrain* as implicit to the burden. The result will be a different sense of the carol's formal experience, one that makes available to the
burden and carol the strange footing of those supplements that emerge in
the reenactment of poetic form through dance.

As before, this reenactment counteracts an analogical relationship where
dance and poem are each like the other in their mutual resolution and symmetry. Instead, the *carole*'s danced *ductus*—with all its experiential quirks,
its virtual arcs, askew and unclosed—habituates the reader to a perceptual
experience that constitutes his experience of the poetic carol's form. As I
have suggested above, what has traditionally been described as the structural independence of the burden has obfuscated our view of its range of
formal relation to the rest of the carol. In what follows, the *carole*'s virtual
circles will intervene into the apprehension of the carol's burden and stanzas to illuminate a formal experience of strangeness and rupture in the relations among those components.

---

43. The noun *refreyn* also appears in *Troilus and Criseyde* 2.1571. Above it translates "Ne
plus bel ses refrais n'assist" (*RR* l. 732)
44. Hollander, 73.

HAND IN HAND

The carol "A child is boren" articulates a relationship between dance and poetry even in the absence of definitive evidence that the poem accompanies dance. Like chapter 2's "Ladd Y the Daunce," this carol incorporates imagery—mainly the "hand in hand" of its burden—that brings familiar dance practice to the surface of the poem, invoking that medial engagement, and perceptual practice, as part of the reader's embodied response. Through the *ductus* of the *carole*, the reader of the carol "A child is boren" experiences its form as a set of decentered and overlapping circular forces. Even as the poem explicitly refers to dancers turning "honnd by honnd," its other language alludes to less apparent virtual circles attendant upon the main embodied dance. This formal experience of "A child is boren," as conditioned in the *ductus* of dance, addresses the poem's two central problems. The first is that it must present a fundamentally uneven exchange—Christ's life for man's—within a form that relies on evenness and balance. The second is that its corrupted state in the manuscript makes it both evenly structured and oddly misshapen. This section will argue that the virtual forces of the *carole* allow the poem's form to accommodate these paradoxes of symmetry and unevenness.

The poem appears as follows in its primary witness, Oxford, Bodleian Library MS Bodley 26; also reproduced here are the indications of the burden in this copy:

Honnd by honnd we schulle ous take,
And *joye* and *blisse schulle we make,*
For the deuel of ele man haght forsake,
And *Godes Sone ys maked oure make.*

A child is boren amo[n]ges man,
And in that child was no wam;
Th*a*t child ys God, th*a*t child is man,
And in th*a*t child our*e* life bygan.

honnd by honnd thane schulle ous take *et ceterum* quod sup*er*ius
dict*u*m est.

Senful man, be blithe and glad:
For [y]our mariage thy peys ys grad
Wan Crist was boren;

Com to Crist; thy peis ys grad;
For the was hys blod ysched,
    That were forloren.

honnd by honnd thanne schulle ous take *and* joy *and* blisse schu[lle]
    we make &c.

Senful man, be blithe *and* bold,
For euene ys bothe boght *and* sold,
    Euereche fote.
Com to Crist; thy peys ys told,
For the [h]e yahf a hondrefo[l]d
    Hys lif to bote.

honnd by honnd *et ceterum* quod prius.[45]

Some scholars, such as Sahlin, seem confident that this text accompanied dance.[46] Greene notes that it is the only English carol whose burden "allud[es] directly to the dancing group" and also points out that its manuscript context in Bodley 26 suggests an association with celebratory secular dance, following as it does a sermon reference to·Revelation 19.9's wedding feast.[47] Greene, however, qualifies the hypothesis that the poem is an actual accompaniment, instead seeing in it an "imitation of the burden of some song for a round dance."[48] This description introduces a degree of abstraction from the embodied dance, complicating its identity as literal dance

---

   45. *EEC* No. 12, 6, dated ca. 1350. In University of London Library MS 657, the third stanza appears independently with the following variants:

Senful man, be blithe *and* bold,
For euene ys bothe boght *and* sold,
    For euery fote.
Thank thou hym, thi pay is told,
For lytyl he yeuyth a hondrefo[l]d
    And lif also to bote.

   46. Sahlin, 58.
   47. *EEC*, clxviii, 346. On this reference, Carleton Brown specifies that "the homily in which these verses occur begins on f. 201b with an exposition of the four locks by which the heart of the sinner is closed, of the several keys which will open these locks, and then of the banquet which Christ offers to those who will open the door to him"; he mentions as well the Franciscan hand in the manuscript. *Religious Lyrics of the XIVth Century* (Oxford: Clarendon Press, 1924), 272.
   48. *EEC*, clxviii.

accompaniment.[49] Further obscuring the poem's relationship to dance is its difference in structure between the first stanza ("A child is boren . . .") and the two subsequent ones. I will address this first stanza after discussing the rest of the poem, suggesting ultimately that its formal difference indicates readerly awareness of the very complexity of relation that this poem bears to dance. To make this case, however, I must first establish some ways that the poem makes the *ductus* of dance perceptible.

The burden makes the *ductus* of dance evident, for its pronouns convey the dance idiom's perceptual practices in a process of leading. The burden's "we" and "oure" mark perspectival positions in a dance, referring to the visual and bodily awareness of others necessitated in the community that standing with hands held creates. Arising at different points throughout the poem as the burden repeats, such pronouns and pronominal adjectives acknowledge medieval dance's perspectival combination of participation and spectatorship, its trajectories of constitutive gaze. Judson Boyce Allen has argued, building upon Leo Spitzer's work, that pronouns solicit the reader of medieval lyric "to perfect or universalize himself by occupying that language as his own."[50] This act of occupation is often construed as relating to penitential, meditative, or other devotional states. But "A child is boren" introduces the possibility that to intone and thus occupy its handholding "we" is to inhabit a perspective generated by habituation to the kinetic collectivity of dance. As it recurs through the poem in the burden's repetition, the set of pronominal references to a performing and spectating group indicates a process of leading the reader by means of continued self-orientation at various points around the circle's network of perspectival trajectories.

It must be admitted that this reading of the burden could reinforce a reading of "A child is boren" that analogizes the structure of the poem to the structure of the dance. Other interpretations of this poem do, in fact, see in the lyric the same kind of symmetrical circularity that characterizes medieval round dance. John Hirsh, for instance, identifies this poem as "complexly read[ing] the Passion into the Nativity" so that "the Nativity . . . marked the point at which the promise of the Annunciation was fulfilled, but it pointed as well toward Christ's suffering, death, and (though this was not always emphasized or even realized in the lyrics) resurrection."[51] In

49. Greene qualifies what he sees as a conversion from a secular dance-song origin to a pious context. Whether or not his motivation to introduce this element of distance between dance and poem is correct, with no direct evidence of the poem's use, neither he nor we can label it as literal accompaniment.

50. Allen, "Grammar," 208.

51. Hirsh, 89.

conceiving of the poem's return to an originating point, Hirsh evokes a device of circularity. Indeed, one might wonder if Hirsh's observation that lyrics often do not explicitly signal resurrection might be explained by the strength of the sense of resolution and return with which their danced origins furnish them. Because of their dance-based structure, that is, lyrics need not make the point about resurrection, and what it fulfills and completes, explicitly. In a reading of this carol that elaborates on details of form, Cristina Maria Cervone narrates the rhythmic and structural effects of the poem that elevate it beyond "mere didacticism." Cervone identifies the spondaic character of the phrase "that child" as creating rhythmic emphasis upon itself as a point of origin in the stanza. When the phrase reappears in the first stanza's final line, it creates a "fulfillment of metre in the concluding four-beat line, which both wraps up and speaks back to the stanza's beginning." Meter, for Cervone, creates an effect analogous to the principle of the Word made flesh.[52] Thus, while Cervone's interpretive agenda differs from Hirsh's, in both cases a discourse of return and circularity obtains.

To some extent, the poem's other stanzas also behave with the sense of resolution for which round dance can act as analogy. Greene suggests, as noted above, that the second stanza's gesture to "mariage" refers to the sermon immediately preceding the carol in the manuscript, which mentions "the wedding feast of the Lamb in Revelation xix.9" [*cenam nuptiarum*]. Even if not performed, the carol is evoked with an awareness of festive dance:[53]

> Senful man, be blithe and glad:
> For your mariage thy peys ys grad
>   Wan Crist was boren;
> Com to Crist; thy peis ys grad;
> For the was hys blod ysched,
>   That were forloren.

In initiating the syntactic construction "for x . . . y," the second stanza emphasizes harmony and unity, not only in the act of the marriage itself but also, ultimately, in a dynamic of reciprocity. The "x for y" construction begins in the second and third lines. While Greene's translation of "peace is proclaimed" for *peys is grad* does not clearly produce an exchange mechanism in this sentence (*for* not really signifying "in exchange for" here), we might bear in mind that late fourteenth-century *peis* carries the resonance of "weight," "measure," and "balance" as well (*MED* s.v. *peis*). When the pen-ultimate line begins with "For," it signifies "for the sake of" or "in exchange for": Christ's blood was shed for thee. This is a slightly different mechanism of "x for y" than that with which the stanza began but is syntactically set in parallel with that opening "For . . ." so that in the echo generated between the two, the reciprocating energy of each is amplified. Through its syntax, the stanza appears to reward certain expectations with which the image of round dance might overlay the premodern carol. The text not only marks the compliant rhythm and shape of an affirming and celebratory dance but also acknowledges the symmetrical circuit of exchange.

The third stanza also seems to begin with an investment in resolved symmetry through an emphasis on the parity that can be implied in acts of exchange.

> Senful man, be blithe *and* bold,
> For euene ys bothe boght *and* sold,
>   Euereche fote.
> Com to Crist; thy peys ys told,
> For the he yahf a hondrefo[l]d
>   Hys lif to bote.

This stanza's first part invokes an ideal of evenness in its declaration that "euene ys bothe boght and sold, / Euereche fote." *Euene* has some shadings. It suggests that the buying and selling occurs evenly; or it happens even, or evenly, for every person (*fote*); or *euene* designates a form of rightness, fitness, or sameness ("just so," "in just that way"). In these different reso-nances, the first half of the stanza emphasizes the balance to which acts of exchange might aspire. Further bearing out this sense is the phrase "blithe and bold" in the first line, where alliteration introduces a sense of seesaw-ing reciprocity not so apparent in "blithe and glad" in the previous stanza. The use of the word *fote* might also, more subtly, suggest regularity and symmetry because of its dual meaning—both "person" and "foot"—with the latter's attendant resonances of dancing (such as the verb *foten* to re-fer to dancing).[54] In its multiplicity of meanings, the *fote* is engaged in the cyclical activity of being perpetually bought and sold. This account might resonate with a danced experience of feet moving and taking each other's

54. *MED* s.v. *fote* 9. *Fote* was also a synonym for "burden"; however, this meaning was not attested until the early sixteenth century, where it is seen in Richard Hill's carol book, Oxford, Balliol College MS 354. See Reichl, 157; *EEC*, clx.

places as a kind of spatial exchange, using the foot to mark and articulate the giving up of one space to take another, only to reprise the movement subsequently. Particularly when the poem juxtaposes the *fote* of the stanza with the *honnd* of the burden, we might perceive the regular, even pacing and spacing of dancers in a revolving and resolving circle linked by limbs. The image of dance generated in the poem might thus analogize the sense of balanced reciprocity in exchange that the carol seems to celebrate through its peaceable lulling of blithe and bold, bought and sold.

In the second half of the stanza, however, such reinforcement of symmetry starts to break down when faced with the asymmetries implicit to the redemptive act. This is a paradox that extends from the paradox of hypostatic union that Cervone identifies.[55] Specifically, the stanza's final three lines express an imbalance between the inconsequential, singular "thee" and the "hundredfold" of what Christ gives up in his dual nature.[56] Christ's redemption of mankind has often been conceived in terms of economic exchange. Jaroslav Pelikan notes, for instance, Hugh of St. Victor's understanding of redemption as a "transaction."[57] In the later Middle Ages, the difficult nature of this transaction is sometimes styled as a "quittance." As Emily Steiner shows, Chaucer's rendering of Christ's sacrifice in this manner emphasizes from a legal and documentary perspective the extent to which "Christ made a special concession to all humanity by absorbing the debt owed to him."[58] It is, of course, a massive debt, as impossible to reconcile evenly: the stanza confronts us with the high value of Christ's life as a sacrifice for mankind. Thus, what began as an ordered exchange comparable to the harmonious reciprocity that a dance might seem to emblematize proceeds in the third stanza to a less manageable dynamic. Here, the tidy shape of the stanza, with its bouncing tails, has somehow to contain what the language of the stanza perceives to be an unwieldily crooked dynamic: each human life in exchange for a sacrifice that is infinitely greater. The stanza contrasts the teeming aggregation of "every foot" in the first short line with the ineffable singularity of Christ's life as a remedy in the second short line.

55. Cervone, *Poetics*, 210.

56. Greene emends the manuscript's "ye" to "he," indicating Christ, here, based presumably on the previous stanza. The error intimates increasing awareness of the exchange's disorienting strangeness.

57. Jaroslav Pelikan, *The Growth of Medieval Theology (600–1300)*, vol. 3, *The Christian Tradition: A History of the Development of Doctrine* (Chicago: University of Chicago Press, 1978), 130.

58. Emily Steiner, *Documentary Culture and the Making of Medieval English Literature* (Cambridge: Cambridge University Press, 2003), 49.

Thus, even as those short two-stress lines might mark the balanced resolution of a danced circle, their relation to each other relies on disproportion. The stanzas gingerly lead up to this asymmetry, which is ultimately at odds with the verse's formal attributes.

But a formal experience of the burden, as shaped by the perception of the round dance's virtual arcs, consists in just such an off-center or uneven dynamic. Let us then return to the burden with this idea in mind. If, as I suggested above, the burden signals the deployment of dance-based perceptual practices, inhabiting that perspectival position could be quite complex when considered in terms of the danced *carole*. The virtual supplement of the *carole* positions the reader to perceive in the burden a complicated set of forces that, rather than resolving simply, create unexpectedly skewed relations. This effect occurs in part through the burden's placement of the word *make*.

> *Honnd by honnd we schulle ous take,*
> And *joye* and *blisse schulle we make,*
> *For the deuel of ele man haght forsake,*
> And *Godes Sone ys maked oure make.*

The burden repeats versions of *make* three times in lines two and four. In the statement "joye and blisse schulle we make" are discernible both a making of joyful noise and, at the same time, the "making" of poetic composition that produces the celebratory verse. In the second use (the fourth line's *maked*), the verb conveys that which is shaped and created but without the poetic resonance. The third time it appears (also in the fourth line), *make* is a noun signifying "mate," orchestrating both a rime riche with line two and a sense of play across line four's uses of *make* between the meanings of creation and companionship. Apprehensionally attuned to the virtual forces of dance, the reader experiences these instances of *make* as the force of a variably resolvable arc. On the one hand, the third instance of *make* leads the reader back to its invocation of *make* in line two. In this transit through the stanza, the additional instance of this word in line four creates not simply a relay between two uses but rather a fuller tracery, three points on a closed circuit of impulsion, traced through repeated incidences of the word *make*, within the verse. On the other hand, the final evocation of *make* as "companion" corresponds less effectively in meaning to the first use of *make* than it does to the first line of the burden, whose declaration of handholding companionship prefigures the sense of more exalted and divine union realized at the end of the stanza. Thus the force that *make* initiates has two possible means of resolution at two different points in the stanza.

A reader attuned to the *carole*'s orthogonal and overlapping forces would perceive the process of being led through the burden as one that traces these sometimes nonaligned arcs of force.

Within this analytic context, the *carole*'s virtual circles cause the burden not only to generate alternate alignments in space but also to render strange its time. Shifting our focus from the single burden to its repetition through the poem, we find a change in the burden's language when it repeats, from "Honnd by honnd we schulle ous take" to "honnd by honnd thane schulle ous take." This is a minor and incidental alteration, certainly within the range of normal variation that occurs across in many burden repetitions. But like the small adjustments in the *danse macabre* manuscripts, it might indicate the reader's importation of habits or memories of kinetic perceptual experience into the textual encounter. In this case, the change reflects the awareness of choreographed conduction through time, because the adverbial *then* introduces a subtle dynamic of causation or conditionality. Whereas the poetic text begins by initiating a circle—"we must take ourselves"—its invocations of the circle in the remaining burdens suggest consequence or subsequence in the phrase "then must we take ourselves"; these circular formations appear as a result of that initial circle, but in the articulation of "thane," they produce a temporal dynamic that fluctuates between the actual and the anticipated: in the moment of intoning the adverb, there is both the present circle and the anticipation of other, future, circularities that the dance creates. In Morris's *L'Allegro*, circles bloom and trace themselves virtually from other circles, anticipated, proleptic, or syncopated in time. The changing adverb in the burden's reiteration reflects a formal experience dictated by that perception of circles always in the process of producing other circles temporally and spatially beyond them.

Through the *carole*'s virtual circles, the burden of this carol accommodates in space and time the strange footing that its stanzas introduce. When the burden frames each of the poem's two final stanzas, it provides an off-kilter spatial model in its placement of *make*: we saw above how the burden traces arcs of force that resolve in ambiguous ways, if at all. That effect experientalizes the stanzas' need both to close their circuits of exchange and to acknowledge the impossibility of doing so in the exchange's fundamental asymmetry. The proleptic temporality of the *carole*'s virtual forces—the reader's perception of which appears in the burden's subtle self-amendments—also establishes a perceptual mode for the stanzas' complex subject matter. The untimeliness of the burden casts into relief the subtle perambulations in time through which the second and third stanzas send Christ and man. Their collective syntax shuttles between the present of

"Com to Crist" and the historical past of the Crucifixion ("was hys blod ysched"); and between man's present fortune ("be blithe") and the perennial state of sin ("That were forloren"). Certainly medieval lyrics elsewhere similarly loosen temporality when dealing with scenes of Christ's life, apprehending one time in another.[59] But in this case, the burden as a set of temporal forces foregrounds the temporal manipulation at work in the stanzas. The network of stanza and burden together thus situates the poem's sense of instability along a temporal axis. Within the context of this formal experience, to pair every *fote* and Christ's life creates an odd, uneven drag underneath the apparently regular marking of measure. In "A child is boren," the estranging forces to which danced idioms habituate a spectator in space and time introduce alternatives to the carol's conventional formal attribute as a closed, home-returning circle. Medieval dance's virtuality constructs the stanza-burden interaction to articulate the difficulties of a sacrifice that at once subscribes to an "x for y" structure while at the same time troubling the mechanics of this circuit.

Stanza-burden relation can also elucidate, finally, how the initial corrupted stanza expresses the complexity of dance's medial presence in relation to the poem. The first stanza replicates the aaaa form of the burden, omitting the two-beat third and sixth lines (with their b rhymes) that the other stanzas include:

> A child is boren amo[n]ges man,
> *And* in that child was no wam;
> That child ys God, that child is man,
> *And* in that child oure life bygan.

Its difference from the poem's other stanzas is attributable to many possible factors. If this material derives from performance traditions of some kind, the kinetic instability of that mode of transmission might have caused a yoking together of two song texts.[60] Alternatively, Greene speculates that the missing short lines indicate scribal error, a "confusion" of the burden's four-line structure with that of the first stanza.[61]

---

59. See, for instance, Grimestone's carol of the Passion "Thu sikest sore" (*EEC* No. 271, 170), which artfully arranges its pronouns and verbs to produce a multivalent sense of temporality for the reader.

60. On dance's literalizing of the motion in *mouvance*, which aligns the instabilities of textual transmission with the exigencies of performance settings, see my "Choreographing."

61. *EEC*, 346.

The irregularity of this stanza further troubles the relationship between poetic and danced media. Stanza 1's inconsistency with the rest makes the poem as such difficult to align with a particular embodied danced tradition, given that a lyric constructed like this would require the melody of the carol to change for part of the performance. It is not simply our lack of knowledge concerning this poem's performance history that is at issue here; the poem's problematic structure complicates its relationship to dance for even a medieval reader bringing those perceptual practices to the poem through his own embodied subjectivity. At the same time, however, the poem as copied on the manuscript page suggests that the text presents itself as a coherent poetic unit, not necessarily an obvious pastiche of different elements from different performance or lyric traditions. It thus raises questions about whether it simply occupies the category of the undanceable or whether, instead, this visual coherence indicates some other kind of relationship it sustains, as an integral text, with performance tradition.

The manuscript folio bears this dichotomy out (figure 24). The differing sizes of the scribe's brackets marking the first vs. the second and third stanzas do appear to make clear the stanzas' significant difference in structure and length. At the same time, however, other aspects of the folio render this first stanza's relation to the rest somewhat more complex. For instance, the contrast between the burden's unlineated copying and the stanzas' lineation (a common copying practice) visually obscures the structural parallel Greene notes between the burden and the first stanza, complicating his attribution of a scribal "confusion" that would want to make them identical. In addition, the first stanza's inclusion of dashes at its line ends, along with its juxtaposition to the abbreviated burden in the right margin, gives it some visual resonance and consistency with the other stanzas. Finally, the placement of the burden notation to the right of stanza 1 confirms its identity as a stanza and not, as the stanza's structure might suggest, an alternate burden. Thus, while on the one hand the divergent stanza undermines the poem's potential as an integral unit of accompaniment to a material dance, on the other its manuscript situation seems to intimate such integrity in some other capacity.

Making this contradiction visible, the copying process sustains a range of medial relations between poem and dance. In its details, "A child is boren" seems conceived on this page as an integral whole and yet contains within itself a break in this wholeness. Some possibilities for understanding the folio include: the visual insistence that it is conventional accompaniment; the reflection of a vestigial dance component in only some of its parts but

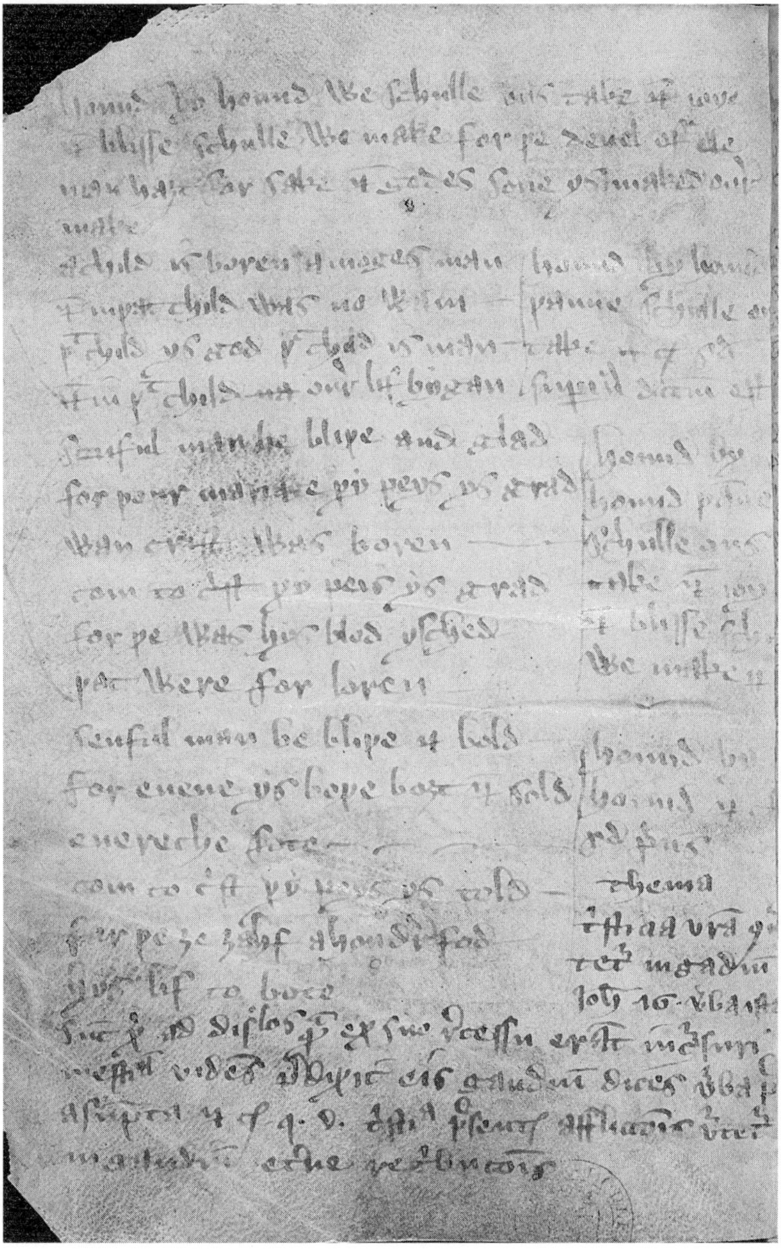

Fig. 24. The Bodleian Libraries, the University of Oxford, MS Bodley 26, f. 202v (ca. 1350). Photograph: Bodleian Libraries, Oxford.

not as a whole; a text responsive as a whole to the ideational trace of dance
but distanced from it in material detail; and, finally, something else entirely:
a poetic object whose internal variation enacts a kind of interstitial placement between the performed and the impossible to perform. In this way, the
manuscript articulates visually how multifarious the space and time of the
danced medium can be even when the poem's language keeps it on its evident surface.

Elaborating on that last possibility, we might say that in the poem's ductile experience of virtual forces, the short lines missing from the first stanza
become not so much absent as virtual. They are beats extant on a different
plane. Modern formalist criticism is accustomed to identifying beats that
exist out of the spatial and temporal ambit of the poem, yet still form a part
of its metrical character. Jonathan Culler and others refer to these beats as
"virtual," but the medieval carol might offer an even stronger basis to evoke
virtus than does the modern poem. A familiar modern example exists in
Derek Attridge's scansion of A. A. Milne's poem "Disobedience." Attridge
identifies a perceptible beat that exists beyond the poem's metrical feet:

> James James Morrison Morrison
> Weatherby George Dupree [beat]
> Took great care of his Mother,
> Though he was only three. [beat][62]

In this case, the four beats of the first and third lines compel the reader to
supply a fourth beat following the second and fourth. The Milne example
obliges the reader to supply additional beats where they do not materially
and sonically exist, beats apprehensible even though not part of the explicit
time and space of the poem's prosody. One might, I suppose, draw a distinction between this modern example and our occluded medieval beats in the
terms of modern intentionality and metric design vs. medieval unintention-
ality or, at best, obscurely reasoned juxtaposition. But such distinctions are
both hard to defend categorically and riskily dismissive of the medieval instance. In "A child is boren," the audible or visible presence of the short
lines' beats in the other stanzas fosters an atmosphere of metric footing that
colors the reader's encounter with the first stanza. Like "Disobedience," "A
child is boren" asks the reader to make space and time for beats not materi-

---

62. Cited in Culler, 151–52. Culler calls the extra beats "virtual" at 152. See also Yopie
Prins on "virtual offbeats" and virtual beats, similarly made space for but not expressed through
articulated sound. " 'What,' " 29.

ally apparent but rather virtual. The difference between "Disobedience" and "A child is boren," what lends the medieval formal experience its unique character, is that in "A child is boren," this impulsion to apprehend the virtual supplement occurs in a conditioning of dance's *ductus* both within and beyond the bodily medium of dance itself.

This reading of the first stanza elucidates the uniqueness of medieval stanza-burden relation. Stanza 1 uses its complex alignment with the burden to reflect the poem's preoccupation with paradox: a paradox in not only its spiritual content but also its relationship to dance. To make this case, we must note that the first stanza's virtual prosody enters it into a relationship to the burden that far exceeds modernity's sense of what formal breakage might mean. This relationship has little to do with the dialectic of sameness and difference in the burden's iteration, as Poe and Hollander conceive of it, with the shard at the burden's core, or even with the notion of one component of the poem commenting upon another. In one sense, stanza 1's very structural consistency with the burden causes a break in the rest of the poem's formal identity, given what would conventionally be a distinction between burden and stanza. But at greater depth, the first stanza's virtual beats interact with the burden to enlarge on another paradox. Stanza 1's positional correspondence with the poems' other stanzas requires that it produce a supplement, apprehensible at the edge of consciousness but dealt out of normal space and time, of virtual beats. Negotiating between its structural parallel with the burden and the virtual supplement that aligns it with the other stanzas, stanza 1 becomes two stanzas superimposed upon each other, which can never both be real at once and which oscillate in their relation to the burden. In order paradoxically to break and not break the poem as a carol, the first stanza draws upon on the skewed arcs of virtuality that both close and do not close. That virtual supplement sustains the ambiguity of the poem's relation to dance as embodied medium. Virtuality makes space for the beats that would align this stanza with the others and thus draw the poem's danceability to the surface. But at the same time, the virtual supplement also expresses dance in the depths: the more obscure and convoluted time created in the structural difference that renders the stanza strangely like the burden. This account describes a stanza-burden interaction well beyond the conceptual frameworks modernity deploys.

"A child is boren"'s virtuality accommodates its medial and conceptual paradoxes. Unlike some other dance-related poems we have examined, this lyric does not employ fantastic, supernatural, or illusory means to signal the *virtus* of the uncanny, forces out of worldly space and time. Reenacting its formal experience in terms of the virtual forces of the *carole*, however, not only introduces the possibility of such an environment but also allows that formal experience to address the poem's most problematic features. In the first stanza, that is, the virtual supplement accommodates the poem's ambiguous relation to dance as embodied practice. In the second two stanzas, meanwhile, form as experience creates asymmetry in time and space to acknowledge the unevenness implicit to those verses' central scene of sacrifice.

THE MAIDEN'S VIRTUAL BURDEN

If "A child is boren" makes evident reference to the hands and feet of dance while rendering more subtly dance's supplementary virtualities, the iconic "Maiden in the mor lay" outlines an opposing dynamic and thus a different relation between dance and poetry. This lyric makes evident in its every feature not embodied dance itself but rather dance's virtual supplement. This characterization of "Maiden in the mor lay," I will suggest, explains its canonicity over time. The relative accessibility of this poem's virtualities to our modern eyes might lead us to think that we do not need dance to reenact this poem's formal experience. I will show, however, that discerning the formal experience of "Maiden in the mor lay" in terms of dance changes our perspective on this poem—and perhaps on medieval poetic form more broadly—by uncovering its possession of what I shall call a "virtual burden."

While in recent years this poem has not tended to receive a great deal of attention, that situation is only a small blip on "Maiden in the mor lay"'s longer record. Perhaps due to its lack of the kind of sociopolitical context that an established new historicist tradition tends to seek, this lyric has suffered some neglect in current critical arenas. An exception is Butterfield's revisiting, to which I shall return.[63] Before the rise of new historicism, the poem enjoyed a long history of admiration and response, one that can be argued to have begun in the fourteenth century itself, as I will suggest below. "Maiden in the mor lay" was once "a field on which D.W. Robertson . . . met his enemies," a text that hosted debate between Robertson and E. Talbot Donaldson concerning the merits of exegetical criticism as opposed to more New Critically-influenced modes of reading.[64] It features prominently in Peter Dronke's 1968 survey of medieval lyric and has reliably served in anthologies of medieval verse. In 2005, John Hirsh's edition of lyrics and carols estimates the Rawlinson fragment, the medieval page

63. Butterfield, "Without," 169–94.
64. Andrew Taylor, "The Myth of the Minstrel Manuscript," *Speculum* 66.1 (1991): 71; I discuss these alternative readings below (see notes 90 and 91).

where "Maiden in the mor lay" uniquely appears in full, to be "the most valuable and important manuscript fragment in all of English literature" at least in part because of the presence of this poem.[65] Something about "Maiden in the mor lay" coaxes a canonical designation from readers even when we no longer clamor to analyze it. Despite—or because of—its mystery and exceptionality, it seems to possess, to a variety of audiences, that "chemical," in Pound's terms, of medieval English verse.[66]

What we have of "Maiden in the mor lay" appears on a page that was added to the beginning of Oxford, Bodleian Library MS Rawlinson D.913 and is dated to approximately the second quarter of the fourteenth century. Its abbreviated prose presentation has been expanded and lineated in various ways, the most frequently printed of which follows:[67]

> Maiden in the mor lay
> in the mor lay.
> seuenyst fulle
> seuenist fulle.
> maiden in the mor lay
> in the mor lay
> seuenistes full
> ant a day
>
> Welle was hire mete
> wat was hire mete
> the primerole ant the
> the primerole ant the.
> welle was hire mete
> wat was hire mete
> the primerole
> ant the violet

65. Hirsh, 75.

66. Pound refers to Old English elegiac poetry here. Ezra Pound, *Patria Mia*, in *Selected Prose, 1909–1965*, ed. William Cookson (New York: New Directions, 1975), 123.

67. Hirsh's lineation, 74–76; I have reintroduced the pointing in the manuscript, though this is vexed because of the expansion. I also silently expand abbreviations, since several abbreviated words are repeated but do not appear in the manuscript. See also Thomas G. Duncan's expansion in *Lyrics and Carols*, 175 (lyric 1.118). Douglas Gray cites Duncan's version in *Simple Forms: Essays on Medieval English Popular Literature* (New York: Oxford University Press, 2015), 225; Butterfield cites the same expansion I reproduce here with slightly different lineation and surveys different editions' lineations ("Without," 169, 170n4, 180–81).

Welle was hire dryng
wat was hire dryng
the chelde water of the
the chelde water of the
Welle was hire dryng
Wat was hire dryng
The chelde water
of the welle spring.

Welle was hire bour
wat was hire bour
the rede rose an te
the rede rose an te
Welle was hire bour
wat was hire bour
the rede rose
an te lilie flour

In the fifteenth century and beyond, it is not unusual for carols in manuscripts to be designated, explicitly or implicitly, as such. Certain medieval
and early modern collections make clear that they understand their carols
as carols through their projects of serializing or anthologizing them. John
Audelay's carols, for instance, sometimes refer to themselves as such. "This
caral I made with gret doloure" (l. 45), he notes in "Dread of Death"; and
also exhorts his audience: "redis this caral reverently / Fore I mad hit with
wepyng eye" (ll. 74–75) in his St. Francis carol.[68] In addition, the *mise-en-page*
and brackets in the fifteenth-century London, British Library MS Sloane 2593
suggest this collection's awareness of its carols as occupying a coherent poetic
category. As Wakelin notes, the arrangement of stanzas, burdens, and brackets in this manuscript's carol texts seems consistent across Sloane 2593.[69] Finally, by the time Richard Hill compiles carols in his sixteenth-century commonplace book, Oxford, Balliol College MS 354, he uses specific terminology

68. Susanna Fein, ed., *John the Blind Audelay: Poems and Carols (Oxford: Bodleian Library
MS Douce 302)* (Kalamazoo: Medieval Institute Publications, 2009), 207, 209–10.

69. Daniel Wakelin, "The Carol in Writing: Three Anthologies from Fifteenth-Century Norfolk," *Journal of the Early Book Society for the Study of Manuscripts and Printing History* 9 (2006):
29. Wakelin argues that Sloane 2593's compiler "seems to have aimed at a tidily coherent book"
(29) and that the Norfolk carol scribes "erased traces of more ephemeral circulation, standardized
the layout, and rubricated and corrected the carols, . . . plac[ing] them in a visual, written tradition" (34).

to designate the carol's burden. What modern critics refer to as the *burden* Hill calls the *fote* on more than one occasion.[70] This usage indicates the carol category to have asserted itself sufficiently to require attendant nomenclature.

"Maiden in the mor lay," meanwhile, is not a carol of explicit or implicit anthologizing in this manner. Appearing earlier, it is instead designated a carol by its triangulation with other references that seem to assert its identity as such.[71] One reference appears in a sermon whose copying Wenzel dates to around 1360.[72] This text addresses the erosion of virtue over the ages of man.[73] In the course of this elaboration, the preacher speaks nostalgically of man's most innocent time, when his food was "fructus qui sponte nascitur," fruit that grows on its own. And with what, the sermon asks, did early man wash this down: "Quis potus?" Switching to the vernacular, it states that the answer can be found "in quodam cantico, viz. karole 'the mayde be wode lay'"; the text then reads "nota in margine: 'the cold water of the well spring.'"[74] The sermon thus categorizes the poem to which it refers—some version of "Maiden in the mor lay"—as a "karole." It is a graceful allusion, initiating, in the embellishment of the Golden Age explication with the figure of the maiden and her slipping stream, the poem's long history of capturing readerly and critical imagination. Naming it does not suffice; the scrawl indicates a compulsion to reproduce the line in all its lyricism, to echo the verse the way the poem echoes itself internally. And in addition to offering this glimpse of an early response to the poem, the annotation confirms that in some capacity, its medieval audiences called this poem a carol.[75]

---

70. *EEC*, clx.

71. For the dating of this text, see J. A. Burrow, "Poems without Contexts," *Essays in Criticism* 29 (1979): 7, which places the copying around 1325; and Taylor, who puts it at a slightly later point in the first half of the fourteenth century ("Minstrel," 71n118). The poem would have a *terminus ante quem* of 1360, the death date of Richard Ledrede (see below).

72. Worcester, Cathedral Library MS F 126, f. 145ra. Siegfried Wenzel, "The Moor Maiden—A Contemporary View," *Speculum* 49.1 (1974): 71.

73. Wenzel, "Moor," 71.

74. The preacher likens this image to the "lubricus ampnis" [slipping stream] that Boethius describes in Book II, meter 5 of the *Consolation of Philosophy* (Wenzel, "Moor," 71–72). Wenzel is "troubled" by the phrase "nota in margine": it could mean that the phrase from the poem is found in the margin of the manuscript from which the scribe is copying, but he also wonders if what appears an abbreviation of *margine* is a corruption of "moor" (72n19).

75. This manuscript might indicate as well that to call the poem a "karole" meant thinking about it in terms of dance. The composite volume containing the reference, Worcester, Cathedral Library MS F.126, additionally includes the sermon *exemplum* narrating a "corea demonum" that I briefly discuss in the introduction. The compiling of both these examples suggests that to call a poem a "karole," in the context of this manuscript, might have implied a consciousness of dance; however, Wenzel does not specify the date of the *exemplum* and seems to think that

Another point in this poem's constellation of reference further reinforces the lyric's possible identity, to its medieval readers, as carolesque specifically in a danced sense. This second reference appears in the *Red Book of Ossory*, a collection of bureaucratic documents and other items by the fourteenth-century Franciscan bishop Richard de Ledrede. Preceding the text of the Latin *cantilena* "Peperit virgo" is a heading that indicates "[M]ayde [y]n the moore [l]ay," which suggests that the Latin poem was intended as its *contrafactum*.[76] The first stanza reads:

> Peperit virgo,
> Virgo regia,
> Mater orphanorum,
> Mater orphanorum;
> Peperit virgo,
> Virgo regia,
> Mater orphanorum,
> Mater orphanorum
> Plena gracia.[77]

Contrafacta like this one offered alternative lyrics to clerks desiring to sings songs, replacing those ditties deemed too worldly or sensual.[78] Unlike the anonymous preacher above, Ledrede appears to have resisted rather than reveled in this poem's beauty. I will address below the question of whether the stanzas of "Maiden in the mor lay" can be made to fit the *contrafactum*'s structure exactly. For now, however, the important point about the *Red Book*

---

its copying is later than the date of the manuscript's "Maiden in the mor lay" reference. "'Gay' Carol," 90.

76. Richard L. Greene, "'The Maid of the Moor' in the Red Book of Ossory," *Speculum* 27.4 (1952): 504–6. See in addition Edmund Colledge, ed., *The Latin Poems of Richard Ledrede, O.F.M.* (Toronto: Pontifical Institute of Medieval Studies, 1974), 26–30; and Richard Leighton Greene, ed., *The Lyrics of the Red Book of Ossory* (Oxford: Basil Blackwell, 1974), 15–17. Elsewhere, Greene notes that Ledrede was trained at the same Franciscan friary in Canterbury that would later house James Ryman, collector of carols (*EEC*, cxvi). See also John Stevens's commentary on this *contrafactum*; he takes its near parallel to "Maiden in the mor lay" as possible evidence that the Latin *contrafacta* in the *Red Book of Ossory* could accompany dance (Stevens, 184). On the complexity of the *contrafactum* as a phenomenon, see Butterfield, *Poetry*, 103-4.

77. Theo Stemmler, ed., *The Latin Hymns of Richard Ledrede* (Mannheim, Germany: University of Mannheim, 1975), 20–21.

78. "... ne guttura eorum et ora Deo sanctificata polluantur cantilenis teatralibus, turpibus et secularibus" (Stevens, 183) [lest their throats and mouths, consecrated to God, be polluted by songs celebratory, base, and secular/worldly].

of Ossory is that this collection strengthens the possibility that medieval audiences viewed "Maiden in the mor lay" as a carol, in whatever sense that might have meant, because of the other texts it includes. For one thing, as Joan Rimmer notes, a number of the poetic texts included in Ledrede's book represent a *"carole* pattern." She believes "Maiden in the mor lay" to be among these.[79] For another, Rimmer identifies other lyric texts in the *Red Book of Ossory* as mimicking the rhythmic signature of the verse embedded in Robert Mannyng's caroling *exemplum* (discussed earlier), another example of a dance-song explicitly referred to as a carol in the late Middle Ages.[80] The manuscript puts "Maiden in the mor lay" in the company of poetry whose verse structure parallels something that was, again, explicitly called a carol in the Middle Ages. The poetic environment of the *Red Book of Ossory* thus potentially supports "Maiden in the mor lay"'s medieval designation as a carol.

J. A. Burrow considers "Maiden in the mor lay" to be a dance song in light of its neighbors on the Rawlinson folio. Immediately preceding "Maiden in the mor lay," for instance, is "Icham of Irlande," a lyric that refers explicitly to dance:

> Icham of Irlande
> Ant of the holy lande,
> Of Irlande.
>
> Gode sire, pray Ich thee,
> For of sainte charite
> Come ant daunce with me
>   In Irlande.[81]

Burrow conjectures that "Icham of Irlande" accompanied a danced *carole,* meaning that its opening stanza is a burden and what remains is part of an originally longer carol. "Icham of Irlande"'s reference to dance and its

---

79. Joan Rimmer, "Carole, Rondeau, and Branle in Ireland, 1300–1800: Part I The Walling of New Ross and Dance in the Red Book of Ossory," *Dance Research* 7.1 (1989): 42. The *Red Book* does contain other forms, such as *rondeau,* and one cannot make a definitive case that Ledrede has categorized "Maiden in the mor lay" among the other carols in his book. Rimmer, however, sees its stanzaic pattern as well as its question-and-answer format as lending themselves appropriately to this dance; she conjectures that it is "an insular residue of a much older and originally more socially significant kind of *karole*" (29).

80. Rimmer, 38–40. Mannyng, 283: "twelue folys a karolle dyȝt" (l. 9016).

81. Burrow, 30.

possible carol form might suggest an analogous identity for "Maiden in the mor lay."[82] Other poems on the page also seem to be dance lyrics or in some way dance-associated. For example, the final poem on the page, a drinking song, includes the verses "Stondeth alle stille / Stille, stille" and "Trippe a littel with thy fot / Ant let thy body gon," which seem to refer to movement practices reminiscent of *carole* dancing.[83] In addition, Burrow identifies the two French poems on the page as dance accompaniments. Like the *Red Book of Ossory*, "Maiden the mor lay"'s own manuscript page, Burrow shows, seems to place it in the company of other dance-songs associable with *carole*, giving it access to this designation.

But these readings leave us with a formal problem, which is that "Maiden in the mor lay" does not offer readers the kind of burden we saw in "A child is boren" or "Ladd Y the daunce"; that is to say, it does not possess the structurally distinct burden that for the most part defines formally the poetic carol. While the ambiguous status of "A child is boren"'s first stanza might make the formal relation between stanza and burden somewhat indeterminate, that poem does reflect, as do other early English carols like "Ladd Y the daunce," a difference in structural character between the burden and the two subsequent stanzas in the carol. Poems that call themselves carols, like Audelay's, also display this feature, suggesting that at some point, the Middle Ages associated the term *carol* with a formally distinct burden; it is not merely a modern imposition. "Maiden in the mor lay," however, exhibits something different. Either there is no discernible burden at all in the extant text or we might (as some critics have) consider its first stanza to be its burden. But in this latter scenario, the burden would possess the same structure as the rest of the stanzas. For this reason, Greene does not include "Maiden the mor lay" in his carol collection. He calls it instead a "variation of the *rondel* which is found nowhere else in English and, as far as can be discovered, nowhere else in Latin."[84] We thus encounter a taxonomic problem whereby the label applied to this poem by its medieval audience does not fit our modern understanding of the term's medieval meaning.

Given that the majority of Greene's examples were recorded in the fifteenth century, it is possible to conjecture that the trait of the distinct burden—indicated as such in the manuscript—developed as the Middle Ages progressed, and earlier texts like "Maiden in the mor lay" were not held to this standard in being considered carols; however, the evidence would be

82. Ibid., 19.
83. Ibid., 32.
84. *EEC* cxvi. See also Greene, "'Maid,'" 506.

ambiguous on this count. Certainly some of the more coherently structured compilations containing carols, like London, British Library MS Sloane 2593 and Oxford, Bodleian Library MS Eng. poet. e. 1, are fifteenth-century examples. It is also the case that London, British Library MS Egerton 613 and Cambridge, Trinity College MS B 14.39 contain versions of a thirteenth-century example lacking a burden (*EEC* no. 191), which enters Greene's carol anthology only because another version appears with a burden in a fifteenth-century witness.[85] At the same time, however, in addition to "A child is boren" as a fourteenth-century example, Grimestone's manuscript contains four poems with formally distinct burdens. Furthermore, the fourteenth-century London, British Library MS Harley 2253 contains "Ichot a burde in boure bryht," whose "Blow, northerne wind" burden is distinguished from its stanzas. Another familiar early example is "Als I me rode this endre dai" ("Nou sprinkes the sprai"), copied in the early fourteenth-century in Lincoln's Inn MS Hale 135.[86] These seem to conform to what would, by the early fifteenth century, be called a carol in terms of the structurally distinct burden.[87] Thus, while calling a poem a "karole" might have been more likely to evoke a specific formal requirement for the burden in the fifteenth century than earlier, some evidence suggests that the expectation of this type of poem existed during "Maiden in the mor lay"'s fourteenth-century transmission. The differences between some of these fourteenth- and fifteenth-century examples reflect Wenzel's observation that the term "karole" could have referred to secular compositions in its earlier use and to religious use as the fifteenth century progressed (although the sacred or secular categorization of the maiden is also somewhat up for debate).[88] But these fourteenth- and fifteenth-century examples suggest that the particular configuration of stanza and formally distinct burden existed across both these centuries, creating at least some question concerning the meaning of the sermon's label for "Maiden in the mor lay."

The problem of the burden affects our sense of the specificity of the danced medium with which the poem might be associated. To explain the preacher's use of "karole," we might construe "karole" in fourteenth-century Middle English to refer not to a precise stanzaic structure for accompaniment but instead to a highly general or variable connection to dance. Rather than attributing

---

85. *EEC*, 125–26; see also clxi. I will discuss this carol below.

86. *EEC* No. 449, 268; and No. 450, 274.

87. Reichl argues that while these two poems reflect the form of the English carol, they also convey in their tone and content something closer to the French *refrain*-poem tradition, engaging in a "deliberate play with popular and courtly modes and styles" (167–68).

88. Wenzel, "Moor," 73.

to the "karole" the formal specificity of a distinct burden, that is, the term simply indicates some sort of song, related in some way to some sort of dance. This is how Wenzel understands the term's use in relation to "Maiden in the mor lay."[89] Other readings of this poem also reflect this approach by conjuring an abstract idea of dance as opposed to a bodily medium. These critics evoke a mysterious, stylized dance environment in order to counteract the Robertsonian exegetical reading of the poem.[90] E. Talbot Donaldson, for instance, reads "Maiden in the mor lay" for its atmospheric qualities, looking to lyric beyond the Middle Ages (such as Wordsworth's Lucy, once full of motion and force) to support his characterization of "Maiden in the mor lay"'s tone.[91] Wenzel exhibits a similar impulse, comparing the maiden to the Dark Lady.[92] John Speirs, meanwhile, ventures furthest in a New Critical direction by arguing for the audience's obligation to consider poetry in terms related to its present reception, rather than reconstructing its own historical terms. His resulting reading of "Maiden in the mor lay"'s incantatory structure responds to its "evoca[tion] of a tranced mood."[93] Presumably the possibility of a danced setting contributes to this tranced mood; this is certainly the case in Peter Dronke's reading. He conjectures a mimed performance accompanying this song, entailing a young girl sleeping on the ground and then swanning

89. Wenzel, "Moor," 72.

90. D. W. Robertson finds "Maiden in the mor lay" an apt vehicle for his method, identifying a series of "figures and signs" that make sense of the poem: seven nights as the time "before the Light of the World dawned"; the primrose as "fleshly beauty"; the "cool water of God's grace"; the "roses of martyrdom" and the "lilies of purity." "Historical Criticism (1950)," repr. *Essays in Medieval Culture* (Princeton: Princeton University Press, 1980), 17. See also Joseph Harris, "'Maiden in the Mor Lay' and the Medieval Magdalene Tradition," *Journal of Medieval and Renaissance Studies* 1.1 (1971): 59–87. Ronald Waldron proposes the "singing games of children" as a context for the poem; in its old sense of "buried," *lay* indicates a childhood attempt to process death. "'Maiden In The Mor Lay' and the Religious Imagination," in *Langland, the Mystics, and the Medieval English Religious Tradition*, ed. Helen Phillips (Cambridge: D. S. Brewer, 1990), 217, 221–22.

91. "Rolled round in earth's diurnal course, / With rocks and stones and trees." William Wordsworth, "A Slumber did my spirit seal," in Ernest de Selincourt, ed., *Wordsworth: Poetical Works* (New York: Oxford University Press, 1936), 149. "Indeed," Donaldson observes (thinking of "She dwelt among the untrodden ways"), "it seems no more legitimate to inquire what the maiden was doing in the moor than it would be to ask Wordsworth's Lucy why she did not remove to a more populous environment where she might experience a greater measure of praise and love." "Patristic Exegesis in the Criticism of Medieval Literature: The Opposition," in *Critical Approaches to Medieval Literature: Selected Papers from the English Institute, 1958–59*, ed. Dorothy Bethurum (New York: Columbia University Press, 1960), 23. Donaldson uses the poem to rebut Robertson's exegetical reading; Greene calls Robertson's analysis "a little classic of misplaced ingenuity" (*Lyrics*, xi).

92. Wenzel, "Moor," 69.

93. Speirs, 63.

into the center of a round dance, where she is offered flowers to eat before moving off "to drink at her well" and eventually falling asleep "again as out of reach as at the beginning."[94] This scene's intricacy is necessarily hypothetical and thus reinforces how abstract the dance is.

Another means to solve the problem of the term "karole" pulls its relationship to dance in the opposite direction. Rather than making the word more capacious, accommodating the idea or practice of any round dance, or any poem capable of accompanying movement in the round, we could seek evidence of more specifically embodied dance protocols in "Maiden in the mor lay." "Karole" would thus acknowledge those choreographic and poetic details. Mullally proposes "Maiden in the mor lay" as uniquely able, among pre-1400 English examples, to fulfill the requirements to accompany a danced *carole*.[95] Rimmer, meanwhile, intervenes into the text's arrangement to render it more carolesque in two ways. First, she suggests that the initial stanza is the burden for the whole, meant to be repeated between the subsequent stanzas.[96] Second, Rimmer proposes that the vocal parts alternate not only between stanza and burden, but also between the questions and answers within the stanzas, with the chorus singing the burden and asking the questions, while the leader sings the parts of the stanza that answer them.[97] This is a thought-provoking approach to the dilemma. It aims to identify within the poem's structure, as given to us, an element that would replicate the responsive and alternating dynamic of the danced *carole*, possibly affecting its attendant dynamics of motion and stillness. Her proposed choreography would effectively create the sensation of kinetic counterpoint between leader and chorus without having to depend on the structural difference between stanza and burden that might otherwise create that experience of difference for performers.

The range of possible relations between dance and "Maiden in the mor lay" has implications for understanding both modern approaches and medieval perceptions. In terms of the modern analytical exercise, these solutions reflect in different ways the limitations with which we have dealt throughout: the difficulty of precise reconstruction, on one end; and on the other the obfuscation, as in the case of *danse macabre*, that inheres in an excessively general performance category. But in this case, the oddity of the

94. Dronke, 196. See also Bédier, 401–2.
95. Mullally, *Carole*, 115.
96. Rimmer, 28.
97. Ibid., 29. Rimmer acknowledges as well that the term *karole* might refer more to the broad category of a dance containing alternating individual and group performance structure than to any particular verse form (25).

form—at least in the instance in which it has survived—at the same time suggests a medieval awareness of this indeterminacy. The play sustained between the medieval designation of the poem as a "karole" and medieval models for what *caroles* as dances might have required to accompany their performances could indicate a somewhat loosened sense, from the medieval perspective, of this poem's relationship to dance. Like the irregularity of "A child is boren"'s copying, the indeterminacy of "Maiden in the mor lay"'s poetic identity sustains a number of possibilities, from a material intersection of dance and musical verse to a sense of dance that is not embodied practice but inheres in the reader's perceptual habits. The medieval audience's ability to call it a "karole," when the poem looks unlike other carols (albeit retroactively taxonomized) from the period, could indicate the medieval audience's self-aware accommodation of this spectrum of relations between dance and verse. In other words, "karole" does not simply designate a nonspecific reference to dance. Rather, it conveys a medieval experience of dance that slides between practice and concept, between bodily and perceptual habit, and as well as the intersection of this continuum with verse. If this poem is, as Gray has called it, "a riddle without a solution," this medial situation might underlie that appearance to us.[98]

In light of these points, I will introduce my own speculation: when apprehended through the perceptual practices of dance, "Maiden in the mor lay" produces a virtual burden. I mean by the term *virtual burden* a carol burden that is apprehended in the mode by which we have seen the medieval world apprehend virtuality and that explains the poem's categorization as a "karole." Could such a burden occur on an alternate spatial and temporal plane in the experience that the poem generates? Could it be a set of beats apprehended as potential and conditionality but with no physical space for them on the page, as "A child is boren" modeled? Would it, apparent in the perceptual mode that sees *carole*'s virtual circles, exist in ancillary and orthogonal ways in relation to the carol? Such a burden would represent a virtual supplement sensed into being in the process of encounter between text and reader, a virtual arc whose apprehension is enabled by habituation to the experiential idioms of dance. Such a burden would break the structure of the poem not in the modern sense of oppositionality but rather in both capitalizing upon and existing outside what are presumed to be the parameters of refrain repetition. In what follows I shall demonstrate why the poem

---

98. Gray, *Simple Forms*, 238.

makes such speculation possible and then return to the question of what this virtual burden might be.

This speculation can be entertained largely because virtuality as an experiential effect is apparent in the poem in a manner that differs from our other poetic examples. Syntax is one aspect of "Maiden in the mor lay" that makes this case. The forces of potentiality and drag—what Massumi understands as the untimeliness of virtuality—structure "Maiden in the mor lay"'s sentences. Theodore Silverstein reads the poem's multiple repetitions as a mechanics of "disclosure."[99] This is true, but the poem's strategies of repetition and deferral seem calculated to accomplish more than revealing what was hidden. R. T. Davies describes such syntactic character as "advancing by partial repetition with an addition." Thomas G. Duncan elaborates on this characterization by comparing "Maiden in the mor lay" to Davies's example "Adam lay i-bowndyn."[100] This comparison helps us to see how both poems use repetition to pull temporal progression back as well as introduce an anticipatory dynamic that pushes it forward. In other words, the poem plots its revelations upon a destabilizing temporal arc. "Maiden in the mor lay"'s repetition of the unfinished phrases "and the . . ." and "of the . . ." interferes with the final three stanzas' overall sense of measure. In one sense, the rhythm of each of these stanzas exhibits an even, lilting, harmonious momentum drawing toward its culmination. But the duplication of the unfinished lines simultaneously introduces another temporal quality. The stanza subtly retards its pace by refusing to resolve itself at the first opportunity. It stretches out a vector of anticipation within a frame of rhythmic regularity. In this way, the stanza's syntax produces a virtual supplement whose force is potentiality in time.

Within the context of this syntactic program, virtuality makes its presence equally known in "Maiden in the mor lay"'s imagistic content. Specifically, virtuality asserts itself through the vegetative *vertu* that suffuses the poem; it is a sense of potential force that shapes its every aspect. The lyric's evocation of the "chelde water of the welle spring," accompanying its "primeroles," violets, roses, and lilies, might lead modern readers to hear echoes of Chaucer's later-fourteenth-century April showers and the prolepsis of burgeoning flowers. Lingering over the General Prologue's resonance, we remember that

99. Theodore Silverstein, ed., *English Lyrics before 1500* (Evanston, IL: Northwestern University Press, 1989), 83.

100. R. T. Davies, ed. *Medieval English Lyrics* (London: Faber and Faber, 1963), 21–22; Thomas G. Duncan, "The Maid in the Moor and the Rawlinson Text," *RES* n.s. 47.186 (1996): 155.

for Chaucer, the "licour" of that spring rain contains the "vertu," the force of potential growth, engendering the spring flower.[101] Even without their echoes in *The Canterbury Tales*, the maiden's water and flowers gesture independently toward this quality of *vertu*. The use of *vertu* to signify what the *MED* calls "quickening" and "vegetative" power, something powerful but "inherent" as opposed to manifested (s.v. *vertu* 3b), is established in Middle English.[102] Most relevantly, it appears in the carol "Ther is no rose of swych vertu," whose *vertu* triangulates maidenliness (of the Marian variety), the force of potential, and the rose.[103] As aspects of nature that contain *vertu*, "Maiden in the mor lay"'s wellspring and its vernal and summer flowers trace this arc of potential force. By placing spring flowers (the primrose and violet) early in the poem and summer flowers (lilies and roses) later, the text further specifies the quality of *vertu* by leading the reader along a trajectory of potential and growth, from the first rose to the reddening rose. In this way the poem's imagery signals the quality of *vertu* to communicate its engagement with virtual forces.

One might argue that because virtuality is so evident in the lyric's syntax and imagery, "Maiden in the mor lay"'s untimely forces display themselves even without consciousness of the *carole*. In cases like "Ladd Y the daunce" or "A child is boren," or in the nonlyric (by modern standards) instance of *danse macabre* poetry, the reenactment of formal experience requires painstakingly crossing these texts with reenacted dance environments to unearth virtual supplements that would otherwise be difficult to discern. But "Maiden in the mor lay"'s virtual supplement asserts itself close enough to the surface—across its very syntax and images—to be an independently manifest quality. If this is the case, what means exist to demonstrate that the poem invites attunement to virtuality in a medieval intersection of dance and verse, rather than simply making virtual elements evident through a contemporary reading practice unaided by the danced heuristic?

The manuscript's use of abbreviation offers an answer (plate 10).

Maiden in the mor lay in the mor lay. seuenyst fulle
seuenist fulle. maiden in the mor lay in the mor

---

101. See the introduction.

102. Some modern theoretical context for this idea exists in Deleuze and Guattari's thoughts on "becoming" and potentiality in terms of plants. *A Thousand Plateaus: Capitalism and Schizophrenia*, trans. Brian Massumi (Minneapolis: University of Minnesota Press, 2003), 11.

103. This carol, in a fifteenth-century manuscript, has a musical setting. *EEC* No. 173, 116; xcviii–civ on this and other carols' connection to the *Laetabundus* attributed to Bernard of Clairvaux. See also Douglas Gray, *Themes and Images in the Medieval English Religious Lyric* (Boston: Routledge & Kegan Paul, 1972), 88–90.

lay seuenistes full ant a day Welle wat hire mete
wat was hire mete the primerole ant the the pri
merole ant the. welle was hire mete wat was
hire mete the primerole ant the violet Welle
wat was hire dryng the chelde water of the
welle spring. Welle was hire bour wat was hire
bour the rede rose ante lilie flour [next item begins]

The strip of parchment containing this poem could once have functioned as a scrap or folded sheet for a minstrel to read (figure 25). Its inclusion of an Anglo-Norman call to dinner supports this use. Andrew Taylor remarks, however, that while the page could make a case for the so-called minstrel manuscript's existence, it at the same time seems to indicate copying by a "highly trained scribe." The use of space and lineation suggests to Taylor some scribal training in a clerical and administrative context: "He might have been a minstrel, but judging by his handwriting he might well have been a bureaucrat at some point as well."[104] In either case, though, the abbreviational protocol emerges as an important component of this text. As Duncan points out, the accident of survival that transmits the Rawlinson version to us does not mean that this is the sole version of this poem; its difference in length from the Latin *contrafactum* suggests that Ledrede, for instance, might have had another in mind. The real interpretive process, Duncan asserts, should therefore involve decoding the abbreviational system itself. If doing so produces an exact correlation between Latin and English, "well and good," but creating this correspondence cannot be the editorial goal with regard to the extant texts.[105] Thus, "Maiden in the mor lay"'s ill fit with the *contrafactum* foregrounds the importance of considering the abbreviational system on its own terms. Whether originating with a bureaucrat or a minstrel, it encodes instructions for intervening into the text to produce a produce a specific formal result.

"Maiden in the mor lay"'s abbreviational mechanics show us a scribe conditioned to apprehend forces of potential. The second stanza, like the first, provides a guide to expand the language of the subsequent stanzas. At the beginning of the second stanza, however, the copyist makes an interesting

104. See Butterfield, "Without," on the (now recto) strip's detachment from the binding (171n6). Taylor, "Minstrel," 71 (citing W. Heuser), 72.

105. Duncan, "Maid," 155. Critics have suggested other means to expand the Rawlinson text to fit the *contrafactum*; Duncan, "Maid," 154n12, enumerates these; he also provides his own relineation at 158–59 and *Lyrics and Carols*, 175. See also Stemmler's transcription and edition of "Peperit virgo," which indicates that, subsequent to the first stanza, all other stanzas are also abbreviated (20–21).

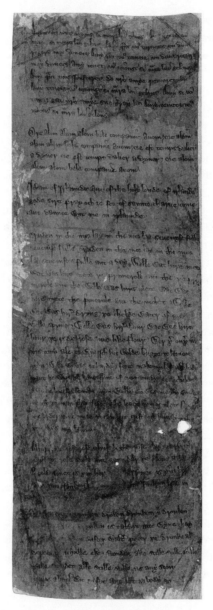

Fig. 25. The Bodleian Libraries, the University of Oxford, MS Rawlinson D.913, now recto (fourteenth century). Photograph: Bodleian Libraries, Oxford.

slip. Opening the stanza, he writes "Welle wat hire mete" instead of "Welle was hire mete."

> Welle wat hire mete
> wat was hire mete

is generally emended to

> Welle was hire mete
> wat was hire mete.

Butterfield notes this "hiccup" and that the use of the phrase of "Welle wat" does not exist in isolation in this poem. In the third stanza, this juxtaposition of "Welle" and "wat" becomes deliberate, seemingly instructing the reader to expand an abbreviation.

> Welle wat was hir dryng

indicates for many an expansion to

> Welle was hir dryng
> wat was hir dryng.

Because the manuscript's text for the second stanza requires no such expansion of its own, including as it does the full first and second lines, the phrase "Welle wat" there cannot intend to fulfill a similar function at the point of its occurrence. Instead, that arrangement of words in stanza 2 anticipates what will become, in the third stanza, a strategy to convey structure. In Butterfield's reading, "welle wat" "illustrates the fine line between abbreviation and error, between compression and poetry," also foregrounding the different techniques of abbreviation within stanzas (what she calls "segments") and across them. The act of transcription itself, she further suggests, produces its own experience of aesthetic enjoyment.[106] I would read her point about the suggestiveness of what we see as error—as well as the idea that transcription and abbreviation can reflect experiences more subtle and diverse than the copying project itself—in terms of the copyist's attunement to force. I would, that is, understand the first "welle wat" to

---

106. Butterfield, "Without," 187–88.

indicate a perceptual mode sensitized to proleptic force. This anticipation of subsequent abbreviational syntax suggests not a look forward to the revelation of content (what other kinds of flowers could she be eating?) but rather the apprehension of the poem's syntactic structure in anticipatory time. The earlier application of the abbreviational syntax generates an arc of force intending toward the point where that syntax might more fully—and diversely—express its function. The scribe's mode of perceiving the poem's main structural attribute is untimely, anticipating the engines by which this repetitive structure will signal itself. In this way, the copying practice of this poem provides a small window onto a medieval interaction with the poem informed by a consciousness habituated to anticipatory, untimely force.

Here the collaboration between the perceptual habits of dance and the text of the poem emerges. The networks the poem seems to sustain with dance—in its companions on its folio and in the *Red Book of Ossory*—become relevant because the scribe exhibits perceptual habits that the culture of dance establishes. The scribal tendency in the parchment strip expresses a practice that we identified in the spectatorship of and participation in round dance. This practice involves perceiving the virtual supplement in terms of time, a momentum underlying the knowledge of what gesture will be articulated next. In the sphere of dance theory, Erin Manning refers to this effect as "preacceleration," and that aptly conveys what the scribe reveals as his perceptual positioning.[107] This sense of anticipatory acceleration could be said to characterize the entire abbreviational strategy, and not just "well wat." In whatever network of dance and verse that "Maiden in the mor lay" spins, the scribe intimates his conditioning by a temporal quality of anticipation that is implicit to dance, inhabiting a proleptic consciousness that intermittently, or interstitially, speeds the pace of the poem's articulation. This scribe might have been, like Lydgate's unfortunate death dancer, a minstrel who shuttled between participation and spectatorship, contacting dance performance in a spectrum of ways. But he could equally have been a literate bureaucrat who simply brought a perceiving consciousness in some way habituated to the experiential features of round dance to his encounter with the poem. In any of these cases, his copying practices illuminate a perception of virtual force conditioned in the intersection of "Maiden in the mor lay" with the dance culture to which its textual network alludes.

107. See chapter 1.

If the technique of abbreviating and expanding the poem's syntactic attributes potentially draws upon a dance-based perceptual mode, this mode
furthermore elucidates the formal experience that the poem produces, the
virtual supplement to its syntactic attributes. In one sense, we have the
suggestive temporal misalignment of a copying practice that accelerates
against a syntax that delays, generating force between those two temporal
experiences. But more specifically, from a perspective habituated to the *carole*'s virtual circles, a reader might perceive the stanzas' delaying impulses
to articulate themselves as force cast out orthogonally to the poem's more
material and evident acts of closure. Each of the final three stanzas, even
unexpanded, is not merely a question resolved with an answer, but also repeats an oscillation between declaration and question: Well was. . . . What
was. . . . Well was. . . . What was. . . . Thus, while at one level the stanza
might appear to mimic the enclosing circularity of a round dance by com-
pleting the answer to the question in its last line, at another, the stanza
also casts forth an ancillary arc in the movement from statement back to
question. The force of potential moves toward fulfillment in the answering
of each stanza's question. But at the same time, the less clearly progressive
exchange between "It was well" and "What was it?" becomes, in dance's kinetic multiplicity of perspective, a different kind of axis-tipping, retrograde
force. This construction speaks to the unstable mood of the *irrealis* that we
have seen before. The attunement to a complex and various set of arcs, cast
immaterially adjacent to or away from the centered circle of the bodily *carole*, thus shapes the ductile formal experience that "Maiden in the mor lay"
offers, illustrating the heuristic relevance of dance even when the poem's
virtual elements might be apparent in other ways.

The poem's syntax, imagery, scene of copying, and formal experience
together produce an environment of virtual force. Indeed, the manuscript's
reliance upon expansion normalizes an approach to the poem where a plane
of space beyond the materiality of the page and its inscription must exist to
make room for what is not there. In relying on a readerly practice of negotiating constantly between what is there and what is not, the abbreviated
poem produces a context for components of ontological ambiguity. Within
this setting might exist a burden as virtual supplement. In some ways, the
poem asks for such a thing. What other burden, after all, might a maiden bear
besides a virtual one?[108] Here we might return to *L'Allegro*'s lesson that the

---

108. *Burden* and *burthen*, though etymologically distinct from the musical term *burdoun*,
homonymically approximate it as a word for "pregnancy" beginning in the thirteenth century
(*MED* s.v. *birthen* 1b).

spectatorial experience of and participation in round dance habituates one to apprehending things only ambiguously perceptible, unearthly, obscured by a scrim or floating in space, and casting forth supplementary forces that anticipate new components. To experience the form of "Maiden in the mor lay" in these terms is to experience the possibility of such uncanny things, answering to the contingencies of round dance's perceptual networks. In light of *L'Allegro*, the first stanza of the poem suggests such supplemental presence. Its repetition of "fulle" emphasizes fullness, the sense that that seven-night period is complete. And yet, it ultimately impels the reader toward the additional day at its end, intimating that even what appears to be articulated as complete, full, and contained always holds the potential of a supplemental element cast away from it—the day from the cluster of nights.[109]

Having cleared some estranging time and space for this virtual burden, we are now faced with the question of what such a thing would be to both medieval and modern audiences of the poem. In order to address this question regarding "Maiden in the mor lay," I shall first turn to Greene's Carol 191, the burdenless poem I mentioned, to provide a frame for further thought about the Rawlinson text. While in modern taxonomy Carol 191 becomes a carol only when it later finds a burden (what Greene calls "the process of turning an already existing poem in another form into a carol"), I propose that in its earlier incarnations the poem's burden is virtual.[110] The earlier copies of the poem have a nine-line stanza that inserts Latin words and short phrases at certain alternating points. The later copy has a shorter and simpler stanza whose abab structure alternates English and Latin, but it also adds a Latin burden, "Enixa e*s*t pu*er*pera" [the lying-in woman is delivered], a hymn line that appears in other extant carols as well (though not as a burden).[111] Compare the thirteenth-century

> Of on that is so fayr and bright,
>   Velud maris stella,
> Brighter than the dayis light,
>   Parens *et* puella,
> Ic crie to the; thou se to me;

---

109. The Latin *contrafactum* draws further attention to the resonant nature of English *fulle* by incorporating into its first stanza the phrase "gratia plena," another fullness that asks ultimately to be even further fulfilled.

110. *EEC*, 399. See also Palti, "Synge," 144–52, on adding burdens to poems.

111. *EEC*, lxxxvi.

> Leuedy, preye thi Sone for me,
> > Tam pia,
> That ic mote come to the,
> > Maria. (London, British Library MS Egerton 613, f. 2r)

with the fifteenth-century

> A lady that was so feyre *and* bright,
> > Velut mar*is* stella,
> Browght forth Jh*esu*, full of might,
> > Par*ens* et puella.
> *Enixa est puerpera.* (Oxford, Bodleian Library MS Ashmole 1393, f. 69v)

The earlier Egerton manuscript calls its text a "cant*us*"; in its refrainless state it cannot be the "cantilena" that Grocheio associates with dance song in his (largely courtly and secular) taxonomy.[112] The first stanza's "Ic crie to the; thou se to me," however, recalls the pronominal play that, I suggested earlier, indicates in "A child is boren" the collectivity and intersubjectivity of danced *ductus*.[113] With this idea in mind, a comparison of the longer, earlier stanza to the shorter, later one (with its burden) can reveal a process in which the perceptual consciousness of dance brings a sense of kinetic collectivity to the Egerton manuscript poem and opens up its possible identities. Perhaps the Latin sonic quality of the earlier, longer stanzas' final lines exerts a breaking, refrain-like force that anticipates its concentration elsewhere, in a later manuscript, as a Latin burden. This burden allows the later song to acknowledge what was carolesque within the earlier one. Such a possibility responds to Nelson's conception of "tactical" relations among lyrics, which are orchestrated in social and cultural practices; the perceptual consciousness of dance enters that network.[114] The virtual burden is thus the force of potentiality that intends toward another experience of the poem already implicit within it, flickering in and out of apprehensibility to its readers.

While "Maiden in the mor lay"'s own formal experience creates untimeliness and ambiguously real space to sustain a virtual burden, speculating

---

112. *EEC*, 126. Mullally, "'Musica vulgaris,'" 4.

113. Other stanzas in the Egerton poem mention "thou" and "thee" and also repeat "him" and "us" in their second sections.

114. Nelson, 13.

about what such a burden might be in its case is more challenging. But Butterfield's proposal that "Maiden in the mor lay" might not cleave to our modern expectations of regularity, and might instead find its wholeness in "a mobile and plural set of potential forms" and diverse amplifications, facilitates my speculation.[115] The virtual burden recruits a specific discourse and cultural practice by which to articulate plurality, irregularity, and—I would say—strangeness. Perhaps the virtual burden is an existing component of the poem—the first lines?—but it could equally be something else.[116] In the space between the Middle Ages and modernity, the idea of the virtual burden crystallizes what the ductile experience of this poem offers readers: an intervening element that breaks into its interstices in a manner that estranges the poem from its own tight coherence but is at the same time characteristic of the carol's medieval experience.[117] From a modern perspective, the virtual burden is perhaps nothing articulable except the force and energy that the dance-literate audience is habituated to perceive. But that possibility is useful in reminding us of the alterity of medieval poetic formal experience. What happens in the repeated space between verses—or even between lines—refuses to respond to modern theories of the refrain because it constitutes itself in a *ductus* responsive to multiple media, on the surface or in the depths.

Here, then, are some aspects of the virtual burden. A virtual burden leads its reader or audience into inscrutable interstices that may or may not affirm the poem's harmonies even as it completes its carolesque identity. In one sense, the virtual burden's kinetic negotiation of space resonates with poststructuralist discourse around blankness on the page, Derrida's "supplementary mark of the blank" that formulates the whiteness of a page as constantly circulating around and folding upon itself.[118] But unlike the Derridean model of white space on a page, the virtual burden of "Maiden in the mor lay" originates from a page that pointedly avoids such white space; the burden must assert itself in a different kind of space and time. The virtual

---

115. Butterfield, "Without," 194.

116. While identical phrasing in the burden and first stanza is unusual, it seems to appear in "Ther is no rose of swych vertu," although some letters in the first burden and stanza are illegible (*EEC* 395, 116).

117. See Zumthor, 231–32, on one notion of poetic coherence, which he renames and specifies as "registre," a network of relations among poetic elements that seems to obtain within and across poems.

118. Jacques Derrida, "The Double Session," in *Dissemination*, trans. Barbara Johnson (New York: Continuum, 2004), 264–65. Wakelin reminds us that in certain manuscript cases, "the carol is not only sound; it is inherently a form of writing, too," where the written activity can assert a kind of Derridean primacy in the constitution of the carol's identity ("Carol," 26).

burden represents the strangest footing of all, able to discompose, in its ambiguous materiality, the poem around it. The virtual burden pushes against the limits of modern discourse concerning the work of the burden, occupying itself with an entirely different spectrum than sameness and difference or simplicity and complexity. Recalling that *ductus* is participatory rather than passive, we might understand the constitution of the virtual burden as dependent upon the reader's perceptual engagement. If, finally, in "Maiden in the mor lay"'s *ductus*, the virtual burden breaks, or breaks into, the poem's harmonious shapeliness in some manner beyond our range of formal experience, that activity occurs on a continuum running between the encounter with dance as a bodily medium and the shimmering and ghostly vestige of that medium in a reader's habits of perception.

As we have seen, there is a chiastic irony in the juxtaposition of "A child is boren" and "Maiden in the mor lay." "A child is boren"'s virtualities are challenging to discern in the midst of an affiliation with dance that appears right on the carol's handholding surface. Conversely, once given a name, the effects of untimely and spatially ambiguous virtuality are everywhere apparent in "Maiden in the mor lay" even though it submerges its relationship to embodied dance more deeply. But the maiden has already been teaching us of this indeterminate relation between surface and depth, between what is in the figure and what is on the ground beneath it. Filled up with, and therefore in a sense composed of, virtuous vegetation even as she also lies upon it, she embodies that interchangeability of figure and ground. With this lesson in mind, we might recognize that even when dance is not cast into relief as a topic, it is a ground that suffuses the experience of the poem. "Maiden in the mor lay" has long appeared to twentieth-century readers as "tantalizing in its isolation and brevity, in the tentativeness of its quasi-hesitant repetitions, and its perplexing form."[119] But the poetic formal experience it elucidates is not unique, because the perceptual habits of dance that shape it are, in a medieval context, conventional. The virtual supplement's generation in these familiar practices renders it an integral, rather than an exceptional, component in the medieval experience of poetic form. "Maiden in the mor lay"'s syntax and imagery simply cast this dynamic into more intense relief than do many other poems; perhaps it is this effect to which both medieval and modern audiences have responded. In the ductile experience of "A child is boren" and "Maiden in the mor lay," virtual supplements unseat whatever neat circularities the comparison of

119. Waldron, 216.

dance and poetry might appear superficially to generate. Across a spectrum
of medial engagement, these reenacted experiences of medieval poetic form
as constituted in dance's perceptual practices disclose what is proleptic, recursive, orthogonal, ancillary, and estranging in the *irrealis*, the time and
space of virtuality.

Dance in the Margins, Dance in the Center

In reenacting medieval dance and medieval poetic form, I have sought, in part, to interrogate some conventional assumptions about the cultural work hat dance can perform. Ballet-based concert dance is sometimes thought, in Jennifer Homans's terms, to have "shrunk into a recondite world of hyper-specialists and balletomanes. . . . [M]ost people today do not feel they 'know enough' to judge a dance."[1] Whether or not this is the case to the degree Homans describes, it is still probably difficult for many to conceive of dance's cultural influence as sufficiently extensive to intervene substantively into other apprehensional practices. Reenacting dance's role in the apprehension of medieval poetry, however, resituates it at a discursive, interpretive, and aesthetic center where it wields influence in textual encounters. And while not every medieval poem's formal experience can be reenacted in terms of dance, such formal experience obtains for a range that includes something as formulaic as an estates-based death dialogue and as singular as a lyric that resembles no other in its capacity to haunt generations of readers.

My case studies suggested that poetic form's dynamic experiences range beyond what modernity and postmodernity imagine possible, and so in this sense, I also place poetic form at a discursive center. In a literary critical context, this act of centering necessarily raises questions about what the attention to form accomplishes, both in the investigation of the Middle Ages and more generally. The roots of this question lie in a critical concern about the nature—and the limits—of formalism's analytic interventions. While these questions and hesitations are familiar to literary scholars, they might

1. Homans, 540, 548.

be surprised to learn how dance history has enacted exactly the kind of marginalizing suspicion historically leveled at formalist preoccupation. Joanna E. Ziegler suggests that Western dance's decline maps onto a twentieth-century critical history that disavows formalist approaches in favor of historicist and cultural studies models:

> it was dance's emergence as an independent medium—not a prop in musicals or opera . . . but an autonomous art form—that was its doing and its undoing at once. As academics shifted their stance on art, beginning in the 1970s and certainly vigorously so by the 1980s, they shifted away from dealing with . . . anything that smacked of Formalism, of New Criticism, of art-for-art's sakeness.[2]

Thus, the current "recondite" appearance of dance might be explicable as a residual perception of its tendency toward purely formal expressiveness rather than a more substantive embedding in examinations of history, society, or politics.[3] Many contemporary choreographers would rightly disagree with this characterization relative to the present state of dance, which has long been politically and socially engaged in many ways. But Ziegler's point outlines an interesting bind in the history of dance: it underwent a shift that freed it from some of its earlier constraints and allowed it to assert an identity as an artistic medium, but in doing so it dealt itself out of an emerging critical conversation that would prove extremely powerful. As throughout, I do not imply here that dance and poetry are analogous in their affiliations with formalism and historicism: dance and poetry obviously do not tell the same story. While in my argument their medial identities have been deeply intertwined, it is also the case that each has its own complicated narrative concerning what defines it as a medium. And yet, Ziegler's account of dance suggests a way to frame a particular literary concern: to the extent that we rely on form to define poetry as a medium, that act might interpretively

---

2. Joanna E. Ziegler, "Skipping like Camels: Or Why Medieval Studies Neglects the Dance," *Medieval Feminist Forum* 32.1 (2001): 26. For a differently inflected narrative concerning modernism, modernity, poetry, and dance in French tradition, see Alice Godfoy, *Danse et poésie: le pli du mouvement dans l'écriture. Michaux, Celan, Du Bouchet, Noël* (Paris: Honoré Champion, 2015).

3. Such formal expressiveness is visible in the work of Michel Fokine, in particular *Les Sylphides* and its crystallization of both the plotless ballet and the *ballet blanc*. On Fokine's critique of artificial mimed gesture in ballet, and his privileging instead of "the beauty of the poses and movements," see his "Theories on the Art of Ballet," in *The Dance Anthology*, ed. Cobbett Steinberg (New York: New American Library, 1980), 17.

limit it, undermining its relevance by reifying certain hegemonic values. Another way to say this might be that while formalist study does not, as Jill Mann points out, necessarily reflect a "flight from historico-political circumstance," Ziegler's history of certain kinds of dance can help us to see how the centralizing of form might appear that way, and how that appearance might compromise our sense of what the study of form can do.[4]

Current critical discourse addresses the literary formalist problem by recasting and politicizing the study of form so as to allow it to undermine, rather than reinforce, what is hegemonic. Caroline Levine reads poetic form to hold the potential to perform real political and social work. As a temporal occurrence, poetic form "competes, struggles, and sometimes even interferes with other organizations of social time," thereby challenging those dominant modes in a socially productive way.[5] Joseph North recuperates formalist study by drawing a distinction between its Brooksian foundation in an inward-turned American Christian conservatism and the British tradition embodied in I. A. Richards, which "oppos[es] any attempt to set up the aesthetic as a self-sufficient category insulated from the rest of life" and reflects a progressive concern with reader, audience, and the contingencies of the material world.[6] Distinguishing these two formalisms clears space for us better to perceive the British theoretical model as offering progressive modes of engagement. For our own sense of what formalism can do, the British model might knock aside the conservative, authority-confirming American New Critical impulse; North proposes through this comparison that "another kind of aesthetics is possible."[7]

But while these interpretations of formalist practice might redress the constraints associated with traditional New Criticism, Levine's and North's renegotiations do not substantially extend beyond the environment of a single, present time. Although she mentions medieval ways of organizing time and space, Levine most expansively demonstrates her point in a reading of *The Wire*. While hardly current by the measures of television, this

4. Mann, "Inescapability," 122.

5. Levine, 53. See also Marjorie Levinson's invocation of Susan J. Wolfson's term "activist formalism," which deploys the study of form to restore the theoretical and conceptual complexity that some critics perceive new historicism to have lost over time. Marjorie Levinson, "What Is New Formalism?" *PMLA* 122.2 (2007): 559; Susan J. Wolfson, "Reading for Form," *Modern Language Quarterly* 61 (2000): 1–16.

6. Joseph North, "What's 'New Critical' about 'Close Reading'?: I. A. Richards and his New Critical Reception," *New Literary History* 44.1 (2013): 144. As he formulates it, "For the Cambridge liberals, the solution to the problem of modernity was education. For the Southern Christians, the solution was piety" (155).

7. Ibid., 155.

series relies upon its engagement of contemporary social issues.[8] North's dichotomy of American and British formalism, meanwhile, sees the religiosity of the former as closely connected to its anti-intellectualism and resistance to theory. It is in this way that he reorients—across the space of modern England and America—what could be central to the study of form. But while religious zealotry can account for a specific benightedness in Brooks's circle, that correlation between what is religious and what is anti-intellectual does not map so effectively onto a longer, premodern history in which intellectual culture was, to a significant extent, religious culture.[9] These reorientations of formalism rely upon their placement within a highly particular postmodern space.

Because my method resituates what is central to the project of reading formally across time, it elucidates the work of form in some different, and I think possibly more expansive, ways that what modernity proposes in its recalibrations of formalist study. Some of my analyses represent recognizable types of hermeneutic interventions. In the case of *danse macabre*, we saw that virtuality might give expression, for example, to a recusant experience of Catholic untimeliness. Similarly, the formal experience of the carol can enable various analytic exercises. We could, for instance, stage a vintage deconstructionist reading of "Maiden in the mor lay," arguing that its virtual burden represents an incursion of *virtus* into the mesh of the poem, rendering the maiden always already unmaidenly and explaining the sense of burgeoning fullness on which the poem seems to insist. Or we could consider the manuscript context of "Maiden in the mor lay" in in terms of danced *ductus*. The "karole" is referred to, we recall, in a sermon that progresses through the degenerating ages of man. How, we might ask, does the poem's proleptic, recursive, and otherwise tipped time interact with this other temporal model? How might that interaction inflect our sense of lyrics' operation in the sermon settings where they frequently appeared? As I intimated earlier, I have chosen not to pursue such routes of analysis precisely because I aim to centralize the account of formal experience and the alterity of medieval poetic encounter that it suggests; however, centralizing the study of poetic form in this manner does introduce these interpretive possibilities, meaning that the method of reenacting formal experience can contribute to readings that articulate certain recognizable stakes, such as those of historicism or book and reader history.

8. Levine, 5, 39, 132–50.
9. North, 147.

As an experience to be reenacted, however, form enables other kinds of interventions as well. Because this method distinguishes itself from the more traditional enterprise of interpreting formal attributes, I would maintain that my readings do not exactly provide "*data* for historical understanding" in the sense that Richard Strier construes the contribution of formalist analysis.[10] Instead, the attunement to experience requires a constant negotiation between past and present. My case studies have asked: What makes the poetic depiction of death so terrifying, and how does this terror rely on a formal experience? What formal experience dictates a medieval audience's placement of a poem within a particular category (like "karole")? In posing such questions, *Strange Footing* renegotiates the relation of modern and postmodern formalist constructs to premodernity. The question about "karole," for instance, compels us to ask: What makes a poem look exceptional to us? What impact does that perspective have upon our account of its medieval identity? In other ways as well, we see medieval poetic form extend beyond the parameters that postmodernity applies to its encounters with literary form. An influential contemporary discourse concerning narrative form's relationship to time, for instance, sets the "oculocentric" drive to see the whole textual articulation at once in opposition to the long narrative's resolution. This theory also challenges both states' dependence upon arresting narrative time in order to perceive form over a period of length.[11] None of these terms, however, fit *danse macabre* poetry's formal experience in time, which is characterized instead by the diverse and simultaneous timescales that a specific *ductus* shaped by medial multiplicity can produce. Similarly, while modern theories of repetition in poetry are predicated on a dichotomy of sameness and difference, the medieval lyric's uses for its burdens, and its means of setting them in relation to their stanzas, plot themselves on entirely different axes.

In other words, at the nexus of medieval dance and verse are more things than are dreamt of in our philosophy: here we find other ways to understand not only what form has done but also what it can do. Investigating this possibility might involve moving away from hermeneutic intervention. Simon Jarvis argues that "the assumption that poetics subserves hermeneutics

10. Richard Strier, "How Formalism Became a Dirty Word, and Why We Can't Do Without It," in *Renaissance Literature and its Formal Engagements*, ed. Mark David Rasmussen (New York: Palgrave, 2002), 210, emphasis in original. Strier goes on to describe "indexical" form, where the formal features of a text are "indices to large intellectual and cultural matters" (211).

11. Catherine Gallagher, "Formalism and Time," *MLQ* 61.1 (2000): 230–31, 251.

presses connoisseurship of verse style so rapidly and so forcibly into inter-
pretative service that it leads to falsified and unconvincing claims about
verse style and its supposed effects."[12] For me the terms of connoisseurship
and the nature of the unconvincing are not so much at stake, but I do want
to tease out an implication of this comment to ask: how might we think
about medieval formal experience, for the Middle Ages and for ourselves,
without immediately conscripting it into the more traditional types of interpretive service?

Framing an answer to this question at the close of this study, I find myself recalling something that the dancer Caitlin Scranton said about *Dance*.
Scranton performs a central solo section accompanied by a film made of
Lucinda Childs dancing the same solo part in the late 1970s. On Childs's
filmed image, Scranton noted: "there is a comforting camaraderie that comes
with her appearance on the scene, and I think it has to do with the fact that
she is set in time, that she isn't going to change even though her movement
might continue to trip me up. . . . When she appears . . . I have this person I
can dance with, this thing that's really solid, that can share the load."[13] This
account reminds us that in the experience of danced virtuality—the experience of those forces that undermine the participant's sense of what is solid
and what is not, what can be expected of space and time—the medieval
audience's engagement is collective. To read with the perceptual conditioning of the *carole*—or the communal installation setting of the *danse macabre*—is to read with many eyes at once. Cervone identifies a "collective
subjectivity" in medieval lyric, a "combined yet distinct 'I' and 'we.' "[14] To
me, medieval poetic formal experience achieves this dynamic by conduct-
ing diverse perspectival trajectories throughout medially complex environments. And in Scranton's terms, there is perhaps an implicit "camaraderie"
in responding to that strangeness and orthogonality of formal experience.
The presence of more than one's own familiar trajectory both produces disorienting strangeness and, at the same time, offers a perceptual mode by
which to understand it.

This is ultimately what medieval poetic formal experience offers to poetic form more broadly. In chapter 2, I proposed that the formal experience of "Ladd Y the Daunce" is a perspectivally-based empathy for a female
speaker whose marginality might otherwise render her inaccessible. In clos-

---

12. Simon Jarvis, "For a Poetics of Verse," *PMLA* 125.4 (2010): 932.

13. Scranton interview.

14. Cristina Maria Cervone, " 'I' and 'We' in Chaucer's *Complaint unto Pity*," in *Readings in Medieval Textuality*, 198.

ing, I wish to revisit and consider further the practices of thought that medieval formal experience enables. The strange footing of medieval poetic form does not simply deploy a series of alternating perspectives in a kind of self-debate. Rather, it conducts the body through uncanniness, disorientation, and decentering that are familiar, accepted, and shared components of the formal experience. This is how, for instance, strange footing can explain the medieval manuscript's presentation of "A child is boren" as a coherent poetic object even though misaligned among its parts. For Levine, form's productivity lies in conflicts among formal manifestations across social, narrative, material, and political realms.[15] Dance, meanwhile, makes its own conflictual or disorienting elements essential to its collaborative enterprise: the toe that is stepped on to diverge from the temporal periodicity of the dance for flirtatious purpose, the eye's chasing of that other, unreal dancer's other turning rhythm. Some of these experiences register as empathetic response. Others, however, compel an engaged and collaborative confrontation with the misalignment or unevenness underlying apparent harmony. For the medieval world, I have aimed to show, such experiences shape the encounter with poetry. In the end, I am not sure that this poetic formal experience can qualify as activist in its effects, and I would join those who feel suspicious of that possibility. But medieval poetic formal experience, conditioned by the cultural practice of dance, might in turn condition an apprehensional mode that resonates in other arenas. At its intersection with the virtual forces of dance, medieval poetic form leads each individual perspective into a decentered state where it must engage in a shared reckoning with estrangement. In this way, strange footing, positioned between the past and the present, the known and the unknown, articulates a thought structure that is enabled in poetry but that contains the force—the *virtus*, the virtue—of a contribution beyond it.

15. Levine, 16–17: "aesthetic and political forms may be nested inside one another ... each is capable of disturbing the other's organizing power." She adds that a goal of her book "is to think about the ways that, together, the multiple forms of the world come into conflict and disorganize experience in ways that call for unconventional political strategies."

ACKNOWLEDGMENTS

I have been extremely fortunate in the support I received while writing this book. I thank my editor Randy Petilos at the University of Chicago Press, along with the Press's readers, for their insightful interventions.

The University of California, Davis, has been my institutional home for many years, and it has made me rich in supportive colleagues and friends. Emily Albu, Gina Bloom, Anna Maria Busse Berger, Joan Cadden, C. M. Chin, Fran Dolan, Margie Ferguson, Claire Goldstein, Noah Guynn, Sally McKee, Anna Uhlig, Matthew Vernon, and Claire Waters are part of a vibrant community of early-period scholars committed to nurturing each other's scholarship. Ari Friedlander and Stephanie Elsky briefly joined this community to my benefit and joy. My weekly dinners with Katherine Lee, Meaghan O'Keefe, and Carey Seal sustained me through this project, as has the companionship of Danielle Heard Mollel, Peter Holman, Marcel Losekoot, Desirée Martín, Colin Milburn, and Gabrielle Nevitt. Mark Jerng, Jon Rossini, and I met regularly to workshop the chapters of our second books; these conversations fundamentally shaped my thinking about this project. Kristen Aldebol-Hazle, Valerie Dennis, Heather Jennings, and Sara Petrosillo, whose dissertations I directed, inspired me with their brilliance and perseverance.

I thank as well Dean Jessie Ann Owens and Interim Dean Susan Kaiser for material forms of support. I am also grateful to the Davis Humanities Institute for their Faculty Research Fellowship, and in particular to the associate director of the Institute, Molly McCarthy. In our staff unit, Darla Tafoya, Melissa Lovejoy, and Mary White guide us through the wilds of permissions and promotions and deserve many thanks for this hard work. I feel special gratitude to Ron Ottman and Elliott Pollard for not only IT support on campus, but also their mentorship in my first experience as a backyard chicken keeper, about which more below.

Beyond my campus, I received a year to work on this book at Cornell University's Society for the Humanities, a treasured time. I thank Timothy Murray, then the Society's director, along with the collegial community of fellows. The Center for Cultural Analysis at Rutgers University provided an invigorating discussion of this material in its final stages. It has been a privilege to watch the projects of Elizabeth Allen, Jessica Brantley, Susie Phillips, and Cathy Sanok develop while receiving their thoughtful responses to mine. I am also grateful to the members of FORMER for their interventions: Arthur Bahr, Becky Davis, Shannon Gayk, Eleanor Johnson, Marisa Libbon, Ingrid Nelson, Sarah Novacich, and Jenny Sisk. And I am delighted to have this opportunity to extend warm thanks, for many different forms of help, to Amy Appleford, Geoff Arnott, Nick Basden and Vivian Hunt, Anke Bernau, Katy Breen, Katie Brokaw, Chris Cannon, Megan Cook, Lisa Cooper, Tim Corbett and Jesus Alvarez-Piñera, Louise d'Arcens, Andrea Denny-Brown, Jody Enders, Mark Franko, John Ganim, Erith Jaffe-Berg, Becky Krug, Kathy Lavezzo, Emma Lipton, David Matthews, Peggy McCracken, the Medievalists of Color, Bobby Meyer-Lee, Chris Nealon, Maura Nolan, Annika Pattenaude, Penn Szittya, Peter Travis, Stephanie Trigg, and Jiayi Young.

I could not have written a book about dance without access to that world. I am grateful to my dedicated ballet teachers and to the inspiring communities—which include everyone from former professionals to adult beginners—with whom I have danced in Davis and Berkeley, CA; Ithaca, NY; and every European city where I took technique class after visiting a library or museum. I am grateful as well for the welcome I received in reaching out, as a researcher, to the professional dance sphere. Caitlin Scranton, of The Lucinda Childs Dance Company, and David Leventhal, retired from the Mark Morris Dance Group, offered brilliant insights. Lucinda Childs and Sally Cohn showed great generosity in facilitating image selection. Karyn Lesuer at the Mark Morris Dance Group provided valuable assistance obtaining images. I thank in addition Jeremy Ganter and Ruth Rosenberg of the Robert and Margrit Mondavi Center for the Performing Arts in Davis.

My good fortune extends to the sphere of family: so many magnanimous souls surround me, daily tugging my heart and pecking my shoes. With their precise attunement to environment, my hens Odette, Odile, and Medora have reconfigured my interactions with the world to make me a more thoughtful and deliberate writer. Niccolo the cat joins my little flock to constitute a much beloved animal family. In so many ways, Carol Clover has helped me to feel at home and surrounded by family on the West Coast, and I am truly grateful. I offer thanks, admiration, and love to my parents

Raju S. K. and Seeta R. Chaganti, my sister Sara Chaganti, and my sister-in-law Samantha DeWitt.

Finally, I dedicate this book to Joshua Clover. In his company I have become a better reader and—I hope—a better person than I could have been without him.

INDEX